# PALESTINE OR ISRAEL

By the same author:

*Seven Fallen Pillars*
*The Secret Roads* (with David Kimche)
*Both Sides of the Hill* (with David Kimche)
*Spying for Peace*
*The Unromantics*
*The Unfought Battle*
*The Second Arab Awakening*

# PALESTINE OR ISRAEL

*The untold story of why we failed*
1917–1923 : 1967–1973

# Jon Kimche

SECKER & WARBURG
LONDON

First published in England 1973 by
Martin Secker & Warburg Limited
14 Carlisle Street, London W1V 6NN

Printed in Great Britain by
Morrison and Gibb Limited
London and Edinburgh

# Contents

# Preface

This book would not have been written had it not been for the encouragement and help of the late Lord Sieff who was, for some 30 years, that rarest of persons – a friend in all seasons. He was also a man with much knowledge and deep insight into the problems and events here discussed. In assembling his own papers, which he placed at my disposal, he had the assistance of the Weizmann Archives, of which he was a Governor, and received much valuable help also from other sources, especially the family of Sir Gilbert Clayton, from the late Mrs Vera Weizmann, and the former archivist at the Weizmann Archives, Dr Boris Guriel. To all those who extended their help to Lord Sieff in this way and to those who similarly assisted me in the carrying out of the work thus started, I would like to express my appreciation. This includes those invaluable pillars of all Middle Eastern students, the Public Record Office in London, Durham University (the home of the Clayton and Wingate papers), to John Presland's invaluable study of Wyndham Deedes, and those others to whom reference is made in the Note on Sources on page 345. It must also include many who have not been specifically mentioned, and Mme Barbara Brosselin for again preparing so excellent an index.

But, above all, this book has become – for it was not intended as such – a tribute to the two men, Gilbert Clayton and Israel Sieff, whose independent and compassionate contribution to the making of Palestine *and* Israel has been greatly underestimated, not least by themselves. However, the ultimate responsibility for this book, its views and iconoclasms, is mine, not theirs, however much they may have inspired them.

*Westhumble, Surrey*
*24 June 1973*

# Selective List of Characters

AARONSOHN, Aaron: agronomist born in Rumania in 1876 and brought to Palestine in 1882, served as agricultural adviser to the Turkish Commander in Damascus 1915 and at the same time organised an underground intelligence service in the service of the British. Later served on Allenby's staff in Cairo and as consultant to the Zionist Commission.

ABDULLAH, Emir: second son of the Sharif Husain of Mecca, of the dynasty known as Hashemite, first negotiated terms of Arab Revolt with Lord Kitchener, 1915, Emir of Transjordan 1921, King of Transjordan 1946, King of the Hashemite Kingdom of Jordan after the annexation of the West Bank 1948, assassinated 1951.

ALLENBY, Field-Marshal Viscount Edmund Henry Hynman: Commander Egyptian Expeditionary Force 1917–1919, then High Commissioner of Egypt until 1925.

AMIN: see el-Husaini

AMIT, Meir: Chief of the Israeli Secret Service in 1967.

AREF EL-AREF: Palestinian Arab politician and historian, served in the Ottoman army during the first world war, founder with Amin al-Husaini in 1918 of the militant wing of the Palestinian national movement.

ASQUITH, Herbert Henry: British Prime Minister 1908–1916, displaced by Lloyd George 6 December 1916.

BALFOUR, Arthur James, Earl of: Prime Minister 1902–1905, Member of the War Cabinet in 1914, Foreign Secretary 1916–1919, Lord President of the Council 1919–1922.

BEELEY, Sir Harold: Secretary to the Anglo-American Commission on Palestine 1946, Minister in Washington, Ambassador in Baghdad and Cairo, Head of Mission to the UN 1959–1960, claims paternity for the Security Council resolution 242 of 22 November 1967.

BELL, Gertrude: orientalist attached to the Arab Bureau in Cairo with special concern for Mesopotamia 1916. Driving power behind the successful attempt to have Emir Faisal named as King of Iraq 1921.

BEN-GURION, David: Head of the Provisional Government of Israel 1948, Prime Minister and Minister of Defence 1949–1953, Minister of Defence under Sharett 1955, Prime Minister and Minister of Defence 1955–1963, one

vii

of the founders and leader of the Israel Labour Party (Mapai) 1948–1965, expelled 1965, formed Rafi Party with Dayan, Peres etc. 1965.

BOLS, Lt-General Sir Louis Jean: Chief Administrator in Palestine 1919–1920.

BRANDEIS, Louis Dembitz: Hon. President of the Zionist Organisation of America 1918–1921, also of the World Zionist Organisation, resigned after differences with Weizmann.

BROWN, George: later Lord George-Brown, Deputy Prime Minister in the Labour Government 1964, Foreign Secretary 1966, resigned 1968. Claims paternity for the Security Council Resolution 242 of 22 November 1967.

CARADON, Lord: formerly Hugh Foot, British representative at the UN 1965–1970, sponsored Resolution 242 of 22 November 1967 in the Security Council for which he claims paternity. Replaced at the UN after the electoral defeat of the Labour Party in 1970.

CLAYTON, Brigadier Sir Gilbert F. (1865–1929): originator of the "Arab Bureau" in Cairo and Director of Intelligence in Egypt 1914–1917, Chief Political Officer of the Egyptian Expeditionary Force in Palestine 1917–1919, Adviser to the Interior Ministry in Egypt 1919–1922, Chief Secretary to the Palestine Government 1922–1925, Special Envoy to the King of Hejaz, ibn Saud, 1925–1927, High Commissioner to Iraq 1929.

CLEMENCEAU, Georges: Prime Minister of France 1917–1920, presided over the Paris Peace Conference 1919.

CORNWALLIS, Sir Kinahan: Director of the Arab Bureau from 1916, on Allenby's staff in Palestine 1918, Foreign Office 1920, Ambassador to Iraq 1941–1945.

CURZON, George Nathaniel, Marquess: Viceroy of India 1899–1905, Member of the Inner War Cabinet 1916, Foreign Secretary 1919–1924.

DAYAN, General Moshe: Israeli Defence Minister 1967.

DEEDES, Wyndham Henry: War Office and Intelligence Officer with the Dardanelles Expedition 1915, Military Intelligence in Egypt and Arab Bureau 1916, attached to Allenby's HQ in Palestine and Syria 1918, Military Attaché in Constantinople 1919, Director-General of Public Security in Egypt 1919–1920, Chief Secretary to the Palestine Government 1920–1922.

DJEMAL PASHA: There were two of them by the same name occupying successively the same position as Military Governor of Syria and Commander of the Turkish Fourth Army in the first world war. The first served until 1916, the second from 1916 until the end of the war.

EBAN, Abba: Israel's Foreign Minister since 1966, previously Ambassador to the United Nations, to the United States, Minister of Education and Deputy Prime Minister.

EDER, Montagu David: founder of the British Psychoanalysts Association, deputy leader of the Zionist Commission in Palestine 1918–1920. President of the British Zionist Federation 1931.

ESHKOL, Levi: succeeded Ben-Gurion as Prime Minister in 1963, died February 1969.

EVRON, Ephraim: Deputy Director-General of the Israel Foreign Ministry 1973, Counsellor at the Israel Embassy in London, Minister in Washington, Ambassador in Stockholm and Ottawa, former principal aide to Pinhas Lavon when Secretary of the Histadrut, the Israel Federation of Labour.

FAISAL I: third son of the Sharif of Mecca, Commander of the Arab Forces against the Turks 1916–1918, Arab spokesman at the Peace Conference 1919, proclaimed King of Syria in Damascus in March 1920, expelled by the French in July 1920, named by the British as Emir of Iraq in 1921, then appointed to be King.

FRANKFURTER, Justice Felix: Professor at Harvard Law School from 1914, associated with Brandeis and Weizmann in the leadership of the Zionist Organisation, legal adviser to the Zionist delegation at the Peace Conference 1919, collaborated with Weizmann in the negotiations with the Emir Faisal.

GASTER, Haham Dr Moses: Head of the Sephardi Jewish Community in the United Kingdom 1887–1917. Close associate of Sir Mark Sykes and keen supporter of his British imperial policy.

HACOHEN, Hillel: Russian-born Hebrew author, first delegate to address the first Zionist Congress in 1897 in Hebrew, settled in Palestine in 1907. One of the recognised spokesmen of Palestine Jewry in its dealings with the Zionist Commission.

HAIKAL, Mohammed Hassanein: Editor of *al Ahram*, the leading Arab newspaper published in Cairo, rated as the confidant and frequent but not always consistent spokesman for President Nasser, but rather less so for President Sadat.

HANKEY, Sir Maurice: Secretary to the Committee of Imperial Defence 1912–1914, Secretary to the War Council and the War Cabinet 1914–1919, Secretary to the Cabinet and to the Committee of Four at the Peace Conference 1919; one of the most influential, if not *the* most influential civil servant of his time.

HELMS, Richard: Director of the Central Intelligence Agency (CIA) until 1972, US Ambassador to Iran 1973.

HOGARTH, David George (1862–1927): like T. E. Lawrence, who was his pupil, successfully combined classical archaeology with political warfare and military intelligence. Head of British School of Archaeology in Athens 1897–1900, Keeper of the Ashmolean Museum at Oxford 1908, Director of the Arab Bureau in Cairo in 1916. Obtained King Husain's approval for British policy in Arabia and Palestine on mission to Jeddah in 1917.

HUSAIN, ibn Ali: Sharif of Mecca, head of the Hashemite dynasty, Emir of Mecca 1908–1916, King of the Hejaz 1916–1924, defeated by the Emir Abdul Aziz ibn Saud, lived in exile in Cyprus 1924–1930, died in Amman 1931.

EL-HUSAINI, Amin: officer in the Ottoman army 1914–1918, deserted to British-occupied Palestine, leader of the militant anti-Hashemite wing of the Palestine nationalists 1918–1920, negotiated with Weizmann and Israel Sieff 1918, escaped to Transjordan to avoid arrest by the British 1920, amnestied and confirmed as Mufti of Jerusalem by Sir Herbert Samuel, the High Commissioner, 1921, President of the Supreme Muslim Council "for life" 1922, supported Hitler regime during second world war.

JABOTINSKY, Vladimir: Zionist writer, orator and activist, formed the World Union of Zionist Revisionists in 1925 in opposition to Weizmann's "moderation", spiritual father of the Irgun Zvai Leumi.

KITCHENER, Lord Horatio Herbert: Field-Marshal, British Agent and virtual ruler of Egypt 1911–1914, War Minister 1914–1916, drowned while on his way to Russia on 5 June 1916.

KOLLEK, Theodor (Teddy): Director-General Prime Minister's Office under Ben-Gurion and Eshkol 1952–1964, Mayor of Jerusalem 1965.

LAWRENCE, T. E.: Assigned to Arab Bureau Cairo 1916, liaison with Emir Faisal in conducting the "Arab Revolt". Considered the Arab cause had been betrayed by the Peace Conferences of 1919 and 1920 in handing administration of Syria to the French. Author of *Seven Pillars of Wisdom*.

LLOYD GEORGE, David: Minister of Munitions 1915–1916, War Minister 1916, Prime Minister 1916–1922.

MARKS, Simon: later Lord Marks, member of the Manchester group which supported and financed Dr Weizmann during the first world war and afterwards, Chairman of Marks & Spencer Ltd.

MCMAHON, Sir Henry Arthur (1862–1949): Foreign Secretary to the Government of India 1911–1914, High Commissioner to Egypt 1914–1916, conducted the negotiations with the Sharif of Mecca which led to the "Arab Revolt" 1916.

MEINERTZHAGEN, Colonel Richard (1878–1967): Chief Political Officer in Palestine and Syria 1919–1920, Military Adviser in the Middle East Department of the Colonial Office 1921–1924.

MEIR, Mrs Golda: Foreign Minister 1956–1966, General-Secretary Labour Party (Mapai) 1966–1969, Prime Minister 1969–

MILNER, Viscount Alfred: Member of the War Cabinet 1916, War Minister 1918, Colonial Secretary 1918–1921.

MONEY, Major-General Sir Arthur Wigram: Chief Administrator in Palestine 1918–1919.

MONTAGU, Hon. Edwin Samuel (1879–1924): Minister of Munitions 1916, Secretary of State for India 1917–1922, strong opponent of Zionism and the Balfour Declaration.

MUSSA KAZEM: Governor of the Yemen under the Ottoman regime, Mayor of Jerusalem and recognised leader and spokesman for the Palestinian Arabs

1918–1920, dismissed as Mayor by the British but became Chairman of the Arab Executive 1920.

ORMSBY-GORE, William George Arthur: Fourth Baron Harlech, Conservative MP from 1910, Arab Bureau in Cairo 1916–1917, Assistant-Secretary to the War Cabinet 1917–1918, Assistant Political Officer assigned to the Zionist Commission 1918, Liaison with the Zionist Delegation at the Paris Peace Conference, British Member of the League of Nations' Permanent Mandates Commission 1921–1922, Colonial Secretary 1936–1938, resigned 1938.

PERES, Shimon: Director-General Israel Defence Ministry 1953–1959, Deputy-Defence Minister 1959–1965, resigned and formed breakaway Rafi Party with Ben-Gurion and Dayan, architect of the National Coalition in May/June 1967, Minister without Portfolio 1969, Minister of Transport and Communications 1970. Largely responsible during Ben-Gurion's Premiership for Israel's French and German connections 1955–1963.

PICOT, Georges François, or, more accurately, GEORGES-PICOT, François: French career diplomat appointed as opposite number to Sir Mark Sykes in the negotiations on the future of Asiatic Turkey which resulted in the Sykes-Picot Agreement of May 1916.

RABIN, Major-General Itzhak: Chief of Staff Israel Defence Forces 1964–1968, Ambassador to the United States 1968–1973.

ROBERTSON, General Sir William: Chief of the Imperial General Staff 1915 to January 1918, principal military oppponent of Lloyd George's "Eastern Policy".

ROGERS, William P.: Secretary of State at the State Department 1969–

ROTHSCHILD, Lionel Walter, Second Baron (1868–1937): Conservative MP 1899–1910, considered by the authorities as the representative figure of Anglo-Jewry.

SAMUEL, Sir Herbert, later Viscount (1870–1963): Liberal MP 1902–1918, member of the Asquith Cabinet 1915–1916, Home Secretary 1916, High Commissioner to Palestine 1920–1925.

SAPIR, Pinhas: Israel Minister of Finance 1965–1968, General-Secretary Israel Labour Party (Mapai) 1969, Minister of Finance 1969–

SCOTT, C. P.: Editor *Manchester Guardian* 1872–1929, friend and confidant of the Liberal Party leaders, especially Lloyd George to whom he introduced Weizmann.

SIDEBOTHAM, Herbert: leader-writer and military specialist of the *Manchester Guardian* during the first world war. His book *England and Palestine* published in 1917 before the Balfour Declaration was a powerful argument for the British-Zionist alliance.

SIEFF, Israel M., later Lord Sieff of Brimpton (1889–1972): Associate and personal assistant to Dr Weizmann 1915–1920, Zionist advocate of a Jewish

State 1916, Founder and principal contributor *Palestine* magazine, Co-founder and member of the British Palestine Committee 1916, Secretary to the Zionist Commission and personal assistant to Dr Weizmann in Palestine 1918, delegate to the Zionist Congress at Carlsbad 1921, President of the Zionist Federation of Great Britain, Founder of the Daniel Sieff Institute at Rehovot, succeeded Lord Marks as Chairman of the Board of Marks & Spencer Ltd.

SISCO, Joseph S.: Assistant-Secretary of State at the State Department with responsibility for the Middle East 1969.

SOKOLOW, Nahum: General-Secretary of the World Zionist Organisation 1905–1909, representative of the World Zionist Organisation in London after the outbreak of war in August 1914, closely associated with Sir Mark Sykes, in charge of negotiations with the French and the Vatican for support of the Balfour Declaration, and with the British Government during Weizmann's absence in Palestine.

STORRS, Sir Ronald (1881–1955): Oriental Secretary in Egypt 1917, Military Governor of Jerusalem 1917, Civil Governor 1920–1926.

SYMES, Lt-Colonel Sir Stewart: Director Arab Bureau 1918, discussed with Dr Weizmann terms of possible Arab-Zionist alliance in June 1918, succeeded Clayton as Chief Secretary to the Palestine Government 1925.

WATERS-TAYLOR, Lt-Colonel L. R. E.: Financial Adviser to the Military Administration in Palestine 1919–1923, encouraged Arab nationalist opposition to Zionists and to British policy favouring a Jewish National Home in Palestine, maintained close and confidential relations with Faisal, Mussa Kazem, Amin and Aref el-Aref.

WEIZMANN, Dr Chaim (1874–1952): Reader in Biochemistry, University of Manchester, Director of Admiralty Laboratories 1916–1919, President World Zionist Organisation and Jewish Agency for Palestine 1921–1931 and 1935–1946, first President of the State of Israel 1949–1952.

WINGATE, General Sir Reginald (1861–1953): Sirdar of the Egyptian army and Governor-General of the Sudan 1899–1916, Commander of the Hejaz operations 1916–1919, High Commissioner of Egypt 1917–1919, led British expedition which occupied Darfur in 1916.

YADIN, Yigael: Lt-General and Professor, Chief of Operations of the Haganah 1948, Chief of Staff Israel Defence Forces 1949–1952, Professor of Archaeology, Hebrew University 1963–

YALE, Captain William: United States' Special Agent in the Middle East 1918. Author of many revealing and self-revealing despatches to the State Department, especially on relations between Great Britain and France.

YARIV, Major-General Aharon: Chief of Israel's Military Intelligence 1960–1972, special adviser on National Security to the Prime Minister 1972–

# Introduction

The real trouble about Palestine – the Palestine conflict, as we have come to know it – was that it had nothing to do with Jews and Arabs. Not in its essentials. Arabs and Jews believed, of course, that they were the principal protagonists when, in fact, they played only secondary and peripheral parts. The Palestine conflict was – and is – an integral element in the relationship of the Great Powers, and it has become more so, not less, since 1915, all the more so under conditions of super-power co-existence – the "peace" of the seventies.

What concerns me here, however, is not to tell again the well-worn account of what has happened in the Palestine conflict since the first world war. That story is already so fully and contrarily documented that the real issues have become obscured rather than illuminated. It is, to be honest, of no great interest any more as to who was right and who was wrong, because it does not really matter any more and because the Jews will not be convinced by the Anglo-Arab version of the history of these 50 years and Arabs will not accept the Anglo-Zionist account of the period. With the passing of the years, the prospect of reconciling these two histories is receding and less promising than it has been at any time.

What I want to do now, therefore, is to take as read this old and new documentation, the rewritten histories and biographies, and ask myself in the wake of it all, "why did we fail"? It is a question that has worried me since 1950 when Israel's glow of independence began to show the first signs of going sour.

Since, and indeed before, then I have spent much time discussing with the principal participants the reasons for the failure to bring about a peaceful settlement in the Middle East. Something like 30 years have passed since I recorded the first such discussion, and circumstances and explanations have changed dramatically since the early 1940s – and they keep on changing. The milestones of this search for a convincing answer were sometimes hopeful, frequently dramatic and often tragic. The only constant was that the explanation for the failure was never wholly satisfactory. Above all, the solutions were never solutions: whether it was the Balfour Declaration in 1917, the Churchill White Paper in 1922, the Royal Commission of 1936, the White Paper of 1939, the Allied victory in 1945, the Anglo-American Commission's Report in 1946, the elevation of Abdullah to Kingship, the UN Partition decision in 1947, Israel's war of independence in 1948, or the emergence of an outstanding Egyptian nationalist leader in 1952. One can go on recording one event or another that was to point the way, but neither the events nor the explanations provided adequate reasons for the repeated failures. Even those who were most intimately concerned, Arabs, Jews, British, Americans, could find no common ground. Times and circumstances changed too often and too quickly for any kind of consistency.

It was after many discussions with the late Lord Sieff, during which we went over his papers concerning his association with Dr Weizmann, that it became evident that there was no single sure way to establish the reasons for failure ; that possibly the only way was to retread the path that led to the present and to see the scene as those who shaped it had seen it. They too, had no common ground. Therefore, the only way we could hope to reconstruct how matters stood then was not by trying to reconcile the conflicting views, but to let them speak for themselves in their own words, private and public.

But one general failure was immediately self-evident: "We" failed because no one was prepared to see the Palestine question in focus. Like the airline advertisements, every contestant saw himself as the hub of the Middle East world. Jew and Arab were both guilty of this mistaken national vanity; but the Great Powers were no less at fault. However, if there has to be an exception to every rule, then it was the British who, alone, had considerable justification in claiming that their role was central and their interests supreme: they were, at the end of the first world war, the dominant power – the only dominant power. They remained as such until the end of the second world war, when Ernest Bevin failed to translate the total military victory into the political aftermath that would have consolidated the military success and maintained Great Britain's political ascendancy in the world for at least another generation, with

xiv

domestic and international consequences that would have transformed the post-war world. It was not the only failure of these 50 years. There were others – none perhaps quite so daunting in their impact as the self-destruction of British power – but in their own way these were mistakes with which we now have to live and for which we will have to pay.

So, if the British were not the only ones to make mistakes, because of their dominant position and the sheer extent of their imperial sway – and because of the imaginative calibre of their policy-makers – these mistakes made a much greater impact than did the mistakes of other parties involved: the Americans, the Arabs, the French, the Germans, the Turks and the Zionists. To begin with, we must, therefore, consider why the British – who had at first everything that mattered on their side – failed on every count. The British had power, the men and the money, the ideas and the means to carry them through; they had both a tradition and experience and they had, when it mattered most, an almost inexhaustible store of goodwill to draw upon. But they failed. Why?

Before we can consider the answer, we have to establish who were the British who were responsible for the failure. They were comparatively few in number: a few ministers, a few soldiers, and a few officials – probably less than 50 in all who really mattered. That they failed is no discredit to them. For they tried and, what is more, they cared for their own. They were imperialists who understood the ground rules of imperialism as well, if not better, than did Lenin, and certainly much better than did the Kaiser or the unlovely French Levant financiers. They did not delude themselves with the ethos and myth of imperialism. They understood what they were after and they had a fine touch in the art of getting it. But they failed. Why?

It is of course always easier to pose these questions than to answer them – especially when there is no simple answer, and even more so when everyone has a ready-made and firmly held view of what the answer should be. Perhaps my main reason for setting out on this work was that I was not certain that I knew the answers after working on the questions for some 30 years, or whether the answers I knew were the right ones. But I wanted to find out.

In the process I have had to revise a number of my own opinions and judgements and to reconsider the accepted role of leading men – such as Faisal and Weizmann, Dayan and Nasser, and of Mrs Meir – and of policies pursued by the Great Powers. Also I came to understand that the real test for both – men and policies – came at two climactic periods at the beginning and at the end of the 50-year span between the Balfour Declaration and its aftermath and the Six Day War and its aftermath, in the two periods from 1917 to 1923 and from 1967 to 1973. I sought therefore to establish the real intentions of the men and powers involved in these two decisive periods in the modern history of Palestine in which the Arab-Israeli conflict became an integral element of the Great Power contest for control and influence in the Middle East as part of their strategic Grand Design and in order to ensure the uninterrupted flow of oil.

Thus the first chapter reflects the British position (with strong French and Russian undertones) during the first period as seen primarily through the private (and therefore more frank) perspective of the principals in London, Cairo and Jerusalem. It is concerned more with intentions expressed in letters, diaries and within the relative privacy of the War Council and Cabinet, rather than with official and diplomatic explanations and their heavy emphasis on propaganda and political warfare. It provides in particular new insights into the remarkable role played by Sir Gilbert Clayton in the shaping of British policy at the time and explains his bold "Design" for a Middle Eastern New Deal in which Arabs, Jews and British would collaborate on equal terms. Clayton played a much more constructive and significant part, as the documentation in this first chapter shows, than did the far more publicised interventions of Sir Mark Sykes. But what emerges here above all else is the unromantic realism of British policy during this period; it had in fact few of the attributes with which it became subsequently identified by pro-Zionist and anti-Zionist historians.

The second chapter considers the Zionist operations alongside the British during this first phase – from 1917 to 1923. It does so largely through the personal views and papers of Dr Weizmann and Lord Sieff, who had been Weizmann's political secretary, personal aide and close friend throughout this period. It also looks at Weizmann through the eyes of contemporary Palestinian Jews at the time when Weizmann headed the Zionist Commission to Palestine in the last year of the Great War and immediately afterwards. All kinds of important revisions of previous judgements were found necessary in the context of the new information and of Weizmann's often contradictory private views as distinct from those he voiced in public or in his diplomatic conversations with British statesmen, American Jews and the Zionists generally. In

xvi

this chapter we also consider the very high degree of collaboration which existed at that time between Dr Weizmann and the British leaders, and with the Foreign Office; this evidently went much further than even Weizmann's closest colleagues had realised. It is worth recalling that Weizmann again made use of these private connections with the British during the second world war and was accused by Ben-Gurion of virtual treason to Zionism in the summer of 1942 because of private links with Lord Halifax, the British Ambassador in Washington.[1]

The often startlingly new information about the Arab nationalist movement in Chapter Three, and especially how active the part played in it by the Palestinians was in the 1918–1923 period, requires some explanation. In the course of my discussions with Lord Sieff about his role with the Zionist Commission we agreed to consult in particular the men and material that had become available in the occupied West Bank territories. Much of this material was at that time unclassified and unsorted in the Israel Government's State Archives; some was in the possession of leading Palestinians living in the occupied areas. The venerable historian, Aref el-Aref, then over 80 years old but still very much in the picture and with massive private diaries and original documents to sustain his memories, was most helpful. But such was the mass of matter, and its state of non-organisation, that it required many months of work to sift, translate and extract what was new and valuable. Virtually all of this was first-hand material, vouchsafed by men such as Aref el-Aref, and as such probably the only remaining so-to-speak eye-witness accounts of that period, much in the same way as the late Lord Sieff was the last remaining survivor of the Weizmann circle at that time who could contribute valuable fresh insights on the strength of his papers and recollections. Two significant factors emerge from this Arab version of events. The first shows how important was the Palestinian role inside the Syrian national movement, and how quickly the Palestinians had emancipated themselves from the control of Damascus; the second factor which required new judgements was the personality of Amin el-Husaini, who gained world-wide fame or notoriety as the one-time Mufti of Jerusalem. Amin emerges as one of the strong personalities in the shaping of Palestinian nationalism and in the making of the Palestinian "rock" on which all Arab policies on Palestine were subsequently built. It was Amin who formulated the

[1] For details of this illuminating episode see my *Second Arab Awakening*, pp. 190–195.

policy of the "Three Noes", which 50 years later Nasser presented to the Arab summit conference after the Six Day War in September 1967.

However, by the end of the first period – in 1923 – Amin's policy of resistance to Zionism hardly mattered any longer in relation to the British position in Palestine. For the British – and the other Great Powers, especially the French – had by then decided against the Arab-Jew syndrome that had been the basis of the Balfour Declaration and the McMahon letters to Sharif Husain. It was too hazardous a gambit and too unreliable an alliance in the securing of the Middle East for their strategic purposes and as their main source of oil.

The Interlude considers the role of this all-important Third Force in the Middle East which Arab nationalists and Zionists had consistently either underrated or misunderstood: oil. As with the origins of the Arab-Israeli conflict, so with the origins of the conflict between the oil companies and the host countries, the essential element that matters is no longer past injustice but present significance and power. The new oil equation could be stated in this way: The Arab countries (and Iran) have the oil; the West has the money which the Arab countries (and Iran) require; and the world at large, especially Europe, Japan and increasingly also the United States and the Soviet Union, must look to the Middle East for their oil supplies during the next decade. It was therefore the oil factor – and not Arab nationalism or Zionism – that fundamentally changed the character of the Middle East and made Israel and the Arab countries indispensable to the United States and the Soviet Union (and thus also to Europe and Japan) in 1973. This was not true of the situation in 1923 or in 1967. The Americans had become aware of this transformation in the strategic assessment of the Middle East; in a sense the visits to Washington by Israel's Prime Minister, Mrs Golda Meir, and of President Sadat's special envoy, Mr Hafez Ismail, in February 1973 were a kind of swan song for the old policy in which the local Arab-Israeli conflict appeared to be the dominant element. It was a policy that had bridged the years between the two decisive periods here discussed in which the local conflict was the principal element in the Great Power struggle in the Middle East. Differences within the Western camp, and uncertainty about the purpose and intention of the British, French and Americans, became increasingly apparent in the decade that followed the Suez war of 1956 and laid the basis for Israel's crisis – in 1966 not 1967 – the subject of the first chapter of Part II.

For by then the tide appeared to be running strongly against Israel and against the maintenance of Western influence in the area. The Arab-Soviet alliance had assumed massive proportions and seemed to be supreme in the Middle Eastern world, and reinforcing it in Africa and in the Mediterranean. The West, through NATO or, more directly, by the United States in the Mediterranean and by the British in the Persian Gulf, seemed either unable or unwilling to intervene. The oil companies were scared and prone to retreat. And Israel's presence appeared to many as possibly no more than a passing phase in the history of the Arab Middle East, much as the Crusader Kingdom had been and of even shorter duration.

Chapter Two of this last part of the book therefore looks more closely at the Israeli situation from the inside, and considers both the shortcomings and the strength which the country had developed, and the narrow line which divided the two during the crisis which preceded the Six Day War. The "Meir Era" and the roots of its inability to bring about a peace settlement with its neighbours and greater harmony within the country, is considered against the background of changes brought about in Israel's social structure. New values have been introduced into the post-June-war Zionism with a strong accompanying emphasis on material wealth and its connections with the Jewish diaspora. This has produced a new solidarity but with the attendant danger – no longer hypothetical – of the strong current of diaspora nationalism spilling over into chauvinism. The price of Israel's contemporary dependence on the United States – and its benefits – is weighed in the light of its respective merits and demerits, and this chapter considers frankly and factually Mrs Meir's role before and during her Premiership in this special relationship. The concluding chapter on the re-entry of the superpowers looks at the other side of the coin: at Egypt's experience with her superpower, the Soviet Union, and, what is of far greater importance, at the superpower assessment of the Middle East. It considers the implications for Israel and for Egypt of the change in the superpower relationship and especially their switch from hostile co-existence to the policy of strategic parity between the Soviet Union and the United States. This has paralysed the superpowers in terms of independent action in the Middle East and compelled them to reconsider the bases of their association with their so-called clients that are clients no more.

In a world situation in which the Soviet Union was increasingly

xix

preoccupied with the emergence of two potential new superpowers, China in the East and the European Community in the West, rather than with the declining world influence of the United States, the position of the Middle East was bound to be central in both strategic and oil terms. As a result we have witnessed a curious reversal of roles to those which had been on stage in 1917. Then Dr Weizmann – and the Arab nationalist leaders – had understood that they had to lock their respective causes to one or the other Great Power coalitions, and, if they wanted to achieve their Zionist and Arab national aims, it had to be with the prospective victor. Both Arabs and Zionists plumped for the Allies and won; they got, more or less, what they had wanted. Fifty years later the two superpowers understood that if they wanted to preserve their influence and interests in the Middle East they would have to lock them to one or the other parties in the Arab-Israeli conflict, to the successful one if they wanted to succeed. The Americans chose Israel, the Russians opted for Egypt. But in the event circumstances were different from those of 1917. Israel's victory in 1967 was total in military terms but not in its political aftermath. As a result, the superpowers had also to adjust their aims alongside those of the local "Powers" in order to achieve a new balance of power and deterrence which applied alike to the local and the superpowers: they had to ensure a de facto form of peaceful co-existence between Israel and her Arab neighbours and between the Arab oil producers and the world's oil consumer countries.

As at the beginning, so at the end, the two sets of forces were intertwined in an intricate interplay; neither could afford to ignore the other and both had to learn from the failure of the past. For the one thing that had changed in these 50 years was that the Middle East had become a matter for world concern because the world's well-being depended on its continued peace, stability and oil. Because of this the Arab-Israeli conflict in 1973 was no longer peripheral but central to superpower strategy and politics, not because of The Book but because of The Oil.

# PART I

## 1917-1923
## THE FIRST CHANCE

# ONE

# The British Approach

The War Council met on 10 March 1915, as usual in the Cabinet room at Downing Street. The Prime Minister, Asquith, presided over the meeting summoned to consider the Dardanelles campaign and the Russian request for a clear statement about British intentions over the future of Constantinople. It was a formidable gathering of talent: the Foreign Office, the War Office, the Admiralty, the Treasury, the Colonial Office, and the leader of the Conservative Party were there: men who ruled the greatest empire the world had ever known – Grey, Kitchener, Churchill, Fisher, Balfour, Lloyd George, Haldane, Harcourt, Bonar Law and Lansdowne. They had met a week earlier to consider these twin problems. The mood had been relaxed and confident. The attack on the Dardanelles was going well and it seemed to be no more than a question of days, weeks perhaps, before they occupied Constantinople, the head and heart of the Ottoman Empire. But they had to decide about Constantinople, which meant in effect about the future of the Turkish Empire for "the Russians wanted an immediate decision" and, in Grey's opinion, it was absurd that "a huge empire such as Russia should have only ports that were icebound part of the year". Moreover, the Council had what is considered reliable intelligence that the Russians were contemplating a separate peace with Germany unless the British ensured Russian possession of the Straits and Constantinople.

None of the members of the War Council were troubled by the thought that the occupation of Constantinople was anything but imminent. What concerned them was the aftermath. Kitchener and Churchill thought that the Turks might be induced by the British to switch sides in the wake of their defeat. Kitchener told the War Council that they should announce to the Turkish public that "we were coming as the ancient friend of the Turks"; Churchill saw even greater possibilities in assuring

3

the Turks before the attack on Constantinople was launched that the British came without any spirit of hostility to the Turkish nation, but were intent solely on ridding Turkey of the pernicious German influence and to restore Turkey's former independence and self-respect. Indeed, Churchill did not rule out the possibility of co-operation with Turkey as soon as the Allies had been successful: ". . . we ought to hire the Turkish army as mercenaries". Grey was not convinced. For one thing it might be difficult to convince the Turks that the British were coming as liberators, while at the same time they were preparing the share-out of the Ottoman Empire with the Russians, Greeks and Bulgars, and possibly even with the Rumanians and Italians. It was Grey's inherent sense of decency that clearly prevented him from mentioning also the French and the British. But if Grey had scruples, his colleagues were not thus burdened.

At their meeting on 10 March, the Prime Minister reminded his colleagues that the Russians had asked for a final solution, not an interim arrangement. Balfour responded with an assurance that he personally had no objections to the Russians getting their way as regards Constantinople and the Dardanelles "provided the other Allies received similar assurances as regards their own wishes. We ought to consider what we wanted, for example, in the Persian Gulf and elsewhere." Lloyd George agreed. The Russians were so keen to obtain Constantinople, that they would be generous in making concessions elsewhere. "It was vital for us, if we made concessions, to say what we wanted in return." Asquith then advised his colleagues that his naval and military advisers also raised no objections on strategic grounds to the Russian claims. However, the naval authorities felt that if Russia was established at Constantinople, then it would be desirable for the British to have another base in the Eastern Mediterranean; they thought of Alexandretta, "the probable terminus of the Baghdad Railway on the Mediterranean". Kitchener agreed. Lloyd George, however, rightly feared that a British claim to Alexandretta might lead to difficulties with the French, and suggested that Palestine would provide far better compensation, "owing to the prestige it would give us". Kitchener stuck to Alexandretta as the most desirable British counter to Constantinople: "Palestine would be of no value to us whatsoever", and he was sure that the French would see reason if the British position was properly explained to them.

Churchill steered the discussion to the broader considerations, reflecting the optimism under which the War Council had met. After the war, he thought, the British position "would be very strong. If we succeeded in shattering German naval power, we ought to be able to build a Mediterranean Fleet against France and Russia." With this in mind, the War Council agreed to Russia's demands: she was to have Constantinople and control over the Straits – subject to the British obtaining their "desiderata" which would be set out in due course and would include Alexandretta. The Prime Minister, writing that day to his young friend, Venetia Stanley, put it more succinctly. The Russians were to have their way, he told her, so long as "both we and France should get a substantial share of the carcase of the Turk".

We have not yet done with this most revealing of War Councils. It met again on 19 March, at first "all rather upset by Churchill reading telegrams . . . announcing the loss of two French and two British battleships and *Inflexible* damaged" in the previous day's battle in the Dardanelles. But the Council was undaunted by this news. A long discussion followed which gave continued consideration to the partition of Turkey which members of the Council believed to be imminent; Churchill alone exhibited some premonitory doubts, but not for long.

To begin with, the Prime Minister informed the Council that the French had now laid claim "to a very large part of Turkey in Asia in return for permitting the Russian occupation of Constantinople and the Straits". These French claims covered Cilicia (the fertile plain between the Taurus Mountains and the Mediterranean), Syria and Palestine. But, said Asquith, the Russians objected most strongly to the Christian Holy Places being in French hands. He had good reasons for turning the attention of the War Council to the demands which Britain's senior partner in the war against Germany was making. For the French were as interested and preoccupied with the future of Constantinople as were the Russians and the British – and, in a sense, their interest was more direct and persuasive. France had more capital invested in Turkey (principally in Constantinople) than all other powers, including Turkey herself, combined. The Ottoman public debt to France was estimated at 2.4 billion gold francs, some 56 per cent of the total Ottoman debt in 1914; French investment in Turkey's private industry at the outbreak of war was 50 per cent larger than Germany's and was estimated to exceed 900 million gold francs; even in the Kaiser's own Baghdad Railway, French investment was larger than Germany's. It was not surprising, therefore, that as the French and British guns pounded the

5

Dardanelles fortifications, French preoccupations, no less than British and Russian, centred on Constantinople. Moreover, the French Quai d'Orsay was convinced "that Churchill's drive to the Mediterranean was in fact a cover to bid for the last link in the British power chain encircling the future Levantine Empire from Cyprus and Suez to Aden and the Persian Gulf".[1]

The French fear of British intentions was not altogether unwarranted as was evidenced by the discussion which followed Asquith's opening remarks about French demands at the War Council. For the moment, the war against Germany receded into limbo as members weighed the imperial interest in the partition of Turkey. Grey wondered whether they ought not take into account the very strong feeling in the Muslim world "that Mohammedanism ought to have a political as well as a religious existence" and whether they should consider setting up "a new and independent Muslim state".

The Indian Government, as always, had the clearest and least inhibited view of the needs of the Middle East. The Military Department, backed by the Viceroy, Lord Hardinge, considered that Turkey in Asia should not be dismembered but, on the contrary, made as strong as possible. It was an opinion worth recording since Lord Hardinge was to occupy the central position of Permanent Under-Secretary at the Foreign Office during the critical years of war and peace-making from 1916 to 1920. The Political Department of the India Office, however, did not share the Viceroy's views. It argued that Turkey should be sacrificed and Arabia made strong.

Kitchener also supported the Arab solution because the Turks would be under strong pressure from their powerful Russian neighbour after the war and this domination would extend also to the Caliphate; thus Russian influence could indirectly assert itself through the Caliphate over the Mohammedan part of the population of India. "If, on the other hand, the Caliphate was transferred to Arabia, it would remain to a great extent under our influence." The "Arab" solution harmonised, moreover, with British interest in the future of Mesopotamia. Again it was the India Office that stressed its significant role. Kitchener believed that, if Mesopotamia was to be left undeveloped, then it might as well be left to the Arabs. "But, if it was to be developed, we should only be creating trouble for ourselves by leaving it to them." All the same,

[1] W. W. Gottlieb, *Studies in Secret Diplomacy*, p. 103; see also George H. Cassar, *The French and the Dardanelles*, p. 92.

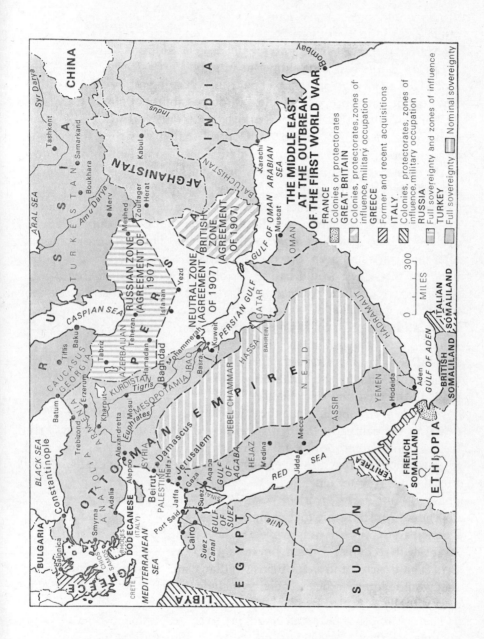

THE MIDDLE EAST
AT THE OUTBREAK
OF THE FIRST WORLD WAR

FRANCE
　Colonies or protectorates
GREAT BRITAIN
　Colonies, protectorates, zones of
　influence, military occupation
GREECE
　Former and recent acquisitions
ITALY
　Colonies, protectorates, zones of
　influence, military occupation
RUSSIA
　Full sovereignty and zones of influence
TURKEY
　Full sovereignty　　　Nominal sovereignty

0　　　300
MILES

"India would expect some return for her effort and losses in Mesopotamia". And the Secretary of State for India, Lord Crewe, agreed that "Basra Vilayet must form part of the British Empire".

Lloyd George had wider horizons in mind, just as, 25 years later, he looked for an ally "to prevent Russia from becoming too predominant".[2] They ought, therefore, not to rule out the possibility of giving Germany "a bone of some sort" in the Turkish share-out, and Churchill, after some initial hesitation, urged the Council that it was time to make a clean sweep and remove the out-of-date Turks from the control of one of the most fertile countries in the world. Turkey had to be partitioned. Asquith then wound up the long discussion with the conclusion that if "we were to leave the other nations to scramble for Turkey without taking anything ourselves, we should not be doing our duty". It was decided to send a stalling reply to the Russians. The first consideration after the Straits had been forced and Constantinople had passed into the hands of the Allies, would be the establishment of a Muslim entity. It would have to include Arabia, and the question would arise as to what was to go with it. The French Cabinet deliberated for another three weeks while the prospect of an early descent on Constantinople receded. Finally, on 10 April 1915, the French Government informed the Russian authorities of its agreement, subject to the ultimate victory of the Entente and to the "realisation by France and England of their plans in the East and elsewhere".

My reason for singling out these meetings of the War Council at the outset of the calling of the British witnesses is that it was so singularly free of humbug and double-talk. In fact, this was a significant element of most of the Great Power exchanges at the time. They required no verbal fig-leaves to hide their desires. For this was the last healthy phase of imperial permissiveness. When Grey spoke of a new independent Muslim state that would embrace Arabia – and won the War Council's support for this project – he meant, as he said, that "the Arabs will recognise British interests as paramount and work under British guidance", and as for British-Indian claims to the Basra province, that would require to be extended to include the Baghdad region and the area actually occupied by Anglo-Indian troops.

There were other potential claimants to shares in the Ottoman legacy so long as they managed to fit into the imperial pattern: Greeks, Bulgars, Italians, Rumanians. But they all had to pass the ultimate

[2] CAB 22/1 PRO; see also M. Gilbert's *Churchill*, Vol. III, p. 356.

test: how much could they benefit their imperial patron? No other considerations entered into the debates of the War Council in London or the Cabinet in Paris. At least one claimant had failed to pass the test and was not even considered at these meetings. In between the 10 March and 19 March meetings which had finally acceded to the Russian demands, and made provisional allotments to the future beneficiaries of Ottoman territory, Asquith told Venetia Stanley in a letter written from Walmer Castle of his thoughts about the suggestion made "in an almost dithyrambic memorandum" by Herbert Samuel that "in the carving up of the Turks' Asiatic dominions, we should take Palestine, into which the scattered Jews could in time swarm back from all quarters of the globe, and in due course obtain Home Rule (what an attractive community!)". Asquith adds that the only partisan of Samuel's proposal was Lloyd George "who, I need not say, does not care a damn for the Jews or their past or their future". Kitchener, Asquith added, continued to favour the annexation of Alexandretta rather than Palestine, "and leaving the Jews and the Holy Places to look after themselves".

This was understandable since the point at issue was not the future of the Jews but, as Herbert Samuel himself had put it in his memorandum circulated to the Cabinet, they had to remember that after the war they would have to live in the same world as 70 million Germans "and we should give as little justification as we can for the hatching, ten, twenty, or thirty years hence, of a German war of revenge". They would have to retain some of the German colonies for strategic reasons, and others to compensate the Dominions and Great Britain herself "which public opinion will demand". But if, instead of annexing German East Africa and West Africa, the British were to seek their compensation in Mesopotamia and Palestine, there might be more likelihood of a lasting peace. That was the issue that was uppermost in the consideration of the future of Palestine, as Samuel and his friends viewed it; they wanted the British to rule Palestine, not the Jews. "To attempt to realise the aspiration of a Jewish state one century too soon might throw back its actual realisation for many centuries more. These considerations are fully recognised by the leaders of the Zionist movement," Samuel assured Asquith and his Cabinet colleagues.

The essence of all discussions by the Allies was emphatically their Great Power interests. The Foreign Office in London and the Viceroy in Delhi looked to a permanent Anglo-Russian alliance to ensure the future peace and the acceptance of British and Russian overlordship in their respective spheres of interest in Asia once Germany was defeated. There was a strong feeling that the Americans had to be kept out of participating in the war against Germany because the Americans would contribute nothing to winning the war while actively interfering to ensure that the Allies would lose the peace.[3] But at that stage, opinion in the Cabinet in London and Paris had crystallised sufficiently to accept that no matter what happened with regard to Germany, the Turkish Empire had to be defeated and broken up. There was some rudimentary discussion about Palestine at various times. Lloyd George thought there might be possibilities in a "partly Jewish buffer state"[4] but he feared that the French would have strong objections. Russia, on the other hand, might prefer Jews to Catholics in the Holy Places. It all depended on imperial interests and calculations, not on Jewish or Zionist desires or aims.

It was much the same with the protagonists of an "Arab" solution. "I conceive it not to be impossible," wrote the British Sirdar of the Egyptian Army and Governor-General of the Sudan, Sir Reginald Wingate, to the Viceroy in Delhi, Lord Hardinge, on 26 August 1915, " that in the dim future a federation of semi-independent Arab States might exist under European guidance and supervision, linked together by racial and linguistic bonds, owing spiritual allegiance to a single Arab Primate and looking to Great Britain as its patron and protector." Wingate was in favour of expressing "pious aspirations" in support of an Arab Union. Hardinge himself did not feel any need for the rotundities of diplomatic imprecision when he discussed with Gertrude Bell the future of Baghdad and of British control over the conquered Arab world after he had taken charge of the Foreign Office in London. They would need to have a really competent man in Baghdad to act as British Resident, he told her. For the rest, "it really would not matter if we choose three of the fattest men in Baghdad or three of the men with longest beards who would be put up as the emblems of Arab rule and who would be ruled through the resident and a certain number of advisers".[5]

But with the halting of the assault on the Dardanelles, the panic

[3] Hardinge to R. H. Benson, 23 June 1915, Hardinge MSS; see also Rothwell, p. 22.

[4] *Scott Journal*, 27 November 1914, p. 113.

[5] Hardinge to G. Bell, 29 March 1917, Hardinge MSS; also Rothwell, "Mesopotamia", p. 280.

expectation of an imminent Allied occupation of Constantinople passed and the new reality of war imposed itself at least on those who were in charge of affairs in London, if not on those who were engaged in its execution in Cairo. Six months to the day after the hopeful division of spoils at the War Council on 10 March, Lloyd George told the Editor of the *Manchester Guardian* over a private breakfast on 3 September 1915 that Russia was finished. He expected the Germans to take both Petrograd and Moscow. Their next move would be to break through Serbia to Constantinople and then to proceed to mobilise the Turks in earnest. Instead of 500,000 men under arms the Turks would have three million. This would make it necessary to send half a million men to Egypt.

The situation was not getting any better. After the Cabinet meeting a week later, on 10 September, Lloyd George was convinced that they had to anticipate a new move by the Germans. The possibility foremost in his mind was that they would break through to Constantinople, "in which case the whole campaign in the East will come to nothing, and we shall meet with terrible diplomatic difficulties", he confided to Frances Stevenson, his secretary and friend. Five days later, on 15 September 1915, he returned to the subject. Things were going very badly; disaster was inevitable. On 5 October Lloyd George repeated to Frances Stevenson what Noel-Buxton had told him the previous day, "that the Germans would be in Constantinople by Christmas" and added his own opinion that this spelled not only the end of the Dardanelles campaign, but the end of " the whole of the Eastern Empire". By 11 October, his secretary noted that Lloyd George was terribly anxious and feared that it was too late to do anything. "The situation daily grows more grave. The Germans seem to have made up their minds to force their way through to Constantinople. Bulgaria has apparently been pledged to Germany for a long time. Greece, through the treachery of her king, has let us down badly." He asked the War Office to let him have up-to-date maps of the Turkish war zone. The only ones they could produce were drawn before the Balkan war of 1912, which showed Rumanian armies on Bulgarian territory. On 12 October 1915, the next day, Lloyd George believed the situation to be "desperate". At least, that is how it looked to the men charged with the conduct of the war in London and Paris.

It was a very different kind of war for the men in Cairo. They had their own stage and they acted out their own parts. While Lloyd George and his Cabinet colleagues were contemplating the impending German

11

descent on Constantinople, the end of the Empire in the East, and attempting to grapple with a war situation they described as desperate and which was getting worse, not better, the High Commissioner in Cairo, Sir Henry McMahon, was putting his signature to promises drafted by his advisers on Arab affairs which committed the British to the establishment of an independent Arab state in Arab territories under Turkish rule. At the time when Sir Henry wrote this now historic letter to the Sharif Husain in Mecca on 24 October 1915, the Government in London could not visualise even a remote possibility that it would be in a position to fulfil these commitments. The prospect of victory had been replaced by the hope for a negotiated peace which would not be too onerous on the British and their allies. But none of this had percolated through to the policy-manipulators in Cairo. In ignorance of the true facts and with confidence in their mission, they proceeded on their set course – a course which was charted increasingly in Cairo rather than in London.

It was in this international setting that Wyndham Deedes landed in Egypt on 30 December 1915, two weeks after his evacuation from Gallipoli after nine months' campaigning against the Turks. There was no mood of desperation in Cairo, none of austerity. Deedes, who had been attached to the meagre intelligence operation at Gallipoli and had been posted to a similar office in Egypt, noted the contrasting mood. The hotels in Cairo and Alexandria were crowded with smart officers and easy-going crowds of soldiers. The officers, he noted bitterly, appeared to have ample time to play polo and they were not alone: there were wives, sisters and ladies of all shades. Everyone seemed to have a good time, Deedes noted. Money was plentiful and so was intrigue of every kind, and his faithful biographer, John Presland, working from Deedes' shorthand diary, found Cairo at that time unique in British imperial history; the most cosmopolitan city on earth.

There were the native Egyptians and their Sultan, enmeshed in the toils of Palace intrigue; there was the British administration, known to leading Egyptians and used to steering a course that would not offend their susceptibilities; there was the imposing array of officers of the British Army, not used to handling Egyptian questions tenderly; there were rich Greek and Syrian merchants; French and Italians long settled in Cairo and Alexandria; Germans, Russians and Rumanians. There were Turks, some loyal to the Government of Enver, some in

12

exile because of it; there were Arabs from all quarters of the Arab world, from the Hejaz, from Palestine, from the Hadramaut, from Mesopotamia, from the land of the Senussi, the Libyan desert. In this vast and motley crowd, there were those who dreamed of Arab independence and an Arab Kingdom; there were Turks who dreamed of the overthrow of Enver and the restoration of a Turkish Sultan; there were Greeks who dreamed of Smyrna, and Italians who dreamed of extending their conquest of Tripolitania, and French with their claims to Syria. And there were those who did not dream at all, but were quietly at work creating disaffection in Egypt . . .[6]

This was the Cairo which greeted Wyndham Deedes with the New Year – 1916. After a few frustrating days of waiting around in Alexandria, he decided to make contact with Colonel Gilbert Clayton who was in charge of the Egyptian Military Intelligence and the nominal Sudan Agent in Cairo. Deedes stayed at Shepheard's Hotel and, with the memory of the Gallipoli disaster and forebodings of more defeats ahead, he observed the crowds of officers and women "who seem to have nothing to do but enjoy themselves. Shepheard's Hotel is more like a carnival than a war."

Deedes knew Clayton and they liked each other. Within a matter of days, Deedes was transferred to the Egyptian Intelligence Service and worked with Clayton in the formation of the curious organisation known as the Arab Bureau, a small group of able and dedicated men who were to permeate the thinking and the policies of the Empire at the climacteric of its greatest expansion and then through the steep spiral of swift decline.

The two men met in Cairo against the background of the German armies storming the forts at Verdun and the Austrians advancing into Albania, the Russians attacking in Armenia and the British withdrawing their last forces from the Gallipoli Peninsula. Clayton told Deedes of the few restless and imaginative men he was assembling in Cairo, and that, like Deedes, he was convinced that it was necessary to change the policies and the methods of the war against the Turks in order to safeguard British interests in the East. He was encouraged and supported in this by the three senior British officials in Cairo, the High Commissioner, Sir Henry McMahon, the Commander-in-Chief, British troops, General Maxwell, and by the Sirdar of the Egyptian Army, Sir

[6] John Presland, *Deedes Bey*, pp. 241–2.

13

Reginald Wingate. To further their purpose, Clayton told Deedes, it was proposed to establish a General Bureau for Near Eastern Turkish and Arab Affairs to be centred in Cairo under the High Commissioner. In the event, it was to be as unique in its way as was the setting in which it was initiated.

The Arab Bureau became a quasi-military and political intelligence service, but not in the then familiar narrow British sense. It had, in those early days, as wide a purpose, if not the resources, as the American Central Intelligence Agency was to develop 50 years later; it became also a powerful political lobby without ever seeming to engage in politics; it decided on the execution of policies it favoured and on the non-execution of policies which it distrusted or disliked; but it did so not on the basis of a specific policy or ideology, nor because of any master-plan. It was done more on the basis of a number of undeclared assumptions, inclinations and prejudices of what was best for the Empire. Reflecting on this way of working during the Dardanelles campaign, Deedes had described it on 8 May 1915 and he now felt that the same could be said of Cairo a year later. "We are such good improvisers, one is told . . . we forever improvise and never organise and the confusion . . . is quite appalling . . . A hundred times a day I find myself saying as I used to at the War Office: How do we come to possess such an Empire and how have we kept it?"[7]

Thus, while the state of the war appeared desperate to the War Council in London, and the Cabinet was preparing monstrous territorial bribes for anyone who would step in to help avert the anticipated disaster, the ten men gathered by Clayton in Cairo viewed the prospect very differently. They were unperturbed by the cruel consequences which might overtake those Arab rulers and leaders who were being encouraged to ally themselves with the British against the Turk. For in a curious way, these men in Cairo simply could not conceive of being defeated by the Germans. They were much more bothered by the fear that their own Governments in London and Paris might frustrate the great opportunities which the war had presented to the Empire in the East. Their immediate preoccupation was not the German, but the Turk.

"We could see that a new factor was needed in the East, some power or race which would outweigh the Turks in numbers, in output and in mental activity."[8] Their understanding of the role of the West in the

[7] Presland, op. cit., p. 150.
[8] Ibid.

Levant convinced them from the outset that these requirements could not be "supplied ready-made from Europe". The solution had to be local and since the challenge was Turkey, the standards of efficiency required would be satisfied by the locally available competition; for "Turkey was rotten".

They judged that "there was latent power enough and to spare in the Arabic peoples". They comprised the largest single component of the old Turkish Empire and they had lived five hundred years under Turkish rule "and had begun to dream of liberty". And despite the now fashionable demoting of Lawrence, he was the frankest and most honest in declaring the purposes that guided the Cairo band. "So when at last England fell out with Turkey . . . we who believed we held an indication for the future set out to bend England's efforts towards fostering the new Arabic world in hither Asia . . ."[9]

What Clayton and his group understood by this has been described by Lawrence. They meant to break into "the accepted halls of English foreign policy, and build a new people in the East, despite the rails laid down by our ancestors". Clayton and his colleagues did not see the Arab revolt merely as a wartime exigency to embarrass the Turks, but as a fundamental change from the traditional policy of safeguarding the integrity of the Ottoman Empire as an essential British interest. In its place, and a more effective instrument for this purpose with greater direct influence, they proposed to raise that "prolific Semitic agglomeration, great in religious thought, reasonably industrious, mercantile, politic, yet solvent rather than dominant in character" – the Arabic peoples, which they judged to have still "latent power enough and to spare to replace the Turkish pillar in the Valhalla of British Eastern policy".[10]

But from his own vantage point in Cairo, his senses still sharpened by the novelty of the scene, Deedes had his doubts. Soon after his arrival, Clayton had requested him to handle the talks with Habib Bey, a representative of Fateh, a secret Arab society representing Syrian nationalists. Deedes was authorised to make clear to Habib the British position on two counts that were to become the source of so much trouble in the years to come – for the British and for the Arabs. The first, fatal, British condition was that "there could be only two parties to an agreement; one was HM Government and the other was *the whole*

[9] T. E. Lawrence, *Seven Pillars of Wisdom*, pp. 56 and 57.
[10] Ibid.

15

*Arab nation.* It was, therefore, incumbent on the various Arab parties to compose their differences, so that they could speak with one voice." (My italics.) The second British condition dealt with the position of France: the British would not bring any pressure to bear on the French in the matter of their differences with the Arabs, and they would not act as spokesman for the Arabs. "It was, therefore, incumbent on the Arabs to make a direct approach to the French for the settlement of differences between them."

Nothing materialised from these initial talks; the small conference of all interested Arab parties which Deedes had contemplated could not take place because the Egyptian authorities had ordered Habib to leave Egypt two days after his talks with Deedes. This, however, was only one of many reasons for Deedes to question the validity of the Arab orientation of Clayton and his friends. He was not opposed to it but he doubted its efficacy as an alternative to concluding a separate peace with Turkey. Deedes was convinced that the Turks would be prepared to make a deal provided they could keep Constantinople and received a number of other not unreasonable concessions. Deedes developed the argument in considerable detail in a letter to Colonel Hankey, the Secretary to the Cabinet and to the War Council, and formalised it in a note he gave to Clayton on 8 April 1916.

This set out Deedes' considered opinion, in the light of his discussions, of the terms of settlement which would be acceptable to the principal Turkish parties and the majority of Arabs.[11] Constantinople and the Straits were to remain Turkish; for the rest, Turkey would withdraw from all territory in Europe. Armenia would be placed under Russian suzerainty. There would be autonomous Arab rule for the vilayets of Damascus, Aleppo and Jerusalem under Muslim Governments appointed by the Allied Powers and guaranteed by them. In the rest of the Ottoman Empire, the provisions of the agreement reached with the Sharif by the High Commissioner and the Arab Bureau would apply, namely "a spiritual and temporal Arab Kingdom" with as yet undefined frontiers. For there were not only the still secret negotiations with the French and the still undeclared British interest to be settled but also the conflicting demands of the Arabs of Iraq, Syria and the Hejaz.[12]

It is rewarding to recall those early days of the Arab Bureau because it was then that the split British personality which was to haunt the

[11] Presland, op. cit., pp. 249 and 258.
[12] Presland, op. cit.

16

Middle East and Whitehall's Eastern policies for the next half-century or more was taking shape. In the note which he sent to Clayton on 8 April 1916, Deedes had a further important reason for seeking an early accommodation with the Turks. He had received a reply from Colonel Hankey to the letter sent in January in which Deedes had advocated support for the Turkish opposition groups and a separate peace with Turkey. Hankey's reply left little room for any hope of approval for such a policy. A separate peace with Turkey, wrote Hankey, was not only impracticable but might endanger Allied unity – and worse. For the Russians, Constantinople was an economic, political and sentimental desideratum "transcending every other" and she might well withdraw from the war as a result. Furthermore – and this passage in Hankey's letter to Deedes shows how little faith in victory there was in Whitehall at that time – "the result of this would be that after the war, Russia and Germany would move together, the financiers would re-establish their position in Constantinople, the German trade would recommence, and Turkey, once again safe, would go back to her incorrigible ways as she did in 1854, 1878 and 1908."[13]

Deedes understood. He warned Clayton to bear in mind the implications of the War Council's policy on the course they proposed to follow in Cairo. And soon afterwards, Deedes had further confirmation of the risks inherent in the Arab Bureau's orientation. With the High Commissioner's approval, he had been conducting secret talks with prominent Turkish opposition leaders in Athens, and these had made considerable progress. But they were particularly instructive for Deedes because of the insight they gave him on many unsuspected aspects of Turkish thinking about a future settlement. During April 1916, the Turks produced a position paper setting out the bases for a settlement excluding Germany, which the High Commissioner, Sir Henry McMahon, described to Deedes as one of the most important papers he had handled since the beginning of the war. What the paper said is evident from Deedes' further comments.

The Arab leaders, he noted, had been having talks with official and opposition Turkish leaders and a tentative agreement had been reached between the Syrian Arabs and the "Saadik Turkish Party" under which the non-Turkish elements of the Ottoman Empire would enjoy full autonomy. The Arab representatives had agreed and Dr Abd-al Rahman Shahbandar, a leading Syrian nationalist (who was later to

[13] Private letter dated 26 January 1916; quoted in Nevakivi, p. 24.

17

play a major part in the negotiations with the British) was deputed to draw up the agreement together with the Turkish representative. Deedes' comment on these talks reflected the dilemma which faced the Arabists in Cairo. "What it comes to is this," Deedes wrote to Clayton, "the Turks today [i.e. the opposition Turks] can offer decent terms with territorial integrity. We can offer independence, but we cannot guarantee territorial integrity, owing to the interests of France in Syria." At about the same time, Deedes received a telegram from Mark Sykes in London, advising the High Commissioner and the Arab Bureau of the terms of the agreement which had been reached with "the French and the Russians as regards Turkey, Syria and the South".

As Clayton, Deedes and their colleagues surveyed the scene in April 1916, the picture was not an encouraging one. Their secret talks with the Turks had foundered because of the irrevocable undertakings to the Russians to cede Constantinople to them – "the one fixed demand on which no Turk, of any political complexion whatsoever, would give way". Their secret talks with the Arabs threatened to run into difficulties over the equally secret arrangements with the French concerning the future of Syria, about which the Arabs knew nothing. On the other hand, Deedes was getting comprehensive accounts of the understanding reached between the Syrians and other Arab representatives with the opposition Turkish parties; and they had information that Sharif Husain, with whom they had been negotiating, was receiving regular monthly payments from the German Consul-General in Damascus. Sir Henry McMahon, the High Commissioner, urged the Government in London to act quickly "before Sharif Husain switched sides and backed the Germans". It was the most common threat at that time used as a bargaining counter by every one of Britain's expensively bought new allies.

The credibility of the British in the Arab world may not have been shaken by the self-contradictory positions of her spokesmen, because as yet they were not publicly known, but the British did suffer greatly in the eyes of Arab nationalists where they had sought favour by the reports of the suppression of the Irish uprising on Easter Monday, and almost immediately afterwards by the surrender of General Townsend with 9,000 British and Indian troops at Kut-al-Amara.

The whole affair began to disgust Deedes and dismay some of his colleagues. Deedes noted with strong traces of bitterness that "these arrangements of course definitely lose our adherence from the Arabs,

Syrian and other Turkish opposition parties".[14] These Turkish opponents of the regime in Constantinople had been to Europe, had established contact with the British, "and were evidently told by HM Government that, if they wish to discuss peace terms, they had better apply themselves to Russia, on whom at the beginning of the war they made a treacherous attack! So much therefore for all my attempts to collect and blend the various movements here in Cairo. At the same time, never having been given a lead as to what the Home Government wished it has been difficult to know how to act . . ." What does it matter anyhow, he concluded; he did not care what happened to the Turks or to Turkey, and still less what happened to the Arabs. All that was left, was the arrangement with the Sharif of Mecca, "a great triumph for Clayton".[15]

Clayton was suitably honoured – or appeased – immediately following the formal notification of the proposed agreement with the French which had so infuriated Deedes. He was promoted to Brigadier-General by the British in April 1916, and appointed an Officer of the Legion of Honour by the French while preparations for the Husain Declaration of Arab independence from Turkish rule were being completed. The pattern that was to shape so much of the coming exchanges and understandings was given its initial contours. Unabashed – unlike Deedes – by the deal with the French and Russians, Clayton prepared to return to London to do his own lobbying for the Arab revolt and for the political engagements which it would entail. He had to make his masters understand what was expected from them.

So far the discussions in the War Council in London, and the parallel talks in Paris and Petrograd, had been conducted with simple directness, without inhibitions about the territorial and strategic requirements of Empire. But now the rot set in. The causes of many failures to come were putting down their roots. The men who were putting them down were not evil men; they were not dishonest double-dealers but able, sincere and imaginative patriots under pressure. They were intelligent and not lightly bemused. Their one standard that mattered was the imperial interest and they were set on preserving it, advancing it and defending it with the limited resources at their disposal, be they Arab, Jew, Greek, Turk or Armenian.

The limitations were not confined to the material, political and

[14] Presland, op. cit., pp. 260–62.
[15] Presland, op. cit., pp. 260–62.

financial. On occasion they embraced also the personal. For the kind of policy on which the Cairo establishment embarked in the spring and summer of 1916 did not allow for mediocrity. It was a dangerous game; it required exceptional nerve and remarkable qualities. For these men had embarked on the largest empire-building operation of the century with their eyes open, without illusions and with a highly developed sense of moral rectitude. It was their misfortune that circumstances compelled them to compromise on all counts.

They were faced by another and more immediately serious problem – and the tragedy was that most of them seem not to have been aware that their guiding hand in Cairo, the High Commissioner, Sir Henry McMahon, appears to have been a man of straw. By all accounts, he was greatly admired long before he came to Cairo while he served in India. He arrived with the reputation of an outstanding administrator and Foreign Minister of the Government of India, and his innate qualities were expected to compensate more than adequately for his limited knowledge of the Arab world and his total lack of the Arabic language. His colleagues have paid tribute to his leadership and know-ledge, to his able negotiations with the Sharif of Mecca and the manner in which he kept the Home Government informed. Lawrence praised him without reserve. But not Laurence Graftey-Smith, who worked on McMahon's staff and on that of five other High Commissioners. He was not impressed by Sir Henry. His distinguished career in India, he recalls, "had left him with no knowledge of Arabic, or indeed French; and he never concealed a basic ignorance of things Egyptian and a real lack of interest in them. He rarely visited the Sultan or met the Cabinet, preferring to leave everything to the various British advisers, whose voluminous reports on this or that aspect of affairs we editorially topped and tailed and sent to London as being Sir Henry's own con-sidered views." The High Commissioner's only visible enthusiasm had been for locusts and his nickname "Loki" became the combination for the Embassy Chancery's safe. Graftey-Smith considered McMahon essentially a political light-weight, and this showed itself, in his opinion, most clearly in his handling of the Arab revolt for which he had political responsibility. McMahon did no more than sign the letters to Sharif Husain which Clayton had actually written.[16] Nor was life at the top all that harmonious, according to Graftey-Smith; disputes between

[16] See Clayton's note to Sir Herbert Samuel, 12 April 1923, quoted by Lord Samuel in the House of Lords, Official Report 20 July 1937, col. 629.

McMahon in Cairo and Wingate in Khartoum and with the Commanding Officer, General Murray, "were frequent and bitter". Confidences, clearly, were not always exchanged, and this may have gone further down the line than one had suspected.[17]

Thus the Foreign Office received a despatch from McMahon on 3 February 1916, regarding an approach made to him by an Italian anti-Zionist leader of the Alexandrian Jewish community, Edgar Suares, who was certain that "with a stroke of the pen, almost, England could assume for herself the active support of the Jews all over the neutral world if only the Jews knew that British policy accorded with their aspirations for Palestine". But Deedes, the man in charge of intelligence, knew nothing of this approach and was not told anything about it at any time in 1916; nor did Deedes or Clayton have any inkling until some time in 1917 about discussions in London about a possible Jewish presence in Palestine. Deedes claimed in his notes, that also the High Commission was not informed of the negotiations with the Zionists, and that their entire effort in Cairo was centred on exploiting the Muslim ferment in 1916. In a conversation with Deedes in August or September 1916, McMahon said that his fear about the Arab revolt had always been less that it would break down than that it would become too potent and make difficulties for the British in the future.

So Clayton and Deedes entered upon the Arab revolt in single-minded ignorance of possible developments with regard to Palestine. For the time being Clayton continued to be mainly concerned to ensure adequate support for the broader implications of the Bureau's Arab policy. Though the war situation was hardly less rosy in the Middle East than it was on the Western Front, he decided to return to London to lobby those most responsible for giving the orders that Cairo would have to execute. He left Cairo for London at the beginning of June 1916 – suitably timed to coincide with the launching of the Sharif's rebellion against the Turks on 5 June. Unfortunately for him, Kitchener, the great progenitor of the pro-Arab policy, was lost in the *Hampshire* the next day, and matters in Cairo were anything but quiet in the aftermath of recrimination after the surrender of Kut to the Turks, the forceful suppression by British troops of a rebellion in the Sudan at the end of May and Turkish incursions into Egypt. But Clayton understood that the key to the situation was in London, not in Cairo. The men who mattered were in Whitehall. He had meetings at the Foreign Office and

[17] L. Graftey-Smith, *Bright Levant*, pp. 20–1.

21

the India Office, he saw officials at the War Office and the Admiralty, and he had many private dinners and talks before he concluded his visit by explaining his ideas to the King. Clayton was satisfied when he returned to Cairo that the imperial purpose of the Arab revolt was fully understood in London. He was also aware of the new complications that he would have to face, and of one possible way by which they could be overcome. But nothing in his opinion must disturb the mounting impact of the Arab factor which he had introduced into the war.

Unfortunately for Clayton, he came away believing that he had effectively convinced the authorities in Whitehall of the significance of the re-orientation of British policy in the East, from emphasis on the Turks to reliance on an Arab connection to ensure British interests. He made the mistake then – which he was to seek to correct later in Palestine – that so many of the British and American Arabists were to commit in his wake; an error which, ironically, was also to become a central feature of Israeli foreign policy. For Clayton, together with his superiors and colleagues of the Arab Bureau, had become convinced that the Arab world as they were shaping it had assumed a central role in imperial strategy. Yet, even as he left London, and the men he had spoken to were giving sympathetic consideration to Clayton's theme, it was not the ideas that mattered at that moment, it was the reality of the war in the West and its outcome – and this was as yet far removed from Clayton's Arab preoccupation.

In the London Clayton left behind there were grave expectations that a negotiated peace might be forced on the Government by circumstances or by American pressure. Lloyd George complained to Lord Esher that if this happened no one had any idea of "what our peace objectives should be apart from vague generalities", and a few days later, on 17 August 1916, the Chief of the Imperial General Staff, General Robertson, wrote to Lloyd George at the War Office about his concern in the event that negotiations were started for an armistice or a peace settlement. This could happen any day, in Robertson's opinion, and he feared "that we may be caught unprepared and find that we have mobilized for peace as we did for war – inadequately and subordinate to France". Possibly even more serious was the immediate concern over the deteriorating relations with President Wilson in Washington. During September, Congress had given the President adequate powers to curb or end all financial and economic relations with the belligerents. It was no idle move and, by November 1916, there was convincing evidence that Wilson had actually contemplated taking the United States into the war on the side of the Germans in the event of the Germans accepting his proposals for a negotiated peace and the Allies rejecting them, as they had given every indication they would.[18]

On 15 December 1916, Lord Robert Cecil, who had joined Balfour at the Foreign Office in Lloyd George's new Government, circulated a memorandum to the Cabinet in which he noted that there was real danger that the United States might cut off the supply of money and munitions in order to compel the British Government to negotiate. It must be recognised, Cecil stressed, "that if he desired to put a stop to the war, and was prepared to pay the price for doing so, such an achievement is in his power".[19]

On the same day, 15 December 1916, the Foreign Office had received a cyphered message emanating from one of its most highly rated agents in the United States, Frederick Dixon, the editor of the *Christian Science Monitor* in Boston. This said that Dixon knew "unquestionably from those engaged in peace suggestions that the object is to involve the Allics in negotiations in the belief that once begun they never can be stopped, and must therefore operate to save Germany. The intrigue is deep-seated here. It includes not only pro-Germans, Zionists, Jews and Bryanites, but members of the Government."[20] Lloyd George's own view was that Wilson was keeping his promise to "pro-German Jews" who had financed his election in return for his promise that he would bring about a negotiated settlement if re-elected.

At home things were hardly any better. His personal secretary recorded Lloyd George's mood on 10 November. "He is feeling very sick with everything . . . He says we have made a muddle of the whole war, and he fears it is too late to do anything." In less intimate but no less forceful terms, Lloyd George prepared a long memorandum for the Inter-Governmental Conference of the Allies in Paris five days later, 15 November 1916. They had made no appreciable impression on the enemy, he argued. The Germans held all their conquests on land and at sea. They had recovered the initiative. Rumania was being overrun. Time was no longer on the side of the Allies. There was no hope of

[18] E. R. May, *World War and American Isolation 1914–1917*, pp. 330–35 and 361–2.

[19] For the best summary of these developments and for detailed sources see Sterling Kernek, "British Government's Reactions to Wilson's 'Peace Note' ", in *Historical Journal* XIII, 4 (1970), pp 727–8.

[20] Cecil Papers, British Museum. Add. MSS. 51092; see also Kernek, ibid.

inflicting a defeat sufficiently crushing in the coming year, 1917, unless they could reinforce their assaults on the enemy by much greater efforts in other theatres of war. But there was little joy coming from these other theatres.

Sir Reginald Wingate had replaced McMahon as High Commissioner in Cairo, and supported if not inspired by Clayton had rejected a proposal by the War Council in London that the French should be encouraged to send as many troops as possible to help hold the Turkish offensive in the Hejaz. Austen Chamberlain, the Secretary of State for India, gloomily told the Council on 2 November 1916 that the issue was now one of preserving the British Empire. The Arab revolt had become a potential liability and threat unless it could be saved from collapse. Chamberlain feared that Husain would come to terms with the Turks unless adequate reinforcements were sent to Arabia. This would enable the Turks to carry out their ambition of inciting a *jihad* throughout the British Muslim empire ranging from India through Afghanistan, Persia, Mesopotamia to Aden and Egypt. Chamberlain set out his views in a memorandum to the War Council on 14 November 1916, but the Foreign Office feared that his cure might be worse than the disease ". . . to allow the French to establish their influence in the Hejaz as predominant over ours will be to abdicate the position that we have always held in the Muslim world". It was hardly surprising that Lloyd George, now at the head of his own administration, should look beyond Clayton's "Arab solution" for a remedy to the grim prospect that faced him in the East no less than in the West.

For Clayton, as we had noted, had completely misread the reaction in London to his advocacy of an Arab orientation, just as Weizmann misread the British meaning of a Zionist orientation a year later. For the time being the interest in the Arab orientation, which Clayton had found so encouraging in London, was entirely dictated by the demands of the war situation; the same was true a year later of the interest shown in Weizmann's Zionist orientation. All that mattered from the end of 1916 until the end of the war, was the outcome of the war. Moreover, the men who made policy in London and Paris had their eyes constantly fixed on Washington and Petrograd. At this stage, not even the prospect of territorial gains was of major concern: War Aims, New Imperialists, Internationalists, Socialists, Zionists, Arab Nationalists, mattered only insofar they had a bearing on winning the war. For Lloyd George and Clemenceau understood much better than their officials and specialists did, that all talk about the future, about territorial desiderata, about new alignments, and new nations would depend on the outcome of the war. The memoranda and committee discussions, the negotiated agreements and deals, which have become such a central feature of our modern discussion and assessments of the history of those days were, at the time, largely irrelevant.

The touchstone was the war. This was Lloyd George's priority when he started to discuss the significance of Palestine in relation to the new Clayton orientation. It was not a question of whether he sympathised with the Zionist or with the Arab orientation: what mattered to him was whether a military advance into Palestine could knock the Turks out of the war more effectively than Clayton's Arab uprising. Insofar as Lloyd George was concerned with the position of the Jews, in relation to the war, his attitude had initially very little to do with the return of the Jews to Palestine. He was rather more preoccupied, as we have seen, with the influence of the American Jews on President Wilson's attitude to the war and on the prospects of a negotiated peace favourable to Germany. It was similarly mainly in relation to the war that he had at times previously expressed his preference for Palestine as an objective over others – such as Alexandretta on the Levant coast. Moreover, Lloyd George, unlike the soldiers and men like Churchill, saw the potentiality of Palestine, not only in the narrow strategic terms of the military, but as part of the broader Grand Strategy of the statesman. He rejected the views of the Chief of the Imperial General Staff, General Robertson, who ridiculed the policy of those ministers who wanted "to waste brain-power over such petty matters" as the Arab revolt and Persia. These ministers, Robertson told Lloyd George on 8 December 1916, two days after he had formed his own Government, "lived from telegram to telegram and attached as much importance to a few scallywags in Arabia as I imagine they did to the German attack on Ypres two years ago". For Lloyd George – almost alone amongst his colleagues – was primarily concerned in not losing the war. It was his opinion that the British Empire was so powerful in the world, that if he managed to hold what they had, with, possibly, some essential "adjustments", then this would be considered a victory. The one big issue for him was not to be defeated in 1917; to remain in a strong enough position to resist a negotiated peace in which the terms might be

25

dictated by Germany or even by a powerful neutral such as the United States.

Given these conditions, Lloyd George ruled out nothing. Thus in the early days of the war, in November 1914, he told the Editor of the *Manchester Guardian* that he would not consider the war to have really succeeded unless all the non-Turkish elements of the Ottoman Empire were set free. The Russians would take Constantinople and Armenia and the British would have Mesopotamia, but the rest of Asia Minor, he thought, might be given to Germany as a consolation prize. It might be possible to establish a Jewish buffer state in Palestine, but it was no more than a passing thought.

But by the following March, at the War Council meeting in 1915, which considered the Partition of Turkey and the Russian demand for Constantinople, Lloyd George's views had clarified to the point where he claimed that possession of Palestine was a specifically British interest. His reasoning, strongly anti-French, was different from that of Curzon, Austen Chamberlain and E. S. Montagu, all of whom were closely linked with the Indian Government; they were primarily concerned with imperial expansion at the expense of the Ottoman Empire, as were the Eastern specialists of the Cabinet, especially Sykes and Amery. Their view, put to the War Committee on 7 July 1916 – about the time when Clayton was in London – was that "unless Turkey was decisively defeated, her alliance with Germany would survive to threaten the British Empire in the East after the war".[21]

Meanwhile, the British had become more deeply involved in the war against Turkey. They had launched the Arab rebellion as a second front against the Turks, but the first front of the British army in Egypt and in Mesopotamia had not made much progress until Baghdad was captured in the spring of 1917. It was a false dawn. The March revolution in Russia had cast a blight over the whole Russian front which cancelled out any of the benefits gained in Mesopotamia. The Arab revolt, instead of acting as a relief for the British forces, had become a regular problem for the War Committee and at the beginning of 1917, Lloyd George noted that "of all issues, the most immediately urgent appeared to be that of ensuring the safety of our Arab allies in the Hejaz".

Lloyd George believed, however, that this was no serious problem. The British Expeditionary Forces in Egypt and Palestine numbered at

[21] Rothwell, op. cit., pp. 126–30.

least three times the men at the disposal of the Turkish commander and they had even greater superiority in equipment and firepower. The situation was such, Lloyd George noted, that in Palestine and Mesopotamia, nothing and nobody could have saved the Turkish forces from total defeat in 1915 and 1916 – "except our General Staff". It was Whitehall, he recorded in a memorable passage, that was the real citadel of the Ottoman Empire, not Baghdad or Jerusalem. "For three years this redoubtable garrison of the effete beat off every attack . . . The War Office saved Gallipoli from falling: for two years it protected the feeble garrison of Palestine from meeting its doom. It did what it could to avert the capture of Baghdad." For two years the Generals had compelled them to stand on the defensive on the Suez Canal against small ill-equipped Turkish forces. Even when the advance of the Expeditionary Force into Palestine was under way, the Chief of the Imperial General Staff cabled to the Commander of the Expeditionary Force, General Murray, that his primary mission remained unchanged "that is to say, it is the defence of Egypt".[22]

The frustrations produced by the Eastern policy – and the fading hopes of success in the West – induced Lloyd George to reconsider British options in the East. He had no doubts that whatever merits there might yet be in the Arab connection, it would not produce an effective contribution to the war independent of the Expeditionary Forces in Egypt and Palestine. At the same time, the French were displaying a pressing interest in the future of Palestine. It was, therefore, with some relief and even hope that he heard about the great Zionist potential in the United States and in Russia. Not least, he had been getting unusually interesting reports of the Kaiser's interest in Zionism and of German projects for the establishment of an autonomous Jewish state on Germany's eastern frontier in the hitherto Russian heartland of the Jews.

Now that he was Prime Minister in charge of affairs, Lloyd George reacted characteristically. He instructed his officials – especially Mark Sykes who was about to set out on a tour of the Middle East to encourage Arab uprisings behind the Turkish lines – not to enter into commitments which would stand in the way of "securing the addition of Palestine to the British area". Unfortunately for Lloyd George, by the time he won the support of his colleagues for his wider strategic concept linked to the conquest of Palestine, the prospect of success

[22] Lloyd George, *My War Memories*, Vol. II, pp. 1080, 1083–85, 1424 and 1864.

27

seemed to recede. The opposition of the War Office increased following the failure of the Nivelle offensive on the Western Front and the marked disintegration of the Russian fronts in Europe and Asia. Always the realist in such matters, Lloyd George's mind turned to the hitherto unthinkable – a negotiated settlement with the Turks "in which Britain would obtain rather less than her maximum aims in the Middle East".[23]

With the growing chaos in Russia and the uncertain outlook of her future military role, the Foreign Office gave careful consideration to the possibilities of a separate peace with Turkey. On the whole, it was the Arabists in the department who made a stand against any such idea, but their reasoning did not impress Lloyd George. Mark Sykes saw the move for a separate peace as emanating from "the Semitic anti-Zionists who are undisguised pro-Turco-Germans". With the exception of Deedes, the Cairo establishment was also solidly ranged against a separate peace with Turkey, and so were the British Zionists gathered round their standard-bearer, Chaim Weizmann, but not the influential German Zionists and the forceful American Zionist lobby. During the high summer of 1917, the confused situation of the war was creating strange bedfellows.

Lloyd George had been impressed by the arguments advanced by those who favoured a separate peace with Turkey which would ensure the elimination of Turkish rule from Arabia and Mesopotamia and ensure a strong British presence; while in Armenia, Syria and Palestine, autonomous native regimes were visualised under Turkish suzerainty and British and French external control. What mattered to him was that, for one thing, they would get rid of the agreement with the French, negotiated by Sykes and Georges Picot, and concentrate on the war against Germany. But he was not altogether sure. When the War Cabinet turned to discuss the possibilities of a negotiated peace during its September 1917 meetings, the issue was no longer that of a deal with Turkey, but of a negotiated peace with Germany, as a result of which, in Lloyd George's opinion, "two great Empires would emerge from the war, namely the British Empire and Germany". There were, moreover, considerable advantages attached to such an outcome: it would exclude American intervention at the Peace Conference and settle the conflicts in the heart of Europe, without American assistance. Germany would restore Belgium and Serbia, return Alsace-Lorraine to France and

[23] Rothwell, op. cit., p. 129.

28

surrender her overseas colonies. In return, Germany would have a free hand in Rumania and Russia and there would be no British opposition to her annexation of Lithuania and Courland. The concept did not outrage the War Cabinet. On the contrary, it was an outcome of the war that would serve British interests at a time when the outlook was anything but promising.[24]

But nothing came of these peace soundings and the War Cabinet returned to consider, among other things, the final shape of the undertaking already given to the Zionists to establish a Jewish National Home in Palestine. After a flurry of last-minute exchanges with the Americans and the Zionists, the definitive version of the Balfour Declaration was given its approval at the Cabinet Meeting on 16 October before the decks were completely cleared at the meeting of 31 October 1917. Meanwhile, Lloyd George had called on the King on 18 October in order to give him an up-to-date assessment of the state of the war. The account of this meeting has to be read together with the imminent formal declaration that was about to be made to the Jews. Lloyd George used no cosmetics for his report to George V. As summarised by Harold Nicolson, he told the King that the Russians and the Italians were out of the battle; it was evident that the French did not intend "to do much fighting"; and the British could not expect great assistance from the Americans during the course of 1918. The British would be expected therefore "to sacrifice the flower of our Army in a single-handed offensive" which would leave them so weak as to be unable to assert themselves or make their will prevail in the Council of Peace when the time came, while France, Russia and America would have had time to recover and have their armies intact.

This, Lloyd George told the King, must never be. It was his duty to ensure that, whenever the climax is reached, England will be at the zenith of her military strength. If, therefore, he could not get satisfactory assurances from the French, Russians and Italians, the British would content themselves with remaining on the defensive in Flanders and curtail their subsidiary campaigns so as to liberate as many men as possible for employment at home. That was on 18 October; on the 31st, the Cabinet decided to make its promised declaration to the Zionists.

Less than a week later, the Chief of the Imperial Staff, General Robertson, submitted a memorandum to the Foreign Office, urging

[24] War Cabinet Minutes, 5, 7, 10, 12, September 1917, CAB 23/4; Rothwell, *War Aims*, p. 106.

that the agreement made with Italy about the partition of Turkey, should be immediately abrogated to facilitate a peace settlement with Turkey. Lord Hardinge, who was now the Permanent Under-Secretary at the Foreign Office, assured the General that Great Britain would renounce the agreement with Italy as soon as the Turks showed a serious disposition towards ending the war by negotiation. First it was French interests, then Italian that were to be sacrificed to the greater need of peace. And who would be next? It looked as if it might be the Zionists.

For in those days, the possibility of making peace with Turkey on terms acceptable to the Turks, was very much in the minds of the Allied leaders. On 28 November 1917, Lloyd George was in Paris for talks with Clemenceau. The French Prime Minister, among other matters, told Lloyd George that he would make peace with Turkey on any terms: he did not want Syria for France, but if Lloyd George could get him a protectorate over Syria, he would not refuse it; it would please some of his reactionaries. However, Clemenceau emphasised that he attached no importance to such a mandate. He agreed with Lloyd George that Palestine should not be given back to Turkey and gave Lloyd George a free hand to negotiate with Turkey and make the best settlement possible.

As it happened, the best terms possible were obtained for Lloyd George by General Allenby and the Palestine Expeditionary Force barely two weeks later, when Allenby formally entered Jerusalem on 11 December. The crisis was by no means overcome, but an important new element had entered into the British perspective for the future, with the direct injection of the Zionist stimulant. Weizmann had conceived what he called "synthetic" Zionism, a synthesis of the visionary ideal and practical politics. He was now to have an active partner who would show himself a master at "synthetic" imperialism, a synthesis of the Arab orientation, the Zionist presence and British imperial interests: the stage was being set for Gilbert Frankland Clayton. Clayton was 42 when Allenby offered him the position of Political Officer with the Palestine Expeditionary Force; he was clearly undecided whether to accept and break his close association with the Sudan in Egypt. He voiced his doubts in a letter to Lee Stack, then the Acting-Sirdar in Khartoum. Stack replied with a perceptive comment which must have reassured Clayton: "I have carefully thought over what you tell me about GHQ wanting you in Palestine," he wrote, "and cannot but own that the work you would be doing there is imperially more important than what you would be doing for the Soudan in Egypt."[25]

Clayton accepted Allenby's invitation, for he was greatly taken by the General. "Allenby is quite splendid. A great commander who carries his whole army with him on the wings of confidence . . ." he wrote to Gertrude Bell as he waited with Allenby at Advanced Headquarters on the approach road to Jerusalem on the day before the British entered the Holy City. It was 8 December 1917; Jerusalem was in sight and so were the politics of the campaign with which Clayton had now to concern himself. "The recent success in Palestine," he confided in Gertrude Bell who was then working at the Arab Bureau in Cairo, "has caused the plot to thicken." France's representative, Georges Picot, had arrived at Allenby's headquarters, but not Mark Sykes, his British opposite. "I am left to face the music of other people's composition – not an easy task." Picot had informed Clayton that the French and British Governments had agreed that an Anglo-French Provisional Government should be set up in Palestine until the end of the war, when some sort of international authority would take over. Clayton told Miss Bell that he had suspected that something of the kind was in the wind, though he had received only evasive replies to his enquiries in London. Therefore, he had urged Allenby to form a purely military administration under his own authority as Commander-in-Chief; Picot "was thus faced with a fait accompli". The time was not yet to talk of politics and government. They had to make sure first that the military situation was secure, for "the fall of Russia may enable the Central Powers to bring very strong forces against us". But politics of another kind could not wait. And Gertrude Bell is put in the picture: "Mr Balfour's pronouncement on the Zionist question has produced a profound impression and caused something very like dismay in Arab and Syrian circles. Mark Sykes talks eloquently of a Jewish-Armenian-Arab combine, but the Arab of Syria and Palestine sees the Jew with a free hand and the backing of HMG and interprets it as meaning the eventual loss of his heritage. Jacob and Esau once more." Clayton thought the Arab was right not to be humbugged by the specious oratory of British sponsors of the Zionist orientation, but he considered it just possible that Zionism might prove helpful in consolidating Arab support for the Sharif of Mecca. "Up-to-date the Syrian Arab has shown the utmost distaste for any idea of a Government in which Meccan

[25] Sir Lee Stack to Clayton, 31 December 1917, Clayton Papers.

31

patriarchalism has any influence." Clayton still had doubts about the future and his experience impelled him "to deprecate strongly incautious declarations and visionary agreements". They had to beat the Germans before all else; "the rest will follow unless we hamper our future action by rash and ill-considered policies now."[26]

After walking with Allenby into Jerusalem on 11 December 1917, Clayton returned to Cairo and wrote a long and tactfully pointed letter to Mark Sykes at the Cabinet Office – the other side of the coin, so to speak, of his letter to Gertrude Bell. To begin with, he told Sykes, "It is probably not realised how absolutely military the whole situation is and how essential will be a purely military administration for some time to come." Moreover, his reading of the news from Europe showed that there was a chance that within two or three months they might be up against a possible German thrust at Palestine without any reinforcements being available to Allenby. All of which pointed to the need for a purely military administration and the avoidance of all commitments for the present. "The less we tie our own hands and compromise the local population at this juncture the better." And then, Clayton proceeds perhaps with less than his customary subtlety: "This brings me to the question of Picot", and he repeats for Sykes' information, Picot's version of the "understanding arrived at between the two Governments". If Picot's account was an accurate rendering of this "understanding", "I have heard nothing of it, and I cannot protest too strongly against any such unworkable and mischievous arrangement."

Clayton next comments on Sykes' "Arab-Jew-Armenian combine". He would try it, but could see no great chance of real success. "It is an attempt to change in a few weeks the traditional sentiment of centuries. The Arab cares nothing whatsoever about the Armenian one way or the other; as regards the Jew, the Bedouin despises him and will never do anything else, while the sedentary Arab hates the Jew and fears his superior commercial and economic ability." He tells Sykes that he had just received an account of a speech by Sykes on the Zionist question, and was troubled by it. "I am not fully aware of the weight which Zionists carry, especially in America and Russia, and of the consequent necessity of giving them everything for which they ask, but I must point out that, by pushing them as hard as we appear to be doing, we are risking the possibility of Arab unity becoming something like an accomplished fact and being ranged against us." No matter

[26] Clayton to Gertrude Bell, 8 December 1917.

32

what Weizmann or Sokolow might say, and whatever Arabs put up by the British may say, they had to face the fact that the Arab did not believe that the Jew, with whom he had to deal, would act up to his high-flown sentiments expressed at committee meetings: "in practice the Arab found that the Jew was prone to extract his pound of flesh." No number of reassuring public declarations could get over this. "We have, therefore, to consider whether the situation demands out and out support of Zionism at the risk of alienating the Arabs at a critical moment."[27]

Two days later, on 17 December, Clayton was writing to Arnold Wilson in Baghdad about the same problems. But there was now an important new dimension that was to play an ever-increasing part in Clayton's calculations and policies. He was rather anxious, he wrote, "about the effect of the tremendous propaganda which is to be carried out in connection with the Zionist movement on Arab opinion here. Mark Sykes is running it very hard, and I have no doubt has good reasons for it." Clayton agreed with Sykes' objective of bringing about an agreed position of the Arabs, Jews and Armenians that would provide the British with "a very strong card at the Peace Conference". Clayton suggested that Wilson should sound the Sharif and other influential Arabs along these lines. Clayton had been doing this himself, carefully and cautiously, and had met with "a certain amount of success". Clayton had his own reasons for pursuing this aspect of Sykes' syndrome. He believed that an Arab state in Palestine could be successful only if it combined Arabs and Jews "on more or less equal terms". The world trend was such that it would not permit a government to exclude any one community from the rights and privileges granted to others – and, in case Wilson failed to understand his generalised assumptions, Clayton elaborated that "moreover, the Jews are an element of great strength if they are incorporated into a state, but are bad enemies if a hostile attitude is taken up".

Meanwhile, Allenby had placed Clayton in general charge at GHQ of the whole administration of the Occupied Enemy Territory of Palestine, and Clayton had to construct the administrative instruments from scratch. Not an easy job, he wrote to Lord Edward Cecil in Cairo on 31 December 1917, "and the presence of Picot and such like does not make the task any easier. Our Allies are all out to stake their claims", not to speak of the conflicting demands of Arabs (Christian and Muslim)

[27] Clayton to Mark Sykes, 15 December 1917.

and of the Jews with which he had to deal. In fact, there never had been a time when the British had to give so much attention to the Jew; furthermore, this time he was a political problem, not a social one, and the British clearly had some difficulty in making this unaccustomed adjustment. However, it seemed easier for Clayton to do this in Palestine than for Balfour at the Foreign Office. About the same time, on 30 December, the British Ambassador in Paris, Lord Bertie, was recording a conversation with the French Ambassador in London, Paul Cambon, who had been telling him of his talk with the Foreign Secretary, Lord Balfour. "Balfour explained his support of Zionism," Bertie noted, "as partly financial and partly political and also senti-mental – viz., the necessity to conciliate the American Jews who have gone in for Palestine and who can supply money for loans, and his own feeling that it would be an interesting experiment to reconstitute a Jewish kingdom. Cambon reminded him that a king of the Jews would be the end of the world. Balfour thinks that such a denouement would be still more interesting." Clayton, however, had no opportunity for such philosophical speculation.

For it had taken little more than a year for the Arab revolt to be downgraded from a major political orientation to an auxiliary military operation. But Clayton was convinced that even if his Arab dream had failed him as an instrument of war, it remained of profound importance as an instrument of peace – but, as he saw it now, only with one all-important proviso: Arab and Jew had to combine on more or less equal terms, as he put it in his letter to Arnold Wilson. Given that, they would command "a very strong card at the Peace Conference" when the future of the Ottoman territories was finally settled. However, more important in the months ahead was who – Clayton apart – could or would play "this strong card"? Only a very few of his colleagues shared his con-viction; some were anxious to play the Arab card but not the Zionist; others were all for pushing the Zionists but not the Arabs. Clayton remained convinced all through that there would have to be a pair – Arab and Jew – to bring about a settlement and he clung to this belief until he saw conclusive evidence that it would not work. How he reached this sad conclusion may show us one reason why we failed to achieve a secure and lasting peace in the Holy Land.

In a personal letter to the High Commissioner in Cairo, Sir Reginald Wingate, dated curiously "5 (or 6) January 1918" Clayton sets out the daunting situation that confronted him in the setting up of an administration in Palestine. Not the least of his problems was that letters from Cairo – less than 300 miles distant – were taking nearly a week to reach him; but he was hopeful. He had a staff at GHQ for his administration "and we have secured a couple of tents and a table or two so all is well". On the other hand, the political situation with regard to Palestine, especially in London, seemed to be extraordinarily vague: "We get our Government's commitments and the aspirations of the Syrians sufficiently complicated by the Sykes-Picot Agreement. Then we get a tremendous rush of Zionism, supported apparently by HMG but disliked by non-Jewish local elements, distasteful to the Arabs and, as far as I can make out, much disliked by Picot."[28]

Picot's role in particular concerned him. "I think I ought to tell you privately," he wrote Sykes, "that it is very clear to me that Picot is far from sympathetic towards our present Zionist policy which he thinks will not be favourable to French interests either here or in Syria." Clayton had heard from several independent sources, Arab and Jew, that Picot's attitude when talking with Arabs on the Zionist question was "not calculated to do away with their feelings of uneasiness or to promote that Arab-Jew-Armenian sympathy which I have – with some success – been at pains to promote". This was all the more significant since Picot had confided to Clayton that he had the promise of the French High Commissionership of Syria, and Clayton wondered wryly whether that included Palestine.[29]

At this stage Clayton was encouraged to assume that he would be backed by the Foreign Office in his effort to maintain the Arab-Jewish balance by keeping French interference at arm's length, when he received from the High Commissioner in Cairo copies of a reassuring three-cornered exchange of telegrams between London, Cairo and Jeddah. The Foreign Office had cabled to the High Commissioner its version of the formula which Hogarth, the Director of the Arab Bureau who was then negotiating with the Sharif (he was now described as king) in Jeddah, was to present to Husain. There were two parts to the message. The first was an assurance: "The determination of the Entente Powers is that the Arab race shall be given full opportunity of once again forming a nation in the world, that this can only be achieved by Arabs uniting themselves and that Great Britain and her allies will pursue a policy with this ultimate unity in view."

[28] Clayton to Sir Reginald Wingate, 5/6 January 1918.
[29] Clayton to Sykes, 26 January 1918.

But it was the second part that encouraged Clayton. The British Government was determined that in Palestine "no people shall be subjected to another", that there must be a special regime for the Holy Places "approved of by the world", and then came the important declaration which Hogarth was to make to King Husain. He was to impress on the King "that since the return of the Jews to Palestine is favoured by Jewish opinion of the world, and inasmuch as this opinion must remain a constant factor, and further, as HMG view the realisation of this aspiration with favour, HMG are determined that, insofar as is compatible with freedom of existing population both economical and political, no obstacle should be put in the way of this ideal's realisation." The purport was clear enough even if the style, especially when translated into Arabic, left much to be desired.

Furthermore, Hogarth was to impress on the King "that the friendship of World Jewry towards the Arab cause is equivalent to support in all cases where Jews have a political influence, and that the leaders of the Movement are determined to bring about the success of Zionism by friendship and co-operation with the Arabs, and that such an offer is not one to be thrown aside lightly."

Wingate received this message on 4 January 1918, and passed it on to Hogarth in Jeddah two days later. Hogarth replied on 13 January that the King had approved of the message, and recognised that circumstances might prevent fulfilment of every minor point of the original agreements; "but he relied on us to notify him frankly of any modification of them and the reasons for same". With regard to the Palestine part of the message, Hogarth comments that "the King was evidently prepared for this announcement and said he welcomed Jews to any Arab country". Husain clearly was making no commitment but he was also raising no obstacles. In fact, it is evident from Hogarth's later report on the ten interviews he had with Husain between 8 and 14 January 1918, that Husain was still primarily taking his cue from the British. As he put it to Hogarth, Great Britain's power was "the great sea in which I, the fish, swim, and the larger the sea the fatter the fish". He could not have put it more succinctly.

However, Hogarth had every reason to be content with Husain's reply – and so had Clayton. For his approval of the Palestine settlement had to be set against his intransigence in other matters, as in his refusal to have any dealings with the Sultan of Nejd, Ibn Saud, who enjoyed the support of the Indian Government. Husain accused him of treachery,

36

of dealing with the enemy and of accepting Turkish as well as British money. (Husain himself had been for a time on the German payroll, and these payments continued during the initial period of his negotiations with the British.) Husain also made difficulties, Hogarth reported, about the makeup of the Hejazi delegation to the "London Arab-Jew-Armenian Committee". The King barred the nomination of any Syrian, Iraqi or anyone who had dealings with the Turks. By comparison, his attitude to the Zionists and the Palestine situation appeared to be almost benevolent.[30]

In Palestine, Clayton was reasonably content with the turn of events. In a long letter to Sykes which he wrote at GHQ on 4 February 1918, he could report with satisfaction that "things are moving very well here". Jews and Arabs were coming together gradually and British efforts had produced a considerable rapprochement, even though this still fell short of cordial co-operation. Muslim feeling against Jews was still strongest in Jerusalem where there was fear that the Jews might control the Holy City and all Palestine. It did not surprise Clayton, for he found that "the Jerusalem Jew of today is certainly not an attractive personality. I look for much from the Weizmann Mission which will bring the Muslims into contact with the really good class Jews."

The pro-British feeling among Jews and Muslims throughout the country and especially in Jerusalem, was most marked and steadily increasing, Clayton tells Sykes. They seem to be convinced that "we have come to stay, and they appear to welcome it". As to the future, Clayton assured Sykes that "there seems little doubt that a plebiscite would result in a large majority in favour of a British Protectorate – various other possible forms of settlement being nowhere. I see practically no evidence among the local population, of whatever community, of aspirations towards independence. Arab national feeling is very weak. France is popular with but a small section, and Italy is nowhere. As regards the Jews, there are no doubt aspirations towards a restoration of the old independent Jewish kingdom, but the majority seem to think that the shadow of a great Power over them is essential, and look to England as that Power."

Clayton qualified his opinions with a caution that these were impressions derived from his experience and they could be inaccurate. But he evidently did not think so because he adds, for Sykes' information,

[30] For exchange of FO telegrams see Wingate Papers and for Hogarth's final report, see *Arab Bulletin* No. 77, 27 January 1918, p. 21.

that "I have urged Lawrence to impress on Faisal the necessity of an entente with the Jews. He is inclined the other way, and there are people in Cairo who lose no chance of putting him against them. I have explained that this is his only chance of doing really big things and bringing the Arab movement to fruition."[31]

In a rather more private letter to George Lloyd (who was to succeed Allenby as High Commissioner of Egypt in 1925), Clayton considered the prospect in the wider perspective of the Empire. He was not happy about "the unfortunate formula" which Sykes had concocted for King Husain and to which the King was induced to agree, at a meeting with Sykes and Picot, to accept from the French in Syria the same treatment accorded to him by the British in Mesopotamia. It was an embarrassing formula, in Clayton's opinion, which placed the British in an awkward position; however, he believed that future developments of the war would relieve them to a great extent of the complications of these agreements "which become every day more out of date". Clayton was confident that so far as his war was concerned and "if we maintain a cautious and watchful attitude (and especially avoid exaggerated propaganda and 'stump' speeches, either on the subject of the French or of Zionism), the time will come, I think, when there will be only two powers in the Eastern picture, namely England and Germany – and if we can 'out' Germany, we remain predominant as the saviours of the Arabs, Jews, Armenians, etc."

But that was not all. Clayton – with all his Palestinian preoccupation – was never parochial. He cautioned Lloyd not to overlook the significance of the advance of Turkish Pan-Turanianism into Central Asia and the resulting switch in German interest from Baghdad to Bokhara. The immediate implication of this, as he saw it, was that England had to remain free from the interference by other Powers in the Near and Middle East. Clayton was therefore of the opinion that their Eastern policy should have two main objectives: the first was to "carry out our Arab policy to its logical conclusion" and achieve a settlement based on the principle of self-determination. The second was to "close down the Arab pages when the Turks are removed from Arab territories, and then turn to Pan-Turanianism and hold out the hand of sympathy to it on the same principles of self-determination". If they failed to do this, Clayton concluded, "the Boche will, and the threat to our Eastern

[31] Clayton to Sykes, 4 February 1918.

38

Empire will be worse than ever".[32] The letter was written the day before the Germans concluded the Peace of Brest-Litovsk with the Bolshevik Government which took Russia out of the war, and the day after the Germans had occupied Kiev, within days of the Turks occupying Baku, and the Germans launching the second battle of the Somme which was to take them to within artillery range of Paris.

However, these wider horizons had to be contracted to allow for more immediate preoccupations. In a brief note to Wingate in Cairo on 7 March, Clayton tells the High Commissioner that he had been to Jerusalem where things were going well though "the Moslems continue to evince great apprehension in regard to Zionist aims, and I fancy the French do not make much effort to allay their fears. The role of saviour of Moslems from Zionist ambition promises some profit."[33] Coming events were casting their long shadow ahead and Clayton read it very clearly.

Meanwhile, in the main theatre of war affairs were going disastrously, bringing new problems to the diplomats and administrators in Egypt and Palestine. To add to their complications, the long-heralded Zionist Commission, headed by Dr Chaim Weizmann, had arrived in Cairo under conditions of considerable political confusion about its status and objectives; there had also been disturbing developments in the contact established between Prince Faisal and the Turkish authorities in Damascus. It was in this setting that Clayton prepared himself for the arrival of the Zionist Commission on which he had set great hope. Their landing in Cairo, as Clayton waited in Palestine, was described in a private letter from the High Commissioner, Sir Reginald Wingate, to Lord Hardinge, the Permanent Under-Secretary at the Foreign Office. Wingate was particularly concerned at the state of the Arab alliance.

"The situation as between the Arabs and Turks," he writes, "has become somewhat critical, and although you will have gathered from my recent letter to Sykes that there is a good deal of method in Feisal's apparent rapprochement with Jemal, we cannot be absolutely sure."[34] However, Wingate believes that the Arab situation will be cleared up by Allenby's military success "and bring the Arabs down finally on the right side". The Arabs had been considerably affected by German and Turkish propaganda, he explains, which had exploited the terms of

[32] Clayton to Sykes, 14 February 1918.
[33] Clayton to Wingate, 7 March 1918.
[34] Wingate to Hardinge, 21 March 1918, Wingate Papers.

peace concluded between Germany and Russia and Rumania under which the Turks regained a large portion of the territory they had lost to Russia; "and it is but natural and characteristic of Arab policy that the Chiefs should trim in order to come down finally on the side which gives them the best terms", Wingate concludes before turning his attention to Weizmann and the Zionist Commission.

He had met them the previous day, he tells Hardinge, and they had a long and interesting talk. "Weizmann is undoubtedly a very clever and capable leader, but I had to warn them to go a little slow in this country, as it is, above all things, Moslem and Pan-Islamic and, as such, does not view Zionism too friendly. I therefore recommended them to feel their way carefully and do all in their power to show sympathy and goodwill to the Arab and Moslem peoples with whom their future must lie." And, as a footnote, Wingate added an extract from a letter which Allenby had written to him and which he thought might interest Sykes. Allenby wrote: "Picot dined at my Headquarters last night [i.e. 20 March] to meet the Duke. Picot is worried about Zionism and I am not sure that he is not right." Hardinge must have felt, reading Wingate's comments that he too shared this feeling with Picot and Allenby. Weizmann and his colleagues, as we shall see, came away from their meetings with Wingate and Allenby two weeks or so later with very different impressions. What had produced the change?

In some curious way, no one among the British officials in Cairo or with the Palestine Expeditionary Force appeared to have a very clear idea of the political intentions of Zionism; the publications of the British Zionists seemed not to be known and the principal information about Zionist intentions came from Sir Mark Sykes at the Cabinet Office. Weeks after the proclamation of the Balfour Declaration there was no kind of Zionist declaration of intent available to those Allied officials and Arab leaders who were most directly concerned with it. It was therefore not surprising that the arrival of Dr Weizmann and the Zionist Commission was awaited in Cairo and Jerusalem with impatience, anxiety and curiosity but meanwhile the Voice of Zion was largely that of Sir Mark Sykes.

It was designed in the first place to reassure the men on the spot – Allenby, Wingate, Clayton – so that they, in turn, could reassure their colleagues and the Arab notables. In this, it must be said, Sykes was more successful than the Zionist leadership in London or the local Zionist spokesmen in Palestine. But Mark Sykes' initiative had a second

40

and more important consequence, whether intentional or not. His various definitions of Zionist objectives and policies set, in fact, the pitch for Weizmann and his Commission. In a sense, Sykes had committed them to his line of action before they had arrived and before they had said a word.

This could be seen in the January instructions to Hogarth as guide for his conversations with the Sharif in Jeddah. It emerged even more closely in the exchanges with the so-called Syrian Welfare Committee in Cairo, which represented Syrian Arab nationalist opinion. On 27 March 1918, shortly after the arrival of the Zionist Commission in Cairo, the Committee addressed a letter to Sykes in which they summed up their understanding of Zionist intention. They thanked him for his advice that they should seek a closer community of thought and aim with the Zionists whose sole wish was to have the right of colonisation in Palestine and of living their national life. They had evidently asked for elucidation from Sir Mark just what this meant and they now confirmed their understanding of Sir Mark's definition of the Zionist position. "We clearly deduce from your letter," they wrote to him, "that all the Zionists demand is liberty for the Jews to settle in our country and enjoy full civil rights." They add that they had received a similar explanation from General Clayton. This was the beginning of trouble. The British presented the Arabs with a rosy image of Zionist intention and the Zionist Commission about to descend on Palestine with a brief stopover in Cairo – would have to live up to it.

Sykes was evidently confident that Weizmann would not let him down, but the officials in Cairo and in Palestine were filled with doubt. All the greater was their relief at Weizmann's attitude, particularly in the case of Allenby and Clayton after Weizmann had spent a night at Allenby's GHQ as the Commander-in-Chief's guest. Clayton writes to Sykes with marked approval and enthusiasm about this first meeting with the Zionist leader. "We are all struck with his intelligence and openness and the Commander-in-Chief has evidently formed a high opinion of him. I feel convinced that many of the difficulties we have encountered owing to the mutual distrust and suspicion between Arabs and Jews will now disappear. An inkling of his real policy which I suspected but which I was never really aware of until his arrival . . . will undoubtedly go far towards removing the fears of Arabs, both in the Occupied Territory and elsewhere." The meeting with the Committee of Syrian Nationalists in Cairo had produced satisfactory results and he

41

expected the same when Weizmann met with leading Muslims in Jerusalem.

In an altogether unexpected sense, the arrival of the Zionist Commission – and especially Weizmann's presentation of the Zionist case – had acted as a catalyst to the thinking of the senior British officials. For the time being, their greatest worry had been removed; their fears of the possible consequences of the Balfour Declaration were at least momentarily stilled, and they could address themselves to other major questions of the war that weighed heavily on them. Clayton lost no time. Hopefully, he saw the new development much as did Sykes and in the same letter, he explained how he now saw the agreement Sykes had concluded with Picot and which carried their joint name.[35] Clayton gathered from information which Sykes had sent him that the Government had decided to let the agreements with the French and the Italians "die gradually until the time comes to administer the coup de grace which may not even have to be given at all". Nothing, however, had been said to the French and he could not see any sign from Picot – with whom he had developed excellent relations – "that he has any idea that such a policy is in contemplation – and he still regards the agreements as his bible". But Clayton had doubts whether he could tell Picot what was in the wind; he would sound him out and begin to impress on him that his agreement with Sykes was out of date, reactionary and only fit for the scrap-heap – words that were hardly music for Sykes' always over-sensitive ears on this particular topic. But Clayton was clearly under the impression – mistaken in this case – that Sykes shared his views on the worthlessness of the agreement with the French.

At the same time, Clayton lobbied Sykes for the other policy initiative on which his heart was set, but which must have been anathema to Sykes: his proposal "to capture" the Turanian movement in Turkey and so prevent its employment by the Germans. Clayton was not advocating anything as radical as a separate peace with Turkey, but once they had achieved a position where they could reasonably say "that we have got for the Arabs what we promised them, then we can logically pursue the same policy and hold out the hand of sympathy to the Turanian movement based on real principles of self-determination".[36]

[35] The Sykes-Picot Agreement provided for the division of the Middle East into British and French spheres of influence – the British taking Mesopotamia and Arabia, the French Syria, the Lebanon, and parts of Anatolia, while Palestine was to be in part British and partly internationalised.

[36] Clayton to Sir Mark Sykes, 4 April 1918.

Clayton's suggestion of "capturing" the Turanian movement was supported by a forceful memorandum from T. E. Lawrence, but the idea received short shrift at the hand of the Foreign Office. In a curt cable to the High Commissioner in Cairo, he was instructed to inform Clayton and Lawrence that their idea "that chauvinistic Pan-Turanianism can be combined with Pan-Arab and anti-German movements" could not be entertained. The Foreign Office gave two reasons for its negative decision. Pan-Turanianism could achieve its objective only on the basis of Armenian and Georgian massacres, and the Greater Turkey outlook of the Pan-Turanians had to be, by its very nature, hostile to any Arab revival "as it is based on the idea of Islam being an appendage to the Turanian movement". Clayton was also to be told that the "pro-Turkish Pickthall group in England had suddenly veered from a violent anti-Arab policy to a pro-Arab anti-Zionist policy". Lastly, Wingate was advised to warn Prince Faisal through his secret channels that a dangerous Turkish intrigue was afoot to bring about a false peace with the Arab movement in order to destroy it or enslave it. Faisal was to be cautioned that Djemal Pasha, the Turkish Commander in Damascus who had made the approaches to Faisal, was quite untrustworthy and concerned only with Turkish interest.[37]

This was but the first indication that, far from having any kind of master-plan, neither the British officials in Cairo and Jerusalem nor the Foreign Office in London were at all clear or agreed about their objectives; nor were they sure about the precise imperial interests involved. They had unchained new forces and they were now finding it difficult to handle them in the classical manner of the Colonial Service, or with the traditional priorities of the Empire. This, together with the nuances and variations of British policy, emerged strongly from a curious exchange of views between Ormsby-Gore, the British liaison officer with the Zionist Commission, Clayton, Sykes and Balfour.

It started with a private letter from Ormsby-Gore to Sykes on 16 April 1918. Ormsby-Gore sent it first to Clayton to read before forwarding it to London. He wrote to Sykes to express his concern over the way in which British officials were dealing with the Zionist Commission and related matters. He also drew Sykes' attention to the pushing methods of the French in furthering their commercial interests. They were spending very large sums of money, he claimed, in developing the port of Jaffa. They had invested £700,000 in that. It was a great pity, in

[37] Foreign Office to Wingate, 23 April 1918, Wingate Papers.

Ormsby-Gore's opinion, that neither the British Government nor the Zionists were doing this sort of thing, and he quoted the belief of the Zionists that the British administration was favouring Muslim Arabs and cited "British ex-Sudan and ex-Egyptian officials" as practising this kind of favouritism. The Jews wanted "deeds and acts to show that the Balfour Declaration is not just a scrap of paper. I shall report this officially."

Clayton did not immediately forward the letter to the Foreign Office. He evidently thought hard about it and its implications. After little more than two weeks in Palestine, the Zionist Commission was clearly dissatisfied with the British administration, and especially with two of its principals, Ronald Storrs, the Governor of Jerusalem, and Pearson, the Governor of Jaffa. This raised some fundamental questions, as well as personal ones, in Clayton's mind, and two days later, he sent Ormsby-Gore's letter to Sykes together with one of his own. At the same time he sent a carefully considered letter to the Foreign Secretary. All three letters, Ormsby-Gore's to Sykes together with Clayton's to Sykes and to Balfour, were despatched on 18 April 1918. Clayton's letter to Balfour is particularly noteworthy for the insight it provides into the policy-making influence of Clayton and his towering impact on the shaping of British policy in Palestine. At the same time, it was also a reflection of the uncertainties at that stage with which the British administration approached the problems of Zionism and Arabism. But above all, it was the first clear evidence of the conflicting emotions with which Clayton was beset and the different way in which he presented these to Sykes and Balfour: in their way, these two letters of Clayton's could be taken as a microscopic presentation of the inner conflict which British policy in the Middle East sought to resolve over the next half-century.

Thus, commenting on Ormsby-Gore's letter to Sykes, which he enclosed, Clayton writes that he thought that some of Ormsby-Gore's remarks "based on a very short experience of local conditions and sentiment may mislead you". Clayton did not think that the French constituted a commercial threat, and in any case they were taking adequate counter-measures. Moreover, it would be foolish to sink that kind of money into developing Jaffa port when it was almost certain that Haifa would become the major port in Palestine. Rather cautiously, he thought Ormsby-Gore's strictures of Storrs and Pearson – "the ex-Sudan and ex-Egyptian officials" – were not justified. And then

Clayton made a quite remarkable personal declaration: "Apart from the fact that support of Zionism is the declared policy of His Majesty's Government," he wrote to Sykes, "I am personally in favour of it, and am convinced that it is one of our strongest cards, but your knowledge of all that has taken place in this area will, I know, lead you to agree with me in the necessity of caution if we are to bring that policy to a successful conclusion." What had Clayton in mind that April 1918, when he conceived of Zionism as one of the strongest cards in the hands of the British policy-makers which – if played with skill – would help to bring their policy to a successful conclusion? Clayton does not spell out his meaning in this letter; presumably, Sykes knew what was in Clayton's mind. Clayton himself simply concluded the letter with a reassuring note that he had been to Cairo and Egypt seemed quiet. He had spoken there to the Arab nationalists, especially Dr Nimr and his friends, and "was much pleased at the evident result of Weizmann's conferences there with leaders of Arab opinion in Egypt".[38]

On the same day, Clayton sent a despatch to the Foreign Secretary which clearly needs to be read in conjunction with his letter to Sykes. In this Clayton addressed himself formally to the question of the Zionist Commission and the complaints which it had made and which were voiced also in the letter to Sykes by Ormsby-Gore. He appreciated, Clayton said, that the Commission had arrived "on a wave of enthusiasm for a great and inspiring project", and had then come up against the squalid details which face those engaged in even the highest enterprises. More to the point were the difficulties felt by the Military administration in Palestine in carrying out the Government's intentions with regard to the Zionists, "in consequence of the fact that, up to date, our policy has been directed towards securing Arab sympathy in view of our Arab commitments. It is not easy, therefore, to switch over to Zionism all at once in the face of a considerable degree of Arab distrust and suspicion." However, Clayton felt that the situation was developing well, the distrust and suspicion was being dissipated more quickly than they had expected "... but in the interest of Zion itself it is very necessary to proceed with caution".

As in his letter to Sykes, Clayton returns to his intriguing main theme. Having in mind their policy in the Middle East during the last three years, he writes to Balfour, "it is obvious that precipitate action will only injure the prospects of a project which, given careful handling,

[38] Clayton to Sykes, 18 April 1918.

45

should give great results". He was fully aware that the Zionist enthusiasts on the Commission might see the necessary delays as evidence of lack of British support, but he was confident that Dr Weizmann fully realised "that the local authorities are only too anxious to help in every way", even if their special knowledge of local conditions led them to delay or turn down schemes put forward by the Zionist Commission. But then Clayton's tone hardens. "Arab opinion in Palestine and elsewhere is in no condition to support an overdose of Zionism just now." The setbacks on the Western Front had made a bad impression on the Arabs to the disadvantage of the British, and great care was therefore essential "in developing a policy which is, to say the least, somewhat startling to those other elements whom we have been at such pains to cultivate during the past three years and to whom we are morally pledged". Moreover, Arab military assistance was of vital importance at that juncture and this was reflected by the Turkish attempts to seduce the Arabs from their British alliance. In conclusion, Clayton requested that the "local authorities be trusted" to carry out the policy laid down and "that they be not forced into precipitate action which might well wreck our whole policy, both Arab and Zionist".[39]

These were the decisive days when the seed was being sown. It was the British who had decided just what should be planted. Two days after Clayton had sent his considered despatch to the Foreign Office, the Director of the Arab Bureau, Kinahan Cornwallis, reported to his superior, Lieutenant-Colonel Symes, that, following the arrival of the Zionist Commission, leading Syrians and Palestinians with whom he had spoken were prepared to acknowledge that the Zionist aims were "not as black as they had been painted", and that under certain circumstances, the Arab population of Palestine "might even benefit from a Jewish 'invasion' ". There remained, however, a deeply felt fear among the local Arabs that Jews intended to govern the country, buy up the land and force the Arabs to leave. These apprehensions, Cornwallis noted, "were fostered not only by their previous experience of a rather undesirable class of Jew, but also by the attitude of the local Jewish Committee, which, possibly owing to a lack of orders as to what course it should adopt, was unable to give them satisfaction". British officers who attempted to allay the Arab fears were handicapped by their own "ignorance of the exact programme of the Zionists". All this changed, Cornwallis notes, with the arrival of the Zionist Commission and the

[39] Clayton to the Secretary of State, Foreign Office, 18 April 1918.

meetings between Dr Weizmann and representative Syrians and Palestinians.

Before we continue with Cornwallis' report, it is necessary to note that here we come to the nub of the problem. For what follows is the implementation of Clayton's, Wingate's, Allenby's and Balfour's injunctions to Weizmann to pursue a policy of caution. Cornwallis now reports, with evident satisfaction, how this policy was applied by Weizmann and understood by the Syrians and Palestinians. "He told them it was his ambition to see Palestine governed by some stable Government like that of Great Britain, that a Jewish Government would be fatal to his plans and that it is simply his wish to provide a home for the Jews in the Holy Land, where they could live their own national life, sharing equal rights with the other inhabitants. He assured them that he had no intention of taking advantage of the present condition caused by the war by buying up land."

Cornwallis notes that "this frank avowal of Zionist aims" had produced a great change of feeling among the Palestinians. They understood that Zionism had come to stay, that it was "far more moderate in its aims than they had anticipated" and that by being conciliatory the Arabs were likely to reap substantial benefits in the future. Such remaining suspicion as there was would disappear if the Zionist Commission stuck to its present attitude of conciliation.[40]

What did not emerge from the Cornwallis report was that Weizmann had played the part set for him by the representatives of the British Government, though it is not at all clear to what extent this was a calculated policy decision by the Ministers concerned. On the contrary, most, if not all, the evidence points to the conclusion that it was Clayton in Palestine who understood from the outset the possible explosive character of Zionism. He sought to bring it into the framework of British interests; it was his initial reaction to Sykes' more fanciful plans that led to the formulation of the "synthetic" British policy, and it was this synthesis, repeatedly elaborated by Clayton, that became the policy of the Foreign Office and of the High Commissioner in Cairo. Most significantly, it was also accepted by Dr Weizmann and became the basis later, as we shall see, for his own formulation of a "synthetic" Zionist programme as he called it with a scientist's precision and without a thought for the possible pejorative political content of the phrase.

[40] Cornwallis to Symes, 20 April 1918, PRO, FO, 371/3395.

47

In short, what Cornwallis reported to Colonel Stewart Symes, Director of the Arab Bureau in Cairo, was the first and seemingly successful interplay between Clayton and Weizmann. Weizmann had his own reasons for accepting Clayton's formula for the Zionist approach to the Arabs, and we shall be able to consider them more closely in due course.[41] But here we are concerned with one of the most intricate and subtle imperial patterns which were being woven by Clayton, then still a comparatively unknown official attached to General Allenby's staff. It was one of the most far-sighted exercises in empire-building undertaken in the history of the British overseas, and it survived – admittedly amidst conflict and crises, but it survived – longer than any other central feature added by the Versailles settlement to the British Empire. And more to the point: it assured the British of their most valuable economic asset which they enjoyed and exploited during the climax of the triumph of the Empire and even more during the critical years of decline. It made possible British possession and control of the oilfields of the Middle East before others joined her, and the harvesting of profits on a scale that has never yet been fully divulged. Had it not been for Clayton's concept of the "synthetic" alliance with Faisal on the one side and Weizmann on the other, this pattern could not have taken shape.

In April 1918, however, the British in Cairo and Jerusalem were still thankful for smaller mercies which were reflected in the informal and private letters Ormsby-Gore sent to Sykes and Hankey. He told Sykes of his growing admiration for the way Clayton was handling affairs in Palestine, and of his considerable alarm at the change in the Arab mood towards the British. "A change on the part of the Arabs towards the Turk is pretty obvious, due to the collapse of Russia, and the Batoum-Kars-Ardahan business, which has gone like a wildfire everywhere. The German advance in the West is also causing them furiously to think. It is my conviction that the Zionists are the one sound, firmly pro-British, constructive element in the whole show."[42]

Ten days later, Ormsby-Gore wrote a personal note to Maurice Hankey, Secretary to the Cabinet and to the War Committee. Ormsby-Gore's position was a curious one: liaison officer with the Zionist Commission, junior to Sykes in London and to Clayton in Palestine,

[41] See Chapter Two.
[42] Ormsby-Gore to Sykes, 9 April 1918, Sledmere Papers.

he had a much closer relationship to Sykes than had Clayton, and he was on more intimate terms with Hankey than was Sykes. In his private correspondence, as distinct from his more formal communications to the Zionist Commission, Ormsby-Gore was that rare individual – a perceptive, independent and articulate junior officer who saw a good deal and was not afraid to speak his mind or get involved with matters that were not strictly his concern as an official or officer.

This showed in every line in the note he sent to Hankey on 19 April 1918: "If this splendid country is ever to be properly developed and still more if it is to be British, it is only the Zionists who can accomplish these two aims. Mark's blessed Arabs are a poor show in this country," Ormsby-Gore tells Hankey. But he was also not dewy-eyed about Weizmann – "[He] is at times too fanatical and too partisan and uncompromising." But he was doing well: "He is very fair and reasonable with the Arabs and rules his own people with a big stick . . . and they accept him as an autocrat." However, Ormsby-Gore has forebodings, and he plunges into high politics in an attempt to rouse Hankey to the seriousness of the situation. "Weizmann's policy is more and more definitely a 'British Palestine' and God knows what will happen if he does not get it." And Ormsby-Gore closes with a look ahead, as he puts it, to the far future. They ought to bear in mind that "the deeper the division between Palestine and Egypt, the better for Palestine and for the British Empire".[43]

Ormsby-Gore's unusual and unorthodox position had been underlined in the letter which the Foreign Secretary had sent to Clayton advising him of the political implications of the Zionist Commission and of the Government's hopes for its success. Balfour makes clear that Ormsby-Gore was to be treated as his representative; he had personally briefed him together with Dr Weizmann, and he tells Clayton that not only will the attitude of world Jewry to Palestine depend on the success of the Zionist Commission, but also that the Mission's achievements "may well play an important part at the Peace Conference". This assumption was one that had greatly appealed to Clayton. It fitted into his own reading of the situation. And so that there should be no room for misunderstanding, Balfour added that he had known Weizmann for many years and had great confidence in his tact and judgement and that Weizmann "is thoroughly to be trusted".[44]

[43] Ormsby-Gore to Hankey, 19 April 1918.
[44] Balfour to Clayton, 2 March 1918.

49

Clayton's first major test came sooner than he had anticipated. Within a matter of weeks after the arrival of the Zionist Commission, he found his political "synthesis" challenged by the Zionists. His formula worked admirably on the level of higher policy, but produced evident anomalies on the practical day-to-day level, and it might then have developed into dangerous animosities, as it did many years later. But it did not at that dangerous time, because of the way Clayton handled the delicate situation.

The threatening storm arrived in a formal letter from Ormsby-Gore to Clayton. This informed that Ormsby-Gore felt duty bound to report the situation that had developed to the Foreign Office "as instructed by Mr Balfour". Ormsby-Gore said he had worded his report as moderately as possible and requested Clayton to forward it to London. However, should the Commander-in-Chief, General Allenby, decide that it would be better for Ormsby-Gore to resign his position in Palestine rather than put his name to such a report, Ormsby-Gore would naturally return at once to his post in the Cabinet Office, because he could then no longer remain responsible for British policy towards the Zionist Commission. And, in a personal note to Clayton, Ormsby-Gore added that he expected Clayton to refuse to forward his report should he consider it either inaccurate or unfair.[45]

Ormsby-Gore's report addressed to Balfour was a formidable indictment of the Military administration in Palestine. It accused it primarily of a lack of understanding and feeling in its dealings with the Jewish population of Palestine. This had undermined Jewish confidence in the impartiality and intentions of the British administration. The Jewish colonists were, in fact, beginning to ask whether the Balfour Declaration was anything more than a scrap of paper? The Jews were reading newspaper reports from the fronts which showed "that by the power of the sword, Germany 'had delivered the goods' to the Jews of Roumania, and has forced the Roumanian Government to emancipate the Jews as part of the peace terms forced on them. They are wondering after all if the British promises mean anything or nothing." Ormsby-Gore proceeded to cite grievances that were submitted to him. When dealing with the Jewish colonists, Palestinian Arabs and Egyptians, often known "Jew-haters", were appointed by the British to decide on the fate of the Jew before the tribunal, even on such routine requests as the permitted yield of the vineyards at Rishon-le-Zion. He reminded

[45] Ormsby-Gore to Clayton and Ormsby-Gore to Balfour, 17 May 1918.

50

Balfour that the Jews enjoyed greater autonomy and a greater sense of community under the Turks than they now did under the British. The British courts were staffed on all levels by Arabs, and the magistrates and judges were Arabs. Jews were compelled to speak Arabic in British government offices, and when Clayton had proposed to attach an interpreter to the staff of each British Military Governor, he was over-ruled by General Money, the Chief Administrator, who thought that this was absolutely unnecessary. "In all these minor details of administration, I note with regret that the prestige and the position of the Jews is being deteriorated while that of the Arabs is increasing in power and arrogance." Ormsby-Gore then weighed the respective value of "the Effendis" and the Jews to the British Empire and had no hesitation in forecasting that the Jews "mean to get Palestine sooner or later. It may be through England in a few years, or through Germany or Turkey in fifty. There is no stopping the Zionist movement now . . . Sooner or later we shall see a Jewish Palestine. Of this I am convinced." He also insisted that the Jews would play an important part in deciding whether Palestine would be British after the Peace Conference, and no less so in the coming post-war struggle for supremacy between the German and Anglo-Saxon civilisations. There was a good deal more along these lines and one rather naïve analysis of the contrasting fine qualities of the Arabs of Arabia and of the desert and the rather poor stuff of the Arabs of Jaffa. Clayton crossed out a few of the more extreme assertions, but he let the major part of the indictment stand and sent it off to London, together with a brief comment of his own.

Clayton sent both documents – Ormsby-Gore's letter and his – first to General Allenby and to the Chief Administrator, General Money. Ormsby-Gore's despatch to Balfour undoubtedly expressed genuine grievances of the Zionist Commission and sought redress on the major question of the status of the Commission in the eyes of the Military administration. On this score, one had to conclude from Clayton's comment that he was in broad agreement with Ormsby-Gore's strictures. But, for the larger part, the Ormsby-Gore letter to Balfour was a somewhat brash affair. He had evidently, deeply and uncritically, imbibed the views of Dr Weizmann without sufficiently distinguishing between Weizmann after-dinner table-talk and his serious approach to politics. Ormsby-Gore was only the first of many others who were so charmed by the man that they did not always separate the charm from the words.

51

Clayton did; and his comment to the Ormsby-Gore letter is a classic statement of its kind. In fact, he advances much the same argument in 200 words where Ormsby-Gore had required 2,000 for his presentation; moreover, Clayton drives the point home without antagonising those whose support he would require to carry through his policy of collaboration with the Zionist Commission. Ormsby-Gore's memorandum reflected Zionist – and Weizmann's – impatience behind the façade of caution and moderation which had pleased Allenby and Wingate so much, but which Weizmann could not sustain: his temperament, his colleagues and the Jews in Palestine would not permit it and they faced the risk, in the wake of Ormsby-Gore's direct appeal to Balfour, of an outright breach with the British administration in Palestine.

Clayton recognised the danger and produced his own formula. It spoke for itself: "To defer all development of Zionist policy and to ask the Zionists to rest content that the assurances given to them will be fulfilled at some future date after the war by a Government, the status and nature of which has yet to be decided, is to present them with a stone in fulfilment of what they regard with some justice as a promise of at least a small portion of bread." Should this happen, Clayton had little doubt that it would result in the withdrawal of Dr Weizmann from his position as leader of pro-British Zionism and in the departure of the Zionist Commission from Palestine. And Clayton warned "this would be a severe blow to British diplomacy in the eyes of the world and afford the German Government a welcome opportunity for extricating itself from what even German statesmen admit to be an awkward predicament. Indeed, the result might well be to throw Zionism into the arms of America or even at worst, on to Germany. Thus the death-blow would be dealt to pro-British Zionism, and at the same time, to any hope of securing Zionist influence at the Peace Conference in favour of a British Palestine."[46]

Clayton's message clearly carried more weight than Ormsby-Gore's, but it had much the same import: Weizmann's and Zionist goodwill were in jeopardy and they were important factors in the final stages of the war and in the making of the peace.

In Cairo, Symes, at the Arab Bureau, saw matters much the same way, but from a distance and with less immediate involvement than Clayton or Ormsby-Gore. This was reflected in the somewhat more

[46] Clayton, "Memorandum", 18 May 1918.

brutal assessment which he made after talking with Weizmann on 9 and 10 June and also with representative spokesmen for King Husain and for the Syrians. When Symes came to summarise his impressions on 18 June 1918, he concluded that the supporters of King Husain in the Hejaz and the Syrian nationalists were firmly opposed to any suggestion of a French dominance in Syria and that both these Arab leaderships would welcome Zionist support for their opposition to the French. They would also prefer Zionist financial support for the new Hejazi state to that from Christian Powers, which might be objectionable in Moslem eyes. Such Zionist aid, moreover, could be the means by which King Husain could establish his complete ascendancy over the other Arab chiefs in the peninsula, "thus creating a better territorial background for his claims to the Caliphate of the Moslems".

From all this, Symes deduced that a situation favourable to the British, for King Husain and the Zionists, could be achieved "if our obligation to France under the Sykes-Picot agreement were finally repudiated and all idea of conserving the privileges of the Palestine Arabs abandoned". Symes believed this to be central to the situation in Palestine and to Great Britain's relations with the Arabs. In any case, this political switch was actually taking place: it was implied, says Symes, in the Government's Declaration in favour of Zionism, and, according to private advice reaching him from London, the Sykes-Picot agreement was already in abeyance and practically defunct. Thus the British position in Palestine and Syria was secured, but there remained the important question (for the British) of the future of Mesopotamia (Iraq). "We mean to stay there in one capacity or another, to create a bulwark against German penetration eastwards, and to develop the great natural resources of the country for the benefit of the inhabitants and our own trade." They would have, however, to obtain the consent of the Peace Conference, Symes adds, in a way that would "give us as far as possible a free hand".

It would not be possible to annex the country and it might be difficult to obtain a formal protectorate over it if there was a peace by agreement. In that case, Symes advised that "we should want all the moral reinforcement to our claim that we can get; and find it expedient and advantageous to pay lip-service to the ideal of [future] political Arab unity." As an alternative, it might even be possible for Great Britain to hold these territories "in nominal fee from King Husain", who would be considered to be the most representative Arab entitled to make this arrangement. It would be preferable to some form of international arrangement which would permit other Great Powers to interfere.

The deal with Husain by which he would lease Iraq to the British clearly appealed to Symes. "Thus might we secure," he concluded his secret memorandum to the High Commissioner, "the substance whilst formally renouncing the shadow of ownership or sovereignty of Arab lands; and, by this renunciation, strengthen our hands against French political penetration in Syria, and allow Syrian prejudice, Moslem partiality and Zionist opportunism to combine and operate on behalf of pro-British and anti-Hun influences throughout the Arab countries."[47]

This was to become the recurring theme of Clayton's preoccupation. His approach was not as harsh as that of Symes; he really did believe that the most effective way of securing the British position in the Middle East was by way of the "compact" with the Arab movement based on the Hashemites (though that word was not yet used) and with the pro-British Zionists represented by Dr Weizmann. He had, in fact, travelled far from those first impressions which he recorded seven months before in his letter to Gertrude Bell while the British troops were on the threshold of entering Jerusalem. He had then approved of the Arab refusal "to be humbugged by the specious oratory of the British sponsors of the Zionist orientation"; he was also dubious, if not contemptuous of the "Meccan patriarchalism" and the Government's visionary agreements and incautious declarations.

That was December 1917; now in June 1918, against the background of the German offensive on the Western Front, the renewed troubles in Ireland, and the Turkish offensive in Palestine and Persia, Clayton had evidently thought deeply about the policy on which he had set his heart and which he believed would best serve British interests. On 17 June 1918, he bared his thoughts at length in another letter to Gertrude Bell, and on the same day, in an even longer letter expressing similar, but not always identical, thoughts to Sir Clive Wigram, his understanding friend and Assistant Private Secretary to King George. Clayton was in confident mood about prospects on the Western Front and expected the Americans to spearhead the final offensive against the Germans; he was better informed, or differently inclined, than the politicians and soldiers who saw the war stretching ahead for another year or two. Moreover, Clayton was sure that the crushing blow against Turkey was

[47] Symes to Wingate, 13 June 1918, Wingate Papers.

only delayed and he took its ultimate execution for granted when he turned to consider the political situation in the Middle East.

A central factor in his calculations was the presence of the Zionist Commission with Dr Weizmann in Palestine. "As you will realise," he wrote in his letter to Gertrude Bell, "it is not very easy to co-ordinate the Zionist Policy of the Government with the Arab policy which we have been pursuing for so long. Still, I do not think that on the broader lines the two policies are necessarily incompatible." Clayton then gives an account of Weizmann's meeting with Faisal, where the two men had established "far more mutual sympathy than I had hoped was possible".

This led Clayton to a new theme – and one which was eagerly embraced by the Zionist spokesmen. "Palestine itself," he writes, "is to my mind outside the real Arab policy except insofar as discontent and disturbance here might react across the Dead Sea and Jordan as well as in Syria. The so-called Arabs of Palestine are not to be compared with the real Arab of the desert or even of other civilised districts in Syria and Mesopotamia. He is purely local and takes little or no interest in matters outside his immediate surroundings." The "Sherifian Movement", the Arab revolt, had left the Palestinians "absolutely cold". The more-or-less educated class in Palestine was against anything which spelt progress or development. Its components – traders, land-owners, and ex-Turkish Government employees – were "shiftless and corrupt by inclination". Clayton did not mince words in the privacy of his letters to Gertrude Bell.

All the same – and it was this that made Clayton the remarkable administrator that he was – "local feeling has to be studied and con-ciliated". The educated Palestinians might find Jewish competition more onerous than they cared for but as far as the Fellah was con-cerned, Clayton thought "that Jewish expansion in Palestine, for which there is adequate room within reasonable limits, will greatly improve the conditions of the local peasantry, provided it is on moderate and liberal lines sketched out by Mr Weizmann". And he proceeded to confide to Gertrude Bell his complete change of attitude to the Zionists in the seven months that had elapsed since he had written to her in December 1917. "There is little doubt that Zionist policy has been of very considerable assistance to us already and may help us a great deal more not only during the war but afterwards. A Palestine in which Jewish interest is established and which is under the aegis of Great Britain will

55

be a strong outpost to Egypt, the invasion of which would raise even more bitter feeling all over the world than did that of Belgium."

As if to explain his changed evaluation of the Zionists, Clayton wonders whether Gertrude Bell was aware that Zionist policy was not as alarming as they had assumed. Zionist policy, he tells her, did not "seek the establishment of a Jewish State, at any rate at present, but aims at the institution of a Jewish home or centre of Hebrew culture in Palestine under the protection of Great Britain". They had not been aware of this until Weizmann and the Zionist Commission had arrived and this had put "a very different complexion on the whole idea in the eyes of our Arab friends who feel that the dangers of Jewish expansion will be greatly minimised if Great Britain is in supreme control".

But he was still somewhat unsure on the way the Arab position would develop. The Sharifians, especially Faisal, had their eyes fixed on Damascus and Aleppo "and nothing else seems to matter to him in comparison with this". It is this that led Faisal to welcome Jewish co-operation as he was quite prepared to leave Palestine alone provided he could secure what he wanted in Syria. Clayton believed that Faisal was wise to enlist Jewish sympathy "as some day he will want money and financial support if he makes good at all", and if the Zionist movement really develops as its leaders expect it would become a powerful ally on the Arab side; its "international character will be all to the good, especially if the roots of Zionism are in Palestine and Palestine is under British control".[48]

It was an impressive insight into Clayton's thinking – but it was not complete. For reasons of his own, Clayton wrote a second letter on the same day to Sir Clive Wigram, the King's Assistant Private Secretary and a man who exercised much influence at Court and among senior politicians and officials. Clayton repeated to him much the same argumentation as he had addressed to Gertrude Bell: he spoke in positive terms about the Zionist Commission and of the "considerable effect" a solid body of Jewish and Arab opinion in favour of independence from Turkish domination would have on the Peace Conference; and he was critical of the "shiftless" Palestinian Arabs of the educated class. But he added a personal note to the summary of the situation he sent to Wigram which he had not put into the letter to Gertrude Bell. "I am personally entirely in favour of the Zionist Policy," Clayton told Wigram. "From the Imperial point of view, it will, if properly developed,

[48] Clayton to Gertrude Bell, 17 June 1918.

56

create a strong pro-British buffer to the north of Egypt and the Suez Canal. If Zionism can be brought into close sympathy with the Arabs it will tend to make Arab ambitions, which we are pledged to support as far as possible, more probable of realisation, and the Jews will introduce the financial and commercial elements by which alone an Arab state can maintain itself."[49]

Clayton was clearly conscious that decisions taken during these June days could make or break the future peace settlement. As his letters show, he believed that there would have to be a negotiated settlement with the Turks and that the success of the British position would rest more on the political case that the British would be able to present with the aid of the Arab nationalists and the Zionists than on the purely military outcome of the Palestine and Mesopotamian campaigns. Thus, after having given more thought to the ideas he had forwarded to Gertrude Bell in Baghdad and to Wigram in London, and after discussing them further with Weizmann and Prince Faisal, Clayton wrote another carefully weighed opinion which he addressed to the Foreign Secretary, with a copy to the High Commissioner in Cairo.

What makes this despatch quite unusually interesting and significant is the way Clayton managed to develop a rather formalistic and polite conversation between Prince Faisal and Dr Weizmann which took place at Wadi Wahaida, near Aqaba, on 4 June 1918, into a strikingly positive encounter. He did this by following up the rather general sentiments expressed by the two men and, in his separate meetings with them, guiding them along lines of thinking which he wanted them to pursue. The views expressed in this despatch to Balfour reflected not so much the opinions of Faisal and Weizmann at their meeting, as views put to them by Clayton subsequently, and to which they gave their approval. What Clayton had achieved in effect was a much more formidable combination than simply the personal meeting of the recognised leaders of the Arab national movement and of the Zionists. For the views formulated for them by Clayton reflected also his personal opinion on how they should proceed further. Thus, his despatch to the Foreign Secretary of 1 July 1918, must rank as one of the significant state papers expressing Clayton's thinking of what British policy should be. Given Clayton's standing and influence at the time, it must have carried great weight with Allenby in Jerusalem, with Wingate in Cairo and with Balfour in London in gaining their approval for a concept, for which

[49] Clayton to Sir Clive Wigram, 17 June 1918.

he had already won Prince Faisal's and Weizmann's support, and which was breathtaking in its daring.

He made his observations in connection "with the problem of co-ordinating the Arab and Zionist policies". To begin with, he noted that for the new Arab states "to depend entirely for economic support on any single Great Power, even although it be Great Britain, is to place the new State in a position of subservience and to destroy even the outward semblance of independence to which the Arabs attach so much importance and without which Faisal cannot hope for their universal adherence". Having said this by way of introduction, Clayton proceeds to discuss, using Faisal's own words, matters which Faisal had not raised at his meeting with Weizmann, and he thus conveyed an extension of Faisal's views on Zionism which were essentially Clayton's. "Sherif Faisal sees in Zionism a force which, if enlisted on his side, may furnish him with the necessary economic support, but which bears what may be described as an 'un-national' complexion. With the help of Zionism, he thinks he may counter international concessionaires of the Vital stamp, French political influence exerted through clericals and financiers, and all these forces which tend towards foreign exploitation and which are detrimental to development on national lines. As regards political support, he recognises in Zionism an 'international' influence which permeates every country from which the future Syrian State may have anything to hope or fear. Finally, behind Zionism and working through it, he reckons on the British Empire on which in the last resort he places his trust."

After this presentation of Faisal's image of Zionism, Clayton turns to Dr Weizmann's projection of the future, again as conceived by Clayton and accepted by Weizmann. "Dr Weizmann realises that the development of those ideals which lie behind Zionism depends upon the establishment in Palestine of a centre of Jewish culture and sentiment, based on the soil itself, to which all Jewry will turn and which will justify its political existence by providing a bridge between East and West. An essential factor to the realisation of this ideal is that the future Jewish Palestine should be linked in close sympathy with the States by which it is surrounded. This is a condition of its development, and, indeed, of its existence."

However, as Clayton proceeds it becomes evident that he sees the British role in this Arab-Zionist marriage of convenience to be more than one of passive benevolence. There must be active pursuit of the policies he had outlined in Faisal's and Weizmann's name. "Thus it is vital to the realisation of Zionist aspirations," he tells the Foreign Secretary, "that Zionism should work hand-in-hand with the neighbouring Arab movement. The two policies, therefore, are interdependent, and it is difficult to see how our pledges to both parties concerned can be fulfilled in anything approaching the spirit in which they have been accepted unless the aims of Zionists and Arabs can be co-ordinated somewhat on the line indicated above. The task is difficult but not impossible."

But, having given Balfour a kind of preview of the great possibilities which his Arab and Zionist policies opened up for the benefit of the Empire, Clayton concludes by coldly placing the responsibility for further action on the British Government. The collaboration between the Arab nationalists and the Zionists was conditional not absolute, and he ends his despatch to the Foreign Office with a warning and a call to action by the Government so as to provide the necessary foundation for the Arab-Zionist British compact on which he had set his heart. "The fact has to be faced that the Arabs and the Zionist movement working together on the lines indicated above must be in direct opposition to the aims of that section of French opinion which favours the Syrian policy and in deference to whose aspirations the Sykes-Picot Agreement was drawn up. No development can take place on the lines suggested by Dr Weizmann's interview with Sherif Faisal so long as the Sykes-Picot Agreement remains in force and until a definite understanding is arrived at with the French Government that it is no longer a practical instrument."[50]

Clayton's letters and despatches reached Whitehall at a crucial moment when the fate of Allenby's campaign in Palestine was at issue. However, when the Supreme War Council met on 3 July 1918, Lloyd George pressed against strong opposition – especially from the military – that they should authorise Allenby to resume the campaign in the autumn. Moreover, the Prime Minister had impressed on the Imperial War Cabinet that there must be no retreat in Palestine. But there was still much confusion between the military and political possibilities and objectives of the Palestine and the Mesopotamian campaigns. This was hardly surprising. For Clayton's and Symes' letters and reports about Hejazis, Sharifians, Jews, Palestinians and Syrians reached London in

[50] Clayton to Foreign Secretary, 1 July 1918, copy to Symes for High Commissioner.

59

the context of a colossal crisis of confidence and mounting doubt about the prospect of outright victory. The German attacks in March and April and again at the end of May had made a deep psychological and strategic impact on the British authorities. Sir Henry Wilson, Chief of the Imperial General Staff, had actually proposed the evacuation of Dunkirk but had his proposals rejected by the French Supreme Commander, Marshal Foch. On 4 June 1918, after a meeting of the Supreme War Council in Paris, Hankey noted in his diary that "the Germans are fighting better than the Allies and I cannot exclude the possibility of a disaster. I see difficult times ahead." Next day, Hankey noted that Milner and Wilson came to see Lloyd George at Downing Street; they discussed "the possibility of withdrawing the whole Army from France if the French crack". Hankey added that it was a very gloomy meeting.[51]

The impact of these events on the principal colleagues of the Prime Minister, and on the Opposition, was reflected in a move by Balfour and Robert Cecil, supported by Asquith and Herbert Samuel, in the House of Commons on 16 May 1918, which has been described by a perceptive observer as "uncommonly like a plea for peace negotiations".[52] There was evidence of a German response, but then Ludendorff stepped in and left the British with no alternative but to fight on. At the same time, the military reports from the Palestine and Mesopotamian Fronts were also not particularly encouraging; they offered little support for the ambitious concepts of Clayton and his friends. Allenby was proposing to launch only a limited offensive in Northern Palestine which would drive the Turks from Galilee but permit them to make their escape. This still left the British forces in Mesopotamia in an exposed position, unsupported by the Russians any longer, since the Turks had occupied Batum in the Caucasus and Tabriz in Northern Persia, and the Germans were established on the Black Sea at Sebastopol. A memorandum presented to the Cabinet on 24 July 1918 by the Chief of the Imperial General Staff, Sir Henry Wilson, saw a direct threat to the Empire developing from this combined German-Turkish advance. There was nothing to stop it from gaining command of the Caspian, proceeding to the conquest of Afghanistan and stirring up the native population of India to revolt.[53] Lord Hardinge at the Foreign Office had no great

[51] Hankey, *Supreme Command*, Vol. II, p. 813.
[52] Paul Guinn, in *British Strategy & Politics*, p. 307.
[53] See Guinn, op. cit., p. 310.

trust in the British holding capacity in the East which was little more, in his opinion than "a big game of bluff".[54]

The possibility of a Turkish-German offensive appeared to be very real and seemed at first to condemn Clayton's proposals to relative unimportance. A General Staff Memorandum submitted to the Cabinet on 11 September 1918, and placed before the Supreme War Council, estimated that the Germans would launch a major offensive against India in 1919, and that a major Turkish offensive on the British positions of the Baghdad-Resht line was imminent. A week later Smuts supported by Curzon and General Cox expressed a similar belief, though Sir Henry Wilson and Balfour doubted it.[55]

At this moment when events of greater and graver consequence almost blotted out the prospect of Clayton's Arab and Zionist policies (and with them also Faisal's and Weizmann's hopes), a new and virtually decisive factor made its appearance and gave Clayton's proposal an entirely new and convincing dimension. As so often with incidents of this kind, it surfaced at a politically critical moment. It arose from steps taken by the Admiralty in 1916 on the recommendations of Admiral Slade to form a British National Oil Company in order to break the dominant hold of the Royal Dutch Shell and the American Standard Oil companies and in order to eliminate the German interests which had been connected with them.

During July 1918 Slade again circulated a memorandum on the significance of the Middle East oil fields on the initiative of the Admiralty Director of Naval Intelligence, Sir Reginald Hall. He sent a copy to Hankey who discussed its implications with Admiral Wemyss on 1 August 1918, and they decided to submit Slade's paper to the War Cabinet with a covering note drafted by Wemyss with Hankey's participation. The gist of it was to urge the importance of oil deposits north of the positions held by the British in Mesopotamia. It was to be a significant move in the shaping of the future of British Middle Eastern interests and more immediately in giving a new perspective to the campaigns in Palestine and Mesopotamia. The trio of British interests, the Arab, the Zionist and the peace settlement had now been joined by a potent fourth. On the same day as Admiral Wemyss dictated his memorandum, Hankey wrote to Balfour and began a campaign of his

[54] Hardinge to Wingate, 29 August 1918, Hardinge Papers.
[55] Eastern Committee, 18 September 1918, CAB 27/24; see Rothwell, *War Aims*, p. 189.

own that was to change the character of British Eastern interests and policy. Hankey urged Balfour to read the Slade memorandum "on the petroleum situation of the British Empire"; it was, in Hankey's opinion, "a most vitally important paper". Oil was going to take the place of coal in the next war, or at least would be of equal importance, Hankey argued. "The only big potential supply that we can get under British control is the Persian and Mesopotamian supply." Moreover, there were important deposits north of the British lines and this might have "an important influence on future military operations". Hankey also wrote to Lloyd George and to the First Lord at the Admiralty, Eric Geddes, to encourage them to press the War Office to resume and extend operations in Mesopotamia.

The War Cabinet was impressed but not altogether convinced, or fully aware of the far-reaching nature of the new element. Balfour told Hankey that the securing of the Persian and Mesopotamian oil-wells would be "frankly imperialistic" and the impatient Hankey noted in his diary: "Fancy allowing such humbug to stand in the way of our vital national needs." The Cabinet decided to refer the matter to its Oil Committee, but this produced an angry protest from Admiral Slade who, according to Hankey, doubted the discretion of Sir John Cadman, the principal man on the oil executive, and suspected his close association with the Dutch oil people, through whom, Slade feared, information might reach Germany.[56]

Hankey's ideas had evoked a quick response from the First Lord. Geddes added his own memorandum in which he urged that it should be one of the British war aims not only to secure the oilfields, but to develop them as a purely British interest, and to exclude all foreign interests. The memoranda and the private discussions worked with unaccustomed speed: by 13 August, Balfour's resistance had been overcome by Hankey, and the Foreign Secretary told a conference of Dominion Prime Ministers that Mesopotamia would have to be the exception to his conviction, that it was undesirable for the British Empire to expand further as a result of the war. It was unthinkable, Balfour added, to let Iraq revert to either Arab or Turkish rule, for the really important factor was that Mesopotamia could supply the British Empire with the one natural resource that it lacked, oil. "I do not care under what system we keep the oil," Balfour told the conference, "but

[56] Roskill, *Hankey, Man of Secrets*, Vol. I, pp. 586–7.

I am clear that it is all-important for us that this oil should be available."

Just how sensitive a nerve Hankey had touched was evident from the extraordinary reversal of priorities which the introduction of the oil factor brought about in the calculations of the Prime Minister. Speaking at the same conference of Dominion Premiers the same day (13 August 1918) Lloyd George explained that he was prepared to give up British control of Palestine to the United States, and surrender one of the German African colonies to the Americans, so as to obtain their approval for British control over Mesopotamia. It was the first of many encounters and clashes between the conflicting interests of oil and the Zionists. But for the moment, the emergence of the oil factor stood the Zionists in good stead. Clayton's letters and proposals suddenly acquired a new urgency and relevance. Although Lloyd George was prepared to trade Palestine for oil, the need to secure the Mesopotamian advance made it necessary also to extend Allenby's objectives, and this made possible the attainment of Arab, Zionist and oil aspirations which were to dominate and haunt British Middle East policy for the next half century. But this is a story in itself and we shall have to consider it in its later setting.[57]

Meanwhile, the great change was taking place in Palestine as Allenby prepared for the decisive September offensive that was to carry him to Damascus and to the rout of the Turkish army. On the eve of the British assault on the remaining Turkish positions in Palestine, Commander Hogarth sent Clayton a "Note" on the way he saw things from his distant station in Jeddah. It seemed to give him a better perspective and more understanding for the realities of the Arab and the Zionist position, and his note is particularly instructive because it is uninhibited and breaks through the polite pretences that covered so many of the Arab-Jew-British relations at that time.

Hogarth's undated note was sent in August or early September 1918, and he dealt first with what Faisal was thinking after his meeting with Weizmann. What he has to say puts a somewhat different complexion on the diplomatic niceties that were exchanged on that occasion, and on Clayton's attempt at a follow-up. Thus Hogarth was convinced that only Faisal, among the Sharifians, understood the real nature of the Palestine problem. "He believes we intend to keep it ourselves, under

[57] See "Imperial War Cabinet Minutes", 13 August 1918, CAB 23/43; also W. H. Rothwell's "Mesopotamia in British War Aims", *Historical Journal* XIII (1970) 2, p. 290.

the excuse of holding the balance between conflicting religions, and regards it as a cheap price to pay for the British help he has had and hopes still to have. He has no idea at all that any of us had ever dreamed of giving it to the Jews."

He then tells Clayton how he understands Weizmann's Zionism, and it is markedly different from Clayton's initial and almost enthusiastic reaction to Weizmann. According to Hogarth, "Weizmann hopes for a completely Jewish Palestine in fifty years, and a Jewish Palestine under a British façade for the moment. He is fighting for his own lead among the British and American Jews: if he can offer these the spectacle of British help, and Arab willingness to allow Jewish enterprise free scope in all their provinces in Syria, he will then secure the financial backing which will make the new Judea a reality. The capitalists will subscribe for Jews in Palestine – but you cannot govern by subscription. However, they will invest in a Jew-advised Syria, and that means success in Palestine."

Hogarth adds perceptively that Weizmann was not yet in a position to make good any promise he made in the name of Jewry. "In negotiations with him the Arabs have to bear in mind that they are worth nothing to him till they have beaten the Turks, and that he is worth nothing to them unless he can make good among the Jews."

Hogarth foresees that as soon as Faisal is established in Syria, the "Effendi class" there, the Christians and the foreign elements will turn against him because he leads a popular movement and his supporters are the peasants in the villages and the poor Muslims in the towns. If, then, British and American Jews, securely established under British colours in Palestine, chose this moment to offer their help to Faisal and the Arab state in Syria, "Faisal would be compelled to accept the help, and with Anglo-Jewish Advisers could dispense with the Effendim, and buy out the foreigners". But Hogarth warns that until the military adventure of the Arabs under Faisal has either succeeded or failed, he did not require Jewish help, "and it would be unwise on our part to permit it to be offered". For the time being, Hogarth was opposed to a meeting between King Husain and Weizmann. It would not be the same thing as the Faisal-Weizmann meeting which was confined to the exchange "of sympathies and sentiments". In conclusion Hogarth ventured to suggest that the possibility of a French presence in Syria was at an end unless the French sent a military expedition there without delay. Even the most perceptive are liable at times to be mistaken, but

64

that was how it looked to the man on the spot in Jeddah at the end of August 1918.[58]

There was a dramatic and swift change of perspective as Allenby's armies swept northwards towards Damascus. The Syrian nationalists were now a real factor in addition to Faisal and the Sharifians and one could detect a new and more reserved attitude to the Zionists in Clayton's messages to London. Writing on 21 September 1918, as the Turkish collapse in Palestine was becoming general, Clayton lent considerable weight to the views of "a somewhat influential Moslem Syrian residing in Cairo" which he proceeds to pass on to the Foreign Secretary.

The Syrian in question, Clayton wrote to Balfour, "shares the feeling of hostility to Zionist aims which obtains among most Syrians in Egypt, both Christian and Moslem, and which no amount of explanation seems to decrease". The views of this man were additionally significant since he belonged to the group that met with Dr Weizmann in March when the Zionist Commission first arrived in Cairo. Weizmann had then thought that he had made a sympathetic impression on the Syrians and the Syrians had expressed reserved approval of what Weizmann had told them. Clayton argues much on the lines of the secret note which Hogarth had sent him from Jeddah, but he ends rather inconclusively by listing all the forces opposed to the Zionists and to Faisal. It was a sign of the times, however, that this time Clayton remained completely non-commital as far as his own position was concerned. Something had changed the fond hopes of the British-Arab-Jewish compact. Was it no longer practicable? Or was it no longer necessary?

The war was drawing to an end. The question now was how much Arab nationalism, how much Zionism was still necessary to ensure British interests at the Peace Conference; they were no longer necessary to win the war. To that extent they had become expendable and both Arab and Zionist bargaining power had thus declined, while that of the British and the French had immensely improved. Clayton was conscious of this change in the balance of political power, but not Weizmann. Five days before the Armistice, and on the day that Georges Picot landed in

[58] Secret note by D. G. Hogarth, undated, probably August or September 1918, Clayton Papers.

triumph in Beirut as the High Commissioner of the Republic of France in Syria and Armenia, on 6 November 1918, Weizmann wrote to Clayton a farewell letter before he returned to London. His letter began with an avowal of his own fight against neutrality throughout the four war years and ended with a sympathetic understanding for Clayton's position. It was an unusually emotional conclusion for Weizmann and Clayton must have appreciated it accordingly. "I pray," wrote Weizmann, "that God may bless your efforts for your and our country and that it may bring you the highest satisfaction that man can attain, namely, realisation of his lifework. You will soon see victory here and elsewhere and then the blessings of an English peace. God bless you, dear General Clayton."[59]

In a sense, Weizmann was saluting a lost cause, an age that had been overtaken when Allenby and Faisal entered Damascus. A new phase had begun and the Zionists would find out in due course what it meant. About a week after receiving Weizmann's letter and blessing, Clayton sent a terse telegram to the Foreign Office in which he set out the changed assessment. For the time being, nothing much had actually changed, only the emphasis was very different.

In his message to London, dated 15 November 1918, Clayton summarised the respective positions of the Arabs and Zionists a week after the Armistice. The Arabs in Palestine, he cabled, "are strongly anti-Zionist and very apprehensive of Zionist aims. They were pro-British in the earlier days of the occupation, but are now showing a tendency to turn towards the King of Hejaz and the Arab Government of Damascus." This changed attitude was due, according to Clayton, to the growing conviction that the British were pledged to support the Zionist programme in its entirety. At the same time, the Arabs are equally sure that the British Government will, in any case, support the new Arab Government and that its establishment in Palestine would greatly reduce the danger of Zionist predominance. Clayton then deals with the Zionists. The followers of Dr Weizmann, he says in his cable, "are strongly pro-British as it is to Great Britain alone that they look for the fulfilment of their programme. They are anti-French and distrust French policy towards the Jews. They are anti-Palestinian Arab, but favourable towards the Arab Government of Damascus, through which they hope to overcome Arab opposition in Palestine." Altogether

[59] Weizmann to Clayton, 6 November 1918, Sieff Papers.

this was a somewhat puzzling message for Clayton to send to London. It lacked his customary strong sense of direction; it read more like an oblique warning that matters were changing and that London should prepare itself for a change of front. That this was happening became more evident from another message sent to London, this time by Sir Mark Sykes, who was staying with Clayton in Jerusalem. It was dated 17 November 1918, and it was addressed to Ormsby-Gore at the Foreign Office. Its unmellowed tone indicated that Sykes, too, had found it necessary to adjust his former ideas to the new conditions and his Zionist enthusiasm was clearly fraying at the edges.

Sykes complained about the lack of leadership among local Jews and the Zionist Commission though Weizmann had only just departed; he claimed that tension in the country had been increased as a result of articles published in *Palestine*, a small magazine which distributed a few hundred copies to interested individuals and which was published by the British Palestine Committee. Most of the contributions were written either by Herbert Sidebotham of the *Manchester Guardian*, by Harry Sacher, also of the *Guardian*, or by Israel Sieff, who was political secretary to Weizmann on the Zionist Commission. All three of the offending articles had in fact been written by Sieff who had never liked Sykes and had suspected his Pan-Zionism from the outset. Sykes was put out by the proposed borders for the Palestinian state which Israel Sieff had mapped in these articles, "one extending Palestine northward to the vicinity of Beirut". There were references to an independent Jewish state which Sykes did not like, and he was particularly outraged by the mention of "Jews beginning military housekeeping on their own account after a period of tutelage". He then demanded from Ormsby-Gore that he should get immediate and straight answers from Weizmann what future boundaries the Jews had in mind and in a curiously revealing second question he asked: "Non-Jews want to know whether the Zionist objective is an independent Jewish state when a Jewish majority is established? Or is tutelage to continue until Jewish and non-Jewish elements jointly demand independence?" It was a curious question coming from Sykes since he must have known the answer better than most. In fact, the question looks more like a set-up for Weizmann whose answer would have provided Sykes – as Sieff had suspected all along – with his justification or excuse to abandon earlier promises made to the Zionists. Sykes' impatience was even more evident in his reference of possible trouble at the "wailing place", his cavalier reference to the Temple Wall. He urged Ormsby-Gore to impress on Weizmann the need to moderate his demands if he wanted to achieve the Zionist objectives.

Thus with the war won and eyes on the Peace Conference, there was an immediate change of climate. Almost overnight, the romantic phase of Zionism in British eyes had faded and a new realism was taking its place. Nor were the Zionists alone in experiencing the chill of the unromantic British. King Husain and Prince Faisal were making the same kind of discoveries as their romantic period was making way for the changed conditions. Sykes, always quick to sense the direction of the wind, was the first off the mark to jettison Clayton's policy of "synthesis"; Sykes had been first in launching the concept of the Middle East comprising the independent Jew, Arab and Armenian in association with the British guarding the road to India; he was first again in his understanding that conditions of peacemaking require different policies to those suitable to the conduct of war and the search for more or less reliable allies. But the mood, and with it the impatience with the Zionists, spread quickly. There was a fair exhibition of it when the Eastern Committee of the Cabinet met on 5 December 1918, to consider the question of Palestine. Curzon was in the chair and among those present were Smuts, Balfour, Lord Robert Cecil, the Chief of the Imperial General Staff, General Wilson, T. E. Lawrence and representatives from the departments concerned.

Curzon opened with a customary discourse for which he had clearly drawn on the messages sent by Sykes, Clayton and on minutes drafted by Arnold Toynbee in connection with them. Curzon referred to the same articles in *Palestine* as Sykes had done in his despatch to Ormsby-Gore – "You have only to read, as probably most of us do, their periodical *Palestine* and, indeed, their pronouncements in the papers to see that their programme is expanding from day to day. They now talk about a Jewish state. The Arab portion of the population is well-nigh forgotten and is to be ignored." There was increasing friction between the two communities and the Arabs had a feeling that the British backed the Zionists, not the Arabs, Curzon said and added that with regard to the future of Palestine "we must recover for Palestine, be it Hebrew or Arab, or both, the boundaries up to the Litani on the coast, and across to Banias, the old Dan, or Huleh in the interior." The discussion then wandered over possible alternatives to Great Britain should she not want to be responsible for Palestine. The only alternative was the United States and there was no great inclination to pass British control over to the Americans.

Lord Robert Cecil and General Wilson were certain that the British would get no thanks for their Palestine policy, but the most instructive, if not illuminating, comment came from the Director of Military Intelligence, General MacDonogh. He thought that the most important consideration was not the border question, but the fact that Palestine was to be "the home for the Jewish people". It was, therefore, of interest to Jews all over the world. He had met a good many of the Zionists and one had put it to him two days previously "that if the Jewish people did not get what they were asking for in Palestine, we should have the whole of the Jewry turning Bolshevik and supporting Bolshevism in all the other countries as they had done in Russia". To which Lord Robert Cecil commented that he just "could conceive the Rothschilds leading a Bolshevist mob".[60]

But it was again, as so often before, the cool interchange of opinion between Clayton and Hogarth that went to the nub of the state of affairs at the end of the year. Hogarth had been on a "flying-visit" to Damascus and into the Transjordan territory and he reported his impression to Clayton on 18 December. In the past, it will be recalled, the senior British officials and also the Zionist leadership had compared the shiftless Palestinians with whom it was almost impossible to collaborate to the fine desert Arab types that were to be found with Prince Faisal. But now Hogarth observed the ugly reality with all the sharp accents of his famous namesake.[61]

The Sharifian princes and the "Hejaz element" which had been introduced into the Syrian government machine, such as it was, and into the unofficial ruling class, "is an evil which urgently calls for removal", the official and semi-official Sharifs should be sent back to the Hejaz for they had assumed "a privileged and oppressive role, and their influence is obscurantist and vicious". The whole business in Syria, "the de-Turkisation of the Arab Government and the education of the Syrians to political independence was going to be such a thankless task that the British would be fortunate to be absolved from it". If the Syrians were prepared to accept French tutelage than the British should gladly let them have it. However, the Syrian Arabs did not see their

[60] Minutes of Eastern Committee, 5 December 1918, CAB 27/42; see also D. Ingrams' *Palestine Papers 1917–22*, pp. 48–50.
[61] Hogarth to Clayton, 18 December 1918.

liberation from the Turks to be such a boon and if they do not get full independence "they would rather have the Turk back and will scheme to get him".

In Hogarth's judgement, and it was one that was highly valued by Clayton, "anti-Jew feeling is as strong – perhaps stronger than ever among all classes of Arabs – and there is little doubt that if we openly and immediately promote a Zionist political state in Palestine, we shall be no more popular than the French in the rest of Syria." But Hogarth's final word was reserved for Weizmann and the Zionists and it was marked by the kind of realism that was liable to be unpopular in Zionist quarters.

"Weizmann's disclaimers," Hogarth concluded, "are not credited, partly because associates of his, both at home and in Palestine, have not always endorsed them. If the Zionists are to come into their 'National Home', they can do it only by suppressing political aims at present and trusting to the slow effect of colonisation and economic forces." If the British occupation continues, they would have to be prepared to face every "sort of intrigues at the hands of various foreign Christian powers" as well as from Jews and Arabs. And the British will have reason to be thankful "if and when the Jewish people is sufficiently numerous and established to take over Palestine".

This would have been a realist's sound advice on which to end the year and to prepare for the peace. But there was to be yet another version of the charade which the British wanted to play with Faisal and Weizmann – and it was not the last.

We may as well first consider the details of the charade before we look at the broader aspects of the policy which had produced it. There is no fixed point at which the play commenced, but we shall be reasonably near the mark if we begin our account on 17 October 1918, some three weeks after Allenby's troops and Faisal's Arabs had entered Damascus. Faisal had become increasingly worried by the absence of any clear British action which would establish an independent Arab Government in Syria. On that day, 17 October, Allenby reported to the War Office in London that he had met Faisal the day before and that Faisal had been very suspicious of French intentions. Allenby reassured him that whatever measures he was taking in Damascus were purely provisional and that all basic questions would be settled at a conference at which the Arabs would be properly represented. "I reminded Faisal," Allenby reported, "that the Allies were in honour bound to endeavour to reach a settlement in accordance with the desires of the peoples concerned and urged him to place his trust entirely in their good faith." Allenby adds that Faisal seemed to be reassured, but Allenby clearly was not. He concluded his despatch with a warning that "any injudicious pushing of their own interests" by the French would confirm the Arab suspicions and forfeit their confidence in both the French and the British.[62]

Clayton also talked to Faisal on 18 October and found that Faisal still had his doubts. However, he told Clayton that he had "implicit confidence in the good faith of the British Government" and in the assurances given him by Allenby. Meanwhile, plans were going ahead for a meeting in Paris sometime in December 1918 at which the British and French Governments wanted to settle their Arab policies. The British were anxious that Faisal should be at hand and used much persuasion on King Husain to allow Faisal to represent him in Paris, despite Husain's mounting – and not altogether unjustified – suspicion that Faisal was being unduly influenced by Clayton and Lawrence.

Faisal's coming was presented to the French as a routine part of British representation, but the French did not accept it as such. In two notes to the Foreign Office, the French Foreign Minister stressed that Faisal would not be recognised as an official spokesman for the Arabs, nor would he be able to participate in the deliberations of the proposed Anglo-French conference. Moreover, the French expressed surprise that Faisal should have been invited by the British without first consulting the French. As far as France was concerned "Arab kingdoms had no real existence and had only a hypothetical character". Faisal would be given the courtesies of a Royal prince but the French Government was adamant that it could not receive Faisal in Paris, which would imply giving him official status. Instead, a French mission would receive him in Marseilles and show him important towns and military establishments likely to interest him.[63]

Meanwhile, Faisal continued blissfully not seeing, or wanting to see, the bleak fate that was in store for him. On 12 December 1918, the High Commissioner in Cairo cabled the Foreign Office a summary of an interview Faisal had given to an Egyptian paper. He had told the interviewer that he was delighted with the statements made by the

[62] Allenby to War Office, 17 October 1918, Tel. No. 1,6906/P, Wingate Papers.
[63] Both messages were handed to the British Embassy in Paris on 29 November 1918, Wingate Papers.

French Prime Minister. "Every Arabic-speaking person would be grateful to the French Government for its determination to ensure that Syria would be enabled to work out its own civilisation and liberty." Faisal expressed further pleasure at the assurance given by Clemenceau that the problem of Asia Minor and Syria would be placed before the Peace Conference as an open issue and that all parties concerned would participate in reaching a settlement.[64]

Nothing could have been further from the truth or the political realities in Paris. But presumably Faisal did not think so; and his British counsellors did not enlighten him. Instead, Faisal was brought to London for a repeat performance, this time with the Zionists who, in turn, accepted Faisal's declarations at their face value. At a dinner given to Prince Faisal at the Ritz Hotel by Lord Rothschild on 21 December 1918, Faisal spoke of the new relationship between Arabs and Jews. "The Arabs are the nearest relations to the Jews," he said replying to the toast by Lord Rothschild, "and have been their constant friends from Baghdad to the Yemen and to Cordova at periods when their treatment by European nations was not all that might be desired. No true Arab can be suspicious or afraid of Jewish nationalism . . . and what better intermediary could we find anywhere in the world more suitable than you? For you have all the knowledge of Europe, and are our cousins by blood." The whole tenor of Faisal's speech suggests that it was drafted either by Lawrence (who made the English translation) or by Sykes; and, again, one is left wondering what was in Faisal's mind when he made these statements. For Faisal must have been as aware as were his British counsellors that the situation in Palestine, and the attitude of the Arab population there, was anything but the idyll he described, and which some days later he and Weizmann incorporated into a draft treaty of friendship, one of the startling curios of this phase of charade politics.

On 20 November 1918, a month before Faisal spoke at the Ritz, the Chief British Administrator in Palestine, Major-General A. W. Money, had reported to the Foreign Office that there was widespread Muslim and Christian apprehension that "Palestine is going to be handed over to the Jews" and he asked for swift Foreign Office action to reassure them about the nature of the Balfour Declaration. On the same day, the Military Governor of the Jaffa District urged that the Foreign Office should form a "Palestine Arab Commission" so as "to keep the

[64] Wingate to FO, 12 December 1918, Wingate Papers.

balance between the races". The Arabs feared not the Jews in Palestine, but the newcomers who were arriving. Mark Sykes also added his opinion that there was a great deal of electricity in the air and that "perhaps both parties think that the moment would be propitious to start a riot in order to draw the attention of the world to their respective claims". Sombre, because it was more to the point, was Clayton's report to the Foreign Office despatched on 6 December 1918, three weeks before the Ritz dinner and the drafting of the Treaty of Friendship.

In this, Clayton took issue with Weizmann who had stated that world Jewish opinion considers that Arab national aspirations have been fully realised "in the new Arabo-Syrian State". Reversing his own earlier position that there was no such thing as Palestinian national sentiment, Clayton reformulated his opinion. "The non-Jewish population in Palestine," he now wrote, "are concerned not with national aspiration, but with the maintenance in Palestine itself of a position which they consider is threatened by the advance of Zionism." As a result there had been considerable excitement and it was possible, in Clayton's view, that anti-Jewish action might be initiated by the Arabs. However, Clayton still had doubts whether matters would go that far. But which ever way one looked at the State of Palestine at the end of 1918, and at Arab-Jewish relations, they hardly reflected the honeymoon spirit expressed by Faisal in London. The charade had taken over from the realities. Nor was this a mere passing foolishness.

As we shall see, it was going to be a long-playing charade; it continued in varying forms for the best part of three years with not only Faisal and Weizmann as the principal actors, but also with the Americans and the French – but why? Why the charade? The answer will suggest itself as we follow the play-acting on its course. And the evidence is conclusive; not supposition, not propaganda, not very pretty.

The change had come abruptly, almost overnight. Put simply, it was the product of the failure of the Grand Design – of Clayton's, and to a large extent also Weizmann's "Design" for the Middle East: it had not materialised; military victory had not produced the political solution. It had, however, laid bare the realities of the Middle Eastern power-game. The Arabs and the Zionists were not the potent force that would decide the fate of the Arab East at the Peace Conference which was expected to be dominated by the standards set by President Wilson's

Fourteen Points and Doctrine of the self-determination of nations; in fact, it did not really matter any more whether they were a potent force or a largely imaginary propagandist force when it came to the crunch. For Wilsonian America and the Peace Conference were in a sense conducting their own charade when it came to the settlement of the Ottoman succession. For, as it turned out, neither Wilson's Open Diplomacy nor the Bolsheviks' Revolutionary Diplomacy were any more decisive at the Paris Peace Conference than were Arabs and Zionists; what mattered in the final analysis were the positions of power and the occupation of captured territories, diplomatic trumps held essentially by the British and the French.

The Grand Design had envisaged Arabs and Zionists as instruments and participants in the acquisition and the safeguarding of British imperial possessions, but with victory it became evident, not least to Clayton, that, far from being the anticipated assets, Arabs and Zionists were rapidly becoming dangerous liabilities, active agents obstructing the creation of the re-adjusted Versailles post-war system based on the crushing military victory over the Germans and the Turks.

The Weizmann-Faisal charade emerged as the result of the kind of brilliant and instant improvisation which has so often been the basis of British imperial policy and which was not entirely absent from the development of Clayton's Grand Design. The proportions of master-plan and improvisation in the contents of British policy varied with the pressures of the time, but the actually planned policy portions were generally much smaller than was credited by outside observers, and sometimes, indeed, wholly absent. So it was with Faisal's speech to the Jewish gathering at the Ritz. The British, as we have seen, had no illusions about Arab-Zionist relations in Palestine and did not expect a five-course meal at the Ritz in Piccadilly to change that one iota. Weizmann also understood the reality and saw the propaganda value of the public encounter with Faisal; and Faisal saw it in much the same light. But in December 1918 it mattered most to the British. It provided a breathing space, time to reconsider the Grand Design before its crucial testing period at the Peace Conference, time to rescue it, or part of it, if possible; time, above all, for necessary adjustments. As with many similar improvised actions which were never really based on clearly thought-out and purposeful decisions, what was intended as a temporary convenience turned into a permanent embarrassment.

In the event, the charade became the most difficult and thankless diplomatic operation in the history of the Empire; more so in its long-lasting effects than the occupation of India. It was neither surprising nor a matter for condemnation that the rescue attempt failed to preserve the Grand Design and that the improvised policies were no substitute. They failed because after Clayton's imaginative concept there was no longer a design geared to the larger interest of the Empire; there was only temporary accommodation, disguised as policy, in search of instant and local diplomatic profit. Policy became largely a question of backing the right horses, and the British – after Clayton – notoriously staked the wrong ones – Arab and Zionist alike.

Thus in the course of time – after the charade had been played out – Clayton's Grand Design was replaced by the Grand Anglo-Oil Design and this in turn became linked to Grand Strategic Design. But both these latter-day concepts were fundamentally different from Clayton's initial imperial vision. This saw the compact of the Empire with the Arabs and Jews not purely as a means to an end; it conceived Arab nationalism and Zionism as essential parts and beneficiaries of his plan to expand and reinforce the Empire in the East. The modern "Design" which replaced Clayton's – oil plus "defence" – was an end in itself which compelled the abandonment of the charade for henceforth Arab or Jewish support was bought or dispensed with as the need arose.

Clayton and his close associates, but mainly Clayton, saw for a few brief months in 1918 the great opportunity which had presented itself to the Empire in Palestine and Arabia, but few of his superiors really understood the full implications of the "compact" with Arab nationalism and Zionism in the way Clayton understood it; Lloyd George and Balfour certainly never did. It showed a much wider perspective than did most of the younger New Imperialists, especially Sykes and Amery and Smuts, who were obsessed by the strategic attractions of either Zionism or Arabism. But in the end the easier road and the temptations of power politics without such difficult and seemingly unnecessary allies triumphed in Paris. But it was not the only reason for the failure of the Clayton's Grand Design. The seed of failure could be found also in Faisal and Weizmann; it was a seed that was to grow into a creature of terrifying proportion in the coming 50 years. Before we turn to that there remains, to chart the milestones of "the charade", the interregnum between the soaring hopes of the Grand Design and its sobering replacement by oil and soldiers, and – disastrously – by Palestine's Little Design. Into the place of Clayton's balance of Arab and Zionist forces moved the special interests. But with the Peace Conference in preparation and session, with the still uncertain attitude and strength of the Americans and the Bolsheviks, it was essential that diplomacy, propaganda and subversion should be anything but "Open". The pretence of an accommodation had to be maintained: between the British and the French, the British and the Zionists, the French and the Arabs, the Zionists and the Arabs and Faisal with everybody. This was the public text. The private faces were different.

On 16 December 1918 the largely as yet uninvolved American Intelligence Agent in the Middle East, William Yale, reported that "in plain English, in spite of a widespread camouflage propaganda in regard to the liberation of oppressed races and the rights of small nations, the British and the French are thinking and working only for their own interests in the Near East". He also noted in his report that after the first public meeting in June 1918, between Faisal and Weizmann, when they had exchanged solemn expressions of friendship and concern for each other's cause, Faisal had hired secret agents to stir up discontent and bitterness against the British and the Jews and to arouse enthusiasm for the Sharifian Party and for an independent Arab Empire under Hashemite rule. Yale stressed that, though the Palestinian Arabs needed no encouragement to oppose Zionism, Faisal's men were exploiting this mood to make political capital out of Arab hatred. Thus, Yale concluded his report, "in all three zones, British, French and Cherifian propaganda is being quietly and more or less secretly carried on against one another".[65]

With the war won, the fear of defeat or of a negotiated settlement favourable to Germany effectively quashed, the latent opposition which had been silent in the face of Clayton's Grand Design when it offered a possible short-cut to military victory, and then to a favourable political settlement, made itself heard once more. It was in the best tradition of the Church that the first warning voice, stated with suitable discretion in private, should have been that of the Roman Catholic Primate of England, Cardinal Bourne, who expressed his views in a letter to the Pope who, in turn, publicised them as his own. Cardinal Bourne's letter was sent from Jerusalem on 25 January 1919. In it, the Cardinal urged that Lloyd George and Balfour should be pressed to make a clear declaration about their future relations with the Zionists. All kinds of Christians and Muslims had approached him about the

[65] See F. R. Manuel, *Realities of American-Palestine Relations*, p. 204.

Balfour Declaration. They felt "that they were being handed over unjustly to those whom they dislike more than their late Turkish oppressors". Cardinal Bourne proceeded to lament that so devout a Catholic as Mark Sykes had "unfortunately, for some unaccountable reason" favoured the Zionists. In the Cardinal's opinion, however, the whole Zionist movement was something "quite contrary to Christian sentiment and tradition . . . that they should ever again dominate and rule the country would be an outrage to Christianity and its Divine Founder". And then neatly mixing his theology with political prophecy, Cardinal Bourne adds that such a course would most certainly mean that the country would come under "the controlling influence of Jewish, which is *German*, finance. Is this really what England desires after recent experiences?"[66]

The point was considered and taken by Balfour, who was going through one of his most attractive periods, at least in his private correspondence and comments, when he tried to persuade his colleagues and subordinates to look at the facts frankly, at least within the privacy of their office, whatever embellishments and explanations they might give to their subsequent policies and prejudices. Thus in a personal letter to Lloyd George on 19 February 1919, while the charade was in full swing, he urged that there should be no, or only carefully controlled, public statements about Palestine and the whole Eastern and Mediterranean question. "The weak point in our position," he told Lloyd George, ". . . is that in the case of Palestine we deliberately and rightly decline to accept the principle of self-determination. If the present inhabitants were consulted they would unquestionably give an anti-Jewish verdict." And Balfour does not shirk the issue or seek an escape into specious formulae. His justification was that their policy with regard to Palestine had to be exceptional just as the position of the Jews outside Palestine "was of world importance". They had a historic claim which the British could meet without either dispossessing or oppressing the present inhabitants. Balfour – evidently speaking of Cardinal Bourne's letter to the Pope – thought that Roman Catholic opposition to Zionist policy could not easily be reconciled with the tenets of the Catholic faith; it was very little to the Catholic credit. He suspected "that the motive of most of them is not so much anxiety about the Holy Places as hatred of the Jews, and though the Jews undoubtedly constitute a most formidable power whose manifestations are not by

[66] PRO, FO 371/4179.

any means always attractive", the balance of wrong-doing seemed to him to be greatly on the Christian side.[67]

Balfour's example appeared to be catching. While the outward formalities proceeded at the Paris Conference, the parties to the charade began to look harder at each other. The Zionists had submitted their draft of the way they conceived the British Mandate for Palestine and this received the minutest scrutiny. The Foreign Office not only scanned the proposed Zionist text, but also intercepted and read private correspondence between Weizmann and his colleagues which was being forwarded by courtesy of the Foreign Office. One such letter which Weizmann had written to Dr Eder, the British Zionist leader he had left in charge of the Zionist Commission in Jerusalem, set off a revealing minute by Lord Curzon, who also had been studying the Zionist draft. Curzon wanted to know from his colleagues just what Weizmann meant by Palestine being turned into a "Jewish Commonwealth under British Trusteeship"? Curzon asked "what is a Commonwealth", and he turned to his dictionary for definitions, and these he quotes in his minute attached to a copy of the intercepted letter from Weizmann to Eder: " 'A State. A body politic. An independent Community. A Republic' . . . What then is the good of shutting our eyes to the fact that this is what the Zionists are after, and that the British Trusteeship is a mere screen behind which to work for this end? And the case is rendered not the better but the worse if Weizmann says this sort of thing to his friend but sings to a different tune in public."[68]

But barely three weeks after Curzon's intemperate but accurate minute, the Foreign Office was again pleading with Weizmann to do just that which Curzon had so roundly denounced. In a letter to Weizmann, Ormsby-Gore, who had been transferred to the Paris Peace Conference delegation, addressed a strongly worded appeal to Weizmann in the form of a personal letter from a friend who was conveying important official advice. The letter, written in Paris, was dated 20 February 1919, and its tone was not that usually employed by Ormsby-Gore and clearly reflected the weighty advice that it was conveying. He began by telling Weizmann that at the coming Peace Conference, Weizmann carried not only a very great responsibility for

[67] This letter and other Foreign Office comments, some revealingly supporting the Cardinal, are in PRO, FO 371/4179.

[68] Curzon minute, attached to intercepted copy of Weizmann letter, 26 January 1919, PRO, FO 371/4153.

his own people, but also to the British Government. It would be idle to deny, said Ormsby-Gore, that Zionism had become unpopular in Palestine and that much of the odium for this would fall not so much on the Zionists and Weizmann as on the British. Therefore, Ormsby-Gore pleads with Weizmann not to make the British task of helping the Zionists even more difficult.

And he proceeds to spell out the terms of the charade in which the British expected Weizmann to fully co-operate. "Let me be perfectly frank with you," writes Ormsby-Gore, "I do not like such phrases as 'Jewish Commonwealth' and 'Jewish Palestine'. They excite fears and opposition . . . I hold so very strongly that 'political' Zionism can but embarrass the British Government," and he therefore asks Weizmann in his capacity as statesman to resist the temptations of the politician "to prophesy smoother things and gain the plaudits of the people who do not know the actual conditions in Palestine". As one who has the success of Zionism at heart, Ormsby-Gore therefore urges Weizmann "to exercise your great influence over next week's congress to ensure moderation, patience, trust and practical evolution rather than press forward claims or to force the pace".

And, just as Allenby and Clayton had assured Faisal in December, so now Ormsby-Gore assured Weizmann: "I believe you can trust the British people and future British Governments to behave honourably and justly, and that it is not necessary to secure a political position which may, to my mind, embarrass you and us in our practical work."[69]

Clayton, for his part, showed increasing distaste for the charade. In two memoranda written on 28 February and 11 March 1919, he documented his disillusionment and the breakdown of the Grand Design on which he had set so much hope. Zionism had become increasingly unpopular in Syria and Palestine and it was no longer possible to discharge all British undertakings. "We are forced, therefore, to break or modify, at least one of our agreements." In the first of these two messages, Clayton appeared to have abandoned all hope for a British solution and proposed that the only and most favourable way out for the British was to ask the Americans to accept the mandate for Palestine while the French would take control of Syria. But then Clayton had second thoughts and in a closely argued despatch (which made a powerful impact on Balfour) came up with an entirely different proposal.

[69] Ormsby-Gore to Weizmann, 20 February 1919.

79

If the British simply support the French claims on Syria, they will suffer serious repercussions among the Arabs in Palestine and elsewhere in the Arab world. Therefore, "if France must have Syria it would be preferable that America, or some power other than Great Britain or France, be given the mandate for Palestine". But Clayton has not much faith in this proposal. Instead, he suggests to Balfour that in order to induce the French to give up their Syrian claim they should be given control over Constantinople and entrusted with the re-organisation and reconstruction of the future Turkish state. This would ensure French control over the future Turkish economy in which the French had an exceptionally large stake and would enable them to control also the southern Black Sea and the Caucasus.

Great Britain would then assume the mandate for the eventual establishment of autonomous Governments in Syria and Palestine with due regard for Arab aspirations and Zionist aims. Such a mandate for Great Britain, Clayton concludes, "would put the seal on British predominance throughout the Arab countries; would render Great Britain paramount in Islam; and would safeguard the Eastern Mediterranean and the routes to Mesopotamia and India by securing control of the Aleppo-Mosul line." In short, it would restore the Grand Design.[70]

Clayton had to wait some months for the answer – but when it came it was the last word and the end of the "Design". It was also to be Balfour's most extraordinary and dazzling position paper; it laid down the guide-lines of the charade they were to continue to play.

Balfour's memorandum was completed in Paris on 11 August 1919, and sent to the Foreign Office only on 19 September. By one of those strange quirks of fate for which there is no explanation, it became Document 242 in the official Volume of Documents of British Foreign Policy,[71] a worthy forerunner of the later charade, the Security Council Resolution 242 of 22 November 1967. There was, however, one major and significant difference between the two: Balfour's version, as distinct from that drafted by Lord George-Brown and Sir Harold Beeley, with the aid of Lord Caradon (all three have claimed exclusive paternity) was singularly free of humbug; in fact, it must rank as one of the frankest diplomatic documents that has emanated from the Foreign Office.

[70] Memorandum by Clayton from GHQ, EEF, 11 March 1919, Clayton Papers.
[71] First Series, Volume 4, 1919, pp. 340–49.

Balfour opened by expressing his disquiet at evident French suspicion of British intentions in Syria, and at the French conviction that the British were intriguing to make a French mandate in the Middle East impossible. The hostile French attitude to the British, Balfour was certain, was due to the French misunderstanding of British policy in Syria and Palestine. But these misunderstandings, Balfour conceded, were brought about by the cause of most misunderstandings – "namely, a very clear comprehension by each party of the strength of its own case, combined with a very imperfect knowledge of, or sympathy with, the case of his opponent. In this particular instance," Balfour conceded, "I have never been able to understand on what historic basis the French claim to Syria really rests." But this was really immaterial, in Balfour's opinion, because they had in all their negotiations accepted that there was a French case and they had therefore to proceed on this assumption and attempt to understand the French position. Balfour proceeded to sketch what Clemenceau might have said in support of his "attitude of resentful suspicion", and made out an impressive case for the French charges of British duplicity. As Balfour puts it, no sooner had Clemenceau agreed to one British demand than the British came with yet another. Clemenceau had agreed to one set of revision of the Sykes-Picot Agreement which would include Mosul in the British zone; he had agreed to the British mandate for Palestine. But then the British wanted to push the frontier of Palestine northward into Syria, and British officers and officials in Syria and Palestine were seeking to create a situation in which a French mandate in Syria would not be possible, so that the British would have to take over Syria as well as Palestine. Balfour spelled out his reasons for believing that there was substance in the French charges of British bad faith despite the firm denials of the British military authorities in Palestine.

He closely analyses the reasons for the inextricably confused position of the Powers in relation to Syria and he sets out to clarify the principal elements of confusion. Unlike almost every other Foreign Office document or report about the Middle East, Balfour does not decry the Sykes-Picot Agreement. It had precisely those elements of realism which, despite its imperfections, could have proved a success if worked honestly and sympathetically by the superintending Powers. "For, as I read history," Balfour noted in passing, "such an overlordship is not alien to the immemorial customs and traditions of this portion of the Eastern world." But, he acknowledges, the Sykes-Picot arrangement was wholly

81

alien "to those modern notions of nationality which are enshrined in the Covenant of the League of Nations and proclaimed in the declaration". Balfour expressed his doubts about the universal efficacy of these new notions, if "by this is meant, as I think it is, that when the Turkish tyranny is wholly past, the Arabs will desire to use their new-found freedom to set up representative institutions, with secret voting, responsible government, and national frontiers, I fear we are in error. They will certainly do nothing of the sort. The language of the Covenant may suit the longitude of Washington, Paris or Prague. But in the longitude of Damascus it will probably get us into trouble."

Balfour then traces with self-critical logic the contradiction between the letter of the Covenant and the policy of the Allies in Syria, Mesopotamia and "in the most flagrant case, that of the 'independent nations of Palestine' ". The question of the allocation of mandates was essentially one of power politics and they had no intention of asking the Palestinians who should have the mandate since that matter was decided by the Great War and the secret agreements between the Allies. As far as Palestine was concerned, "the Powers have made no statement of fact which is not admittedly wrong, and no declaration of policy which, at least in the letter, they have not always intended to violate".

Having thus demolished his own policy and those of his allies, Balfour proceeds on the same level of utter frankness. Clearly drawing on Clayton's 11 March memorandum, he concluded that since the literal fulfilment of the Anglo-French undertakings to the Jews and Arabs was incompatible with the facts "we ought, I presume, to do the next best thing". And the next best thing for Balfour was to restore all the war-time agreements and undertakings on the basis of existing power factors.

The Sykes-Picot arrangements between Britain and France were to stand with some unimportant modifications; French control over Syria was to be extended into Anatolia so as to include Alexandretta in the French scheme; and British control of Mesopotamia would be extended northwards to embrace the oil fields of Mosul; frontiers should be determined by economic and ethnic considerations rather than by strategic safeguards "against so remote a possibility as a war with France". The British would take firm control of Palestine and seek to extend its northern frontiers to the Litani River in southern Syria and take in the valley on both sides of the Jordan. Balfour added considerable detail to his proposed policy and called for further expert examination.

But what he meant was that the Middle East settlement would be dictated by the Governments in London and Paris and not by the Arab Bureau in Cairo or by Allenby or the Zionists or any pressure group such as that constituted by the American oil interests. Balfour's memorandum also sounded the retreat from the policy of a British compact with the Jews and Arabs, as the legitimisation of the British presence in Palestine and Mesopotamia. It was barely two years after Clayton and his friends had begun to build their Grand Design that Lloyd George called a meeting of interested parties at Trouville on 10 September 1919 to consider the future frontiers of Palestine. The minutes of that meeting read like the epitaph for Clayton's effort:

*Mr Bonar Law* asked what was the value of Palestine?
*Lord Allenby* said that it had no economic value whatsoever. Its retention by the British would keep our minds active for the next generation or two. He anticipated great trouble from the Zionists. There had been so much Zionist propaganda that Jews who had been dispossessed in Poland and Russia were actually marching now to Palestine.
*The Prime Minister* pointed out that the mandate over Palestine would give us great prestige. He asked which the Field-Marshal would prefer, Palestine in British or French hands?
*Lord Allenby* said that if the French were in Syria, they might almost as well be in Palestine. In any case they would give us great trouble.

In the end, the meeting agreed that it would not be practicable for the British to give up Palestine even if they wanted to, that the French presence in Syria would have to be tolerated, that French control over the Hejaz Railway would constitute a potential security threat and would have to be prevented, and, lastly, that the British could not lay claim to Syria. On this inconclusive note, the discussion petered out.

It was a defensive, even defeatist and lame conclusion to the Grand Design, it was bereft of the power of decision. It set the pattern of future British concern for Palestine and for what became known as the Fertile Crescent – Syria, Mesopotamia-Iraq and Transjordan. It was strategic, economic and to some extent politic – but hardly imperial. If Clayton's Grand Design had been the product of an expanding, expansive and liberal imperialism which in itself was something of a

83

contradiction of terms, then the new "Design" was that of a contracting, preservative and somewhat authoritarian imperialism which sought to hold what it had, as best it could, on the most profitable terms possible. And oil was becoming profitable, extremely so; orange-juice was not. Arabs mattered, Jews did not; at least, not any longer once the popular myths of the British upper class were recognised as such and the Zionists were found to be neither the secret weapon of international finance nor of an international Bolshevik conspiracy. In fact, it took the British about two years following the Balfour Declaration to evaluate the Zionist factor at its actual worth once there was no longer a war situation in which the Zionists mattered, and there was a new world in which there was no longer a Germany or a Russia in which Zionist influence counted for anything. And the United States – the only country where the Zionists were to some extent able to impress their views on the Government – was withdrawing from the arena of world power politics.

Thus it soon became evident to the British delegation at the Paris Peace Conference, and to the Imperial General Staff at home and its representatives in Cairo, that the Middle East settlement would not have to be tailored, as they had feared, to either Wilsonian, Bolshevik or Zionist specifications; it would have to be negotiated and agreed with the French along the anticipated and prepared diplomatic lines. It was this – and not the Balfour Declaration or the Zionist orientation of the British Government – which in the first instance undermined the prospect for Clayton's Grand Design. For it imposed on the British the necessity to ensure, despite the deal with the French and abandonment of Prince Faisal in Syria, that the British were the Arabs' best friend. The Government proceeded to demonstrate this to the Arabs naturally where it least hurt British interests – in Palestine and also, to a lesser extent, in the French-controlled Levant.

There was yet another reason for the British change. From 1917 onwards – until some time early in 1919 – the British had viewed the Zionists with their influence on world Jewry as a welcome, necessary and desirable ally who could help to win the war against Germany and Turkey by its influence in the United States and Russia, and thereafter help also to win the peace for Britain. But all that changed during 1919. In Paris and in Palestine, the Zionists were no longer necessary, and no longer desirable; they were becoming a problem and even an embarrassment. They were no more a welcome ally; they were admitted to the Middle East on British sufferance, not of right. The Balfour Declaration was no longer seen as a British obligation negotiated between equals, a British *quid* for a Zionist *quo*; the British now preferred to see their Zionist commitment as an act of generous charity in a moment of absent-minded or desperate rashness which could not be undone, at least not yet. But it could be rendered largely ineffective. This was not too difficult in view of the still inherent weakness of the Zionists and of their own admitted inability to live up to their promises.

Thus, the charade was played out. There was to be a Jewish National Home in Palestine, but not yet. First, there had to be agreement with the Arab representatives, but agreement on what? Did that mean that there had to be Arab consent for every Zionist action by the British? Did it confer a veto on the Palestinian Arabs? Official British policy on these points was always ambivalent; it had to be under the terms of the charade; it had to be explainable, if not altogether credible, alike to Arabs and Jews and it had to have the appearance of benevolent neutrality towards both for the benefit of the League of Nations. It had, in fact, to mean all things to all people, following the hallowed practice of the Foreign Office which was so vividly described by Lord Caradon during the discussions at the United Nations of the ambivalent British draft, which became the Security Council Resolution 242 of 22 November 1967.[72] Two days before the Security Council met to vote on that resolution, a discussion took place in the Working Committee which had prepared the text of the resolution. The Indian delegate informed Lord Caradon at the meeting that they understood the British draft to mean full Israeli withdrawal from all occupied territories as had been stressed in a speech by the British Foreign Secretary to the Assembly, and that India would vote for the resolution on that understanding. Lord Caradon, after consultations with London, came back with the British reply a few hours before the Security Council convened. If the Indians pressed their interpretive declaration, then Caradon would respond by stressing that it was his understanding that, under the terms of the resolution, each delegate was entitled to his own interpretation. In the Council meeting, after the Indian delegate had repeated his interpretation of the resolution, Lord Caradon explained the essential elements of the British draft resolution – and it will stand also for most of the British declarations made on this subject during the

[72] See Appendixes I and II for text of declaration and of the resolution.

85

playing out of the charade. Lord Caradon said that he was sure "that it will be recognised by us all that it is only the resolution that will bind us, and we regard its wording as clear. All of us, no doubt, have our own views and interpretations and understandings. I explained my own when I spoke on Monday last. On these matters, each delegation rightly speaks for itself."

That took place half a century after the events we are concerned with here, but the practice had changed little, if at all. It underlined the contention that we shall not be able to fathom what was at the back of the British mind in the aftermath years of the Balfour Declaration by dissecting official statements. Far better guidance can be obtained from the less-guarded comments made in more private circumstances by the men who either made or influenced decisions. Lord Curzon, for one, provided an admirable example of such uninhibited outspokenness under conditions of privacy. He gave us, among many other examples, a vivid insight into official thinking as we reach the winding-up phase of the Grand Design in a series of minuted comments attached to reports sent to him during the drafting of the British mandate for Palestine.

Thus Curzon in a Foreign Office minute on 20 March 1920: "It all turns on what we mean. The Zionists are after a Jewish State with the Arabs as hewers of wood and drawers of water. So are many British sympathisers with the Zionists . . . That is not my view. I want the Arabs to have a chance and I don't want a Hebrew State."

Curzon, again on the same day, commenting on the same topic: "I think the entire conception is wrong . . . a country with 580,000 Arabs and 30,000 or is it 60,000 Jews (by no means all Zionists). Acting upon the noble principles of self-determination and ending with a splendid appeal to the League of Nations, we then proceed to draw up a document which reeks of Judaism in every paragraph and is an avowed constitution for a Jewish State. Even the poor Arabs are only allowed to look through the keyhole as a non-Jewish community. It is quite clear that the mandate has been drawn up by someone reeling under the fumes of Zionism. If we are all to submit to that intoxicant, this draft is all right. Perhaps there is no alternative."

But in a further comment to a report from Vansittart in Paris, Curzon minuted on 21 June 1920, that he was "quite willing to water the Palestine mandate which I cordially distrust", and he elaborated in comment to a later report by Vansittart, on 6 August 1920, that he was

86

not prepared to recognise "that the connection of the Jews with Palestine which terminated 1,200 years ago, gives them any claim whatsoever. On this principle, we have a stronger claim to parts of France."[73]

Curzon was, of course, not alone in holding these views either in the Foreign Office or in the military establishment. Allenby, also, had travelled far from the enthusiasm of his first encounters with Weizmann two years previously to the disenchantment with the Zionists reflected in his messages at the time of the Paris and San Remo Conferences. Thus on 6 May 1920, he warned the Foreign Secretary that the "appointment of a Jew as first Governor will be highly dangerous". The Arab population of Palestine would view the appointment of Herbert Samuel as in effect "handing the country over at once to a permanent Zionist administration". Allenby felt certain that when Samuel's appointment became generally known, there would be a general Arab movement against the Zionists and "that we must be prepared for outrages against the Jews, murders, raids on Jewish villages, and raids into our territory from the East", if nothing worse. It was a very different picture of Weizmann that Allenby now presented to the Foreign Office in a cable noting the high feeling between Arabs and Jews. "I have had an interview with Weizmann this morning," Allenby reports. "He was in a state of great nervous excitement, shedding tears, accusing the administration of Palestine as being anti-Zionist and describing recent riots as a pogrom. . . ."

The Weizmann Zionists whom Balfour and Clayton had nursed and encouraged as the more moderate element among the Zionists that would not frighten the Arabs with their intentions were clearly put out of their depth by the turn of events – and this applied also to Weizmann himself. They had come to believe their own propaganda about the British and about their emotional attachment to the vision of Zionism. They admired and trusted the British and the British way of life, and men such as Clayton had confirmed them in their trust. And now in their hour of disenchantment they had to find convincing explanations for this British "betrayal". Weizmann and his friends suffered from the same difficulty that Balfour had so ably diagnosed in his Peace Conference memorandum of August 1919. The Zionists, like Balfour's British, were able to understand and appreciate their own position, but

---

[73] PRO, FO 371/5199; the whole section is usefully assembled in Doreen Ingrams' *Palestine Papers*, pp. 94–97.

not that of the other party. The only explanation under these conditions was to look for evil-minded conspiracies. Thus the British had suspected the French, and some Zionists and Arabs. And now the Zionists found instances of British officers and officials at work against them. In some cases they were real enough; in others, the circumstances were more dubious. We shall come to consider these in more detail in another place (see Chapter Two); what concerns us here is to appreciate the deteriorating political climate which began to tell on the British administration in Palestine.

Between March 1920 and 1921, the power factors had been reversed: the Zionists were on the defensive, complaining and retreating and had moderated their demands; they were no longer operating from positions of strength. But the Arabs had seized the initiative; they were on the offensive, they were aggressive, extreme in their demands, and effective.

Thus the British were confronted by the demands of the Haifa Congress of Palestinian Arabs in 21 March 1921. It described the Balfour Declaration as "an act of modern Bolshevism, pure and simple". And it proceeded to present five demands to the British administration which were as extreme in their intent as those formulated by Fatah 50 years later. They demanded that the British Government abolish and reject the concept of a national home for the Jews; the formation of a Palestinian Government based on the Arab majority in the country; the halting of Jewish immigration; all legislative measures by the British to be halted pending the formation of an Arab national Government; and the cancellation of the division of Palestine from Syria and Transjordan.

Before the British administration could fully absorb the implications of these demands, however remote their prospect of implementation, they were presented with the Haycraft Commission's Report on the disturbances in Palestine in March and May that year. It was the first official document of its kind that delved closely into the causes, real and imagined, which lay behind the mounting Arab bitterness against the Zionists. And two days after the publication of the Haycraft findings, on 12 August 1921, the official Arab delegation which had come to London for negotiation with the Colonial Secretary, Winston Churchill, informed him that they did not recognise Dr Weizmann or the Zionist claim, that they would not meet with Weizmann or conduct negotiations through him. They recognised only the British Government.

The British response was confused. Such extreme demands did not fit into the pattern of the charade. However, the British – and also Weizmann – thought that the Arabs might still be persuaded to continue the game. Thus on 8 November 1921, a secret meeting took place between the Zionist leaders and a young Syrian nationalist leader, Riadh-es-Sulh. They drew up a Draft Basis for Discussion for an Arab-Jewish Entente. But there was as little substance behind this display of goodwill as there had been in the first Weizmann-Faisal encounter in June 1918. For the pressures that mattered came no more from the moderates, but from the extremists, and, for the time being, these were far more effectively operated from the Arab than from the Zionist side.

The British began to give way a little. They asked the Zionists to appease the Arab demands with some concessions. Weizmann refused because the Arab demands were such that they called not for concessions from the Zionists, but for submission. When the Zionists refused to concede anything worthwhile to the Arabs because they had nothing that they could afford to concede, the British stepped in with selective appeasement of the Arab demands, mainly at the expense of the Zionists. The British-Arab alliance might then have taken shape and would have put paid to any but the most modest dream of Zionists, but the Arabs refused. They wanted no concessions from the Zionists; they wanted no Zionists, no negotiations with Zionists, and no deal with the British that involved the Zionists. The British were thus left politically out on a limb. They had to go on playing their charade without either Arab or Zionist participation – and they continued at it until the charade was exploded in their faces by the survivors of the Nazi concentration camps.

The British failed in the crucial years between 1917 and 1922 because they believed that an accord in Palestine was possible; first, in Clayton's time, with the participation of Arabs and Jews, and then, after the Peace Conference in 1919, mostly without Jews, and at times also without the Arabs. But the central theme of British policy after the failure of Clayton's policy of a compact was to turn the Palestinian Arabs into the instrument for the legalisation and justification of the British presence in Palestine in place of the Zionist Commission conceived for this purpose. This policy might have been possible and it might even have been successful if Palestine could have developed outside the pressures of interested Great Power politics. But it did not. And the British failed at the first attempt, though not without a degree of honour and a refreshing amount of official frankness – at least, in private.

The British failure was compounded by that of the Zionists and that of the Arabs. But the time has come to consider how it was and what it was that brought about the estrangement between the British and the Weizmann Zionists. For it lies at the root of most of the troubles that were to come. We can do no better than close this chapter and open the next with the critical evidence of one of the best, most sincere and selfless British friends that the Zionists have had, the bitter letter which Wyndham Deedes, Chief Secretary to the Palestine Government, addressed to Sir John Shuckburgh at the Colonial Office on 22 November 1921.

They had always known, Deedes tells Shuckburgh, that their policy was unpopular with the Arabs. But until some time early in 1921 this unpopularity had fallen principally upon the Zionists. But matters had changed. British reputation used to be sufficient to ensure the goodwill of the people, but no longer in Palestine. And the reason for this, Deedes finds, "was in the association with the British administration of another Body, the Zionist Commission". The partnership might have worked and might have been tolerated by the Arabs if the British and the Zionists had professed the same aims. But it was not so. Deedes continues to explain how dangerous this partnership must appear in Arab eyes "when the least trusted of the two partners professed an Extremist policy and announced its intention far and wide of bringing the other partner 'into line'!" As a result the Arabs believed that every measure taken by the British in Palestine was inspired by the Zionists and impotently accepted by the administration.

Deedes was particularly concerned when on 3 June 1921 Herbert Samuel, the High Commissioner, pronounced a new policy designed to win Arab support. Deedes saw this as a great opportunity. The British had spoken and the Arabs expected the Zionist partner to fall into line. "But no. No reorientation of Policy took place in the Zionist Organisation . . . HMG's recent Declaration of Policy was declared by the Zionist Organisation to be wholly unacceptable, a betrayal and much else of that nature . . ." The Arabs waited to see if the British would insist on their Zionist partner accepting the new policy. But nothing happened and the Arabs could draw only the one conclusion which they did draw – that the British were "bound hand and foot to the Zionists, that the statement of the 3rd June was mere dust thrown in their eyes, and that

90

all Legislation here was and would continue to be inspired by Zionist interests . . ." And Deedes concludes his letter by proposing that the special position allotted to the Zionist Organisation in the mandate should be abolished.

At about the same time, General Sir Walter Congreve, the Officer Commanding British troops in Egypt and Palestine, addressed a circular to Commanding Officers in order to explain official policy to the troops of the Palestine Garrison. General Congreve explained that whilst the Army was supposed to have no politics, there were exceptions, such as Ireland and Palestine where the sympathies of the Army were on one side or the other. "In the case of Palestine, these sympathies are rather obviously with the Arabs." Those responsible for the application of official policy were "anxious that it should at least be clearly understood . . . that they would never countenance any policy which inflicted oppression or hardship on the Arab population . . . The British Government would never give any support to the more grasping policy of the Zionist Extremists which aims at the establishment of a Jewish Palestine in which Arabs would be merely tolerated." The British, the General concluded, would not countenance a policy "which made Palestine for the Jew what England is for the Englishman". And there was more.

It was a long, long way from the Great Design. In a matter of some three years, official British policy had come a full circle from the Grand to the Little Design. The reasons for this had to be sought not only among the British or in British policy, but also among the Arabs and especially the Zionists. What was it, then, that had so embittered a friend of the Zionists such as Deedes and had confirmed men like Curzon in their opposition to the Weizmann Zionists? Was it the greater understanding of the Palestinians' just cause or was it the need for Arab friendship and oil? Or was there something wrong in the Zionist leadership, in Zionist policy and philosophy?

It was Wyndham Deedes' sensitive and perceptive approach to the problems of Palestine and Zionism that pointed at the root of the trouble: the Zionist Commission was conceived and intended to be a major instrument of British imperial policy in Palestine, a function about which Weizmann and his colleagues were largely oblivious. But as it became operative in 1918, the Commission found it increasingly difficult to reconcile British and Zionist interests and as it opted more and more for Zionist as against British objectives, it contributed to the

91

erosion of the British-conceived compact and brought on the expressed impatience and antagonism by friends such as Clayton and Deedes, and such critics as Allenby and Curzon.

What then was the Zionist Commission; what did it do and what were its Zionist objectives that so annoyed the British? For the answer, we must first go to Manchester in the summer of 1913.

# TWO

# The Zionist View[1]

But why Manchester? Why not Pinsk or Berlin? Why not Petrograd or Paris? Why not New York or London? The seed of Zionism had been sown in each of these political gardens but had failed to flower; everywhere except in Manchester. Why? What was different; what was it that gave political life to the Zionism which came from Manchester, which transformed it from propaganda to politics?

There were, of course, all kinds of reasons, but the catalyst was the presence there of a group of young men and women, without much wealth and influence, but with unbounded enthusiasm and a remarkable sense of loyalty and understanding, who had become deeply impressed by the Zionist presentation made by Chaim Weizmann, a lecturer in Chemistry at Manchester University. Israel Sieff was one of the young men, Simon Marks was another. Together with Harry Sacher and their wives, they were drawn into the political world of Zionism by Weizmann; modestly and locally at first, without any indication of what was to be in store for them.

Zionism, the ten million Jews in the world, and the Great Powers unknowingly on a collision course provided the setting but did not unduly impinge on their daily life. The Reverend Simon continued to deliver his Sabbath morning sermons at the Higher Broughton Synagogue, and the reputed 30 synagogues on Cheetham Hill proceeded on their less formal course, each according to its own lights and the particular East European origin of its congregation. An experienced manager for a tailor's shop in Manchester was offered 55 shillings a week and glad to get the job; others were paid no more than £2 a week,

[1] Much of the information in this chapter – the parts are indicated in the text – is based on the private papers of Lord Sieff and on numerous discussions and interviews about them over a period of ten years or more.

rent free. Cope's advertised that their fish were "still wet with seawater", flannel shirts were 4/6d and pure silk stockings 1/4d.

The July calm that year – 1913 – was rippled by the excitement caused by a picture hung in the Summer Exhibition of the Royal Academy by Edgar Bundy. It was described simply as "Finance", and depicted a pure blond Englishman surrounded by cigar-smoking, evidently opulent financiers with somewhat over-emphasised semitic features in a situation that left little to the imagination. The picture and the Royal Academy were denounced by the Jewish papers and from many Synagogue pulpits as an outrageous display of antisemitism. But outside Jewish circles there appeared to be little interest in either the Jewish indignation or in the artist, or in the Academy's protestations of innocence.

Yet the incident was curiously revealing; it illustrated once more how psychologically and socially isolated from his English surroundings the Jew – even the English Jew – had remained. In fact, he lived in two separate worlds. For six days every week he read the solid pages of the *Manchester Guardian* and became a part of the scene it recorded, but on the seventh day he turned to the pages of the *Jewish World* and the *Jewish Chronicle* and it was difficult to believe that these papers were concerned with the same world as the *Guardian*; they simply never met: The greater world reflected in the *Guardian* during these months of 1913 was one, in both of which Sieff and Weizmann had a consuming interest.

Even though we could not then know or fully appreciate the implications of the advances that scientific research had made that year, we had a sense of great things happening, though I had no inkling of how much my later life was to be linked to them. Professor J. J. Thomson published his findings on the application of rays of positive electricity to chemical analysis, Rutherford brought the atom to life, Niels Bohr made his revolutionary discoveries about the nature of atomic structure, Geiger completed his research into many aspects of radiation, and Einstein published his Theory of General Relativity. In France, Proust and Peguy were exciting the literary world; in Germany, Thomas Mann had published *Death in Venice*, and at home, D. H. Lawrence had shocked many people with his *Sons and Lovers*; Sickert, Sargent, Epstein, Eric Gill and Stravinsky had produced paintings, sculpture and music that roused mounting controversy and interest.[2]

[2] Sieff to J.K.

The political background was filled with great drama: Home Rule for Ireland, the clash between Government and the Lords, the struggle of the suffragettes. But what began to preoccupy Sieff more than anything were the implications for the future of the Ottoman Empire at the end of the second Balkan war.

This, then, was their outside world. Manchester was very much part of it, not only because of its own unique local press represented by the *Manchester Guardian* but also because Manchester had made its own contribution to the mainstream. They had no feeling of being provincial outsiders. They possessed the Hallé Orchestra under Sir Charles Hallé, and, after his death, conducted by Hans Richter. Manchester University was an institute for higher learning which housed scientists like Ernest Rutherford and William Henry Perkins, philosophers like Samuel Alexander and historians such as Tout. Also on its staff was Dr Chaim Weizmann.

Manchester was the centre of Britain's growing chemical industry, the home of Brunner Mond which was to become Imperial Chemical Industries and of Aniline Dyes, a great concern of which Charles Dreyfus, a one-time leader of the Manchester Zionist Association, was the chairman. Manchester Jewry, moreover, was a pleasant society. Numbering about 30,000 it was drawn largely from the Jews of Eastern Europe, part of the 3½ million Jews who had been leaving Russia and Poland for the Western world during the preceding 30 years.

There were not many Jews of German origin in Manchester; most of them had assimilated to their Christian surroundings or had been actually converted to Christianity. The smallish number of Sephardi Jews, with their Spanish background, did not play any noticeable part in the life of the community. But on the whole, they were a homogeneous group, though with different levels of prosperity. They did not, however, suffer unduly from the snobberies such as were to be found in Germany in the relations between the German Jews and the *Ostjuden*, the Jews who had immigrated from Eastern Europe. In Manchester, there was a certain freedom of association and tolerance between the "old settlers" and the new immigrants:

The family remained the centre of our Jewish society; it counted for a great deal, as was perhaps best illustrated by the breach between the young Harold Laski and his father, Nathan, who was a leader of our community, when Harold decided, at the age of 18, to marry

95

against the wishes of his parents. It was admittedly a great blow to his father and mother when he married a gentile, but they reacted with the then customary harshness and a lack of understanding compassion.[3]

But, in the main, they were an integral part of the excitement of liberal progress and of the preoccupation with world affairs which the *Manchester Guardian* reflected; "all the same, one part of us remained elsewhere. We were obsessed by the problem that found little attention in the world at large – not even in the *Guardian*. We found that other world in the Jewish weekend papers and in the information brought by an endless stream of visitors and emissaries, many of them seeking financial help, from the Jewish ghettoes of Eastern Europe."[4]

There was one feature that turned up every Thursday and Friday in the Jewish papers in a matter-of-fact way, as if it was an ineluctable law of the universe: no fuss, no excitement; just one of the routines of the golden summer of 1913. A report from Constantinople would record the massacre of Jews by the Bulgars during the final phases of the Balkan war; another from Warsaw noted anti-Jewish riots in different parts of Poland. Messages reported Jews leaving Kiev in the wake of the excesses that had accompanied the Beilis trial, Jews departing from Salonica, riots against Jewish students at the Czernowitz University, the Minsk Synagogue surrounded by Tsarist police, restrictions on Jews in Odessa and attacks on Jews in Persia. Expulsion, outrages, arrests and searches, restrictions and attacks, the names changed, the routines never.

"In Manchester we seemed to be at a safe distance from that hostile world, and yet we felt part of it. On a Sunday 13 July 1913, the Ancient Order of Maccabeans, of which I was an active member, had called a meeting to consider the situation."[5] It was to be addressed by the Sephardi Chief Rabbi, the Haham, Dr Moses Gaster, by Neville Laski, Samuel J. Cohen and Dr Weizmann. It was an important meeting, for it showed the essential difference between the two Zionist leaders, Gaster and Weizmann. Gaster spoke passionately of the Zionist link with England; Zionists, he urged, should help Britain to maintain her position in the Eastern Mediterranean, in East Africa and India. He was prepared to risk Ottoman wrath in Palestine and declare forthwith

[3] Sieff to J.K.
[4] Sieff to J.K.
[5] Sieff to J.K.

the Zionist connection with Britain. By contrast, Dr Weizmann showed, as he was to do so often on later occasions, that he was not a man who would be carried away by words. He also hoped for a Zionist alliance with Britain, but the conditions would have to be right for it. At that time, such a step would be a grave mistake. The situation in Europe was far too uncertain for Zionists to commit themselves in this manner. It would be wrong, Weizmann insisted at that stage for Zionists to rely on any European Power other than the "present master of Palestine – Turkey". Everything else, he insisted, was playing with words and with the hopes of their people:

> It was the first indication of the workings of the mind of the Weizmann I was to get to know so well. Facts mattered, power mattered, realism mattered. In the event, I met Dr Weizmann almost casually; he clearly was not impressed at first sight, but it was to be the beginning of an association and friendship that was to last for 40 years. Even more profoundly, it was the first step on our road to the making of a state, a Jewish State in Palestine.[6]

There was, of course, no homogeneous Zionist movement in 1913, any more than there was a unitary Jewish people. They were divided by environment, education, upbringing and, above all, by the outside pressures which shaped their lives as a people. But they were also united by these same pressures and by the imponderables of history and religion. There was then no simple definition of the Jewish people, any more than there is now. Zionism understandably meant entirely different things to the Jews in the Russian pale and to the Jew in Berlin; and there was no less of a chasm, though it might not have been quite so evident to the eye, between the Zionism of the German Jews and those in Manchester:

> The outbreak of the Great War was to bring home to us not only the existence of this gap, but it was to turn it into an unbridgeable gulf – or so it seemed to us at the time. It was only in later life that I discovered that nothing in public life or politics is ever quite so absolute as it might appear to the contemporaries.
>
> It is my conviction now, as I look back on those years in Manchester, when Dr Weizmann was far from being the accepted leader of the Zionist movement, that it was then that he exercised his most

[6] Sieff to J.K.

lasting act of leadership. For it was then that he became the – self-appointed – spokesman for the Jewish people, not for Russian Jews, not for English Zionists, not for any group or sect other than the Jewish people. He surmounted the differences and divisions of our people with a remarkable act of faith and he imposed it on the outside world. It was an extraordinary achievement because it was to take years before the Jewish people were willing to accept his concept, let alone his claim to leadership. It was no doubt one of our great tragedies that our people failed to understand this in 1917 and in the years that followed. We had to wait 50 years – until June 1967 – before world Jewry effectively united in its support for the Jewish state for which Dr Weizmann had struggled through the fog of war in 1917.[7]

Admittedly, back in the summer of 1914, the Weizmann circle in Manchester had no real inkling that they were on the eve of a great revolutionary upheaval. As Zionists, few of them – if any – were prepared for it. "We often talked of the prospects of a Jewish state in Palestine, but I doubt whether many or any of us actually believed it would happen in our time. Nor were we encouraged by the initial impact of the war on Jewish and Zionist thinking."[8]

At first, the course of events was quite unlike what the Manchester Zionists had anticipated. The Zionist leadership had been preoccupied since the revolution of the Young Turks in 1908 with the fate of the Ottoman Empire and its domination over Palestine. Events did not bear out the early hopes expressed by Max Nordau, then the foremost living Zionist and contemporary of Theodor Herzl, that the revolution in Constantinople was in effect the realisation of the Charter which Herzl had sought.

On the contrary, the nationalism, often turned to chauvinism, of the Young Turk leaders, forced the Zionist leaders to become increasingly circumspect in their public pronouncements. The fact that a number of the principal members of the Young Turk movement were of Jewish origin and were amongst the most nationalistically minded Turks, did not make matters any easier. But, as happens so often in similar circumstances, public men are inclined to make a virtue of necessity and it soon became difficult to distinguish between those Zionist leaders

[7] Sieff to J.K.
[8] Sieff to J.K.

who really believed that the Zionist future was inevitably linked to the Ottoman suzerain of Palestine, and those who were convinced that the Ottoman Empire was approaching its dissolution but understood that it would not be politic to say so, or even to act on this assumption. The fate of the Jews still living under Turkish rule, and not least of the 100,000 in Palestine, depended on continued Zionist discretion.

With few exceptions, this was the accepted view of both leaders and followers. The community of Zionist and Turkish interest was stressed by the President of the World Zionist Organisation on every possible occasion. It was proclaimed as a centre-piece of Zionist policy at the Zionist Congress in Hamburg in 1909 and repeated at every formal meeting of the leadership. Vladimir Jabotinsky resigned his position as editor of the paper published by the Zionist Organisation in Turkey because the leadership had allowed a member of the executive to publish a book which advocated the establishment in Palestine of a Jewish nationality, with its own security forces, speaking Hebrew and possessing the right of self-taxation. Jabotinsky felt that to distribute such views in the name of the Zionist Organisation was to court the deportation of the Zionists from Ottoman territory, if nothing worse, and the closing down of the Zionist press and of Zionist activities.

Sieff mentioned this to illustrate the difficulties under which they laboured even when it came to public discussion. The growing gap between public expression and private belief was, therefore, only inadequately reported in the public records of those days. There were, of course, individuals who did not believe in discretion: Joseph Cowen, a leading member of the English Zionist Federation, was one of them. Both publicly and privately he urged English Zionists not to let Zionist policy be dictated by the German, Austrian and Russian Zionists, but to grasp the great opportunity which confronted them and to seek their future by association with the Franco-British Entente.

Many of the younger Zionists in Manchester – Simon Marks, Harry Sacher and Sieff – sympathised with Joseph Cowen. So did Dr Weizmann, but he insisted that they should be guided not by sympathies, but by realities. And as matters stood, the Ottoman rule over Palestine was still very real and they had everything to lose at this stage if they sought to challenge the Turks in public.

When war came, the Zionist movement had to pay a heavy price for the lack of adequate discussion about its policy in such an eventuality. The leadership was divided in its attitudes and loyalties. There was no agreement as to precise Zionist objectives. Zionists were split along the geographical and national divisions of the movement while the World Zionist Organisation sought safety in a general disengagement from the conflict by declaring its neutrality.

These were difficult weeks in Manchester, all the more so because of the suddenness with which the fact of war descended on the Jewish community. In the discussions in the Jewish and Zionist press in the month preceding the outbreak of the war, there was not the slightest evidence that they were heading for such an armed conflict. On 17 July 1914, the annual meeting of the Manchester Zionist Association was concerned primarily to encourage Hebrew education, the formation of a Zionist lending library and the winning of new members:

> The greater world issues did not appear on our agenda. The only crisis which figured in our minds was the growing tension over the situation in Ulster, and I have a vivid impression still of the firm tone of the *Jewish Chronicle* during that last week of peace, expressing concern over the possibility of war in Ireland and counselling the Jewish community to stand aside from that conflict and not become a party to either side.[9]

If that was to be the Jewish attitude over the danger on their door-step in Ireland, how much greater was the temptation to contract out from the conflict that involved the hated Tsar of Russia with the Austrian Emperor who had always been a consistent friend of the Jews. In fact, the Jewish and Zionist leadership was most concerned at the prospect of Britain becoming involved in the war as an ally of the Russians. The *Jewish Chronicle* faithfully reflected this feeling in its uninhibited warning which made a great impression on its readers on the last day of July 1914. It expressed its sympathy for the Austrian Emperor, and for the Serbs, and expressed the devout hope that England would not be dragged into the hostilities. Such action, claimed its Editor, Leopold Greenberg, would amount to an outrage and a crime. The flower of British youth should not be sacrificed to Russian interests in a quarrel which was none of its seeking. He urged Jews to ensure that England would stand solidly for neutrality and peace. The war still seemed a long way from Manchester.[10]

[9] Sieff to J.K.
[10] *Jewish Chronicle*, 31 July 1914.

100

In private, guided by Dr Weizmann, we began, however, to speculate further afield. How would this third Balkan War, as it seemed to us, affect the future of the Ottoman Empire? We reached no firm conclusions other than that henceforth, the equation of Zionism and Turkey might have to be drastically revised.[11]

Meanwhile, war came despite the injunctions of the Jewish leaders and with war came also its soul-destroying conformism. The same Mr Greenberg who had a week earlier told Anglo-Jewry to keep out of the war, and that to associate itself in any way with the Russian Tsar was an outrage and a crime, was now in the forefront of those who preached that rather excessive patriotism which is one of the least attractive by-products of all wars, no matter where they happen and when they happen.

I still shudder when I recall the injunctions which were addressed to us by Mr Greenberg now that the British Government had failed to take his advice. In type larger than he had ever used, he told us that since England's cause was now our cause, we must set aside all scruples, including our feelings about Russia. Under the circumstances, there was possibly nothing else that the Jewish leadership could do, but we all – including Dr Weizmann – felt that it could have been done with greater dignity and self-respect.[12]

This loud protestation of Jewish conformity was expressed in a famous – or notorious – recruiting poster which the *Jewish Chronicle* had produced and which became the slogan for all occasions: ENGLAND HAS BEEN ALL SHE COULD BE TO THE JEWS, JEWS WILL BE ALL THEY CAN BE TO ENGLAND. Added to this were warnings disseminated by the Jewish press telling and assuring its readers that paper money was safe, banks were sound and that trading with the enemy was wrong. All this infuriated many loyal Jews. It was so patronising in its assumptions. Much of it came from the Anglo-Jews who were anxious to be cleared of any taint that German Jews or Russian Jews hostile to the Tsar might undermine the support of the Jewish community for the war.

Manchester felt this rather strongly. It was an integrated Jewish community in which the majority had Eastern European origins:

[11] Sieff to J.K.
[12] Sieff to J.K.

We did not feel that we had reason to explain or apologise for being Jews. We were loyal, but we did not have to make a fetish of it. We were also Zionists and we now began seriously to establish an identity of interest between our Zionism and England at war. And we were fortunate to have Dr Weizmann to guide us on our course.[13]

Public expression of official Jewish opinion was aimed at countering the popular identification of Jew and German; at the same time, there was no mistaking Jewish uneasiness at being in the same camp as the Russians who had been – and probably still were – conducting pogroms against the Jews under their rule. When Israel Zangwill wrote a letter to *The Times*, during the opening weeks of the war, in which he gave expression to this feeling of disquiet about the high price that England and English Jewry had to pay for the Russian alliance, the Chief Rabbi and other Jewish leaders rushed letters to the paper to explain what Zangwill had meant, and that he was casting no aspersion at Britain's powerful Eastern ally; in vain did Zangwill protest that he was sufficient master of the language to say himself what he meant. But the incident was symptomatic of official Jewish nervousness at the time. This, however, exceeded the bounds of propriety when the *Jewish Chronicle* began about a month after the outbreak of the war to deny neutral reports of further Russian pogroms against Jews, especially in the Lithuanian capital of Vilna. The paper said that such reports were enemy concoctions.

Dr Weizmann had been holidaying in Switzerland when war came. He returned to London and immediately impressed on his Manchester friends a sense of urgency, an understanding that they were faced by a choice which might well decide the future of Zionism:

It might advance the implementation of our dreams into our own time, or it might compel us to delay it for generations to come. For more than anyone, he was aware to what extent the future policy of the Ottoman Government might decide our fate.[14]

There was much talk at the time about the desirability of compelling Turkey to stay neutral, despite the treaty which she had concluded with the Kaiser. The war against Germany would be so much easier if Turkey would not be a partner to it:

[13] Sieff to J.K.
[14] Sieff to J.K.

But as we discussed the situation in Manchester, we came to understand the dilemma which we had to resolve. If Turkey agreed to stay neutral, she would exact a formidable price for such an undertaking. Britain, France and Russia would have to undertake to ensure the integrity of the Ottoman Empire within its 1914 frontiers. It would rule out any hope of a Jewish State, independent or merely autonomous, in Palestine.[15]

On the other hand, if the Turks were to side with the Central Powers, then the Zionists would be freed from the limitations of policy under which they had operated since the revolution of the Young Turks in 1908 – and even before. It would then become possible to develop the community of interest of England and Palestine into a working alliance which would benefit both parties. This thought was uppermost in Zionist discussion during the first autumn of the war. It was resolved when the Turks entered the war. "I must admit that when the news came on 5 November 1914 that we were at war with Turkey, our Manchester circle was greatly relieved."[16]

Weizmann and the Manchester circle began to think along new lines, and were very much on their own in doing so. The official Zionist leadership had in fact maintained its headquarters in Berlin, but had established a kind of liaison "Bureau" in Copenhagen which had declared its total neutrality in the war. In effect, the German Zionist leaders were fully supporting the Kaiser and the Russian Zionists were supporting the Tsar. Under the prevailing conditions and police regimes one could hardly blame them, but most of the German and neutral Zionist leaders went considerably further than merely paying lip-service to the German cause; they really believed that right and might were with the Kaiser:

Our disillusion in Manchester reached its fill when Turkey entered the war and the American Zionist leadership justified Turkey's policy in view of the threat from Russian and allied interests which sought the dismemberment of the Ottoman Empire. The organ of the American Zionists went so far in its passion for neutrality as to justify the expulsion of thousands of Jews of Russian origin from Palestine.[17]

[15] Sieff to J.K.
[16] Sieff to J.K.
[17] Sieff to J.K.

The more Dr Weizmann saw the official Zionist confusion, the more he urged his Manchester colleagues to clarify their thinking and to be ready to act independently of the World Zionist Executive. Admittedly, their resources were limited, but not their enthusiasm. Dr Weizmann's demands were modest, extremely so by modern standards. They had to find the cost of his fare to London, be it to meet Balfour or Lloyd George, and, when necessary, to enable him to stay overnight. On these occasions either Simon Marks[18] or Sieff travelled with him and looked after his needs and acted as secretary or *chef de cabinet*. Simon Marks believed passionately in the Zionist-British connection and he was an unashamed and outspoken imperialist at the time, a time when it was considered neither shameful nor pejorative to describe oneself as such.

Sieff did not quite agree with him in the emphasis which he placed on his imperialism. "I shared his faith in the British connection but, like Weizmann, I believed it had to be rooted in our common but separate interests. I was passionately conscious at the time of my Jewish nationality and I had given expression to it in a letter which I had written to Dr Weizmann shortly before the outbreak of the war, on 18 May 1914. I told him that I wanted to be an active Zionist and I asked him to put me on the right path; I did not want to be a dilettante dabbling in Zionism, but to do useful work 'to improve the welfare of my nation and further the development of my national cause and culture. I hope you will not regard me as an "English Jew" enthused momentarily by a vision, but as a hundred per cent Jew, *sans epithet*.' " There was a special reason for Sieff's reference to the "English Jew". Weizmann had experienced both rebuff and disappointment from the most representative members of Anglo-Jewry and had developed an understandable scepticism about their lip-service for the Zionist cause. At this time, in fact, his mood bordered on an outspoken distaste of the patronising English Jews. It was Sieff's intention to reassure him.

When, therefore, Dr Weizmann returned to Manchester at the commencement of the autumn term of 1914, all their attention was focused on the decision that was about to be taken in Constantinople. Weizmann was impatient with the official Zionists in London who were

[18] Simon Marks was Sieff's brother-in-law; he had married Sieff's sister, Miriam, and Sieff had married Marks' sister, Rebecca. They became partners in business and politics; Simon Marks, later Lord Marks, was the Chairman of Marks and Spencer Ltd and Sieff the Deputy Chairman.

anxious about their neutral position. He decided, therefore, to act alone. With the help of his friends he made contact with the Editor of the *Manchester Guardian*, C. P. Scott, and renewed his acquaintance with Balfour and Lloyd George. When Scott proposed to take Weizmann to meet Herbert Samuel, "a Jewish Cabinet Minister", Weizmann was clearly upset at the prospect of having to meet what he described as an "English Jew". In the event, he overcame his resistance and was glad he had done so, but his more generalised resentment against the uncomprehending English Jews died hard, and one had to admit that it was not without cause.

It took time for Weizmann's independent Manchester policy to have effect. The process was not facilitated when, in November 1914, the World Zionist Executive sent two of its foremost members to take charge of Zionist affairs in Great Britain. Henceforth, Nahum Sokolow and the Russian Zionist Dr Yehiel Tchlenov (who returned to Russia after a few months) were the two accredited spokesmen of the World Zionist Organisation, and, since the parent body had declared itself for neutrality, that was also the official position of its two eminent representatives in the United Kingdom. Weizmann did not like it and did not agree to abide by this policy. "Our circle in Manchester proceeded on its separate way."

> Life was not easy for Sokolow. He was a sensitive man, with a panache for words and language, and he was not happy with his limited mastery of the English tongue. He had no office to work from, no staff and a somewhat equivocal position in wartime England as the spokesman and representative of an organisation whose *de facto* headquarters and most powerful section was in Germany, and was known to be collaborating with the German Foreign Ministry and the German military authorities on the Eastern Front. But both Weizmann and Sokolow were unquestionably personalities and they made an impact on whoever they met; there was, however a fundamental difference in their approach which became increasingly emphatic as the months passed and Dr Weizmann decided that the Zionists had to cast their lot with the British – but on what basis?[19]

About this time, the Russian Zionist leader Vladimir Jabotinsky passed through London and Manchester, but made no headway with his project for a Jewish Legion. The War Office had turned him down;

[19] Sieff to J.K.

the British Army, he was told, had no room for "fancy formations". Insofar as there was any understanding for Zionism, it came from those who were attracted by its biblical features, by the concept of the redemption of the wandering Jews or of their conversion to Christianity in the Holy Land. English Zionism at that stage, whether that of the Jews or the Gentiles, had little political basis and no political programme linked to the prevailing wartime conditions: it was a dream, a hope, an aspiration without any clear understanding of how it was to be achieved. What distinguished Weizmann during the formative months of 1915 was that he sensed that this was an opportunity of hitching the Zionist star to the British imperial wagon and he was determined that he should do this even though he had no idea as yet where it would lead him and how he would get there; but somewhere along that road lay the future of Palestine and its Zionist link.

Weizmann had kept us informed of his talks in London. He had been encouraged by the responsive attitude of Lloyd George and impressed by the detailed interest shown by Herbert Samuel. He was understandably delighted that a Jewish Cabinet Minister should be so openly favourable to the establishment of a Jewish state in Palestine. The two men met together far more often than is evident from their respective memoirs, and many of the most striking sentiments of the memorandum which Samuel sent to Asquith, the Prime Minister, in November 1914, and circulated in a somewhat amended form to the Cabinet in March 1915, were, in fact, formulated by Weizmann. Many of the sentiments, but not all. In the end, there remained a fundamental difference in the approach to a Jewish state in Samuel's proposals and Weizmann's concept. It is the reason why Samuel's memorandum remained stillborn, apart from obtaining a few polite sounds of approval from some of his Cabinet colleagues. The significance of these was later rather exaggerated as was the general impact of the Samuel memorandum.

I am not minimising the part played by Herbert Samuel, or the encouragement which we derived from the fact that we had a Zionist sitting in the Cabinet, but Dr Weizmann immediately recognised the difference between his Zionism and Samuel's. Samuel saw the establishment of a Jewish state in Palestine as a British gift to the Jews for which Jews would express their gratitude by serving British interests in the Levant. Dr Weizmann was certain that such an

106

approach would be fatal to the idea of Zionism and the genuine prospect of an independent Jewish state. He looked through the other end of the Samuel telescope. Zionism had to be a Jewish gift to Britain – arrogant, presumptuous and ridiculous as the idea might have appeared during the first winter of war. Indeed, I doubt whether it had been fully shaped in Dr Weizmann's mind by that time. But he used to come back from London convinced of one thing: that we would never succeed if we approached the British Government in the character of a suppliant.[20]

Weizmann considered it essential that they should speak to the British as equals and that, in order to do this effectively, they would have to convince the British of the importance of Zionism as an element in winning the war and, even more so, the peace. Samuel had grasped all this and he had incorporated it in his memorandum to Asquith, but he had failed on the crucial issue, as Weizmann saw it: he had presented the cause of Britain as a Jewish interest; Weizmann was sure – and the certainty grew on him with the years – that Zionism was a British interest.

It was these contrasting attitudes that were to make all the difference to our work. For it became clear to us in Manchester what we had to do. In a sense, we had to believe and act as if we were the spokes-men for the Jewish state; we had to emphasise the British rather than Jewish features of Zionism. And this we proceeded to do with all the self-assurance of youth and confidence in the justice of our cause and of its practical importance to Britain at war.[21]

Dr Weizmann was anxious not to arouse the opposition of the official Zionist Federation in London, or of the two representatives of the World Zionist Organisation, Nahum Sokolow and Dr Tchlenov. He therefore submitted a report to them on 7 January 1915 in which he reassured them about his work in Manchester. It was merely recon-noitring work, he told them, and that they had been careful not to commit themselves, or the Zionist Organisation, to any definite course of action.

I was to understand in later years just why Dr Weizmann wrote this report. It was a constant fear of many of the official Zionist leaders –

[20] Sieff to J.K.
[21] Sieff to J.K.

107

and even of Ministers of the State of Israel half a century later – that they might be committed to a definite course of action. Dr Weizmann was cast in a different mould. He never shirked responsibility or hesitated from taking an initiative even if it was not formally authorised; but he also understood when not to advertise his personal activities. All through 1915 we were in this state.

We worked quietly; we made no fuss. We had to overcome a good deal of inherent prejudice in public opinion and in government offices about the real nature of Zionism. We came across this profound misunderstanding of Zionism in all kinds of places, in newspapers and books, and, even more, in the privacy of the drawing rooms where still so much politics was shaped. A typical example was the publication in 1915 of a massive history of the Turkish Empire by Sir Mark Sykes, who was to become our great friend and guide along the road to the Balfour Declaration. In his book, he says that the Young Turks, who had overthrown the Sultan in 1908, supported Zionism because it was compounded of a mixture of bad Cosmopolitanism with the power of finance.[22]

It was this type of attitude that Sieff and his colleagues sought to overcome, as was also the widespread suspicion of Zionism as a German movement with its headquarters in Berlin and Vienna, and with powerful strings operated through the German-Jewish bankers of New York. There was, of course, an element of truth in this. The German Government had been far quicker off the mark than the British in recognising the importance of the Zionist and Jewish factor in the war, and they had made an impact on some of the powerful Jewish banking houses in the United States. Because of all this Weizmann felt it all the more urgent to stress not so much the Jewish aspect but the British interest in Zionism.

We were fortunate early on in our endeavours to make the acquaintance, through Harry Sacher, of his fellow leader-writer on the *Manchester Guardian*. Herbert Sidebotham belonged to that small group of journalists during the Great War who were men of great education and sensitivity, and no mean historians in their own right. And by good fortune, their devouring interest was in the future of the Ottoman Empire; their concern with Palestine was but a natural extension of this.

[22] Sieff to J.K.; see also Mark Sykes, *The Caliph's Last Heritage*, p. 509.

Among them were men who were to make great names for themselves, or had already done so: Wickham Steed of *The Times*, an imposing personality with his imperial beard and great height, an undisputed authority on the Hapsburg Empire and the emergent national movements, including Zionism; Alfred Zimmern, who was to become the foremost interpeter of classical Greek democracy; R. W. Seton-Watson, a protagonist for the new nations at the outset of the Great War and foremost historian of British foreign policy, and Arthur Greenwood, a lecturer in Economics at the University of Leeds, who was to become an outstanding personality in the Labour Party and one of our greatest friends.[23]

It is sometimes forgotten – especially in Zionist circles – that these men had an immediate and greater impact on public opinion in 1914 and 1915 than official Zionist propaganda. They saw the problem of Zionism in political terms and they spoke to a much larger public than did the official Zionists. That was why Weizmann – and the small circle in Manchester – believed so much in the importance of quiet diplomacy.

We had an early example of this when, at the end of 1914, about the time when Samuel was sending his memorandum to Asquith, Macmillan's published a paperback of some 400 pages edited by Alfred Zimmern, called *The War and Democracy*. The contributors were Seton-Watson, Dover-Wilson, Arthur Greenwood and Zimmern. A substantial section dealt with the future of the Ottoman Empire in Asia. Seton-Watson presented a penetrating case for a Jewish State in Palestine alongside the developing Arab national movement, and gave us great encouragement in our work by his outspokenness.[24]

It is high time, Seton-Watson wrote in one of his contributions, that Jews should realise that few things do more to foster antisemitic feeling than the tendency to sail under false colours and conceal their true identity. He hoped that the war would provide a new and healthy impetus to Jewish national policy; the Zionist national Jew was winning the admiration of the world. He proposed that a Jewish state be established in Palestine as one of the democratic war aims of the Allies, though like so many Englishmen at the time – and since – he could not bring himself to trust Jews with the government of Jerusalem. That was

[23] Sieff to J.K.
[24] Sieff to J.K.

to have some form of international control. All the same, the Manchester circle was greatly encouraged by this public presentation, but soon realised that it was not enough. "In order to be effective we would have to give more precise political direction to our work and throughout 1915, we sought ways and means of doing this most effectively."[25]

I have already mentioned Herbert Sidebotham. With him, we began to develop a relationship in which we inspired and educated each other. He became convinced that the deadlock on the western front would have to be broken in the East, and he told me on more than one occasion that the first step towards an effective Eastern political policy was to convince the Government of the essential character of an Eastern military policy.

Our discussions of this problem proceeded over weeks and months; personal problems intervened and caused delays, the impact of the war did likewise. But by November 1915 we had sufficiently clarified our thoughts for Sidebotham to put them on paper and propose to C. P. Scott, the Editor of the *Manchester Guardian*, to publish them as editorial policy. The curious thing about Scott at this time was that though he had become most friendly with Dr Weizmann and some of us, and had assisted Dr Weizmann in his meetings with Lloyd George and Herbert Samuel, he had never confided to his staff – and especially Sidebotham, who was the *Guardian*'s leader-writer and *Student of War* – that he supported the Zionist cause. Be that as it may, it was a great day for us when on 22 November 1915 the *Guardian* printed a long editorial article, opposing the French proposal that the main allied effort against Turkey should be aimed at Salonica and arguing that it would be dangerous to leave the Suez Canal as Egypt's frontier with Turkey which Britain would have to hold. Proceeding almost entirely on the basis of military need, with only slight imperial undertones, Sidebotham proceeds to argue the case for a Jewish Palestine as a buffer between Turkey and Egypt and as an important link across the land bridge between Europe and Asia – especially with India.

Dr Weizmann called us as soon as he had seen the *Guardian* that day, and suggested that we should approach Sidebotham with a view to expanding his article into a memorandum which Weizmann

[25] Sieff to J.K.; see also R.W. Seton-Watson in *The War and Democracy* (1915), pp. 283–291.

wanted to submit to the Foreign Office. We felt, however, that this was too important a document to prepare in haste. We produced many drafts, consulted many friends and critics, and made many changes before the document was ready for presentation to the Foreign Office in May 1916. The memorandum was 8,000 words long.[26]

But meanwhile, the political climate changed. By the time Sidebotham had completed his assignment, the Gallipoli expedition had failed, and the British Government was looking for a new policy in the Middle East. Sidebotham's memorandum pointed the way, and also urged the establishment of a Jewish state in Palestine as a part of the British Empire. But for Sacher, Marks and Sieff, working with Sidebotham on the preparation of the memorandum had been a significant experience. Even before they had completed the final draft they had become convinced that their work would have to be done differently if they wanted it to be effective; they had to turn from casual propaganda to organised exploitation of the Zionist solution, and they had to make the most of the support they had received.

We decided therefore, with Dr Weizmann's blessing and encouragement, to form the four of us – Sidebotham, Sacher, Marks and Sieff – into an *ad hoc* committee, and thus, the British Palestine Committee was born in April 1916. Simon Marks and I raised the necessary finance, we took offices in Norfolk Street, Manchester, and engaged a secretary. We were full of high hopes and excited expectations. We despatched several hundred circulars and some personal letters to potential sympathisers, and we waited for their response. It turned out to be a sobering experience.[27]

Out of the hundreds of letters they had despatched, only ten replies dribbled back; five were non-committal acknowledgements and two were outright negatives, including one that shook Sieff personally. It came from Sir George Adam Smith, the author of the *Historical Geography of the Holy Land*, a book that had made a great impact on him and on many Zionists. Lloyd George sent for a copy at the Paris Peace Conference, as a guide to the future borders of Palestine.

[26] Sieff to J.K.
[27] Sieff to J.K.

111

He [Smith] condemned our proposal – and in a way, pointed to a weakness in the purely utilitarian approach on which we had embarked. The whole idea of a Palestinian nation was wrong, he said in his letter. Palestine, as such, never has been, and never would be, a nation. He was probably more right at the time than we would have granted him. But it did underline the importance of stressing the fact that what we sought was not a Palestinian state but a Jewish state.[28]

The positive replies came from Sir Flinders Petrie, the well-known archaeologist, from Lord Carson who had come so close to leading the Ulster rebellion against the Asquith Government, and, a little later, most valuable and encouraging support from C. P. Scott, the Editor of the *Manchester Guardian*. It was hardly world-shaking, but it was a truer picture of the power of British Zionism than the image of influence over finance, the press and the politicians. Gradually, as their ideas began to crystallise in the summer of 1916:

We began to hear rumours and then reports of the negotiations which the Foreign Office had been conducting with the French and the Russians for the dismemberment of the Turkish Empire, and especially of their plans for the future of Syria and Palestine. In particular, we heard of the supposedly secret talks which Sir Mark Sykes had been having with the Frenchman, Georges Picot. They had been together in Petrograd and were said to have reached an agreement for the division of spoils and the establishment of a Great Power condominium in Palestine. The more I heard of this, the more disturbed I became. For I had become convinced that we had to make our arrangement for the Jewish state in Palestine with the British, and alone with the British. Any form of international control or condominium would introduce conflicting issues and probably frustrate our aims. Dr Weizmann thought that I was over-anxious about this. He also wanted an arrangement with the British, but he was not so immediately concerned with perils of the Sykes-Picot talks. As for Nahum Sokolow and the English Zionist Federation, they seemed to have no objection to an Anglo-French condominium in Palestine. I felt it my duty to impress on Dr Weizmann the danger of compromising on this question and, also, I was not too sure about Sir Mark Sykes' intentions. Sokolow and others attempted to reassure Dr Weizmann and thought me to be unduly alarmist, but

[28] Sieff to J.K.

112

the more I heard from Sidebotham and others about Sykes' peregrinations and inclinations the more insistent I became in my warnings.[29]

The British Palestine Committee shared Sieff's disquiet, and decided, with Weizmann's enthusiastic support, to publish a magazine to be called *Palestine*. It was to be printed on good paper under the prevailing wartime conditions; it would be confined to eight pages and carry two major articles and some short notes. It was to be published as a monthly at first, and sell for two pence per issue. Between 400 and 500 copies were to be distributed to members of parliament, churchmen and publicists.

How little impact Weizmann's arguments had made on the official Zionists in London was again reflected later in the year, while Sieff was actively engaged in planning the first issues of *Palestine*. In October 1916, the Zionist Organisation presented a detailed memorandum to the Government setting forth its ideas.

We were horrified to discover that this assumed that joint British and French control over Palestine was just as likely and desirable as purely British control. In the preamble to this Zionist declaration, it said that it was based on the assumption that "Palestine will come under the suzerainty, or the protection, or within the sphere of influence of Great Britain or France or under the joint control of both Governments". We set ourselves to correct these dangerous assumptions which were largely accepted by Dr Weizmann. Above all, therefore, we in Manchester felt we had to convince Dr Weizmann that this was an issue on which Zionists dare not compromise.[30]

Sieff therefore wrote again to Weizmann on 4 December 1916. Weizmann had urged them to do nothing without the approval of "Jimmy" Rothschild, but they were getting restless because they could get no clear idea from Rothschild as to what he considered to be a desirable policy. Sieff put all this in his letter of 4 December 1916. They wanted to participate in the meeting between Weizmann and Rothschild. Sieff told Weizmann that:

"As far as the British Palestine Committee is concerned, we are at a standstill until we know what form our propaganda is to take. If it is to be quiet and more or less subterranean, then we need Jimmy's help;

[29] Sieff to J.K.
[30] Sieff to J.K.

if it is to be public, then we shall need to discuss it with Jimmy, to find ways and means which will conform (if we think it desirable and advisable) with Jimmy's ideas on this subject. Of course, we appreciate that Jimmy's help to us would be invaluable, but, at the same time, we feel that at this critical time – when the Government will have to decide on an Eastern campaign – we ought to have a definite policy and work it until it is demonstrated to be a failure."

It was because of this and because we were becoming even more aware of the poverty of official Zionist propaganda, that we approached the publication of *Palestine* with a sense of urgency. Apart from Dr Weizmann's personal efforts at persuasion, our case was going by default.[31]

One reason for this was that, with the exception of Weizmann – and of the Zionist leadership in Berlin on the other side – there was no real attempt made to relate the Zionist aspirations to the conduct of the war. Sidebotham argued strongly that this should be the principal function of the British Palestine Committee: they were to provide a sound political foundation for the historic Zionist case in the present world situation.

It was to this that we addressed ourselves. As we prepared our arguments and surveyed our potential friends and opponents, we became ever more aware of the pervasive influence of Sir Mark Sykes. His shadow began to fall over every aspect of the future settlement in the Near East. It dominated, so to speak, all our discussions, and it was this consciousness of his influence and outlook that largely dictated the character and the contents of the first issues of *Palestine*.[32]

Sykes had by that time won considerable reputation as a friend of the Arabs, concerned to advance their political interest against that of their Turkish overlords.

This was of great interest to us in the British Palestine Committee. We were greatly worried by the information, coming from trustworthy sources, that Sykes had made an arrangement with the French about the future government and frontiers of Syria and Palestine. Our concern was further increased when we heard that Sykes had been appointed to the Cabinet Secretariat but then, suddenly, we were told by Sokolow and the Sephardi Chief Rabbi, Dr Moses Gaster, that

[31] Sieff to J.K.
[32] Sieff to J.K.

114

they were in touch with Sykes, that he was an ardent pro-Zionist and was providing assistance and advice to the Zionist leaders. Most of my Zionist colleagues were relieved and delighted: Sokolow had been completely charmed by Sykes and would trust him and rely on his counsel in all matters. Weizmann was also impressed by the brilliance, wit and enthusiasm of Sykes, and even more by his detailed understanding of the diplomatic processes.[33]

In return, Sykes sought Zionist understanding and support for the policy with which he had been charged. He was to conciliate French susceptibilities about Syria, but to detach the Palestinian question from the Syrian, and to conserve intact as far as possible the special British interests in Arabia. He had succeeded in convincing Sokolow – and, largely through Sokolow, also Weizmann – that the best solution for the Zionists would be an Anglo-French condominium over Palestine. That would ensure French support for the Zionist cause and it would leave the French content with the proposed Syrian and Arabian settlement. Despite the confidential reports that reached Weizmann from the Continent, and the growing volume of rumour about Sykes' discussions with the French, the Zionists knew nothing specific at that time about the conclusion of the formal Sykes-Picot Agreement which had been signed by the British, French and Russians on 16 May 1916.

In the light of the unease created by these reports, the British Palestine Committee decided to devote the first issues of *Palestine* to the presentation of its views against the plans for a condominium, or the partition of Palestine, and to spell out precise Zionist proposals for the future boundaries of the Jewish State. Thus the stage was set for the explosive publication of *Palestine*.

The first issue appeared on 26 January 1917, and across the front page of every issue during the next two years we carried two mottoes. The first stated that the British Palestine Committee sought to reset the ancient glories of the Jewish nation in the freedom of a new British Dominion in Palestine. The second was a quotation from the *Spectator*. This read as follows: "If he [Lord Beaconsfield] had freed the Holy Land, and restored the Jews, as he might have done, instead of pottering about with Roumelia and Afghanistan, he would have died Dictator."[34]

[33] Sieff to J.K.
[34] Sieff to J.K.

115

I must add here that the word "dictator" had not the same connotation in this context as it would have today, fifty years later. It meant then no more than that Disraeli's authority would not have been questioned as it was at the end of his years because of his unhappy Eastern policy.

No sooner had the first number appeared, on 26 January 1917, than Sieff became aware that their arguments had reached their target. Weizmann called him and transmitted a strong complaint from Sir Mark Sykes that the contents of the first number of *Palestine*, which pressed unequivocally for a British-controlled Palestine, was a great embarrassment to him when he met the French. To emphasise the seriousness of the complaint, Weizmann wrote to Sieff stressing the importance of not upsetting Sykes or his work.

Encouraged by Sidebotham, Sieff persuaded Sacher and Marks not to accept the proposition that they should not openly discuss the policy pursued by Sykes although it had evidently been approved by the official Zionist bodies. After much heart-searching, Sieff decided to stand by his guns, and wrote to Weizmann on 4 February 1917, just as the second issue of *Palestine* was in the process of distribution:

. . . It is our duty to insist upon a British Palestine in every conversation the Zionists have with Sir Mark. I do not think one ought to underestimate the weight of Sir Mark's opinion on the real F.O., and I believe that the real F.O. will lean on the advice of Sir Mark to a greater degree than we perhaps imagine. In other words, assuming that, after Sir Mark has thrashed out the whole Palestinian problem with the Frenchman, he comes to the conclusion that a condominium is desirable – temporarily or permanently – it will be very difficult for us Zionists to persuade the real F.O. that a purely British Palestine is the right solution. So that our duty is to attack the danger at the source – i.e. to demonstrate to Sir Mark the evil and dangerous results which would follow a joint administration of Palestine . . . Again, I cannot too strongly insist upon the danger of allowing Sir Mark to believe that we Zionists can agree to a condominium, which impression he will obtain, and rightly too, if we do not combat this idea right at the outset. After all, we do not come to him as beggars, but with something to give. Without us Zionists, his Palestinian problem is going to be a very difficult one and he must be made cognisant of this. As the first number of *Palestine* states, Jewish

116

Zionists must be regarded by English people not as mendicants of British generosity, but as applicants for a political accommodation which they hope later richly to repay . . .[35]

Two days after Weizmann had received Sieff's letter on 7 February 1917, he had his first formal meeting with Sir Mark at the home of Dr Gaster. "I was not present but Harry Sacher attended on behalf of our group; Lord Rothschild was there, so was Herbert Samuel, James de Rothschild, Weizmann, Sokolow, Herbert Bentwich and Joseph Cowen. Gaster presided. Judging by what I was told after the meeting, it was a muddled and inconclusive affair, largely because of Gaster's inept handling of the meeting. Moreover, the account that Weizmann gave me of his discussions with Sykes and Sokolow on 10 February, three days after the meeting at Gaster's home, was quite different to the account subsequently incorporated into the official report of the Zionist Executive. In fact, what had taken place at Gaster's was the exact opposite to the version later presented by the Executive to the 12th Zionist Congress."[36]

> According to what Weizmann told us after the meeting – and I have been able since to confirm this version from the notes of the meeting in the Gaster archives – Gaster suggested that France should be invited to act as protector of the Zionists in Palestine, and Sykes said that the Foreign Office was not likely to make difficulties for such a proposal coming from Zionists. The idea was again raised at a private meeting at Sykes' home in Buckingham Gate which took place on 10 February, three days after the more formal gathering at Gaster's. Present were Weizmann, Sokolow and Sykes. Weizmann told me afterwards that Sykes had again expressed his annoyance at the editorial policy of *Palestine*. He told Weizmann that the paper ought to popularise the Zionist cause without mixing it with politics. We should stick to straight pro-Zionist propaganda and not antagonise the French by our insistence on the over-riding British interest in Palestine. Our articles in *Palestine* had made his negotiations with the French much more difficult, and he urged Weizmann to curb our pro-British enthusiasm.
>
> After we had heard of Gaster's incredible suggestion that responsibility for Palestine should be given to the French, and the surprising

[35] Sieff to Weizmann, 4 February 1917.
[36] Reports of the Executive to 12th Zionist Congress, Pt 1. Political Report, p. 10.

support which Sykes gave to this opinion of the Haham, we concluded that Sykes and Gaster had arranged to make this proposal to the meeting to ease Sykes' thorny path of negotiations with the French. In any case, the whole affair roused both Sidebotham and myself to the conviction that we would have to make a public stand on this issue, notwithstanding the complaints which Sykes had already addressed to the Zionist leaders about the editorial conduct of *Palestine* and despite Weizmann's personal appeal to me.[37]

Accordingly, the issue of *Palestine* for 15 February dealt in detail with the boundaries Sieff had proposed for Palestine:

We added a detailed map of the proposed frontier for good measure. I had by then made a close study of the geopolitical problem of Palestine and had been guided in my thinking by Sidebotham who had a sixth sense about these questions. We had reached the conclusion that the northern frontier of Palestine should be slightly north of Sidon and moving inland to include the Hauran and Golan Hills. The eastern frontier would run parallel with the Hejaz railway, between ten and twenty miles east of the railway. This would include within the borders of Palestine the best part of the rainfall area of what came to be known later as Transjordan. As for the southern border, we printed a separate article arguing strongly for the need to incorporate the Sinai peninsula in Palestine, both for the sake of the defence of the Canal and the greater security of Palestine.[38]

Sykes, confronted by this open defiance, despatched a furious message to Weizmann on 16 February 1917, and Weizmann, in turn, wrote a fairly strongly worded letter to Sieff in which he pleaded again that he should contain his enthusiasm so as not to embarrass Sykes.[39]

I replied on 19 February, the day after receiving Weizmann's second letter of complaint. By now I was certain that we were right and that Gaster, Sokolow and the London Zionists were inclined to be too uncritical about Sir Mark Sykes. I was now convinced that Sykes was primarily concerned – as he should have been – to further British interests with Zionist help. I may have done him an injustice,

[37] Sieff to J.K.; see also the account in *Two Studies in Virtue*, by Christopher Sykes, pp. 194–98, and *Balfour Declaration*, by L. Stein, pp. 370–77.
[38] Sieff to J.K.
[39] Weizmann to Sieff, 17 February 1917.

but I was very much on my guard. Looking back now on the tragically short life of Mark Sykes, I admired his brilliance and perspicacity but I am more than ever convinced that there was something ambivalent about his attitude to and enthusiasm for Zionism.[40]

All this surfaced in a letter which Sieff wrote to Weizmann:

"I must confess that I was very much surprised at first at the attitude taken up by Sir M. But, after reading your letter through again, the whole matter became clear and definite. There is no doubt in my mind that Sir M. has come to an agreement with the Arabs and his interest in Jewish political aspirations in Palestine is only secondary. The very fact that he claims part of the Hauran and the Hedjaz Railway for the Arabs is proof positive. I am sure that you will concede that to us Jews, Palestine without the whole of the Hauran and the Hedjaz Railway, means not only a cramped and restricted Palestine without any hope of extension, but also a Palestine continually threatened by a strong Arab group which will make our position East of the Jordan precarious for all time. Added to which the Arabs will have the advantage of the Hedjaz Railway which, to us, is of vital importance. I have no doubt that Sir M., in holding France up to us, has been trailing a 'red herring' across our path – in the same way as Monsieur has been trailing the 'red herring' of Italy. The difficulty is not France, but the Arabs – and this Arab problem is the key to the whole situation. Now then, I ask you, must we sit down and say nothing? Is it not our duty to ourselves as well as to the future of Israel in Palestine to fight this Arab agreement? Is Jewish development in Palestine to be stifled before the Jewish political State is born? Yes, our articles do enormous harm, but it is harm in the right direction. It may harm the Arab kingdom, but that is no concern of ours. The only thing that troubles me is that you may be having worry added to your daily life which I want to avoid as much as I can. And in this connection, therefore, you may diplomatically hint that you are not responsible for the 'hot headed youths' of the British Palestine Committee. Of course I know you agree with us, but your position is very awkward. We shall talk about this when I see you on Wednesday evening."[41]

I wrote this letter with a heavy heart, but also with a sense of

[40] Sieff to J.K.
[41] Sieff to Weizmann, 17 February 1917.

relief. I felt that I had not established my position in relation to the contemporary politics in Zionism, and I had also achieved a relationship with Dr Weizmann which combined friendship and mutual trust with dissent and criticism. Dr Weizmann never took kindly to critics because he felt that they wanted to undermine or minimise his work. My impression at the end of this particular clash was that Weizmann was a little impatient at the seriousness with which we treated our publication and at our insistence in parading our principles, but at the same time he gave me to understand that he shared our concern and was not altogether unhappy that someone other than himself should give voice to it.[42]

In fact, it was evident to Sieff that Weizmann was rather more worried by his first encounters with Mark Sykes than he was prepared to show. He was disturbed by the evident interplay between Sykes and Sokolow at the Gaster meeting. Sir Mark had suggested that the Zionists should become a party to his talks with the French representative, Georges Picot, with whom he had been discussing the future of Palestine and Syria.

Sykes had so worded his proposal that the obvious name to suggest for participation in the talks with the French was Nahum Sokolow. This did not please Weizmann. He thought Sokolow far too gullible where Sykes was concerned and he feared that Sykes and Picot would get the rather naïve Sokolow so involved in their schemes that the Zionists would be in no position to criticise the Anglo-French project for the Levant, although at the time we knew nothing about the agreement with the French which Sykes had signed in May 1916.[43]

Meanwhile, Sokolow left for Paris and Rome, and his reports from both places confirmed the fears of the Manchester circle. He was easy-going in his diplomacy, inclined to accept generalisations rather than specific formulations. The weeks he spent in Paris were to give Weizmann and his Manchester associates a great deal of trouble. All the more so, since the Americans were beginning to play a much bigger part in the political discussions. The American-Jewish press was virtually unanimously in favour of a Great Power condominium over Palestine, either an Anglo-American condominium or one that also included the French.

[42] Sieff to J.K.
[43] Sieff to J.K.

120

We kept up our pressure on Weizmann to impress on Mr Justice Brandeis, the influential American Zionist leader and close friend of President Wilson, that it was in the Zionist interest to have only one Power to deal with, and that he wanted Britain as the trustee. But then we heard to our distress that Sokolow had advised Brandeis that he was hopeful that there would be either a British protectorate or a joint Anglo-French arrangement for Palestine. Sokolow's permissive attitude to French participation brought home also to Weizmann the need for a firm stand on this question, so as to leave no doubt in the minds of our friends.[44]

Weizmann's negotiations for a declaration of support for a Jewish National Home in Palestine by the British Government were making encouraging progress, but the British Palestine Committee – and especially Sieff – felt that public opinion, Jewish and Gentile, was not yet adequately prepared for the event. The Annual Conference of the English Zionist Federation which was held in February appeared to be wholly out of touch with the great events that were taking shape. Sieff pressed Weizmann to call a special conference of the Zionist Federation which would primarily address itself to the political situation as it affected the Jewish National Movement and to consider the disturbing news from Palestine where the Turks were deporting and harassing the Jews.

The special conference met in London on 20 May 1917. But even at this gathering of Zionists, Weizmann discovered that he had to walk warily. The creation of a Jewish Commonwealth, he told them, was the final aim, but it would be achieved only through a series of intermediate stages. One of these was the protection of Palestine by one of the Great Powers; he thought it might be Britain "acting in agreement with her Allies".

The reason for Dr Weizmann's cautious formulation had to be sought in Whitehall. There had been a marked shift of attitude in the Foreign Office. The Foreign Secretary, Mr Balfour, had been persuaded that the British position at the Peace Conference, or in a negotiated peace settlement with Germany, would be greatly strengthened if the British protectorate over Palestine was shared, not by France, but by the United States. Accordingly, when Balfour went to Washington in May 1917 and met with Justice Brandeis, he told Brandeis that the

[44] Sieff to J.K.

121

British favoured a condominium for Palestine in which the United States would participate. But the worst was yet to come. President Wilson and his Secretary of State, Lansing, were still hopeful of detaching Turkey from the German alliance. Their attitude was shared to a disturbing extent by the American Zionist leaders, among whom German influence was still considerable.

> Thus while we were working hard to ensure that only a British protectorate over Palestine would be considered as acceptable by the Zionists, the American Zionists were prepared to support a separate peace with Turkey which would leave the Turks in authority in Palestine and allow the future of the country to be decided by the uncertainties of an unspecified Peace Conference.[45]

It was a difficult and untidy situation that called for great tact and patience on Weizmann's part. Brandeis also had been won over into supporting Balfour's idea of an Anglo-American condominium, and he sent an outstanding American Zionist, Felix Frankfurter, to convince the Weizmann "group" to abandon its insistence on a purely British protectorate. Frankfurter had a strong case when he pointed out that while Weizmann wanted a British protectorate, not even Balfour, the Foreign Secretary, backed his claim. On the contrary, Balfour wanted to have the Americans involved in the Middle East. Frankfurter urged that this would be of immense benefit to the Zionists. In the end, Weizmann convinced Frankfurter of his determination to oppose any form of condominium. "It struck us as extremely odd that we should have to be more insistent on British suzerainty than the British were themselves. But we knew what we were doing – and why – and I am certain now that all the facts are known to us, that we were right to make the stand we did."[46]

Weizmann returned from his meeting with Morgenthau in Gibraltar in the middle of July, and turned at once to the discussion about the British Government's statement which was in the process of being drafted. He found it increasingly difficult to cope with the nagging criticisms and obstacles from the official Zionist Federation; and he found Sokolow's unpredictability to be the cause of quite unnecessary problems. Suddenly, Weizmann seemed to be able to take no more of this. "He sent me a short note saying that he was resigning his

[45] Sieff to J.K.
[46] Sieff to J.K.

122

Presidency of the Zionist Federation and added for good measure that he had become convinced that the Zionists were 'bankrupt'. He was bitter, tired and despondent."

Sieff wrote to Weizmann the next day (17 August 1917):

"I cannot refrain from telling you how perturbed I am at the situation which has arisen in the Zionist world in London. I am far from believing that any words of mine can persuade you to radically alter the decision to which you have arrived, nor can I convince you that Zionism is not bankrupt. I am convinced that you would not take such a serious step – fraught with danger to the whole movement – without having good and sound reasons. What those reasons are, is not clear to me, though, in view of my affection towards you, I have sensed them, rather than understood them. Your assertion that Zionism in England is "bankrupt" has not yet been proved. No real test has been made. Give the Zionists a lead. Who knows – they might successfully pass through the fire or not. If they do not, you can then dissociate yourself from them. As I told you last night, I am gradually arriving at the conclusion that the majority of Jews do not deserve Palestine. There are one or two *Rara Avis*. They will develop their own free Jewish life in Palestine under any circumstances. The rest have not yet got the spirit of sacrifice. . . ."

Neither Dr Weizmann's autobiography nor any of the Zionist histories deal with the causes of this incident nor with any aspect concerning it. As far as Sieff recalls, he discussed the problem with Weizmann before Sieff left for a brief holiday with his family. Dr Weizmann abandoned his intention to resign, but he was still in an unhappy mood when he returned home.

He had been getting complaints from local busybodies about not being suitably consulted and honoured, and I tried to reassure him with another letter. I was close enough to him to understand how much agony, frustration and annoyance he was suffering in these weeks during which he was approaching the climax of his efforts. My main concern – and that of my friends, Simon Marks and Harry Sacher – was to ensure that he could concentrate on the principal issues without being bothered by all the pettiness and jealousy that was unfortunately a part of Zionist politics – as indeed of all politics.[47]

[47] Sieff to J.K.

Sieff wrote to Dr Weizmann about this on 3 September 1917, when they had returned to Manchester. "So far as the mass herd goes, it will only awaken when someone gives it a violent jolt – e.g. pogroms, or a British-cum-Allied declaration that henceforth the war is being continued on behalf of the Zionist movement. It is very hard to drive out the *galuth* spirit. My advice to you, however, is quite simple. Don't take any notice or account of complaints. You will never get any help from glory-seekers and the complaints only cover some ulterior motive. . . ."

The crisis passed, though still largely unexplained, and we approached the stirring days of the Government's policy declaration. But our interests were now less with the formal document that we were to get than with the practical realities that were to follow. The Balfour Declaration* was a milestone, a most important one, on our way. It was a means to our end. But whether it would matter in the final analysis depended in the first place on a complete allied victory over the German and Turkish Empires, and on the manner in which we succeded in laying the foundations of a Jewish state before the Peace Conference began to dispose over it. My principal preoccupation in the autumn of 1917, remained the geopolitics of the Eastern campaign. My "penchant" for geographic study, about which I had written to Weizmann, was fully occupied with the realities of the war situation and the discussions about the frontiers of the Jewish State. I use the term "Jewish state" deliberately for this was our objective at the time; we never thought of anything else or anything less. We knew that we might have to approach our goal in stages, but at the end of the line, not too far off, we saw a Jewish state in association with the British Empire. So did our friends and opponents. The discussion about Zionism in that autumn of 1917 was the discussion about the desirability or otherwise of a decision by the Government that would lead to the establishment of a Jewish state in Palestine.[48]

In Sieff's view the Cabinet realised this, so did the British Ambassador in Paris, Lord Bertie. Balfour certainly did, though Sieff had his doubts about Mark Sykes; Amery, Ormsby-Gore, Lawrence and the other members of the Arab Bureau in Cairo, Hogarth, Cornwallis and Clayton took the same view. The devaluation of the concept of in-

* See Appendix I.
[48] Sieff to J.K.

dependence into a watery national home had not yet taken place. "The Balfour Declaration was considered by its authors and by us as an undertaking that would result in the creation of a Jewish State."

All this was fine, but Sidebotham never tired of impressing Sieff and his friends in Manchester that it was entirely dependent on the successful outcome of the war. This was also Sieff's view, and he was none too sanguine about the prospect. In September 1917 he had some correspondence with Vladimir Jabotinsky who had sought to create a Jewish Legion to fight with the British in Palestine, but had got no further than permission to recruit a Zion Mule Corps. On 29 September 1917 Sieff told Jabotinsky: "You have, I know, been up against the supineness not only of the British Government but what is, in my opinion, much worse, of the Jewish masses. If Palestine is to be Jewish, it is only the few who will be worthy of it . . . You will no doubt have read the military article in this week's *Palestine*. It is the black truth, and we want the British Government to know it. They are messing up the Eastern campaign and sacrificing it to the fetish of the Western Front . . . There is no doubt that Germany's new military orientation is in the East."[49]

The Weizmann circle was understandably elated with the Balfour Declaration, yet in some ways it served only to underline the gap they still had to bridge. More than ever, they became aware of the lack of understanding for the Jewish position among the English, the ruling upper classes and the popular working classes.

The Jew was a financier, a Germany sympathiser, a Bolshevik or whatever you may think other than what we set out to be. We had, we felt, to restore the historic Jew, the link with our land, and the significance of both to whoever wanted to rule the East. The choice before us was limited: we had to ally ourselves either with the Democracies or with the Central Powers, Germany and Turkey, or we could make common cause with the revolutionaries in Russia. Our choice was dictated by our sympathy for Britain and by our own interest. But others did not see it that way. We therefore set ourselves to educate public opinion.[50]

Their new periodical, *Palestine*, was one of the means, but they needed more. Sidebotham wrote a small, closely argued book, *England*

---

[49] Sieff to Jabotinsky, 29 September 1917.
[50] Sieff to J.K.

*and Palestine*, which can still be read with profit and they published books and pamphlets. What mattered most, however, was that they had something to say and were fortunate to have men like Sidebotham, Sacher and Norman Bentwich to say it well.

The historical argument, advanced by Sidebotham, was that already Alexander, Caesar and Napoleon had clearly realised the tremendous importance of Palestine as a bridge to the possession of the East. Alexander used Jewish colonists to confirm his hold on Egypt; Caesar's idea was to use Palestine as a stepping-stone to the establishment of a Roman Empire on the Euphrates, and he thus anticipated Napoleon's project in the campaign of 1799. If the policy of Alexander, Caesar and Napoleon was pro-Jewish it was so because they considered the Jews and their country as a keystone in their imperial projects. This, Sidebotham argued in *England and Palestine*, held good to an even greater extent of the conditions that would govern the stability of the British Empire in the East in the years after the Great War.

Sidebotham dealt also with the emergence of the Arab nation. The project of reviving Arab power side by side with the Jewish state, he pleaded, was the strongest of arguments for compromise and adjustment of Arab claims where they seemed to come into conflict with those of the Zionists. But in all their discussions of the future frontiers of the Jewish state, in *Palestine* or in Sidebotham's *England and Palestine*, what may be called the young Zionists had never any doubt about its dimensions. It was impossible, Sidebotham wrote, "to exaggerate the importance of the country East of the Jordan to the future of the Jewish state"; he wrote that in 1917 before the publication of the Balfour Declaration.

We knew what we were doing. For while we were seeking to ensure a realistic and viable Jewish state, we were oppressed by the information that even so good a friend as Mark Sykes was thinking in severely restrictive terms about the Jewish state. On 13 October 1917 – two weeks before the Cabinet took its decision on the Balfour Declaration – Sykes circulated a memorandum about future British policy in the Levant. It barely mentioned the Jewish role in Palestine other than in terms of very limited local rights, and at a public meeting in December, Sykes warned the Jewish leaders to see their problem "through Arab eyes".

It was thus that we turned to the formation of a Zionist Commission that was to go to Palestine as the key to our future. Dr

126

Weizmann had invited me to act as the secretary of the Commission and I was most happy to accept. For I had come to understand from what he told me that not only the fate of the Balfour Declaration but also the prospect of a Jewish state would depend largely on what the Zionist Commission would be able to achieve. We were, in fact, to lay the practical foundations of our state while war was still raging, and the future uncertain. It was to be our act of faith and to this now I devoted all my efforts. For we were to create the *fait accompli* that might well be decisive in the negotiations at the Peace Conference. Few people understood the significance of the Zionist Commission; Balfour did, Allenby did and so did we.[51]

What Sieff did not know then was that the British – Balfour, Sykes, Clayton, Allenby, Ormsby-Gore – had an entirely different function mapped for the Zionist Commission than had Weizmann or Sieff. What Sieff also did not know then – nor did Weizmann – was that the Zionist Commission was to be not only the root of their greatest achievement, but also the source of their most serious problem. It marked the most challenging period of Weizmann's leadership of the Zionist movement, and of the political means which he employed to further the cause.

For, quite apart from the political implications of the Zionist Commission, which were considerable, there was also the curiously ambivalent position of Dr Weizmann himself. A careful study of all the records of the Commission and its related documents, as well as prolonged discussion about them with two members of the Commission – Lord Sieff and Sir Leon Simon – suggest that there were aspects of Weizmann's conduct at the time which remain to be more fully explored and explained. Sieff had been aware of it from the time Sir Mark Sykes appeared as Weizmann's guiding light, and, in retrospect, what followed was too good to be altogether coincidental. When I discussed this with Sieff in May 1967, he recalled that Weizmann had come back to Manchester from London after his first meetings with Sykes in February 1917, and had told Sieff and other members of the British Palestine Committee that they ought to take into consideration the agreement which Sykes had made with the French and the Russians, though Weizmann would not divulge any details of the arrangement of which Sykes had evidently informed him. Sieff's subsequent two letters to

[51] Sieff to J.K.

127

Weizmann[52] expressed his disquiet, also that of Sidebotham, Sacher and Marks, at the way in which Sykes' policy-making "was allowed to slide on without anybody being made aware of its dangers because nobody knew just what Sykes had agreed with the French and Russians". But Weizmann evidently had been told a great deal more by Sykes and was prepared to go along with it.[53]

Thus it was again a year later, at the beginning of 1918, when the Zionist Commission prepared to leave for Palestine. By now, one of the main British objectives in the Middle East had undergone a considerable change. It was no longer to seek to implement the agreement which had been made with the French, but to undo it. This was summarised in a "Secret and Confidential" paper on the Zionist Commission prepared by the War Office for the General Staff, and which used as its source, amongst other intelligence material, private letters and telegrams which were despatched by the Intelligence Directorate for the Zionist Organisation. The Zionist Commission, this paper said, "was planned by Dr Weizmann in conjunction with the Foreign Office". This planning covered also the political and economic objectives of the Zionist Commission, and clearly went much further in the extent of mutual arrangement than Sieff or any other of Weizmann's colleagues realised or appreciated. Thus, what was particularly stressed in these "Notes on Zionism" for the General Staff was that Weizmann's policy of seeking a purely British protectorate in Palestine "conflicts radically with the Sykes-Picot Treaty", and that "one of the main political aims of the Zionists is to obtain the abolition of that treaty and to substitute for it a British Protectorate over the whole of Palestine".

A second point, evidently no less important for the War Office authors of these "Notes", was to stress the significant role which Weizmann was playing in convincing President Wilson of the importance to the United States of "a non-Turkish Palestine" and of impressing on him that "a Jewish Palestine must become a war aim for America". There was no need in the paper to stress again that in Dr Weizmann's political dictionary a "Jewish Palestine" was synonymous with a "British Palestine". But the connection was clearly established in the citation of a long extract from a private letter by Dr Weizmann to the American Zionist leader, Mr Justice Brandeis, addressed to him at the Supreme Court in Washington. The letter had been given by Weizmann

[52] See pp. 116–119, above.
[53] Sieff to J.K.

128

to the Intelligence Directorate for speedy and safe despatch to the United States.[54]

It was an unusually buoyant letter which Weizmann had written to Brandeis on 14 January 1918; it was also the most complete statement of Weizmann's public position in the weeks before leaving for Palestine at the head of the Zionist Commission. He appealed once more to Brandeis to join with him but he knew already that he could not do so. It was essential that Brandeis should understand what Weizmann will have to face in Palestine when he gets there, and Weizmann proceeds to itemise the problems: "The French are making themselves as disagreeable as possible. They pose as the conquerors of Palestine . . . as the modern Crusaders." The British naturally resented this, but they were anxious not to have any friction with the French because that would upset also the Arabs and introduce complications with the Italians. In rather lurid terms, Weizmann explained to Brandeis the position of the Christian Arabs, the "so-called Syrians" who are behind the "abominable agitation, semi-antisemitic, semi-anti-British, which is carried on at present in certain French newspapers". These "Syrians" were supported by French financiers, Jesuits "(not the Vatican!)", and by some rich Jewish anti-Zionists "like Reinach and his friends". All these were united in their hatred of Britain but dare not attack the British openly; so "they preach a crusade against us". Weizmann then dwells on the role of the Bolsheviks, who were appealing "to the darkest forces in Russia and Central Asia", hoping to spread their propaganda to India and Egypt. After the Russians, Brandeis is warned of the Germans, who pretend to be the friends of Turkey. Clearly, with an eye on the still latent American fear of German-Ottoman domination, he assured Brandeis that "the Germans well know that a Jewish Palestine, initiated by Great Britain and supported by America, a Palestine which stands in friendly contact with a free Armenia and an independent Arabia, means a death blow to the combination of Islamo-Prussian-Turanian domination of the East. This is why Germany is so very much perturbed about the British Declaration given to us."

But if the Germans and Turks have their way they would crush Palestine, Armenia and Arabia out of existence, spread their influence as far as India and become the modern version of Tsinghis-Khan

[54] *Notes on Zionism*, Secret & Confidential, for the information of the General Staff; three papers dated February and April 1918, and February 1919; B19/22, 100–2/19 H & S 6839, wo, pp. 10 and 16.

equipped with Krupps' guns and poison gases, wireless telegraphy and U-boats – "a danger to Europe and America alike". The only hope of the Zionists was that Great Britain should retain Palestine; but she could do so only if the Jews of the world would demand it, and if the two powerful democracies of England and America work together for it in opposition to "the pseudo-democratism of the Bolsheviks and their Jewish cosmopolitan satellites".

Weizmann's letter proceeds relentlessly, at inordinate length, and with uncharacteristic language to describe a kind of "Protocols of Zion" in reverse operated by a kind of conspiracy "(the cohesion between the various groups is perhaps not sufficiently intimate to warrant the term 'coalition')". Weizmann lists them for Brandeis' benefit:

"Jesuits with branches stretched across Austria-South Germany (think of Erzberger and the Centre Party in the Reichstag!), Syrians with Syrian-French financiers as expressed in the ambitions of the *Crédit Lyonnais*, *Banque de Paris et Pays Bas*, and, who knows, perhaps Caillaux and Bolo, their Jewish Associates like Reinach, Lucien Wolf and this so-called Jewish influence stretched across to Salonica and to the pseudo-Jewish members of the Committee of Union and Progress, like Djavid Bey, etc. Your own Morgenthaus, Elkus and Edelmanns belong to the same species."

And Weizmann added that, with the exception of the Jesuits, all these were people "striving for worldly power and financial gain, and they see that their ambition will crumble to pieces if the Zionists get hold of Palestine under the aegis of England".[55]

Before we consider the extraordinary language and far-reaching implications of this letter to Brandeis, we have to take note of one further feature on which Weizmann puts great emphasis. They have to remember, he warns Brandeis, that the Zionists will enjoy British support only so long as Zionist activities in Palestine do not lead "to an increase of jealousy on the part of France and all the forces that centre round it". They must not give the impression that they are acting as a cover for the British so as to enable them to annex Palestine. "These circumstances set a limit to our immediate possibilities in the Holy Land during the period of occupation. Our activities must therefore be of such a nature as to meet these objections."

What emerges from this letter, and from a second letter which

[55] Weizmann to Brandeis, 14 January 1918.

130

Weizmann sent to Brandeis two days later was that it was composed as much, if not more, by Sykes as by Weizmann. Weizmann acknowledges in his second letter that he was in close touch with Sykes about the information he was passing on to Brandeis. It was, in fact, more of a letter seeking President Wilson's support for British policy than an appeal to Brandeis for American Zionist support for Weizmann's Zionist policy. It points at one of the least illuminated chapters of Zionist history and of Weizmann's personal relations with Sykes. Everything in these letters, and in the War Office's intelligence "Notes" about them, suggests the conclusion that there had been a secret "deal" between Sykes and Weizmann the precise nature of which can only be deduced from these documents. Perhaps, it was more of a personal understanding, never spelled out as such, by which Sykes would assist in keeping the French out of Palestine and Weizmann would ensure Jewish and American support for the British solution as against that of the French. For Weizmann's letter to Brandeis is written in a language so uncharacteristic of Weizmann and so typical of Sykes that there can be little doubt about it having been inspired by Sykes and written by Weizmann as if copied from a brief. But as he was inclined to do at times – Leon Simon notes this in his diaries of the Zionist Commission – Weizmann was more royalist than the king on such occasions. He was so enthusiastic an advocate that he was inclined to overdo it. Sykes evidently thought so; when Weizmann showed him the first letter to Brandeis, he suggested some modification in the description of French policy. In the end, Sykes drafted a corrective memorandum himself and asked Weizmann to enclose it with the second letter to Brandeis. But the upshot was the acceptance by Weizmann of the general outline of policy sketched by Sykes in return for the sustained support for the Zionist Commission by Sykes.[56]

There was, however, a second aspect of Weizmann's letters to Brandeis that required clarification for it revealed a peculiarity in Weizmann's outlook which affected also other and later Zionist leaders and which was to become a source of recurring difficulty. Weizmann suffered – as did Nahum Goldmann and Eban after him – from a political defect which can best be described as "selective hearing": they heard only what they wanted to hear. This was especially evident when Weizmann's accounts of his meetings with soldiers and statesmen are checked against other versions. There were two striking instances of

[56] Weizmann to Brandeis, 16 January 1918.

131

this in his second letter. In the first he tells Brandeis of his meeting with Lord Reading, Britain's Ambassador to Washington; Weizmann recalls that they had quite a satisfactory conversation. In fact, an independent account of the meeting, and particularly Reading's own version, indicate the extreme caution on Reading's part; he made no commitment beyond the official word of the British Government. The second example is rather more indicative of this diplomatic defect. Weizmann talked about the way some people were rather timid about expressing their support for the Zionists; not so "our friend Sir Mark Sykes". He had once more shown, he tells Brandeis, "his deep understanding of the position and he has informed both the Egyptian authorities and the Arab Chiefs including the King of Hedjaz, that Zionism is a *fait accompli* and that the publicly declared policy of Great Britain is a Jewish Palestine".

As a result of Sykes' "bold and honest telegrams", Weizmann continues the tale, "the king of Hedjaz telegraphed back to say 'the Jews are welcome in any Arab country' ".[57]

The actual text of Sykes' telegram to Sir Reginald Wingate, the High Commissioner in Cairo, hardly warranted such conclusions. It was not despatched until 13 February and its relevant portions advised Wingate that the "object of the Commission is to carry out, subject to General Allenby's authority, any steps required to give effect to the Government's declaration in favour of the establishment in Palestine of a National Home for the Jewish People". The Commission would also have as its important function the establishment of good relations with the Arabs and other non-Jewish communities and to act as a link between the military authorities and the Jewish population and interests in Palestine. However, the operative paragraph in Sykes' telegram to Wingate stressed that "it is most important that everything should be done to obtain authority for the Commission in the eyes of the Jewish world and at the same time to allay Arab suspicions as regards the true aims of Zionism".

Weizmann was impressed by the support which the Zionist Commission was to get; the limitation which Sykes had specified seemed unimportant to him; yet it was to become the central theme of the diplomacy of the Zionist Commission. It was also to launch Weizmann on a course of diplomatic opportunism from which there was no turning back. Thus the Brandeis letter, so clearly concocted together

[57] Weizmann to Brandeis, 16 January 1918.

with Sykes, became a watershed in Zionist diplomacy and established a relationship between Sykes and Weizmann which evidently went much further in its private understanding than any of Weizmann's colleagues knew and which only Sieff, at times, suspected.

The working of this understanding began to show itself clearly during the first meetings of the Zionist Commission on the way to Palestine; the first in Rome on 11 March 1918, the second on board the *Canberra* in Taranto on 14 March, and the third in Cairo, with the High Commissioner present, on 22 March 1918. The Sykes-Weizmann theme was advanced on a step-by-step basis and it was done initially by the representative of the Foreign Office and liaison officer of the Commission, Major the Hon. W. Ormsby-Gore. The first meeting at the Excelsior Hotel in Rome, was in low key and largely routine. Weizmann was depressed. He did not like Rome which, with its elegant crowds and officers in smart uniforms, did not look like a city at war. "Rome oppresses me," he wrote to his wife. "It is too alien, and everything here speaks to me of the triumph of others over us."

It was at the second meeting, on 14 March on board ship at Taranto, that Ormsby-Gore elaborated on the instructions which he had received from the Foreign Office for the Zionist Commission. Weizmann was in the chair and Sieff acted as secretary. But it was Ormsby-Gore who was doing the explaining. Weizmann confined himself to saying that they would be meeting Sir Reginald Wingate and other prominent Egyptian officials when they arrived in Cairo. They would be asked searching questions and it was therefore necessary to be quite clear and definite "as to what our intentions were for the future".

It was again Ormsby-Gore, not Weizmann, who elaborated on these intentions of the Commission. In the first place, they had to appreciate that there was a total misconception among the Arabs about the aims and aspirations of the Zionists, "and this misconception was shared by English officials". Wingate had only the vaguest idea as to the practical meaning of Zionism. It must be borne in mind, Ormsby-Gore stressed, that the main misconception in the East with regard to the Jewish National Home was "that it was thought to mean the establishment of some form of Jewish Government in Palestine at the end of the War". It was important therefore that they should all give the same answer as to the political objective of the Commission, "how far it is limited" and what they meant by a National Home.

On 22 March 1918, the Zionist Commission, accompanied by

Ormsby-Gore, called on Sir Reginald Wingate at the Residency in Cairo. Wingate expressed his thorough sympathy for the Zionist ideal and said that he had been greatly impressed by the Jewish colonies in Palestine which he had seen during a recent visit. He understood that the idealistic motive behind the Jewish return put the colonisation of Palestine on an entirely different plane from the attempts at the Jewish colonisation of America and elsewhere. Weizmann responded and agreed with the distinction Wingate had made and said it was this difference which would guarantee the ultimate success of Zionism.

Wingate then proceeded to dwell on some of the difficulties that confronted the Commission and embarked on a speech that rather startled Weizmann. The Arabs, he said, were nervous and suspicious of the Zionists. They feared that they intended to establish a Jewish Government in Palestine after the war and that the Jews planned to expropriate and expel those Arabs who were in Palestine. The situation was further complicated, Wingate continued, by the fact that various agencies were at work to dissuade the Arabs from trusting the British and to revert instead to Turkish rule. The best plan for the Zionist Commission, Wingate counselled them, was to ignore the Arab politicians and to concentrate instead on the really influential Arabs, particularly the religious leaders. The British had found this the best method of conciliating native opinion in the Sudan.

It was then that Weizmann made the declaration that he was to repeat over and over again; it was without a doubt his part of the deal he had struck with Sykes and for which Ormsby-Gore had prepared the ground at the first two meetings of the Commission. He was most anxious to meet with and to satisfy the real Arab representatives, Weizmann said "There was no intention whatsoever of expropriating or displacing the Arabs now in Palestine, nor of setting up a Jewish Government in Palestine in the near future." The Jews, Weizmann assured Wingate, "wanted Palestine to be a British Colony or Protectorate. He thought that the opinion of the Jews, thrown into the scale in favour of British Palestine (which for us meant a Jewish Palestine) would have some weight at the Peace Conference." In Weizmann's judgement, "there was a complete accord between British and Jewish interests in regard to Palestine, and it should be realised that those who worked against the Jews were working also against Great Britain".[58] Wingate was evidently and pleasantly surprised by this

[58] Minutes of 3rd Session of the Zionist Commission, 22 March 1918.

patriotic definition of Zionism, and naturally welcomed it after the fears he had harboured that the Zionist Commission intended to set up a Jewish administration. All this was so moderate, so reasonable and confirmed the advance views Sykes had transmitted to him from London. But two members of the Commission were more than somewhat disturbed by this unexpected intervention by Weizmann. He had not said anything about it either to Sieff or to Leon Simon. Sieff kept his own counsel but could not rid himself of the earlier unease at Sykes' intervention. Leon Simon noted in his diary that Weizmann's stress on the identity of British and Jewish interests was a little too much for his liking. He also noted that Weizmann had told some of them privately that he had persuaded Wingate to send a telegram to the Foreign Office in which he said that he considered that any anti-Zionist was also anti-British.

This had been a noteworthy occasion. For Weizmann had gone out on to the political slope prepared by Sykes and it proved to be slippery and fateful. It was followed three days later, on 25 March 1918, by the fourth meeting of the Commission. Its main feature was a report on the meeting between Weizmann and Clayton. The account of the encounter was given, however, not by Weizmann but once more by Ormsby-Gore. This was all the more curious in view of what transpired in the course of this discussion. Here were two men of outstanding intellect and original thinkers who had devoted themselves with unique single-mindedness to the problem of Palestine, the defeat of the Turks, and the role of the Arabs in the Ottoman succession. Yet – to judge from Ormsby-Gore's account to the Zionist Commission – Weizmann and Clayton talked like a couple of parrots repeating the pre-arranged words of a brief, almost totally identical with the conversation earlier with the High Commissioner. In the words of Ormsby-Gore, Weizmann's exposé of Zionist policy made an excellent impression on Clayton. Amongst the points brought out was the misconception in the mind of General Clayton that the Zionist programme included the immediate establishment of a Jewish state after the war. Clayton had also expressed the opinion that there was no Arab problem west of the Jordan. Support for the Arabs was purely a war measure, whilst he saw the development of Jewish colonisation as a permanent asset to Palestine.

Weizmann came away from these meetings with Wingate and Clayton pleased and impressed with his reception and by the promise of British support; but he also had some nagging doubts. Something was not quite right. "I cannot explain it," he wrote to his wife from Cairo, "but nevertheless I begin to sense something." It seemed to him that Zionist propaganda in Europe had been understood in Cairo "in an entirely perverted sense". All the British authorities in Egypt were convinced that the Jews intended "to found a Jewish state immediately, and that the first step would be the confiscation of all land and the enslavement of the Arabs". Weizmann tells his wife how when he explained to Wingate and Clayton that the Zionists wanted a British Protectorate, and why, they were wide-eyed with surprise "and both assured me that if this is the case there will certainly be no difficulties with the Arabs. Imagine, my darling, my surprise at encountering such a trend of thought and such ignorance."[59]

Moreover, as happens so often, Weizmann "the great charmer" was himself charmed by Allenby, Clayton, Wingate. "Despite the lack of understanding by the British authorities," he confided to his wife, the British were honest and frank and "so long as we are in contact with the British it is very pleasant and agreeable". But the local Jews in Egypt were quite a different proposition. They were not openly opposed to Zionism; they were just not interested. They constituted High Finance in Alexandria and in Egypt generally. "They are all related to each other . . . millionaires and getting richer daily." He did not want to condemn them "but looking at this crowd one gets the shivers and feels uncanny". There was much noise, flag-waving and emptiness. Fortunately, Weizmann concluded, the Palestinian Jews were different; they had "a new sense of realities, and a sincere and honest approach".[60] He reached this conclusion before he had met the Jews in Palestine. That shock was yet to come – for both parties. But he did meet in Cairo with a representative group of Syrian Arab nationalists who had been chosen by the British authorities for this purpose. The three Arabs, Shukair Pasha, Dr Nimr and Solieman Bey Nassif, expressed their pleasure at meeting Weizmann and the Commission and the hope that they would be able to work together in harmony and understanding. Weizmann replied in the same manner but added "for the sake of perfect frankness" that one of the main tasks of the Commission, with which they had been charged by Mr Balfour, was to prevent land speculation in Palestine. On the broader political aspect, Weizmann said that it was their earnest wish to live on friendly terms with the Arabs.

[59] Weizmann to Vera Weizmann, 24 March 1918.
[60] Ibid.

136

They were making no claim for a Jewish monopoly of the administration of Palestine, which he understood was the principal Arab fear. In particular, Weizmann said, he wanted to remove the misconception which seemed to be very common among Arab leaders that the Zionists wished to establish a Jewish state in Palestine immediately after the war. What Zionists desired to see as a result of the war was "a British Palestine which would act fairly and justly toward all groups which inhabit the country".

The Arab leaders expressed their complete satisfaction with the Weizmann Declaration. Soleiman Bey Nassif added that there was room in Palestine for another million inhabitants without affecting the position of those already there. Ormsby-Gore cautioned the group, however, that the British Government had so far made no claim for a British Palestine, but Weizmann replied that "no matter what the British Government thought of the establishment of a British Palestine, the Zionists wished to see such a solution as a result of the War".[61]

Thus Weizmann had made his initial contribution to Clayton's Grand Design – without seemingly being aware of it. The inter-play of these three remarkable political manipulators – Clayton, Sykes and Weizmann – was proceeding as if moving according to a master-plan. In one sense they did: the three men had all had very similar ideas and objectives and they understood each other and each other's special interest without having to spell it out. But there was one major snag. The three, together with Allenby, were not an orchestrated quartet following a single score. They were four soloists, each convinced of the primacy of his chosen instrument. They all believed in much the same means in getting what they wanted, but they had different priorities and separate objectives.

Weizmann's awakening to the realities of Palestine came fairly swiftly in the wake of his initiation into the Cairo world of British Middle Eastern thinking which, in its way, was closer to his own than Sykes' had been with his more insistent pressure to recognise the requirements of the war situation and of Great Britain's French ally. However, a very different mood awaited him in Palestine from the comparatively small group of dedicated Zionist settlers. There was an air of almost religious awe in the anticipation of the coming of Weizmann and the Commission.

[61] Appendix 10 to the Minutes of the Zionist Commission on the Conference held on 27 March 1918, at Shepheard's Hotel in Cairo.

On 13 March 1918, Mordechai Ben-Hillel Hacohen, one of the most representative and genuine Zionist pioneers (and later Arthur Ruppin's father-in-law) noted in his diary that he had received a cable from London that the Zionist Commission was on its way. He added his own thoughts:

> Before the Commission left, Weizmann had an audience with the King on March 7th which is very important. This is very important for the King only grants an audience in cases of great political significance. The King was evidently aware of the great value of the mission on which Dr Weizmann was embarking and gave his royal blessing to the Balfour Declaration. Thus the King's audience commits the British Government to do its best to realise the Balfour Declaration and ensure that it should not become an empty promise. Blessed be the Almighty![62]

Sykes probably knew what he was doing when he tried to persuade Weizmann to call off the visit to the Palace because the Arabs might misconstrue it. The Palestinian Zionists certainly did read more into it than was warranted; but so did Weizmann.[63] The Palestinian Jews met with Weizmann and the Commission only a month later when Hacohen and his friends sat for three evenings with Weizmann while he gave a full account of the events leading up to the Balfour Declaration and of their future intentions. The emphasis, however, was very different from that of Weizmann's earlier meetings with the British authorities and the Arab representatives. This was understandable but the gap between the two presentations was such that Weizmann was, in the event, never able to close it.

It led him further and irrevocably down that slope of Zionist opportunism on to which Sykes had inveigled him. In fairness to Sykes it has to be stressed, however, that Weizmann had not been a reluctant partner in this risky political collusion. On the contrary, Weizmann went into it willingly and with his eyes open. And in fairness to Weizmann, his reasons for doing so were based on his consummate understanding of the requirements of realistic politics, especially when such realism had to be practised on behalf of a cause such as Zionism that had no visible or real position of power from which to operate. Despite everything that he had said or written about the world standing of the

[62] Hacohen Diary, MSS.
[63] See *Trial and Error*, p. 268, for Weizmann's version.

138

Zionist movement, Weizmann knew that its actual power in the world of 1918 bore little resemblance to its image in the minds of the world's statesmen, especially the British, the Americans and the Arabs. He accepted Sykes' "deal" because he understood that he had really no choice, or so he believed. He was probably right; but he also gave hostages to the future which have bedevilled Zionist relations with the Arab world from the moment when it became evident, towards the end of 1918, that Weizmann would not be able to close the credibility gap which he and Sykes had opened.

How wide Weizmann's gap was from the outset became evident from his briefing of Hacohen and his friends at the three meetings which Hacohen recorded in his diary. Weizmann told of the lone fight he had conducted with only a few helpers in England while the whole upper strata of Anglo-Jewry had been opposed to him, and how they had managed to convince the British Government of the significance of Zionism largely because of the help given them by the Editor of the *Manchester Guardian*, C. P. Scott. Sokolow had meanwhile worked on the French authorities and obtained their support for the Balfour Declaration.

Weizmann was firm in his belief that the British Government is not going to deceive the Jews. They had made their decision with open eyes and in all honesty and had made "Palestine for the Jews" as their slogan. This is now a political reality, for the English understood that the Power which first undertook to give Palestine to the Jews would gain great political advantages. Jewish sympathy is no small matter in politics.[64]

Weizmann continued his report on the following day and again dwelt on his confident trust in the British Government: their intentions were sincere "and we are on the eve of our redemption". And on the third evening of Weizmann's report – "we are not tired of listening to him" – Hacohen noted in his diary of 9 April 1918, "Dr Weizmann read to us from the letters he had brought for General Allenby from Balfour and Lloyd George. We were thus convinced that the British Government treats the Declaration with great earnestness; they may deceive whomsoever they decide to deceive, but they will not deceive us and will help us to achieve the Declaration." And Hacohen concluded his detailed account of the three long meetings with the self-assuring assertion that

64 Hacohen Diaries.

"one can trust Weizmann; it seems that we have found in him the right man".

Yet Weizmann did not really believe himself all that he had conveyed to these trusting Palestinian Jews. His doubts about the British were stirred from the outset along with his irrepressible admiration for them. He wanted the British to be as he described them to Hacohen and his group, but in his heart he saw the British as he talked about them in the privacy of the evenings with Israel Sieff, or as he described them in his letters to his wife, Vera, which, incidentally, with his other letters, were scrutinised, copied and assessed by the British Intelligence Directorate in Cairo before they were forwarded to their destination. Weizmann had dined with Allenby at GHQ before meeting Hacohen and had afterwards written about it to his wife, his first letter to her from Palestine. Writing from Tel Aviv on 6 April 1918, he gives her his impressions of Allenby: a great man, intelligent, well-read, direct and interesting "but I cannot say that he understands or appreciates the moral and political value of the movement". Weizmann says he had explained to Allenby the Zionist programme in great detail "and, of course, such explanations are always brought up sharp before the Arab question which seems much more acute here than in Egypt".[65]

Weizmann was clearly troubled by the unexpected intrusion of the Arab question on a scale which he had not anticipated. He shared his thoughts, after the dinner with Allenby, with Israel Sieff and also with Leon Simon. They had just received, through Clayton, the memorandum drawn up by the Arab representatives after their recent meeting with them; Weizmann and his colleagues wondered what they should make of it. Its tone and contents were starkly different from what the same men had said when they met together; they were wholly irreconcilable with the Zionist standpoint. "I am trying to maintain in my own mind an attitude of sweet reasonableness towards the Arabs," Leon Simon noted in his diary for 7 April 1918. "But when one . . . reads these absurd demands and . . . sees the Arabs who walk about here, it is not easy to prevent oneself from slipping into a pronounced anti-Arab frame of mind. I simply cannot see the elements of an *entente*." He wanted the Commission, however, to resort to persuasion or "bribes" to win the support of the Arab leaders rather than bring in the heavy hand of the British Government "which might not be too readily at our disposal though certainly General Clayton and others here seem

[65] Weizmann to Vera Weizmann, 6 April 1918.

140

to be quite disillusioned about the Arabs". Simon, a senior British civil servant, was an acute and accurate observer with a strong liberal bent, and recognised the Arab problem that loomed ahead. So did Weizmann but he did not seem fully to comprehend its implications.[66]

Weizmann had come very much under the influence of Aaron Aaronsohn, a man in his early thirties, a charmer, brilliant, as Sieff described him, an agronomist of note who had grown up in Palestine, spoke Arabic and was convinced that there existed a fundamental hostility between Jew and Arab. This was, Simon noted at the first meeting of the Commission, "a thoroughly bad beginning". Moreover, Aronson was not liked and rather suspected by the Palestinian Jews. But Weizmann had clearly taken to him and listened to his expert views on the local Arabs.

Much to Sieff's and Simon's regret, Weizmann accepted Aronson's counsel on the problem which the Arabs presented within two weeks of the Commission's arrival in Palestine. In a way, one cannot blame Weizmann, for the shock of confrontation with the Arab reality in Palestine was considerable. It bore so little relation to the picture presented by Mark Sykes. Weizmann had kept to his part of the bargain. He had said all the things Sykes had wanted him to say to the British and to the Arabs, and he had left unsaid all that Sykes wanted kept quiet. He had met the Arab leaders and reassured them; he had explained the limited demands of the Zionists to the British in Cairo and in Palestine, but it had been of no avail.

On 16 April 1918 Weizmann wrote to Ormsby-Gore about his impression that the political atmosphere in Palestine was not as favourable as they had wished and, indeed, had a right to expect. They were particularly concerned, Weizmann noted, by "the attitude of Arabs and Syrians and the way that attitude is regarded by the military authorities". They had found among the Arabs a state of mind which "seems to us to make useful negotiations impossible at the present moment". Weizmann had clearly been put out by the contrast of his meetings with Arab representatives in Cairo and the Palestinians – particularly as Clayton and other British officials had indicated before-hand that the Palestinians were a negligible factor and need not be considered seriously. This was a view that was naturally welcome to the Zionist Commission and one to which they clung with great tenacity

[66] See Leon Simon Diary for 7 April 1918, MS, p. 25.

even in the face of mounting contrary evidence. The Zionist Commission set the tone in this matter for Zionist and Israeli policies that were to dominate Zionist thinking and actions for half a century.

Weizmann's letter to Ormsby-Gore was a watershed in Zionist relations with the Arabs. Weizmann, who had shown such pertinacity and diplomatic staying power during his negotiations in London for the Balfour Declaration, found himself baffled by the Palestine Arabs within a matter of two weeks. Leon Simon, who was most anxious to work together with the Arabs, felt much the same. So did Clayton and Ormsby-Gore. There was thus every reason for Weizmann's sense of utter frustration. But why did he give up so easily? For once one gets the impression from Weizmann's presentation of his case that he was motivated by other than political considerations. He tells Ormsby-Gore with evident shocked surprise that the Arab speakers at an Arab entertainment at which the Military Governor, Sir Ronald Storrs, had been present, had used "the kind of language which would be appropriate if an attempt were on foot to enslave and ruin the Arabs of Palestine. They had called on the Arab nation to awake from its torpor . . . Palestine was and must remain a purely Arab country . . . and the speeches concluded with the expressions 'Vive la Nation Arabe, Vive la Palestine Arabe'."

Weizmann contrasts the spirit at the Arab meeting with that of the mood of the Jews who met the same day in Jerusalem to welcome the Zionist Commission. Here was the Arab crusade against the imaginary Zionist enemy with its expression of intransigent and aggressive nationalism; and there were the Jews, absolutely loyal to Great Britain and sincere in their desire for peace and friendship with the Arabs. Weizmann believed that this was an accurate description of the state of affairs, just as his successors during the next 50 years have all along believed sincerely in their unrequited desire for peace. Neither Weizmann nor his successors seemed to be able to comprehend that there could be Arab unease, suspicion and fear of the Zionist incursion and that it might require more than some reassuring words and Weizmann's charm to persuade them that they had nothing to fear from the Zionists. The thought did occur to Weizmann. But after two weeks in Palestine he was convinced – and he may have been right – that "the Arabs, so far as we can tell, are not in a frame of mind in which any explanations offered by us would receive serious attention". But Weizmann may likewise have been mistaken. Instead of probing deeper into the Arab

142

opposition and resentment, he handed them over to the British. It was their duty now to explain the exact meaning and scope of the Balfour Declaration to the Arabs . . . "it should be made perfectly clear to them that this declaration represents the considered policy of HM Government, and that it is their duty to confirm it".[67]

Two days later, on 18 April 1918, Weizmann wrote to his wife. He was clearly under the shattering impact of his first visit to Jerusalem: ". . . it was sad – very sad. We have so little here – hardly a single Jewish institution to delight the eye or the heart. But instead, how much alien power, threatening and austere – Minarets and bells, cupolas reaching up to the skies; a constant reminder that Jerusalem is not a Jewish town." His heart cried out, he confided to his wife, when he saw the Jewish quarter, ". . . . filth and infection, indescribable poverty, century-old ignorance and fanaticism. To organise Jerusalem, to bring some order into this hell, will take a long time and need much strength, courage and patience." He was unhappy, he told her, with the conduct of the local English authorities. "They are really too narrow-minded and appear to be quite unable to orientate themselves. They make terrible mistakes, but the worst of it is that they always give preference to the Arab. We meet it at every step. They suspect the Jews – quite undeservedly because the whole Jewish population met them with understandable delight."[68]

But a week later we meet an entirely different Weizmann and we get a taste of the chameleon-like character of his diplomacy, his oblique approach to his target, and his ingrained opportunistic understanding that in politics there was no other way of being successful. This is not the place to make a judgement but rather to look more closely at the evidence. On 18 April he had written about his concern at the British lack of understanding to Ormsby-Gore and to his wife, and he had underlined the total Arab opposition which led him to conclude that no deal was possible with the Palestinian Arabs. On 25 April Weizmann wrote a report to Brandeis in Washington. But this time the emphasis was very different.

In this letter it was the Jews, who with their critical mind "did not fully appreciate the weight of the words expressed by the British Government" in the Balfour Declaration. The Palestinian Jews understood its real value only after they had come into contact with the

[67] Weizmann to Ormsby-Gore, 16 April 1918.
[68] Weizmann to Vera Weizmann, 18 April 1918.

143

British army of occupation. "Every British soldier who entered a Jewish colony considered it his pleasant duty to tell the people that they have come here to wrest the country from the Turks and to hand it over to the Jews." The non-Jewish community in Palestine, especially the Arabs, Weizmann tells Brandeis, interpreted the Declaration as an intention of the British Government to set up a Jewish Government at the end of the war and to deprive the Arabs of their land and expel them from Palestine. They looked upon the Zionist Commission "as the advance guard of Jewish capitalists and expropriators and, naturally, received us with the greatest suspicion".

Weizmann then proceeds to make a statement which was in stark contradiction to what he had written to Ormsby-Gore and his wife a week earlier. "It is true that the British officials have tried their best before our arrival to allay the suspicions of the Arabs both in Egypt and in Palestine." It had not been easy for them, Weizmann adds, because they themselves had had so little information about the Zionist movement and its intentions. Moreover, the Military Authorities were naturally primarily concerned with winning the war and to maintain just and fair conditions in the country. "It is very difficult indeed to find any objections against such a view," and they had therefore to keep a restraining grip on their own more ambitious Zionist schemes.

All the same, "the Chief Political Officer here, General Clayton, and his Assistant, Colonel Deedes, know the movement, sympathise with it and consider a Jewish Palestine as the only worthy aim and possible ultimative solution. But they have not received perfectly clear instructions from Home and have been left a good deal alone, so that even they suffer from a certain vagueness which exists in their mind."[69]

On 30 April 1918, Weizmann sent a copy of this letter to his wife and told her of the speech he had made in Jerusalem on 27 April. It was an impressive performance in which Weizmann had again, in the most solemn way possible, reassured the Arab notables present that the Zionists had come to live in peace with the Arabs of Palestine, that they wanted political power vested in one of "the civilised democratic Powers" to be chosen by the League of Nations and that "once more we see rising a strong and regenerated Arab political organism which will revive the glorious traditions of Arab science and literature so much akin to our own." The Arabs had replied to his speech very amiably, he

[69] Weizmann to Brandeis, 28 April 1918.

told his wife, "but it is difficult to trust them . . . I consider that it is unnecessary to bother any more with the Arabs for the present; we have done what was asked of us, we have explained our point of view sincerely and publicly; let them take it or leave it. If the Government would only take it upon itself to settle this thing with the Arabs that would be all that is necessary."

With every passing day. Weizmann appeared to drift – privately – ever further from any possible accommodation with the Arabs. On 19 May he saw Allenby again and he wrote to his wife about the meeting on the following day, 20 May 1918. Weizmann was evidently most dissatisfied with the manner in which the British were treating the Arabs and his uninhibited comments to his wife provide an insight into his thinking which is not evident from his more formal and public speeches and reports. "The fact is," he tells her, "that the local English administration is de facto preserving the Turkish machine, with the difference that previously you had Turks at the head of the big departments and now you have Englishmen drawn from the Egyptian, Sudan and Indian administrations. The Turk ruled with sword and fire and kept the Arab trash in submission. The Jews were then the predominant element. Now what happens?" Weizmann then describes how the British mete out the same justice to Jews and Arabs, but the Arabs do not understand such conduct without the use of the whip. They therefore consider the British to be weak.

As a result the Arabs had become "arrogant towards the Jews and haughty; Arabs and Syrians – our enemies – crowd all the offices and de facto rule the land". Weizmann thought he had made this clear to Allenby "a just and honest man, and an exceedingly sympathetic person . . . Allenby himself is for us and with us, but he is a soldier and the Commander-in-Chief." Therefore the political initiative, Weizmann tells his wife, must come from London and, on Allenby's initiative, Weizmann proposed to write a personal letter to Balfour. "If London would indicate that the Declaration is to be made into a living thing in Palestine now, and that this is necessary, then Allenby will gladly help us in everything. He is doing much already but he is tied by the rigid framework of military requirements."[70]

There was a basic inconsistency in Weizmann's reading of the Palestine situation which was to become a built-in factor in future Zionist policy, a degree of utilitarian opportunism which at times

[70] Weizmann to Vera Weizmann, 20 May 1918.

appeared to exceed the politically permissible or necessary. Thus, in his letter to Ormsby-Gore, Weizmann blames the British administration in Palestine for the disappointments of the Zionist Commission; in his letter to Brandeis, the blame is put rather on the failure of the Jews to appreciate what the British are doing, and in the letters to his wife, responsibility is placed largely on the Government in Whitehall. What does emerge from these letters, and from the discussions Weizmann was having about his next planned move, was that he was not at all certain where British power in Palestine really resided: was it with Allenby and the local military; was it with Clayton and the Arab Bureau; was it with Sykes and the Foreign Office in London; or was it with Lloyd George, Balfour and the War Cabinet? Who had the decisive say? It was not an easy question to answer – then or now.

Weizmann had broached the question when he met with Allenby on 19 May, and Allenby had advised him that the only effective lever that Weizmann could pull was Balfour and that he should put his views before him. This, Weizmann decided, he would do. He began to draft a letter and to discuss it with Ormsby-Gore and, at a further meeting on 25 May with Allenby; he also showed the draft to Hillel Hacohen in order to obtain the reaction of the Palestinian Jews, and he finally despatched it to London on 30 May 1918. It was a majestic, almost arrogant document; it was also a fateful one – more so than any of those concerned with its despatch could realise.

What Weizmann evidently failed to observe in composing the letter was the impact that it would make on the reader – and especially on Balfour, Sykes and the Foreign Office. He should have been fore-warned after he had shown the draft to Hillel Hacohen on 23 May 1918. For what had struck Hacohen most strongly was that after marshalling such forceful argumentation, Weizmann should have asked for so little in practical terms: to be permitted to establish a Hebrew University, to be allowed to acquire the land adjacent to the Wailing Wall and the so-called waste-land in Southern Palestine. Such requests sounded strange to Hacohen. They should hardly have been necessary after the proclamation of the Balfour Declaration. They had built the Haifa Technion under the Turkish regime and there had been neither fuss nor difficulty; if they had had the necessary money they could have bought the Moghrabi Quarter adjoining the Wailing Wall! Such matters surely did not need the Declaration. And as for the derelict lands in the South, this was simply a matter for the British Government. Hacohen

146

was quite sure that it would not make this land available to the Zionist Commission.[71]

It was not the only undertone of doubt about the Zionist Commission during the days when Weizmann drafted his "Note" – for such it was – to Balfour. In a curious way, Weizmann and the Zionist Commission were living in a political vacuum of their own making. They were clearly oblivious of the lively exchanges that were going on about their work – and about British policy in the Middle East – between London, Cairo and Jerusalem. They saw Allenby, Clayton and the situation generally that confronted them entirely through Weizmann's eyes – and these were focused on a very narrow front. He had become preoccupied with the British estimation of the Arab factor in general and with the Arabs of Palestine in particular, and he proceeded to communicate his own views on this sensitive topic to Balfour. He did so, moreover, in his own most imperious manner and he did so – for once – with utter disregard for the circumstances and the timing of his intervention. Both were disastrous for this purpose. For even as he wrote his letter, Weizmann was preparing for his journey to meet Prince Faisal and to seek an understanding with him. He mentions this intention in his letter to Balfour and he assures the Foreign Secretary that he meant everything he said in his speech in Jerusalem about friendship and collaboration with the Arabs. But it must have sounded oddly unconvincing and possibly insincere to Balfour in the light of so much else that was in Weizmann's letter and which was so revealing about Weizmann's and the Zionist attitude towards the Arabs.

In the course of his long letter, Weizmann developed the Zionist concept of the Arab, not in one rounded assessment but in a series of asides and interjections. They revealed an odd outlook as he prepared for his journey to Aqaba to meet the Emir Faisal as the leading Arab representative. He noted at the outset that the Commission arrived in Palestine at an unfortunate moment when, as a result of the Allied setbacks in France, the campaign in Palestine had come to a premature halt and the great hopes raised by the capture of Jerusalem had not been realised. "The Arabs, who are superficially clever and quick-witted, worship one thing and one thing only – power and success," and this had led to much whispering in the bazaars and the cafes that the Turks were still all-powerful and merely biding their time before they came back. "This has naturally made the British authorities rather nervous and,

[71] Hacohen Diary for 23 May 1918.

147

knowing as they do, the treacherous nature of the Arab," they had to be on guard so that the Arabs should have no cause for grievance or complaint. "In other words, the Arabs have to be 'nursed' lest they should stab the Army in the back. The Arab, quick as he is to gauge such a situation, tries to make the most of it."

Weizmann then recounts the now familiar story of the misrepresentation of the Balfour Declaration and how German agents assisted in turning anti-Zionist agitation into anti-British propaganda. He also reminds Balfour how many non-Jews "always envisage only one type of Jew – the financier, the exploiter, the stockbroker". Zionism – "what a tragic irony" – was identified with the capitalistic exploitation of poor and ignorant natives who had to be protected by honest officials against the all-powerful Jew. They did not see that the rich Jews were the opponents of Zionism. "You will therefore realise, dear Mr Balfour that we found ourselves in an atmosphere very unfavourable to our work. The British viewed us with suspicion, the Arabs with hostility and the rich Jews of Egypt with indifference." There were exceptions: Allenby, Clayton, Deedes and Ormsby-Gore gave great help to the Jewish cause. "I should be guilty of lack of taste if I were to express my appreciation of the personalities mentioned in trivial words of gratitude. I am convinced that history will register their deeds as among the finest achievements of British statesmanship." Weizmann was not a man who believed in half measures when it came to turning a phrase.

Weizmann's indictment continued unrelentingly: but the British were only the heads of the administration; down below the old Turkish machine had been left intact: "the offices are filled with Arab and Syrian employees who have certainly not changed their mentality with the change of master. The fairer the English regime tried to be the more arrogant became the Arab." He knew the language and the ways of the country, he "is a *roué* and therefore has great advantage over the fair and clean-minded English official who is not conversant with the subtleties and subterfuges of the Oriental mind. So the English are run by the Arabs."

It was a situation "fraught with grave danger" for the Jews, Weizmann explained to Balfour. The rule of "brutal numbers operates against us" since there were five times as many Arabs in Palestine as Jews. "The result is that the Jews are practically handed over to the Arabs. This system does not take into account the fact that there is a fundamental qualitative difference between Jew and Arab. The Turk being himself

148

of inferior culture saw in the Jew a superior to himself and to the Arab, and so, by virtue of his intelligence and his achievements, the Jew held a position in the country perhaps out of proportion to his numerical strength." Weizmann made no bones of the conclusion which he drew from the British practice: "The present system tends, on the contrary, to level down the Jew politically to the status of a native, and in many cases the English Administrator follows the convenient rule of looking on the Jews as so many natives."

Weizmann warns Balfour not to overestimate Arab support in the war in terms of long-term assets: ". . . the somewhat shifty and doubtful sympathies of the Arabs represent in the long run infinitely less than the conscious and considered policy of the majority of the Jewish people which sees in a British Palestine the realisation of its hopes and aspirations." The policy pursued by the British at present would tend towards the creation of an Arab and not a Jewish Palestine which would be controlled by the "dishonest, uneducated, greedy and unpatriotic" Palestine Arab effendi class. Balfour is assured by Weizmann that Allenby, Clayton, Deedes and – more surprisingly – also Storrs share the views expressed in this letter and the proposals which Weizmann makes in some detail for development of the country without waiting for the Peace Conference. And this leads him to what he calls the heart of the Arab problem.

For the crux of Zionist relations with the Palestinian Arabs, he wrote, was economic, not political. "From the political point of view the centre of gravity is not Palestine, but the Hedjaz, really the triangle formed by Mecca, Damascus and Baghdad." In fact, he was about to set out to meet the son of the King of Hedjaz and to impress on him that if he wanted to build a strong Arab kingdom only the Jews would be able to help him with the necessary money and organising power. The Jews would be his neighbours and present no threat to him; indeed, they would be the natural intermediaries between the Hedjaz and Great Britain, and they would protect the Hedjaz from becoming a French dependency. "With him I hope to be able to establish a real political entente. But with the Arabs of Palestine – in whom so far as I can gather the Sharif is little interested – only proper economic relations are necessary."

Weizmann concluded by reminding Balfour magisterially of the importance of what the Zionist Commission does for the Peace Conference: the voice of the representative Jews of Palestine, "I venture to

149

think, will not pass unheard". But this would depend on it becoming evident to the Jewish people "that during the period of British occupation the foundation of the National Home had been laid in Palestine".[72]

This extraordinary letter became in its way a basic state paper on the Zionist attitude towards the Arab problem; it dominated Zionist thinking and policy for the next half-century with all the complexities and contradictions of Weizmann's initial formulation. But to complete the picture we have to consider a second, follow-up, letter which Weizmann sent to Balfour on 17 July 1918, seven weeks later, before he had had any reply to his first letter. Weizmann had no way of knowing whether Balfour had received his first letter. The July letter is especially significant for it expresses not only Weizmann's views but also Clayton's opinions. So much so, that we have to assume that Clayton was a party to his second letter and that there had been much consultation and collaboration before it was actually despatched. For one thing, the horizon of this second letter is much broader than that of 30 May.

Weizmann reiterated again that Faisal would need the kind of support that he could get only from the Zionists. "I am informed by the most intimate counsellors of Faisal that he desires nothing better, and that his desire will take tangible form as soon as the military position allows. The so-called Arab question in Palestine would therefore assume only a purely local character and, in fact, is not considered as a desirous factor by all those who know the local situation fully."

Again echoing Clayton's Grand Design – possibly belatedly – Weizmann turned to the Sykes-Picot Agreement and argued Clayton's case for him. "The continuance of the agreement and all it stands for," he told Balfour, "is a constant source of embarrassment here." But the significance of this intervention by Weizmann was less in what he said than in why he said it and in the way he said it. For he proceeded from this firm suggestion to Balfour to reconsider British policy with regard to an agreement reached with France (and Weizmann here appears to be backtracking on his earlier arrangement with Mark Sykes) to raise the whole question of British authority in Palestine.

After apologising to Balfour for remarks which strictly speaking were not his concern, Weizmann pointed out that:

General Clayton, who has very deep knowledge of all questions

[72] Weizmann to Balfour, 30 May 1918.

concerning Egypt and Palestine, and with whom we have had the great privilege of working all the time, is certainly hampered in his work by the fact that both the Residency and the Arab Bureau are also exercising direct influence on the policy. It is only human that these centres should sometimes work quite unconsciously against each other. . . . The interests involved are so serious and so far-reaching for the welfare of the British Empire in the East that a definite co-ordination and direction of policy seems imperative.

It is evident that Weizmann would not have written this without Clayton's knowledge and consent. Moreover, he would hardly have known of this situation or of its far-reaching implications to which he refers unless he had been thoroughly briefed by Clayton – or put up by Clayton to write in this strain to Balfour. There is every sign that once in Palestine Weizmann not only lost the nervousness with which he was afflicted during his interviews with ministers and others in London,[73] but acquired a sense of confidence and authority which he had previously lacked; it was this new bearing that many British and most of Weizmann's colleagues in Palestine mistook for arrogance. That, at least, was how Sieff saw the sudden evolution of the new Weizmann. There was another contributing factor to this change – Clayton. Weizmann began to find Clayton's concept of the Grand Design, even in its state of eclipse, far more sympathetic than Sykes' pattern of Arab-Armenian-Jew. He also found Clayton a more sympathetic personality than Sykes. Above all, Weizmann trusted Clayton as he trusted few men and as he did not trust Sykes.

But there were those who doubted the wisdom of Weizmann's new orientation in the footsteps of Clayton. Four days before Weizmann despatched his letter to Balfour – on 26 May 1918 – Hacohen had another long conversation with Weizmann in which Weizmann told him of his plans for the meeting with Faisal which had been scheduled for the following week, and Hacohen reported the discussion in his diary entry for 26 May. Weizmann had said that "the aim of the journey was to negotiate with the son of the King of the Arabs about the future of the Arab question in relation to the Jews and to the frontiers of Palestine. Professor Weizmann intends to impress on the son of the Sharif the extensive benefits which the Arab Kingdom will derive from its Jewish neighbour. . . ." Weizmann evidently repeated the formula

[73] Sieff to J.K.

151

he had used in his letter to Balfour on 30 May. But Hacohen was evidently not impressed. He wondered whether Weizmann would succeed in influencing Faisal and even more whether such influence was really necessary? The Arab national movement, Hacohen noted in his diary, does not depend on the Sharif, and it does not really matter very much whether the Sharif agrees with it or not:

> One knows that Arab consent is of no value and that an Arab promise is not a promise. We have to hope that the execution of our policy does not have to depend on Arab consent and that the achievement of our aims will not be dependent on Arab agreement. But if Dr Weizmann considers his journey to be necessary, and if the British Government also thinks that this trip is not a waste of time, then there must be something behind it. God speed.[74]

In fact, we know from Clayton himself (see above, pp. 57-8) that it had been his idea that Weizmann should meet with Faisal, and the whole encounter had been largely engineered by Clayton. If Weizmann had been aware of this – as he must have been – he gave no sign of this in his private or public utterances at the time. Indeed, he successfully convinced himself and others of a far-reaching significance of the meeting with Faisal which was hardly warranted by the circumstances but which was precisely what Clayton had hoped to achieve. Thus within days of denouncing Arab untrustworthiness in his letter to Balfour he concluded a compact with the Emir Faisal which Weizmann for one was evidently prepared to accept not only at its face value but with the added premium of his own interpretation and of Clayton's flattering praise which Weizmann inhaled with evident delight. Clayton had written to him from GHQ to tell him that he had informed Balfour of the outcome of Weizmann's visit to Faisal and that Balfour had telegraphed to say "that the satisfactory result attained meets with the warm approval of His Majesty's Government". Clayton adds that he was further directed "to convey to you Mr Balfour's appreciation of the skill and the tact displayed by you in arriving at a mutual understanding with the Sharif Faisal".[75]

Weizmann had also received a letter from Colonel Deedes in which Deedes told him that he was sure that Weizmann's mission would be a success. "Your personality disarms suspicion and carries conviction,

[74] Hacohen Diary for 28 May 1918.
[75] Clayton to Weizmann, 17 June 1918.

and your tactful persuasiveness makes friends. Your cause has undoubtedly progressed here while you yourself have won many friends and admirers. Please count me among the latter."[76]

Weizmann sent copies of these two letters to his wife when he wrote to her on 17 June after his return from the Faisal meeting. From these letters by Clayton and Deedes, "the most important members of the political administration here", he tells her, "you will see what they have to say about me, and the position I have succeeded in winning for myself here". He also sent her a copy of his letter to Balfour and adds that his views in the letter "are shared by General Clayton and even by Allenby himself; they have wired home in almost the same sense". Weizmann then tells his wife about Faisal. "He is the first real Arab nationalist I have met. He is a leader! Fairly intellectual, very honest and very picturesque! He is not interested in Palestine, but he wants Damascus and the whole of Northern Syria. He spoke with great bitterness of the French desire to meddle in Syria and expects much from collaboration with Egypt. He looks upon the Palestinian Arabs with great contempt and hardly regards them as Arabs at all."[77]

Weizmann had reported to the Zionist Commission the day before and here again he appeared to maximise Faisal's expressions of goodwill and minimise his evident reservations. He appeared also to be offering Faisal much more than he was getting in return. He went to great lengths to reassure Faisal that "we did not wish to establish a Jewish State in Palestine but were willing to live under the suzerainty of Britain". Jews and Arabs had parallel interests, Weizmann impressed on Faisal, "thus it was possible for the Jews, who were a great force, to help him to realise his great ambitions. We could help him towards Damascus and the territory to the north," which should not be encroached upon by the French.

Weizmann had clearly approved of this political and propaganda gambit and on his way back from the meeting with Faisal he stopped in Cairo to report on his meeting to the High Commissioner and to Colonel Symes at the Arab Bureau. In his later accounts to the Zionist Commission of these meetings, Weizmann said that he had discussed with the High Commissioner, Sir Reginald Wingate, how the Zionists proposed to deal with the Arab question.

"Assuming Arab interests lay outside Palestine," Weizmann said,

[76] Deedes to Weizmann, 30 May 1918.
[77] Weizmann to Vera Weizmann, 17 June 1918.

then it was in the interests of the Jews and the British to establish an Arab belt extending from Mecca to Damascus and on to Aleppo. It would be impossible, however, for the Arab authorities in Mecca to rule effectively over so diverse an area. It would therefore be necessary for the British to step in. But such a move would meet with Arab suspicion and factions would form, intrigue and unrest would follow and extend also to Egypt. "The only people who could organise a real Arab belt would be the Jews for they had the money and the necessary people to do it. The Jews were an oriental people and the Arabs would take things from them which they would fear to take from a Great Power. . . ."

Weizmann concluded this part of his report by adding that the High Commissioner had welcomed this concept as important and statesman-like and one that could be tackled. Before returning to Jerusalem, Weizmann had also stopped over at General Headquarters to report to Allenby and to Clayton; he also talked with T. E. Lawrence, who shared his views on the Arab question, according to Weizmann's report. As a result it was decided to call a conference to define the political orientation of the Zionist Commission in relation to the Arab movement. Those taking part would be Clayton, Deedes, Lawrence, Ormsby-Gore and Weizmann. The conference did not materialise; nor did the Zionist political orientation in relation to the Arab movement.[78]

It was hardly surprising. For the encounter with Faisal hardly warranted the massive superstructure which Weizmann had built on it. Faisal had committed himself and his father to nothing other than willingness to accept Zionist financial and political aid in the attainment of the Hashemite goal. The Arab national movement – and certainly the Palestinians – were in no way involved. One further matter cannot have escaped the notice of a man like Clayton, and surely not that of Balfour who had just received a batch of letters from Cairo and Jerusalem, all tabulating Weizmann's discontent with the progress made by the Zionist Commission in its relations with the British authorities and the Palestine Arabs. It must have seemed somewhat incongruous that Weizmann, seemingly unable to obtain minimal and routine Zionist objectives in Palestine, and having difficulties with the local Jews and with his colleagues in London, saw the Jews as the only effective force to be able to organise the Arab world from Mecca to Baghdad and Damascus. It is a little surprising that Weizmann himself should not have been

[78] Minutes of the Zionist Commission's 17th Meeting, 16 June 1918.

154

aware of the inherent incongruity of some aspects of his Arab policy.

Barely three weeks after making his confident reports, which at times bordered on the self-satisfied, Weizmann was writing again to his wife but in a very different strain. He had observed the arrival of the American Red Cross mission – "camouflaged missionaries supporting the Arab cause" – and he was evidently feeling the strain of reality overtaking the hopes and dreams which he had enjoyed in the wake of the meeting with Faisal. "I remain alone – a voice crying in the wilderness! . . . There is great danger. I am no alarmist. I have got used to things in Palestine but I am deeply indignant at the procrastination practised by Sokolow and the others in London. They have given us no help, absolutely none and have left us to be devoured by the local administration which is completely ignorant of Zionism."

Forgotten are the plans to save the Arab world; the problem was nearer home:

Instructions must be sent to Allenby that they must open the road for us here; that the Jewish population of Palestine cannot be classed, in the eyes of the Administration, on the same level as the Arabs . . . otherwise it will be bad for us . . . I request this statement: otherwise I shall have to come out into the open about all this, and that would be a catastrophe . . . Get these instructions sent – instructions in principle that the way should be opened for us in Palestine, and that we should be treated as the founders of the Jewish National Home, and the future masters of Palestine. Allenby is only waiting for that. He has read my letter to Balfour and agrees with it. Men and Money![79]

It was high summer in Palestine, little more than three months since their arrival, and Weizmann was becoming not only impatient but at times almost desperate. By now he was fully aware of the abject poverty, the absence of talent and worldly understanding, and of the deep psychological gulf that divided him from the great majority of the Jews in Palestine. There were a few exceptions, very few, but not enough to make any impact on the generally dismal picture. He talked at night to Sieff of his near despair, of the need to revise their entire Zionist perspective and their hopes for a Jewish State because of the poor human material they had found in Palestine, and the failure of their colleagues in London and New York to back them up.[80]

[79] Weizmann to Vera Weizmann, 11 July 1918.
[80] Sieff to J.K.

Weizmann began to dislike going to Jerusalem. "There is nothing more humiliating than our Jerusalem! All anybody there does is to profane and to besmirch our holy things," he confided to his wife. "So much falseness, so much bigotry, lies and avarice, it is difficult to imagine." He is shocked by what Jewry pays in charitable contributions to the inhabitants – "£3,000 a month, the equivalent to the budget of a good European university". And for what? The worst of it, he tells Mrs Weizmann, was that the whole system was accepted and – most dreadful of all–"sanctified by religious tradition". To fight this system it was their duty to overhaul everything, "and to use the situation created here by the fact that full power is now in our hands to make clear the full horror of the situation to the whole Jewish world".[81]

But it was not only the religious grip of Jerusalem that drove him to seek compromise, to make deals, to obtain what was possible. The more he saw of his own army and the more he assessed the resources at his disposal, the more bitter he became with his own colleagues. In one of his last letters to his wife before returning home, he pours out his heart. It was as much a warning for those who would follow him as an accusation to those who were supposed to march with him.

"If we fail in our work," he wrote to Vera Weizmann on 19 September 1918, "it will not be because of the English or the Arabs, but solely because of our own Jews! The other day one very notorious Englishman, no doubt of great ability, told me: 'you know, Dr Weizmann, there *is* no Zionist Movement, but there is your devilish ingenuity!' God! What a lot of truth in the negative part of that remark." Weizmann then tells his wife that he had not seen much of the Jews in Palestine ". . . it is our people and we have no other. Small consolation perhaps but what can one do? We must resign ourselves to that as we resign ourselves to the physical features of Palestine – its rocks and sands and barren Judean hills. A hard road – with Arabs and other obstacles to be overcome. And how many precious lives it will cost . . . But I am inwardly fortified by the struggle because there is something in the air here which inspires you to great deeds." And for the first time in his letters, while speaking of his weariness, he talks of Sieff: "Israel is an angel; without him it would have been difficult to bear many things."

It was a situation of which the local Jewish and Zionist notables seemed singularly unaware. They lived in a small but very real world of their own and they found it difficult to understand Weizmann and his

[81] Weizmann to Vera Weizmann, 1 July 1918.

colleagues who represented another world. There were a number of memorable men of character among the Palestine Jews, without whose pioneering and dreaming there would have been nothing for Weizmann to build upon. But they were not aware of their own shortcomings and some later historians and Zionist politicians have compounded this error.

Weizmann saw all too clearly the unrepresentative character of local Zionist notables. They had admirably liberal sentiments with regard to their relations with the Palestinian Arabs; they drafted a model constitution to which no Arab leader could have objected. What they did not seem to understand – and to this extent they failed to understand the singularly exclusive character of the Arab nationalist movement – was that with such a constitution there would have been no independent Jewish existence in Palestine, neither cultural nor political, neither a National Home nor a State. Weizmann understood this, and he also understood the need for an understanding with the Arabs, an understanding between equals. He conceived this possible with Faisal, since both the Hashemites and the Zionists were equally client movements of the British. This was also Clayton's design. But such an arrangement presupposed that the British were willing to play their part. But they were not. Confronted by Clemenceau and the French, they abandoned Faisal; confronted by international pressure, the Palestinian nationalists and the Arab independence movements, they abandoned the Zionists, as under further pressures they abandoned later also the French and the Hashemites and, in the end, in the face of American pressure and Jewish resistance, their own position in Palestine.

Without British support Weizmann's Arab policy – whatever it might have been – would have been doomed to failure. Weizmann seemed to sense this, almost from his arrival in Palestine, when he abandoned all efforts to reach a realistic political accommodation – and not a propaganda arrangement – with the Arabs. There is nowhere any evidence that Weizmann or the Zionist Commission, or the Zionist Organisation intended any serious follow-up to the Faisal talks and tentative agreements. They were considered – by Weizmann and by Faisal – as convenient window-dressing. Both men were realists. They understood that there was no other basis on which they could collaborate. Weizmann did not trust the Arabs. Faisal did not trust the Jews. Neither trusted the British. There was much pretence by all concerned but they no longer harboured illusions. It would have been a healthy and promising climate for the development of Clayton's Grand Design. But the design was finished and done with. It had been effectively killed.

The Zionist Commission had arrived in the spring with high hopes and a grand idea and now as Weizmann returned home in late summer, the hope had evaporated as the war had been won and the grand idea, the Grand Design, was abandoned. But this was due to no accident and to no error on the part of the British or the Zionists. It was due to the old political maxim that the strongest political power is the man who knows his own mind. That was Weizmann's power that won him the Balfour Declaration; that was Lloyd George's power that won him the war; that was Clemenceau's power that won him the peace, and that was Haj Amin's power that enabled him to frustrate the Great Design and put in its place what he conceived to be the Greater Design of Arab unity.

Thus, when Weizmann departed for home in September 1918 his mission and that of the Zionist Commission was in effect at an end. They had come to lay the foundation of a Jewish state and they left with Palestine set to become an Arab state – and it probably would have become one but for the Hitler holocaust and the second world war. It would have become an Arab state because as the alternative to Weizmann's evolutionary vision of a Jewish State, the Palestinian Arabs had set their own vision of a Greater Arabia, and after the war it was the Arabs that could offer the British the kind of inducement that enabled the Zionists to obtain the Balfour Declaration.

The Weizmann Commission had failed just as Clayton's Grand Design had failed. Both did so for a variety of reasons, as we have seen. But at the root of both failures was the inability of the British and the Zionists to evaluate the Palestinian Arab factor. It was not only those who devalued the Palestinian Arabs who were mistaken, foremost among them Clayton and Weizmann, but also those who over-valued them among the Zionists and the British. They foundered on the Palestine Arab rock, which we now have to consider.

# THREE

# The Arab Reaction

The Arab historian and diarist, Aref el-Aref, had noted that before the Great War there had been no hostility shown to the Jews by the Muslim Arab notables and publications in Palestine. He recalled that the Christian Arab paper in Jaffa, *Falastin*, did print critical articles on the Jews, presenting their penetration of Palestine as a form of invasion with the ultimate aim of gaining complete domination over the Palestinian Arabs. But with the Young Turk revolution in 1908 Arabs and Jews joined forces to make the most of the greater political freedom. They sought to bring about reforms that would lead to an autonomous Syrian state which would provide Jews and Arabs alike with a better life. And when Jews bought land from the Arab effendis, they devoted some of their profits to contributions for the national cause of the Arabs.

The Arab leaders – or at least the more enlightened among them – had heard of the Zionist dream "to conquer Palestine", but they were not unduly concerned by it. They knew that no Turkish Government would agree to the Zionist political aims. The usual Arab response at the time, in the years before the outbreak of the Great War in 1914, was that governments come and go but people remain in their lands. They were confident that the Jews would never present a real danger because of the unshakeable common front of Arabs and Turks on the one issue that no Arab-Muslim country must be deprived of its Islamic character.

When the Arab leaders realised that the Young Turk Government had no intention of implementing its promises of Arab autonomy, they decided to explore the possibility of enlisting Jewish-Zionist support for the Arab national ambitions. They delegated Negib Shukeir, one of the Arab nationalist leaders in Constantinople and Editor of the

159

Arab periodical *Fyam*, to sound out certain Zionist leaders about possible collaboration against the Turks. Also drawn into these discussions were three prominent Arab members of the Turkish Assembly, Said el-Husaini and Nashashibi from Jerusalem, and Faris el-Khouri from Beirut. The Zionists, according to the contemporary Arab reports, urged that Southern Syria (Palestine) should be excluded from the proposed aim of a Greater Arabian state and should be made available for Jewish colonisation. In return, the Jews would help to win Arab autonomy from the Turks, principally by providing financial support.

The Arab delegation reported at the end of these talks that nothing had come from them since they had become convinced that the Zionists were concealing their real aim of domination over the Palestinian Arabs with their offers of help and co-operation.

The Arabs also came to suspect the Jewish delegates were in fact acting as Turkish agents, enlisted by the Turks and their German associates, for the purpose of damaging the Arab national movement. They knew that the origin of political Zionism was German, that its leaders were German Jews and its headquarters was in Berlin. They now considered, for the first time, that the possibility of a Turkish-Jewish front against the Arabs could not be ruled out.[1]

It was natural, therefore, under these changing conditions, with the evident anti-Arab emphasis of the Turkish rulers, that the Arab nationalists should have been receptive to the overtures from Egypt and the British. Egyptian Arab papers openly called on the Syrians to re-orientate the national outlook in line with British thinking, and "Kitchener's secretary visited Damascus, Jaffa and Haifa where he made contact with local notables and made available substantial British subventions for Arab national requirements." He argued, as did the Egyptian Arab press, "that with British support for the Arab cause it would be possible for the Syrian-Palestinian Arabs to stand up to the Zionist danger". For the national Arab leadership there was, however, still one further problem: the British were not the only power offering support. There was also a strong pro-French lobby, encouraged and richly financed by Neguib Azouri supported by a group of very rich Lebanese Christian Arabs in Paris. What decided the Muslim Arabs of Syria, Iraq and the Peninsula to opt for the British was primarily the

[1] For the sources quoted in this chapter, readers are referred to the Introduction, p. xiii, and to the Note on Sources, p. 345.

fear of the French because of their emphasis on the Christian connection. The British were thought to be free of this taint. Either way, the Arab leadership had become convinced, with much heartsearching and many second thoughts, on the outbreak of the war, that their best chance of national liberation was to be found in alliance with the power opposed to Turkey and Germany. On the eve of the war the Central Committees of the nationalist societies moved out of Constantinople, first to Beirut and then to Damascus, where they established the secret headquarters of the Arab Party of Independence, the common front of the former "el-Fattat" and "el-Ahd".

The Arab revolt was no more started by the uprising against the Turks by Sharif Husain than Zionism was launched by the Balfour Declaration and Dr Weizmann. However, both these events – the Revolt and the Declaration – because they were linked with British war aims, turned the Arab and the Jewish national movements from largely platonic protest movements, into immediate and major political factors. But it had been touch-and-go in April and May 1915 whether the Sharifians would opt for the Turks or for the British. In the end, the Syrian Arab nationalists presented Faisal with the so-called Damascus Protocol which set out the basic terms of independence and of collaboration with the British. It became the basis of the Sharifian negotiations that led to the Arab revolt even though the British did not accept all its initial stipulations, especially the territorial demand for a single Arab state from the Indian Ocean to the Red Sea and the Mediterranean. But in the opinion of Aref el-Aref, it was neither Syrian nationalist pressure nor British gold that finally decided Sharif Husain to revolt against the Turks; it was el-Aref's well-documented opinion that the Sharif raised the banner of revolt only when the Turks had rejected his demand to be recognised as the hereditary ruler of the Hejaz and his request that the Arabs sentenced to death should be reprieved by Djemal Pasha. Djemal had them hanged in April 1916 and had refused to give any undertaking to Husain. Instead, he organised an expedition to Mecca to appoint a new ruler in Husain's place. The Sharifians had no choice left but to seize the opportunity and the leadership of the revolt.

While the military success of the revolt – and indeed of the Allied cause to which Husain had attached himself – was still finely poised in the balance at the beginning of 1918, the Arab leaders were exposed to a series of political shocks, followed by a supreme temptation. They

161

managed to overcome them all, but it was not easy and they left their mark. First came the revelation by the Bolsheviks that the British had made a secret deal concerning the Arab lands promised to Sharif Husain with the French and the Russians. Then came the proclamation of the Balfour Declaration and its implication on the future government of Palestine, and, to cap it all, early in 1918, an emissary from the Turkish Governor in Damascus, Djemal Pasha, arrived at Faisal's headquarters near Aqaba. Faisal and Djemal had been in touch through intermediaries throughout the period of the revolt, but this time Djemal made his most ambitious and tempting move.

He described for Faisal's benefit the situation between Faisal and his allies as Turkish and German intelligence had presented it. The British were planning the artificial partition of Palestine and Syria; Palestine would become a Jewish State and Syria a French Protectorate. Faisal would be a puppet of the British, the French and the Jews. Djemal therefore appealed to Faisal to halt the Arab war against the Turks and to form a common front of the Arab Army with the Turkish 4th Army which was under Djemal's command. Together they would liberate Southern Palestine which Allenby had occupied and install Faisal as King of the Greater Syrian Arab Kingdom. Djemal's emissaries also informed Faisal that the Turkish Government was in the process of negotiating a separate peace with the French and British Governments. Once that was settled the Turks and the Arabs would combine to impose a truly Islamic settlement on the area. Faisal replied that he would have to submit these proposals to his father in Mecca and the King would make the final decision. Meanwhile, Faisal agreed that his communications with Djemal should be kept secret from the British "and from Lawrence".

Faisal kept his secret lines to the Turks open until September 1918, throughout the period of his talks – and those of his father – with the British and with Weizmann. According to Aref el-Aref, by the summer of 1918 – when Faisal and Weizmann met – the Turks were prepared to accept all the Arab demands, and there were moments when Faisal and his advisers were inclined to listen. For he was puzzled and worried by the British. They had not been frank. They had not told him about the Balfour Declaration, nor about the agreement with the French. He had first heard about Balfour's Declaration to Lord Rothschild promising the Jews a National Home in Palestine from Palestinian Arab leaders who, in turn, had heard about it from their Palestinian Jewish

162

friends. Faisal, when told about it, at his headquarters camp at Wadi Waheida asked for Lawrence and Joyce, the British liaison officers with his troops. They told him that the reports of the British undertaking to the Zionists were malicious rumours spread by the Turks in Syria in order to undermine Arab faith in Britain. But Faisal was alarmed and informed his father who demanded an explanation from the British. As a result, Commander Hogarth was sent to Jeddah to explain the position to Sharif Husain with regard to Palestine and to the secret treaty with the French.

The account of Hogarth's message which Aref el-Aref related is somewhat different in emphasis from that which Hogarth gave.[2] In long talks with the King "Hogarth persuaded him that the reports of the Balfour Declaration were greatly exaggerated by the Turks and the Jews; the actual position, as explained by Hogarth, was that England had need of Jewish support in the United States in order to win the war as Russia under the Bolshevik Government had deserted her allies and had become pro-German. Under these conditions the support of America was essential for the entente and for that purpose it was necessary to win over the American Jews to help organise American military power against the Germans and their allies." Aref el-Aref noted that the Sharif was satisfied with this explanation and published a statement in the Mecca newspaper *el-Kibla* at the end of February 1918 in which he assured Christians and Jews that the Arabs of the Hejaz, "now liberated from the Turkish yoke" would respect the Holy Places of all religions, and, with his eye firmly fixed on the Balfour Declaration, added one further significant assurance and made an even more significant omission. "We are willing," the statement in *el-Kibla* continued, "to receive into our fold those Jews who intend to settle in the Arab countries as our brethren, and we shall give them all protection for their loyal citizenship under Arab rule." Husain meant this. He accepted the British assurances about the Balfour Declaration at the face value put on it by the British with whom he had discussed it. What he understood by the Balfour Declaration he made clear in his statement in *el-Kibla*. It was not questioned by the British or by the Zionists.

Even so, Arab concern was not stilled. In Cairo a group of Arab nationalist leaders, including such representative figures as Rafiq el-Azm, Dr Shahbandar and Hassan Himada, addressed a memorandum to the High Commissioner, Sir Reginald Wingate. In this they expressed

[2] See Hogarth's report in the *Arab Bulletin No. 77*, p. 37 above.

their confusion as to the status of British undertakings given to the Arabs, the French and the Jews. Wingate sent the enquiry to London but no formal reply was received. Instead, the Arab records note, British officials of the Arab Bureau in Cairo clarified the situation in response to the memorandum. It was pointed out in this reply that the British Government had given four undertakings concerning the future of the Arab territories. The first to King Husain in 1915; the second to the French in 1916; the third to Lord Rothschild in 1917; and the final one to the Arab Nationalist Committee in Cairo in 1918. "The only valid declaration was the last one made to the Committee in Cairo which stipulated Arab national independence in a Greater Arab state with King Husain as the titular sovereign of all Arabs."

This British declaration by the Arab Bureau, recorded by Aref el-Aref, was communicated to Faisal and by Faisal to his father. It provided a decisive element in the Arab rejection of the peace initiative from the Turks who were poised for another offensive and vastly superior in numbers to the British. They had offered Faisal most of the demands he had made to the British and some more. Faisal had not rejected the Turkish offer out of hand because he had become deeply distrustful of the British and greatly offended by what he considered their double-dealing. But this categorical clarification by the Arab Bureau about the Balfour Declaration was precisely what Faisal and his father had wanted to hear. They were reassured and not unduly bothered by its singular anonymity. It had all the credence in their eyes as if King George in person had underwritten the promise.

Their joy was shortlived. Late in March 1918 the Zionist Commission arrived in Cairo. "It was received with much pomp and ceremony by the British authorities, by the High Commissioner, by General Allenby and his staff, by the British-led Egyptian Government and by Egypt's rich Jews." The Arab Committee was greatly disturbed and enquired at the Arab Bureau what this portended. "The British officials could hardly conceal their confusion. All they would say was to advise the Arab leaders to establish contact with the Zionist Commission. But privately, some members of the Arab National Committee were told that the arrival of the Commission had come as a complete surprise to the Arab Bureau and to the British Army Commanders. It was the outcome of the civilian political intrigue in London against the military commanders in Cairo and at the front." The Arab Bureau agreed to send one of its senior members, Colonel Cornwallis, with Rafiq el-Azm

164

as representative of the Arab National Committee, to report to Sharif Husain in Jeddah on the arrival of the Commission.

Rafiq el-Azm has recalled the anger with which Husain received them, and, in his presence, summoned Colonel Arnold Wilson, the British officer with the Sharif, and Cornwallis and ordered them to inform Cairo that he demanded the immediate recall of the Zionist Commission to London. Wilson asked for a twenty-four-hour delay so that he could consult with his superiors in Cairo and the Sharif agreed. Faisal had also been summoned by the Sharif and was similarly alarmed. He asked Lawrence to proceed immediately to Cairo and report on the situation there. Lawrence suggested that it might be advisable to go first to Jerusalem and consult with Storrs before going on to Cairo, and he did that.

From Jerusalem, Lawrence sent a messenger to Faisal with a report on his consultation in Jerusalem. "Storrs is most worried about the Zionist Commission," he reported to Faisal, "and believes that its arrival in Palestine will have grave consequences for the Arab cause and that its ultimate significance may be no less than the occupation of Jerusalem by the British in December 1917." But something happened to Lawrence's messenger on his way back to Faisal. He turned up only after much delay and after Wilson had received a reassuring answer from Cairo. This enabled Wilson to tell the Sharif that the most authoritative explanation of the Zionist Commission's function was "that it was little more than a relief mission to the stricken Jews in Palestine, rather along lines of similar missions by the Red Cross. Its principal purpose was to assist the Jewish religious congregations in the Holy City and to look after the schools for Jewish children etc." Wilson told the Sharif more about the collaboration that had already been established between the Zionist Commission and the Arab National Committee in Cairo and about their respective roles in Palestine. It was all very reassuring and Husain relaxed somewhat though he retained his basic suspicion of the British. He told Rafiq el-Azm to go back to Cairo and to keep his eyes and ears open and to report everything that he saw and heard – and suspected.

In the meantime Lawrence had been investigating the objectives of the Zionist Commission on his own account. He had questioned Arabs and Jews in Cairo and talked at length with officials of the Arab Bureau and he was introduced by them to members of the Commission. "When Lawrence returned to Faisal's headquarters, he reported that

165

there was something unexplained about the objectives of the Zionist Commission and that they had come evidently with some secret mission on behalf of the British Government. The nature of the mission was known only to a few senior officers in Allenby's headquarters, Lawrence added, and the Arabs would be well advised to remain on guard against any possible danger from this quarter." In particular, Lawrence counselled Faisal to expedite the Arab Army's advance on Damascus so as to ensure that they occupied Syria before any political settlements were made that could jeopardise the Arab interest.

Rafiq el-Azm, for his part, had returned to Cairo and had also met with Dr Weizmann and the Zionist Commission. He reported his impressions to the Sharif. From his preliminary talks with the Zionists, he advised Husain, he was convinced that Dr Weizmann and the Commission were going to Palestine with a plan to turn the country into a Jewish state and that behind this plan were the British who were determined to disrupt any possible formation of a United Syrian state. For the first time, the Syrian nationalists in Cairo were beginning to wonder about the role of the Sharifians, Husain and Faisal. They had been suspiciously lacking in energy in resisting the onward march of the Zionist Commission. "Could it be that they had made a deal with the British at the expense of the Palestinian Arabs?" The accusation against Faisal was all but openly made and relations between the Arab National Committee and Faisal were virtually broken off.

Faisal reacted angrily and accused the Syrian nationalists of having remained passive in the actual struggle against the Turks; they were pursuing a separatist policy inimical to the concept of a Greater Arabia and he charged them with being under the influence of the Christian-Arabs who preferred the French orientation to the British alliance. But Faisal could not still the whirlwind of rumour that had arisen. He was not interested in the fate of the Palestinians, it was said; he was quoted as having described them as "a rabble of mixed origin, corrupted by foreigners, not pure Arab stock but, like the Egyptians, outside the mainstream of the Arab nation". Faisal and his father were said to be totally dependent on the British and they were ready to sacrifice the Arab cause to preserve their British connection. The first victim of this alliance was to be the Palestine Arab.

Thus as the Zionist Commission left Cairo for Palestine the breach between the Syrian Arab nationalists in Cairo and the Sharifian leaders in Mecca and at the front was acute. Suddenly, Palestine had become an issue not only between Zionism and Arabism but also the test case between the Sharifian-dominated Arab nationalists and those who identified Arab unity with the formation of a Greater Syria comprising Syria, Palestine, the Lebanon and Transjordan. Overnight, as the Zionist Commission travelled to Palestine, the main issue which confronted it had been transformed and the Arab, British and Zionist alignments were forced into new groupings. The British were clearly aware that something was not going according to their plan. When the Syrian Arab nationalists asked for permission to go to Palestine at the same time as the Zionists they were told that they had better wait for the arrival of Sir Mark Sykes who was said to be due to arrive shortly.

The ceremonial and enthusiastic welcome of the Zionist Commission in Jerusalem was watched with apprehension by the Arab notables. The Mayor of Jerusalem, Mussa Kazem Pasha, and the Mufti of Jerusalem, Kamel el-Husaini, were in constant touch with the British Military Governor, Colonel Storrs. Storrs' advice to them, as they reported it to their colleagues, was that it was the official policy of the Government in London to promote Jewish interests in Palestine. But Storrs gave them to understand that the military commanders in the country did not like this policy. He advised them to form a united front of all Palestinian Arabs, Muslim and Christian, and formulate their own views of the policy of the London Government. If they did that, Storrs promised that he would ensure that their views and wishes were conveyed adequately to the British Government.

Accordingly, at a conference between the Arab notables and Storrs soon after the arrival of the Commission in Jerusalem:

Mussa Kazem reminded Storrs that the British had come as the liberators of the Arabs from Turkish rule and he hoped the British would now stand by their promise. Palestine was an Arab country, a part of Greater Syria. At this point Storrs interrupted him and asked Mussa Kazem whether the Palestine Arabs supported the Sharifians and Faisal's army. Kazem replied cautiously that this was an internal matter that concerned only the Arabs.

What Storrs did not know then was that at the actual time of this conference Mussa Kazem had already been informed by the Arab National Committee in Cairo of their doubts about Faisal, and the

Palestinian notables were careful therefore not to identify themselves with the Sharifians. In conclusion, Storrs appealed to Mussa Kazem and the Mufti that they should meet the Zionist Commission so that they could judge for themselves. "At first, Mussa Kazem hedged. He had to consult with the notables of Jaffa, Gaza and Hebron before he could take a decision. But then he learned that the Mufti, Kemal el-Husaini, had secretly met with Dr Weizmann at the offices of the Sha'ria in Jerusalem and that Storrs had been the intermediary in arranging this private talk." It was indicative of the mood of the times that neither Weizmann nor Storrs record this meeting in their memoirs, nor the typical aftermath that followed it. When the Arab notables, including Mussa Kazem, heard of the meeting they accused the Mufti, not of meeting Weizmann behind their backs, but charged him with having accepted a gift from the Zionist leader. The Mufti's explanation that Weizmann, by way of customary courtesy, had presented him with a copy of the Koran was treated with derision and there is no way of knowing whether this was so or whether the gift had been of a more material kind. Aref el-Aref records drily that, whatever the truth, it was noted after the meeting that the Mufti was far less radical in his attitude to the Jews and sought to persuade the Arab notables to co-operate with Dr Weizmann and the Zionist Commission.

The initiative for such collaboration came again from Storrs. He invited the Arab notables and the Zionist Commission for a joint meeting to which he had also asked the heads of the Muslim, Christian and Jewish religious groups.[3] Weizmann made one of his familiar conciliatory speeches, stressing their common Semitic origins, denying any intent of Zionist domination and promising much prosperity for all citizens. Storrs translated Weizmann's speech into Arabic and the Mufti replied, thanking Weizmann for dissipating Arab fears and welcoming the prospect of Arab-Jewish collaboration.

"Some of the Arab notables present were visibly irritated by the Mufti's speech but they said nothing. For the Palestinians felt their own weakness and they were at this time – in May 1918 – also under considerable pressure from the representatives and agents of Prince Faisal," who had told them, as Aref el-Aref recalls, without actually spelling out the precise meaning, that if the Palestinians wanted to benefit from the

[3] Though the invitation for the meeting came from Storrs, it would be fair to assume that the initiative for it – and the authority – came from Clayton and that he made use of Storrs' special relationship with the Arabs for this purpose.

successes of the Arab Army, they had to show their support in a suitable fashion: Faisal wanted Palestinian volunteers for his Arab Army.

The Arab notables decided that it would be wise to accede to Faisal's thinly disguised ultimatum. They appointed Amin el-Husaini, a young Arab officer who had recently deserted from the Turkish Army, and who as the younger brother of the Mufti was well connected, to lead a Palestinian unit which he was to recruit and organise. Altogether, he assembled, according to his own report, some two thousand Palestinian Arab volunteers who joined Faisal's forces in Transjordan. The officers among these men were to become a significant link between the Sharifians and the Palestinians and a powerful instrument in Amin el-Husaini's advancement.

After his first brief reconnoitring of the state and purpose of Faisal's Army, Amin el-Husaini came back to Jerusalem and asked Mussa Kazem to summon a meeting of notables. "Mussa Kazem agreed and it did not pass unnoticed by his colleagues that he appeared to be greatly influenced by the dynamic and incisive personality of the young Amin. Together they became the first – and, some were inclined to say later, also the last – effective leadership of the Palestinian Arabs. Mussa Kazem had held the position of Governor of the Yemen under the Turks, a status equal to that of the Sharif of Mecca. He had many important connections among the Arabs and the Turks and he was Mayor of Jerusalem until he was dismissed by Storrs in 1920. But he continued the close collaboration with Amin, his cousin, when Amin became the Mufti of Jerusalem and Mussa assumed the office of President of the Arab Higher Executive which he held until his death in 1934.

Amin reported to the notables assembled by Mussa Kazem that he doubted whether Faisal's Army would really liberate the Arab lands. He suspected the Sharifians – he called them Hashemites – of much too deep involvement with British imperialist politics. He was certain, he said, that Faisal and his father "had become the servile instruments of the British and that there was no prospect of winning Arab objectives in Syria and Palestine if the Arab cause remained tied to and controlled by the British".

The young Amin now made his first direct intrusion into Palestinian Arab politics in relation to the British and the Zionists. He counselled the assembled notables "to provide or play off the French against the British, and the Jews against both. He warned them that unless the Palestinian Arabs succeeded in driving a wedge between the British and the Jews, the British will establish their rule over the Arab world with the help of international Jewry which will be centred in Palestine. He concluded by telling Mussa Kazem to make the most of his Jewish contacts in Jerusalem to obtain information about the links between the British and the Zionists."

Amin had also something to say about the relations between the British and Faisal which he had discovered while at Faisal's head-quarters. These made it necessary for the Palestinian Arabs to treat the British Military Administration in Palestine and the Arab Bureau in Cairo with great reserve and caution. He reported that he had met and talked with Colonel Lawrence "who, it was obvious" was Faisal's superior. "Lawrence had bitterly complained to Amin about the Palestinian contingent in Faisal's Army. They were unreliable, un-disciplined and they incited the Hejazi Arabs to disobey their com-manders. He would never appoint a Palestinian to any political position, Faisal had told Amin. When Amin questioned Lawrence about 'the British Rothschild letter', Lawrence had replied that 'it was a good thing to tame the Levantines with a Jewish rod'." Amin concluded that if the alliance between Faisal and the British succeeded the Arabs in Syria and Palestine would have to submit to the rule of the Bedou-Hashemites. Moreover, Faisal himself had completely absorbed the British view of the situation. "He saw the principal danger to the Arab future as coming from the French. He had told Amin that in view of this threat he was prepared to collaborate even with the devil himself, let alone with the Jews, to resist the French invasion of Arabia."

Whether this had been Amin's intention or not, he roused great anxiety among the Palestinian notables – but not so much about the Zionists as about the British-Hashemite alliance. Mussa Kazem decided therefore that this was the time to establish closer contact with the Zionist Commission but to do so without the knowledge of Faisal and the Hashemite agents in Jerusalem. The meeting was privately arranged and it was one of the most representative of its kind. Dr Weizmann came with his deputy, Dr Eder, Leon Simon and Israel Sieff, who acted as their secretary. The Arabs were represented by Mussa Kazem, by the Mufti of Jerusalem, Kamel el-Husaini, the Mayor of Jaffa, Abd el-Rauf Bitar, the Editor of the Cairo paper *el-Mukkatam*, Dr Faris Nimr who had come specially from Cairo, by Amin Tamimi, Haj Tewfiq Hamad and Shibli Jamali, who acted as the Arab secretary. The atmosphere at the meeting was free and easy and Jews and Arabs were completely relaxed. Weizmann spoke of the need for the total dismemberment of the Ottoman Empire and for the formation of a Greater Arabia "which will inherit the Turkish Empire. With the aid of Jewish capital and Jewish experts the Arabian Peninsula will be revived as a great civilisation comparable to its golden age in the Middle Ages. It was the Zionist intention to help establish this Great Arab state under the Hashemite dynasty. This Arabia will then join in a Confederation with Palestine where Jews will have their national and spiritual home."

Mussa Kazem also spoke of past Arab glories and welcomed the prospect of Jewish help. But he warned the Zionist Commission that the Western way of life followed by Zionists was a hindrance to their collaboration. He wanted to know whether Jews living in Europe would be prepared to abandon their Western links, especially as it was said that the Jews were the leaders of the infidel Godless Bolshevik movement in Russia and in Germany. He produced a pamphlet called *The Elders of Zion* which had been given to him by a British officer in the Administration. He wanted to know whether the Zionists were connected with these "Elders of Zion"?

Professor Weizmann replied that the Zionists were against the Bolsheviks and that they were helping England and the entente to get rid of the Bolsheviks in Russia. As for *The Elders of Zion*, Dr Weizmann claimed that it was a forgery perpetrated by the old Tsarist government in order to damage and oppress the Jews. He emphasised again that his Commission was not going to establish a Jewish Government but would support the British administration which would be the Trustee for the Arabs and Jews in Palestine.

At this stage of the discussion, the preliminary niceties began to make way for the realities. It was evident that Mussa Kazem had been closely briefed by his cousin Amin for he now began to change the direction and emphasis of the proceedings. He asked Weizmann about the proposed role of the French in Syria; where did the Zionists stand in relation to the partition of Syria? The Arabs of Greater Syria and of Palestine specifically wanted no Western domination but full independence. And then he came to the crunch of the Arab argument:

As for the Jewish National Home in Palestine, they were not opposed to it, provided the Zionists presented their desires direct to the

171

Palestine Arabs and accepted Palestine Arab sovereignty in all matters concerning Palestine. Mussa Kazem added that he had been assured by the British Military Administration that nothing will be done by the British in Palestine which would run counter to the legitimate Arab desire for self-determination. Moreover, Mussa Kazem indicated that he was still in touch with the Turkish authorities in Damascus who were anxious to establish friendly relations with the Palestinians on the basis of complete Arab national independence.

But it was the Mufti, Kemal el-Husaini, with whom Weizmann had established the closest and most friendly association, who explained the Palestine Arab position to the Zionist Commission in the clearest and sharpest terms. For Weizmann and the Zionist Commission had walked, seemingly unaware, into the trap which Amin had set for them. Amin had warned his cousin and his brother, the Mufti, that there was a conspiracy to defraud the Palestinians by the British with the help of Faisal and the Zionists. And in his speech to the meeting, in which he had stressed the close link of the Zionists with the Hashemites and the British, Weizmann had played Amin's hand and had confirmed – without knowing it – the warnings which Amin had brought back from his visit to Faisal's headquarters. Mussa Kazem was clearly impressed by Amin's foresight and his reply to Weizmann had an edge which had not been evident before. It was, however, comparatively mild to the words which the much-maligned Mufti now addressed to the Zionist Commission.

To Weizmann's evident surprise, Kemal el-Husseini, singled out the Hashemite alliance of the British and the Zionists as an insuperable stumbling block to collaboration. Speaking as the head of the Muslim community of Jerusalem, he explained that neither the Muslims of India nor of Iraq would support a Hashemite and pro-British orientation, and, more to the point, nor would the Palestinian Arabs. He repeated what he had said previously to Professor Weizmann, "that the Arabs would treat the Jews as brothers", but the Jews must recognise Arab supremacy in Palestine. He knew that the Jews had dreamt for generations of their return to the Holy Land and they would be welcome to do so under Arab rule. The Arabs would guarantee them all the religious facilities in Jerusalem. They believed that the Almighty had imposed upon the Muslims of Jerusalem the

172

guardianship of the holiness of Jerusalem and they would not tolerate any interference in the execution of this task by foreigners, be they English or Jewish.

Weizmann and his colleagues were clearly disconcerted by the Mufti's declaration and Weizmann sought to turn the discussion from the political to the religious level by talking about the bitter irony if the Moslem world now stood aside after the Christian world had acknowleged the Jewish rights to Palestine. But, inevitably, the discussion slipped back into its political grooves when Weizmann inquired what then was the Arab position: with whom should the Zionist Commission negotiate, with the Hashemite rulers or with the Syrian and Palestinian nationalists? Mussa Kazem sensed the trap that Weizmann had set for him and answered on lines which Amin had earlier suggested to him. He told Weizmann that provided the Zionists undertook that if and when they proposed to deal directly with the Hashemites they should ensure that the Palestinians and Syrians were kept informed and would participate in these direct talks as equal partners, there would be no difficulties. "Dr Weizmann replied that he accepted Mussa Kazem's formulation in principle and would authorise a member of the Zionist Commission to maintain contact with Mussa Kazem's group."

Following this "secret" meeting, Mussa Kazem formally informed Clayton of what had transpired and, more privately, discussed the proceedings with the Military Governor, Colonel Storrs, and with the Chief of Staff, Colonel Waters-Taylor (a great friend of the Arabs in Palestine and strongly opposed to the British-Hashemite alliance). He also nominated his cousin, Amin el-Husaini, to remain in touch with the Zionist Commission as had been agreed by Dr Weizmann. To his great surprise Mussa Kazem next heard from Storrs that Weizmann had gone to Aqaba on Allenby's orders to meet Prince Faisal. Neither Mussa Kazem nor Amin had been told by the Zionist Commission, as they had undertaken to do, that such a meeting had been arranged and that Weizmann would meet Faisal alone. The meeting was followed by a wave of contradictory rumours as to what had taken place. There were reports of secret agreements, of Weizmann going to the Hejaz to meet the Sharif himself and conclude a pact with him, and that Faisal had sold out the Palestinians to the Jews. Mussa Kazem asked Faisal for information and was told by a member of Faisal's staff "that the Prince had received Dr Weizmann as a matter of courtesy at the request of

General Allenby who wanted Faisal to meet this great scientist; nothing more. British officials told Mussa Kazem that the purpose of the meeting was to demonstrate the common front of Arabs and Jews against French political ambitions in the Levant."

Appeals to the British in Cairo and Jerusalem were of no great avail. The Arabs were told that the Hashemite and Zionist orientation had been decided upon in London as part of the British imperial design and the Palestinian Arabs would have to fend for themselves as best as they could. This they began to do. They consulted with Storrs, Waters-Taylor and others and they were given to understand that British policy hinged on British support for Zionism. This, the Palestinians were told, was the weakest link in the British policy chain and it was on this the Arabs should concentrate their struggle. Moreover, "Mussa Kazem and his Palestinian friends became aware of the divisions among the British in Cairo and Jerusalem". On the whole, the British in Cairo – the High Commission and the Arab Bureau – supported the Hashemite connection, but the local British military administrators in Palestine were in general in favour of supporting the Syrian-Palestinian Arab nationalists. They were opposed to the Zionists in Palestine and to the French in Syria. But most important for the Palestinians was the encouragement and advice they received from these British officials to organise themselves and to unite against the advances of the Zionists. Thus, when the Palestine Arab delegation returned from the festivities in Damascus following its occupation by the Arab Army, they called a meeting of the notables of Jerusalem and Jaffa and demanded that all Jewish immigration to Palestine be halted.

In response to this demand, presented to the British by the Mayor of Jaffa, al-Bitar, British officials, and in particular the Military Governor of Jaffa, "explained that there was nothing final about the British support for the Zionists and that everything remained to be negotiated at the Peace Conference. Sir Mark Sykes would be arriving soon, al-Bitar was told, and would discuss Arab demands with their leaders." There was no mistaking the changed mood in the streets and among the nationalist politicians. There were no more suggestions of collaboration with the Zionists. Even those who might still have wished it, or believed in it, remained silent.

The leaders in Damascus published their Manifesto with the slogan "Palestine is Our Land", a part of Greater Syria. The Manifesto was distributed in all towns and villages in Palestine and was read with great enthusiasm by all classes of Arabs. In Palestine an additional manifesto was produced with more specific slogans. These were typical of the changed atmosphere: "Save the Mosque of el Aqsa from the Jewish Invader"; "Protect the Holy Sepulchre"; "The Yarmuk will flow with blood but Palestine will not belong to the Jews"; "All Jews are Zionists!" The atmosphere became tense; but the main outcome of this campaign was that on the issue of Zionism it had united all sections of political interests and religions of the Arab world; the supporters of the Hashemites and their opponents, the pro-British and the anti-British, the advocates of a Greater Syria and those who denounced such a move, Moslems and Christians. When Sir Mark Sykes arrived in December, he was overwhelmed by the extent of the Arab united front against Zionism. The anti-Zionist movement in Palestine became the prototype and the example for other Arab states to follow. The demonstrations by the Arabs made a deep impression on Mark Sykes. He was reported to have said to Storrs that there was at least one major issue on which all the Arab factions have a common voice – Zionism. But despite the instant success of the anti-Zionist campaign it produced no real political dividends, and when Faisal left for Europe it was not only the Hashemites who were in a precarious position but also the whole Arab movement.

Allenby's capture of Damascus initiated a period of Arab setbacks and defeats. The French were installing themselves in Syria, the British in Iraq and in Palestine, and they had with them the Zionist Commission. Sykes' visit had brought little real comfort though many comforting words. Lawrence advised Faisal to seek an understanding with the Zionists. They were powerful and could influence President Wilson and American policy, and, what was more to the point, they were the only possible ally prepared to help Faisal obtain his Syrian crown.

Faisal allowed himself to be persuaded by Lawrence for he had no evident alternative. Faisal's mistake, however, was to allow his British advisers to conduct the negotiations with the Zionists. Mark Sykes was in Syria and Palestine at the time and the details of the talks were conducted in London by his deputy, A. J. Toynbee, by Ormsby-Gore and by Lawrence for Faisal while Weizmann had with him the Palestinian Aaronsohn and the Secretary of the Commission, Israel Sieff and, somewhat later, the American Professor Felix Frankfurter. The Foreign Office was kept informed of the progress of the talks and, it must be assumed, guided the British and the Zionists in their presentations.

Faisal was clearly not aware of this, nor did he seem to realise that what was taking place was not so much negotiations between Dr Weizmann and himself as an arrangement arrived at between his British advisers and the Zionists which was to be presented to him for approval.

Even so, when it came to the crux of the discussion, Faisal maintained the Arab position from which he had never wavered since his first meeting with Dr Weizmann. Although Faisal tried to be more conciliatory than other Arab leaders, he made it very clear again to Dr Weizmann and his friends that any agreement between them had to be based on the assumption that Palestine would be an Arab state which would allow the Jewish home to be developed and given a special status within the Arab state. In view of the feelings of the Arabs of Syria and Palestine they should not speak of Palestine as a Jewish state. If Dr Weizmann agreed to this arrangement then Faisal would provide a seat for the Palestinian Jews in the Syrian Arab Government,

> This was not what Weizmann had asked for. He had put it to Faisal that both Arabs and Zionists had the same problems. Both had to rely on British support and both were opposed to the French expansion into Syria and Palestine. Weizmann said that the Arabs had to recognise Jewish aspirations and, in return, they would use their influence to bring about a Great Arabia on the lines of the Sharif Husain's agreements with the British in 1915. But Weizmann surprised Faisal by two qualifications which he added to his statements – evidently at the behest of the Foreign Office: Palestine would be excluded from the Greater Arab state and so would the Christian-populated coastal stretch of Syria, the Lebanon, so that French claims in the Levant could be satisfied.

At this point Lawrence intervened in the discussion and proposed that they should draft an agreement between Weizmann and Faisal which would incorporate all relevant points which they had discussed. It was decided that Lawrence and Sieff should prepare the draft and then submit it to Toynbee for the British Government's approval before presenting it to Faisal and Weizmann for signature. Faisal wanted his political secretary, Awni Abdul-Hadi, to be also consulted by Lawrence and Sieff.[4]

[4] Abdul-Hadi's account of these talks, quoted by Aharon Cohen in his *Israel and the Arab World*, p. 142, appears more as an exercise in self-justification than as a factual version of what did take place.

But while these talks were proceeding in London, conditions in Syria and Palestine were rapidly deteriorating. Violent verbal opposition to Zionism had become the order of the day. Politicians and notables vied with each other in the denunciation of the Jews. The Syrian newspapers were filled with radical criticism of the Zionists. The Zionist Commission in Jerusalem reported this to the British Government and to Weizmann, and Weizmann in turn protested about this to Faisal. Faisal sent a special messenger to his brother Ali whom he had left in charge in Damascus that he should take measures to halt this anti-Zionist campaign and to stop the publication of such hostile articles in the Syrian press. "Ali replied that there was not much he could do as the campaign was encouraged by British agents who were inciting the Arabs against the Jews in Syria and also in Palestine." Ali provided no specific evidence for this charge and it was more likely that the real cause of the trouble was the waning influence of the Hashemites in Damascus and Ali's ineffectiveness in particular.

The reason for the erosion of Faisal's influence and for the militant attitude to the Zionists after Faisal had left for Europe could be found in the new Arab leadership that was making its views felt in Damascus. It emanated largely from a group of young Palestinians who had achieved positions of considerable influence among the Syrian nationalists. Foremost among them were two young men, Amin el-Husaini, who had moved for the time being from Jerusalem to Damascus, and a Palestinian officer in the Turkish army who had recently been released from captivity in Russia, Aref el-Aref. When Faisal and Weizmann raised this with the British they were told that the trouble had been stirred up by French agents.

Meanwhile Lawrence and Sieff had agreed on a draft treaty and showed it to Faisal and Weizmann. Faisal asked that the word "Palestine" should be substituted for "Jewish State" and Weizmann substituted "Hejaz" for "Arab States". It was also agreed to hasten the completion of the Treaty in view of the disturbing news from Damascus. They also discussed the Jewish representation in the Damascus Arab Government. Weizmann suggested Aaronsohn but Faisal said it would be unwise to have a Palestinian. Weizmann then proposed Dr Eder who had been his deputy in Jerusalem, but Faisal expressed the desire for a younger man and pointed to Sieff as his choice. Weizmann agreed. They discussed a few more improvements in the text of the Treaty and the draft was returned to Lawrence, Sieff and Toynbee for the preparation of the definitive text. Before they parted, Faisal asked Weizmann whether he could exert his influence with the French to obtain their agreement to the settlement which they had reached. But Weizmann could see no possibility for such a step. Any such move would have to come from the British Government, he told Faisal. Faisal signed the agreement with Weizmann on 5 January 1919, the day after he had shown Weizmann the Arab demands which he was to present to the Peace Conference and to the British Government. The two steps were closely linked in Faisal's mind and they explain the reservation which he attached to the agreement when he signed it. The British asked that the existence of the agreement and its text should be kept secret, but Faisal sent a copy to his brother Ali in Damascus and to his father in Mecca.

I want to pause here in the presentation of this Arab account of how the Arab leaders saw and reported the proceedings and insert Weizmann's and Sieff's accounts as given in their private letters and reports and in personal conversations with the author. More than almost any other occurrence, this not only illuminates the contrasting understanding and intentions of the British and the Zionists which is reflected in the account of their respective attitudes, but it also shows how very differently the Arabs and the Zionists assessed the situation, their relationships and their respective objectives. Who was right and who was mistaken, and what were the reasons for this stark contrast in the reading of the facts as given, whether they were Machiavellian or the product of personal shortcomings, are matters which we shall consider later when we have the full evidence before us. First, then, here is the record of these events as seen by Weizmann and his colleagues at the time, not as they came to be presented in the unfortunately garbled account in Weizmann's memoirs for which he personally was not wholly responsible.[5]

Before leaving for Europe in the autumn of 1918, Faisal had approached the Zionist Commission in Jerusalem with a request for an "advance payment" on the financial assistance which Dr Weizmann had promised him as part of the understanding they had reached at their meeting in June. Dr Eder, who was in charge of the Commission's affairs in Weizmann's absence, cabled London on 27 October 1918 for guidance. Weizmann replied by cable and explained the reasons for

[5] Weizmann's *Trial and Error* was not edited by himself because of failing eyesight.

rejecting Faisal's request in a letter to Eder.[6] Weizmann said he had consulted with Lord Robert Cecil at the Foreign Office and also with Lawrence, Hogarth and Herbert Samuel and they had "come to the conclusion that unless a proper political arrangement is arrived at with Faisal, and such an arrangement is ratified by the British Government, we should not advance any money". It might easily be misinterpreted, Weizmann added, by their Jewish and non-Jewish enemies. They might claim that the Zionists were seeking to place Faisal under an obligation, make him their debtor and so prejudice the negotiations with him and with the British. "I quite understand that nothing of that nature is contemplated but we run the risk that malevolent people would make such insinuations." The Foreign Office was still advising him to lead a Zionist mission to Sharif Husain and to discuss political and technical assistance with him but to leave financial matters until later. Weizmann also advised Eder that he was keeping Clayton fully informed of these developments. Weizmann remained in constant touch with Lawrence who had assured him that there had been no change in Faisal's attitude about the general lines of co-operation on which he and Weizmann had agreed at their June meeting. These decisions were "still adhered to by him and his advisers".[7]

On the same day, Weizmann had also written to Clayton in Jerusalem and informed him of his close collaboration with Lawrence and Hogarth with regard to the policy which the Zionists should adopt in their relations with Faisal. He explained again the reasons for not advancing money to Faisal at this time but that they wanted to be of assistance to him "with the consent of His Majesty's Government and after we have arrived at a clear and frank arrangement with Feysal, an arrangement which must be approved by General Allenby, yourself and the Government here". In his talk with Lord Robert Cecil, Weizmann informed Clayton, they had agreed that Weizmann should see Faisal again as soon as possible and discuss the details of co-operation with him. Meanwhile, Weizmann proposed that the British Government should look to Faisal's financial needs:

I have pointed out to my fellow Zionists that the fundamental principle on which co-operation with Feysal must be established is that whatever we do there must be done in the same spirit and under

[6] Weizmann to Eder, 5 November 1918.
[7] Weizmann to Eder, ibid.

the same conditions as we do things for ourselves. On no account must an impression get abroad that the Jews, whether they are Zionists or non-Zionists, are trying to hunt for concessions in Damascus and are making use of Feysal's financial embarrassment in order to lay their hands on the newly created Arab Commonwealth. Nothing would be more disastrous than that, and that is why we have to be so particularly careful now in our negotiations with Feysal.[8]

Three days later, on 8 November 1918, Weizmann was attending the third meeting of the "Advisory Committee on Palestine" which met at Herbert Samuel's home in Porchester Terrace. Samuel was in the chair and also present in addition to Weizmann were Sir Alfred Mond (later Lord Melchett), Robert Waley-Cohen, Sokolow, Sieff, Stern and Cowen; Ormsby-Gore was there "in a consultative capacity". The meeting was concerned with the proposals which the Zionists should make about the future sovereignty of Palestine. Samuel "thought that a formula could be formed wherein the Committee could ask for a British Trusteeship of Palestine for a time, until the development of the country would allow the question to be considered. In any case, the Committee might suggest to the Government that the ultimate development in contemplation was a Jewish State." At this point Weizmann intervened to stress "that whether the formula asked for a protectorate or trusteeship it was absolutely essential that it should indicate that the ultimate object was to make Palestine into a Jewish Palestine.[9]

The Committee met again, two days later on the eve of the Armistice, to continue the discussion about the form which sovereignty should take in Palestine. It was resolved that the Government should be informed "that the form of sovereignty most acceptable to the Zionist Organisation was an unqualified British Protectorate over Palestine". Sokolow then raised the question of the exercise of this sovereignty in relation to Jews and Arabs. From the chair, Samuel elaborated by adding that where the Jewish Community was a compact body it should have as much self-government as possible. But Weizmann went much further and insisted that they must face the fundamental question which was here involved.

[8] Weizmann to Clayton, 5 November 1918.
[9] Minutes of the Third Meeting of Advisory Committee on Palestine, 8 November 1918.

The principle of self-government which Samuel had stressed was "a right and proper principle and would prevent the majorisation by the Arabs. Although the Jews were numerically inferior, they were qualitatively superior, and it was necessary to safeguard this superiority from being overwhelmed in the first period by mere weight of numbers. Conditions therefore must be established in Palestine as speedily as possible to allow for the creation of a Jewish majority."[10]

Weizmann, it must be remembered, was stating a cold fact; he was not advancing a racist doctrine. All the same, his basic thinking in this inner circle of Jews, not all Zionists, was far removed from that which he expressed in his letter to Clayton or in his encounter with Faisal. But Weizmann was becoming increasingly obsessed by the difficulties which they had to overcome and the prospects which faced the Jews in Eastern Europe – a factor that was always present in his mind when he talked to the British and to the Arabs. He wrote again to Eder about this, later that month, and shortly before his meeting with Faisal.

He told Eder that news was coming in from Poland of renewed anti-Jewish progroms and he doubted whether they could do anything to stop them though they had taken steps to do so. "I am quite sure that the position of Jewry in Eastern and Central Europe after the war will be worse than ever and the emigration will simply be enormous with the difference, I'm afraid, that America and England will be less ready to receive Jews than before," and, he added prophetically, that this pointed "to one fundamental fact – that we must have Palestine if we are not going to be exterminated." He realised that the Arabs were becoming restive, "but does it amount to much? We know that it is not serious and I am not so very sure whether all this noise is not engineered by some of our 'friends' ".[11]

Weizmann also told Eder that he had sent a telegram to Sykes in Palestine to assure him, as Sykes had requested, that there would be no official Zionist demand at the Peace Conference for a Jewish state in Palestine.

Weizmann's account of the meeting with Faisal on 11 December 1918 at which Lawrence acted as interpreter reads like the scenario of a love-feast. They mutually denounced the Sykes-Picot pact. Faisal spoke of the benefits which Zionism would bring to Palestine and the

[10] Minutes of Fourth Meeting of the Advisory Committee on Palestine, 10 November 1918.
[11] Weizmann to Eder, 26 November 1918.

181

welcome which it would have from the Arabs. He could not understand why there should be conflict between Jews and Arabs in Palestine for there was none elsewhere in any Arab country. The trouble, he was sure, was promoted by intrigues from outside the country. "As for Sursuk and other Effendis, he did not trouble his head about them. He assured us on his word of honour that he would do everything to support Jewish demands and would declare at the Peace Conference that Zionism and the Arab movement were fellow movements and that complete harmony prevailed between them." He would try and get the British as Trustee Power for Arabia and he hoped the Zionists would support him.

Weizmann's account of Zionist intentions was similarly tailored for the situation. There was no mention of Jewish statehood or of a Jewish majority. He stressed the need for land reform of the land now in the hands of effendis and usurers and he added his belief that there was room for four or five million Jews if all available land was fully utilised. Faisal concurred with the view that there was no shortage of land in Palestine. Judged by Weizmann's account, this interview with Faisal was mainly noteworthy for what was not said – either in the discussion between the two men or in Weizmann's account of it. There was no mention of the Committee of Three (Lawrence, Toynbee and Sieff) that was to draft a treaty; there was no mention or explanation for the rejection of Faisal's demand for a financial advance on future arrangements, no discussion of Arab sovereignty, of Jewish representation in the Damascus Government. Not only did Weizmann minimise what happened at this meeting, but his autobiography ignores it altogether, and so does Leonard Stein in his authoritative history of the Balfour Declaration. He has no more than a passing reference to the discussion that took place at the Carlton Hotel.[12]

Yet almost immediately after the meeting with Faisal, Weizmann cabled to Eder – through the Foreign Office – that he had had "a most successful interview with Faisal, who found himself in complete agreement with our proposals. He was sure that he would be able to explain to the Arabs the advantages to the country and thus to themselves of a Jewish Palestine," and that Faisal would spare no efforts to support Jewish demands at the Peace Conference.

[12] For Weizmann's account – there are two slightly differing versions – see Note on the interview with Emir Faisal at the Carlton Hotel, 11 December 1918, Colonel Lawrence acting as interpreter.

The telegrams were forwarded to Eder through Clayton but the Chief of the General Staff in Cairo queried who had authorised Weizmann to use the government prefix for telegrams which exempted them from censorship?

Somehow Weizmann appears to have convinced himself that all was going well only a few days later. Gone is the gloom which had settled on him when he had written to Eder on 26 November before his meeting with Faisal. First came the meeting with Faisal which reassured Weizmann about Faisal's intentions. Then, a week later, he had a long private meeting with Lloyd George and Herbert Samuel just before the Cabinet was due to discuss the role of Palestine in British peace strategy. Lloyd George was at his flattering best and this did much for Weizmann's morale. But what gave him most encouragement was the dinner which Lord Rothschild gave for Prince Faisal on 21 December 1918. Among those present were Lord Milner, Lord Robert Cecil, Lord Crewe and Lawrence. Faisal made just the sort of speech that Weizmann had hoped for and Lawrence had drafted. "All present were very much impressed," he wrote next day to Aaronsohn who was in Paris for the Peace Conference preparations, "and realised that there is a real basis for an alliance between us and him."[13]

It was in this state of near – and rare – euphoria that Weizmann saw out the fateful year of the Zionist Commission and prepared for the realities of the Peace Conference in Paris. His mind was focused firmly on Faisal and the advantages which the agreement reached with him would provide in the presentation of the Zionist case at the Peace Conference. He was not unduly impressed by the Arab agitation in Palestine and Syria. But it made its mark on Faisal.

We return now to the Arab account of the aftermath of the meeting in London between Faisal and Weizmann. Faisal made his presentation of the Arab case to the Peace Conference on 6 February 1919. He asked for Arab independence from the Turkish border in the north to the Indian Ocean in the south but, more significantly and deliberately, he mentioned neither the agreement which his father had made with the British nor the British promise concerning Palestine to the Jews. He did, however, put great emphasis on President Wilson's stress on the right to self-determination and invited an inter-Allied commission to sound Arab opinion in the countries concerned.

[13] Weizmann to Aaronsohn, 22 December 1918.

Later that month, Dr Weizmann presented the Zionist claim for a Jewish State in Palestine to the Peace Conference. Faisal was greatly annoyed by the way in which Weizmann had formulated the Zionist demands and considered this to be a breach of the secret agreement they had concluded in London. All the more so, since Faisal himself had deliberately avoided all reference to Palestine in his own presentation so as to avoid a clash in public on this issue.

Faisal's fears were soon realised. When news reached Damascus of the claims advanced by the Zionists at the Peace Conference it produced immediate repercussions throughout Syria and Palestine. Denunciations in the press were followed by violent and angry demonstrations and in Jaffa the first conference of the Moslem Arab-Christian Societies proclaimed that the Arabs would never submit to the Zionist foreigners. There were demonstrations against the Zionist policy throughout Palestine. The British Military administration sought to reassure the Arab leaders; they were told that nothing had yet been decided and that the Arab view would receive the British Government's careful consideration. The Arab leaders were told by Storrs that their views would have much greater weight if they spoke with a single voice to the British authorities.

In Damascus, the two principal Arab parties announced that elections would be held for an Arab National Congress. This met in Damascus in July 1919 and proclaimed Syria's national independence under King Faisal and resolved at the same time "to reject demands for a Zionist Republic in Southern Syria, known as Palestine". It also proclaimed its opposition to Jewish immigration into any part of Syria but promised that Jewish citizens would enjoy the same rights in the country as any other citizens. "Independent Syria will be established within the natural borders of Syria, including Palestine, Transjordan and the Lebanon." The Congress also issued a National Charter for the Arabs of Palestine which prohibited the immigration of Jews and the sale of land to Jews and claimed full national independence for Palestine as an integral part of Greater Syria. Meanwhile, Faisal was undergoing a painful political education. He had returned from Paris to Damascus and had attached to him by the British a former senior officer of the Arab Bureau in Cairo, Colonel Kinahan Cornwallis.

Cornwallis impressed on Faisal that his most effective step towards his Syrian crown would be to take a strong stand against Zionism in

184

Palestine and to identify himself with the Palestinian nationalists. Moreover, Cornwallis explained that such a step would also open the way for Faisal's reconciliation with the French.

Cornwallis had not been alone in impressing on Faisal the need for political re-orientation. Faisal also heard from American friends in Paris, and from others, that it was certain that the British proposed to hand over control of Syria to the French. He realised that in future he would be more concerned with the French than with the British and that he would have to find a common language with them. And there was no better way, he believed, than by promoting Arab national claims in Syria and Palestine and using these as his trump card in obtaining French support for a greater Syrian Kingdom under his rule linked to a French Mandatory regime. Faisal prepared for a second trip to Europe in the summer of 1919 with these ideas in mind. But the Arab nationalist leaders in Syria and Palestine were more concerned with the Zionist threat than with the Hashemite ambition. They began to direct their agitation more against the Jews in Palestine than against the potential danger of a French take-over. One reason for this was that the Palestinian *Istiqlal*, Independence Party, which operated out of Damascus found that in Syria it was hamstrung by Faisal's dominating position and policy and moved its headquarters to Jerusalem. "However, they had Faisal's tacit blessing to concentrate their agitation against the Zionists in Palestine."

The two men who emerged as the driving force behind this new activity were Amin el-Husaini and Aref el-Aref. They were the recognised leaders of the new Arab radicalism. They preached "direct action" and mass protest against the Zionists and especially against Jewish immigration. "Their call was enthusiastically taken up by the Arab communal and religious leaders in Jerusalem, Jaffa, Haifa, Nablus and Hebron. They summoned their followers to battle for the liberation of Palestine by the sword in a holy war against the Jewish invasion." Suddenly, Palestine had become the centre of militant Arab nationalism.

This was more than the British had bargained for. They had their own troubles in Egypt following the riots in April 1919 and the heavy-handed British suppression of those held responsible. They wanted to lessen the tension in Palestine while they were thus preoccupied in Egypt. They therefore proposed to the Zionist leaders that they should approach Faisal with a view of reviving the Faisal-Weizmann agreement concluded in January. But Faisal informed the Zionist emissaries who came to see him that the Zionists should now deal with the Palestinian Arab leaders in Jerusalem since he was for the time being preoccupied with the French.

He told David Yellin who had come to see him on behalf of the Zionist Commission that the London Agreement with Weizmann had been concluded on the assumption that the British were the masters of the Levant, but the British had betrayed him to the French. He advised Yellin to negotiate with the Palestinians, to moderate Zionist claims and to abandon Zionist hopes of becoming the dominating element in Palestine. They should recognise Palestine as an integral part of Greater Syria and act accordingly.

What most disconcerted the Zionist emissaries was a further message which Faisal asked them to take back. He told them that under the changed circumstances he would prefer in future to deal with Zionist leaders who were not too involved with the British Government. He would prefer not to meet with Weizmann again but rather with Professor Felix Frankfurter with whom he had established friendly relations after their first meeting in London in December 1918.

However, Arab nationalist policy was anything but clear or consistent. While Yellin was in Damascus with Faisal, another Zionist emissary, Elmaleh had contacted the Jewish communities and the pro-French Arab nationalists in Beirut and Damascus. He was told that the real purpose of the anti-Zionist agitation was not to harm the Jews but to isolate the British. They had betrayed the Arab national cause and deserted Faisal and if the current agitation succeeded, the British would be left only with old King Husain sitting in the midst of a desert in Mecca.

The press campaign against the Zionists was only a convenient smoke-screen for this policy, Elmaleh was told, and it had as its aim the establishment of a Greater Syrian state under Faisal. In this Syria the Jews would enjoy limited autonomy for their religious and cultural development under Arab rule. But they must understand that the Arabs would never allow them a political status of their own because the Zionists would always remain dependent on the British for the achievement of their Zionist ambitions.

186

There was further evidence that the Zionists were making a determined attempt either to sound out Arab opinion or to seek some kind of accommodation with the Arab nationalists in order to further their own case at the Peace Conference. For in Jerusalem, two local Palestinian Jews – Hillel Hacohen and Eisenberg – came to discuss the situation with Mussa Kazem on the recommendation of the Mufti of Jerusalem.

Mussa Kazem informed them that he had lost his earlier faith in the Zionists. He now saw that the British backed them because they were shrewd and rich and he considered the Zionists to be a menace to the Palestinian Arabs. He advised Hacohen and Eisenberg to go to Damascus and make their submission to the Arab Government there as the subjects of an Arab Kingdom.

All these conversations were seen by the Arabs as preliminary to the coming of the American Mr Justice Brandeis – "a close friend of President Wilson" – to Damascus. Faisal especially had prepared himself and the Arab Congress that met in Damascus in June 1919 for this encounter. Brandeis had arrived in Palestine and "had a number of conferences with Allenby, Storrs and other British officials. He had heard from them their views of the Zionist Commission and of its arrogant behaviour to the Arab majority. He was informed by them of the Arab restiveness caused by Jewish radicalism, conceit and aggressiveness." Mussa Kazem finally catalogues the long list of Arab grievances when he met with Brandeis and was convinced that Brandeis had gone away greatly troubled by what he had heard in Jerusalem.

Following preliminary discussions in Paris and Jerusalem, it was agreed that a high-level Jewish mission led by Brandeis would meet with Faisal in Damascus. News of this arrangement roused new hope in Faisal and his colleagues. Faisal decided to postpone his planned journey to Europe and prepared detailed proposals which would enable the Americans to assume mandatory responsibility over Greater Syria. "Faisal was convinced that American Zionism was much less dangerous than the British variety." He also prepared statements stressing the demand for a unified Greater Syrian state, the opposition to British and French mandates, and the Arab opposition to the Balfour Declaration. Then Mussa Kazem formally invited Brandeis to be Faisal's guest in Damascus. But Brandeis informed Kazem that though he was anxious

187

to make the journey to Damascus he had been dissuaded by the British – and by Weizmann – from proceeding with this mission to Faisal.

This was the end of the American dream for Faisal, of the hope that the United States would bail him out and take over control of Syria and Palestine from the French and the British.

Moreover, he now was convinced that, since the British had abandoned Syria to the French, his concessions to the Zionists had become pointless and that his best policy henceforth was to work for the elimination of the Zionist presence and influence with the help of the French. By doing this, he would pacify his Palestinian radicals and possibly succeed in saving the unity of Syria by including Palestine as well as Syria in the French mandatory regime.

Faisal had been told by Allenby (at their meeting in Damascus in May 1919) that the main reason why the British had given in to the French over Syria was because of their commitment in Palestine. Faisal discussed this with his advisers and they reached the conclusion – on the advice of several senior British officials in Palestine and Syria, who had appointed themselves as confidential advisers to Faisal, and whose commitment to the Arab cause was total – that the only way to get rid of the Zionists in Palestine was to get rid of the British. But the British would leave Palestine only in the face of overwhelming military considerations; they had therefore to find convincing military reasons that would persuade the British to pull out. Intense Arab nationalist agitation could have the desired effect provided the British were enabled to retain control of the land-bridge from Aqaba to Mosul and Iraq. "Faisal decided to discuss this question with the French High Commissioner in Beirut, Georges Picot and sound him out as to further negotiations."

It was in line with these discussions – and with Faisal's and Picot's tacit approval – that the radical young Palestinians stepped up their anti-Zionist campaign. They also had received adequate financial help to enable them to start a paper. In September 1919 the first issue of *Syria el Jenoubia* (*Southern Syria*) appeared in Jerusalem under the editorship of Aref el-Aref and Hassan el-Boudeiri. Its uncompromising tone left little to the imagination. The first issue proclaimed that "if our protests are not heeded, we shall pass from words to deeds; we shall exchange words for swords, and in place of ink we shall use blood". There was a huge demonstration in Jerusalem led by Mussa Kazem

188

and Amin el-Husaini. In the mosques throughout the country fiery sermons denouncing the Zionists were preached.

More discreetly, Amin began to organise small secret groups known as *Fedayoun*, suicide squads who were to terrorise the Jews and their British supporters. These movements, moreover, were greatly influenced by the news from Turkey where Kemal Pasha had started the career which led, not long after, to his successful war of liberation against the Greek invader backed by the British. The notion was taking root that the Arab nationalists could emulate the Turkish example and do to the Jews what the Turks were doing to the Greeks. The immediate effect of this was, however, that during Faisal's second absence in Europe the focal point of the Arab nationalist struggle moved from Damascus to Jerusalem – and with it came the feeling in the Arab camp that the Palestinian Arabs were destined to be the vanguard of the struggle against the British and the Jews – a feeling further reinforced by the rapidly mounting Arab distrust and disappointment in the Hashemite dynasty. The Syrians were still waiting to see some worthwhile results from Faisal's European negotiations and they were becoming distinctly sceptical of what they came to look upon as Faisal's "political game".

It was thus that in the winter of 1919/1920 a Palestinian entity came into effective existence as an independent factor in the Arab world which gave a new tone and sense of purpose to the Pan-Arab national movement. The Syrian nationalists were inclined to join with the Palestinians instead of the Palestinians following the Syrians as hitherto. The new leadership was concentrated in Jerusalem rather than Damascus and though the rank-and-file remained predominantly Syrian the leaders were Palestinians; Amin el-Husaini, Aref el-Aref, Rafiq Tamini, Izat Darwasa, Mouein al-Mahdi, Ibrahim Kassem Abdul-Hadi and Salim Abdul-Rahman.

Meanwhile Weizmann had returned to Palestine in October 1919. Urged by the British to renew his contacts with the Palestinian Arab leaders, Weizmann sought a suitable opportunity. It was created for him by the British Governor of Jerusalem, Colonel Storrs, who pressed Mussa Kazem to arrange such a meeting. The Arabs were opposed to the idea of again talking with Weizmann but Storrs persuaded them of its possible advantages. Accordingly, they met at the house of Dr Tich, a well-known Jerusalem physician. Mussa Kazem came with his usual colleagues, including Amin. Weizmann came with Sieff, Dr Friedenwald, an American Zionist, and the Italian Bianchini. In the discussion which ensued there was a strange reversal of roles by Weizmann and the Palestine Arabs. It was known that Weizmann had maintained in all his discussions with the British, and with some Arabs, that the Zionists were prepared to deal with Faisal or any other recognised head of an Arab state, but not with the Palestinians. They were not an entity that the Zionists recognised.

"This time, however, much to the surprise of Mussa Kazem, Weizmann proposed that there should be direct negotiations between the leaders of the Palestine Arabs and the Zionists without interference from Arab leaders outside Palestine, be they Hashemites or Syrians." It was the first time that the Zionists had made such an offer and the Arab delegation was confronted with this unexpected turn; for this is what they had asked for in their many private talks with the British and the Zionists. Some members of the Arab delegation, especially Amin, expected Mussa Kazem to take up Weizmann's proposal, if only to see just how seriously the Zionists meant it.

But Mussa Kazem would not hear of it. The Palestine Arabs, he told Weizmann, were an integral part of the Arab nation; they were fighting their national war for a common Arab cause and would therefore not be separated from the rest of the Arab world, especially not from their Syrian brethren. Weizmann then asked Mussa Kazem whether he knew that there was already agreement between the British and French to partition Syria so that Southern Syria, Palestine, would come under a British mandate and the North, with the Lebanon, under French rule? Mussa Kazem replied that the Arabs would not recognise such a partition and would fight against it in Syria and in Palestine and he spoke with enthusiasm of the example set by the Turkish leader, Kemal Pasha. The Arabs, he told Weizmann, could easily find a common language and a common cause with the Turkish nationalists. He stressed that this would become an immediate issue should Faisal in his current negotiations in London and Paris accept such a partition of Syria. If that were to happen, the Arabs of Syria and Palestine would rise against the Hashemites and open the whole of the Near East to Turkish armed resistance in a common front with the Arabs. This would compel the British and the French to withdraw their troops from Syria.

"At this point Weizmann interrupted and asked the Arab delegates whether they realised that behind the Turkish uprising under Kemal

190

Pasha stood the Bolsheviks. The Entente Powers would never permit Bolshevik expansion into Palestine or Syria. They would not withdraw their troops as Mussa Kazem expected but deploy more military forces to clear the Near East of the Bolshevik danger." Mussa Kazem doubted Weizmann's claim. All the more so, he said, since British officials had informed him that "the Zionists were flooding Palestine with Russian Bolshevik immigrants". Weizmann denied this and maintained that the Russian Jews who were coming to Palestine were anti-Bolsheviks who had fled from Russia because of the policy of the new rulers there. It was quite absurd, he said, to equate Zionists with Bolsheviks and at the same time identify them with the British Government. "Jews and Arabs, Weizmann urged, should co-operate with the British in Palestine to make the country prosperous for the Arab fellaheen and for the Jewish settlers." Mussa Kazem rejected this argument. The Arabs, he told Weizmann, would prefer to remain in their present state rather than permit foreign penetration whatever its economic advantages, and concluded that there was really nothing more to say. Weizmann expressed the wish that they should meet again and Mussa Kazem agreed – but only after Faisal's return from Europe and when Greater Syrian unity had been re-established.

Faisal arrived in London on 18 September 1919. He met with Lloyd George on the following day, and again four days later. He also talked with Curzon and Allenby who had been summoned from Cairo to be present. But the man who spelled out the upshot of these conferences for Faisal was Lawrence. He did not mince his words. What all this meant, he told Faisal, was that either Faisal accepted the Anglo-French agreements on the partition of Syria and the future of Palestine or he would be brushed aside by the British and they would find another Arab leader who would collaborate with them. Faisal felt that his old British friends had deserted him and that he had to look elsewhere for help. So he turned again to Weizmann and sought his assistance in his further negotiations with the Powers. He told Weizmann that he proposed to go to the United States with a representative Arab delegation, and request President Wilson's help against the British and French intrigues. He thought that in the light of the favourable recommendations of the American King-Crane Commission which had made its report to the White House on 27 September 1919, and had not supported Zionist claims to Palestine or the French mandate for Syria, the President might respond favourably. However, in return for

Weizmann's assistance, Faisal undertook to seek full co-operation with the American Zionists under Mr Justice Brandeis' leadership. He suggested to Weizmann that they might form a joint Arab-Zionist delegation to see the President.

Faisal had evidently given much thought to his proposal under the impact of the desertion by the British.

In return for the support of the Jews in the United States, he told Weizmann, he would order the Palestine-Syrian extremists to halt their anti-Zionist campaign and to establish instead a common front with the Jews against the British in Palestine. Moreover, once he had Wilson's support he would seek an accommodation with the French in Syria, so as to force the British to abandon their plan for the partition of Syria. The Zionists would be able to establish their national home in Palestine, protected by the Americans, while the Arabs would form the Greater Syrian state which would include Transjordan and Iraq and together with Palestine would form a Hashemite Confederation. He promised to obtain his father's support for the plan since King Husain was also under great pressure from the British. He informed Weizmann that he, Faisal, was already in touch with Kemal Pasha and that he believed that the Turks would support his plan. The French, he said, were also secretly in contact with the Turkish nationalists, and thus a powerful front against the British could be established. He had heard from Kemal that he would be happy to have this Arab support. Lastly, Faisal requested Weizmann to keep his proposals completely secret as he did not want the British to know about them at this stage.

Weizmann was not prepared to join Faisal's intrigue against the British. He told Faisal that it would be fruitless for the time being to appeal to the United States in view of the President's shaken position. In fact, the Americans were withdrawing from all their commitments in Europe and the Near East and even from the League of Nations which they had fathered. He advised Faisal not to go to the United States as the situation there was not propitious for their purpose. Weizmann had already decided to cancel his own journey there. He told Faisal to wait until the Franco-British negotiations had established some sort of stability in the Levant.

As for the Turks, Weizmann said, he had no confidence in Kemal Pasha whose movement was fomented by the Bolsheviks. He was not

192

satisfied with the British administration in Palestine and intended to launch a public campaign for a return to the policy to which the British had pledged themselves in 1917. But he urged Faisal to rely on the British and oppose the French. He had private information that the French position in Syria was very shaky and that the British would soon oust them from Syria. Thus Jews and Arabs had a common interest in shaping their policy in association with the British. Moreover, the British were also negotiating with the American Standard Oil Company to provide it with concessions in the Mosul oilfields. This would ensure American backing for the British – and, if they went along with them – also for the Arabs and Jews.

Faisal was not reassured. He wanted to know in practical terms what the Zionists could do to assist the Arab cause. Weizmann replied that the Zionists would provide financial support and specialist advisers who knew how to handle the French. Weizmann thought it would be a sound move on Faisal's part to have with him in Damascus some Zionist representatives from Palestine or London, but Faisal said he would prefer Americans, especially Professor Felix Frankfurter whom he greatly respected. Weizmann resisted the suggestion. He said that it was not feasible to send an American Zionist to Damascus because of the American position of neutrality and because of French opposition to any kind of American intervention in their zone of influence in the Near East.

After the meeting, Faisal discussed it with his advisers. He was convinced now, he told them, that the Zionists in London were completely dependent on the British and acted, in fact, as British agents in all matters concerning the politics of the Near East. Soon afterwards, Faisal left for Paris. He departed with a heavy heart and the knowledge that he could no longer depend on British support.

In Paris he came under the influence of the Emir Michel Loft-Allah, a powerful Syrian landowner who led an influential committee of Syrian nationalists, mostly large landowners, which he had formed in Cairo, and which had influential links with leading Egyptian politicians. Faisal proposed to him that he should sound the French Government for his plan that the French should take the mandates for Syria and Palestine and reunite the Greater Syrian state under a common French mandate with Faisal as King.

Loft-Allah was a thoroughly bad influence on Faisal. He was convinced that the young Syrian nationalists were little more than a revolutionary rabble with radical ideas fed to them by the British military. He suggested to Faisal that he should get rid of them and of the British and work with the responsible landowners who enjoyed much influence in France. Once again under pressure, and feeling cut off from his old friends, Faisal agreed and requested Loft-Allah to inform the French that he would recognise their rule in Syria provided they unify Syria with the Lebanon and Palestine and recognise Faisal as the titular head.

Faisal's chief adviser on his European mission was General Haddad Pasha. He enjoyed Faisal's absolute confidence and had been kept informed of the secret talks with Weizmann and with Loft-Allah. None the less Haddad betrayed that confidence when he suddenly left for London and informed the British of Faisal's plan to work with the French. "The British took immediate counter-action. They informed the Arab leaders in Jerusalem of Faisal's intentions and urged them to intensify their anti-French campaign with the slogan 'Greater Arabia with three Centres – Mecca, Damascus and Baghdad'."[14]

The diplomatic struggle between the British and French over the future organisation of the Middle East continued to centre on their respective positions in Palestine and Syria. The British had reconciled themselves to French rule in Syria but still sought to extract the best possible frontiers for Palestine and Iraq. They accepted Faisal's new French orientation so long as it was not used to encourage opposition to the British in Palestine. The British had been content with Weizmann's loyal role when tempted by Faisal to join in an anti-British campaign and so win French support. They were clearly less sure of Faisal – and they appeared to care less what he did. Faisal had the impression before he returned home in January 1920 that the British had largely discounted him as a serious factor and that they were now more interested in the Palestinian Arab leaders and in French policy than in Faisal's Syrian Kingdom. Faisal had concluded a number of agreements with the French and Clemenceau had expressed his appreciation to Lloyd George for the assistance which the British had given him in getting Faisal to accept the French presence and the French terms.

[14] This was the slogan which Weizmann had coined in his letter to Balfour on 30 May 1918, see page 149, above.

194

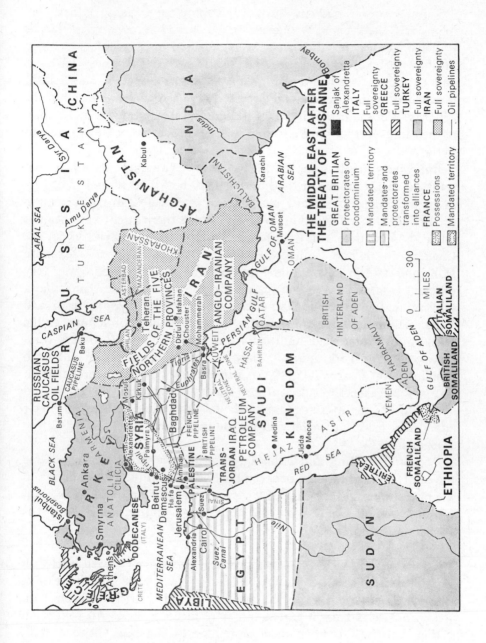

THE MIDDLE EAST AFTER
THE TREATY OF LAUSANNE

GREAT BRITAIN
Protectorates or
condominium

Mandated territory

Mandates and
protectorates
transformed
into alliances

FRANCE
Possessions

Mandated territory

Sanjak of
Alexandretta
ITALY

Full
sovereignty
GREECE

Full sovereignty
TURKEY

Full sovereignty
IRAN

Oil pipelines

0    300
MILES

195

Faisal, however, had few illusions left about the meaning of his agreements with the French. With every signature he wrote, he knew that he was signing away his authority as King of the Syrians – unless he could produce yet another policy to satisfy his impatient followers in Syria and Palestine. So once again, when he felt let down by the British, threatened by the French, and criticised by the Arabs, he turned to the Zionists. Weizmann was in Palestine and Faisal suggested a resumption of their talks further on Weizmann's earlier project when he returned to Syria.

But when Faisal stepped off the French warship at Beirut and returned to Damascus on 14 January 1920 he found himself faced by more pressing problems and by the unexpected defeat of Clemencau in the French General Election. Whatever hopes there might have been of an accommodation with the French Government over Syria under the Clemenceau regime, vanished with the appointment of Alexandre Millerand as the new Prime Minister. His own reception was very different from his first homecoming the previous summer. He found a Government installed in Damascus composed of Syrian, Iraqi and Palestinian nationalists who owed neither allegiance nor support to the Hashemites. Some had returned from exile in Europe, others from service with the Turkish army. They were members of prominent Arab families with a strong Pan-Arab orientation who were prepared to accept the Hashemite rulers as a means to an end, but no more. And since Faisal was no longer the evident key to victory, they and their supporters made no secret of their doubts about the function of the Hashemites.

Without intending, and without even being aware of it, Faisal became the catalyst in the division between the Syrians and the Palestinians and the progenitor, so to speak, of a separate Palestinian identity, of what was to become known as the Palestinian entity and, later, the Palestinian nation.

To understand what happened next it is necessary to dwell briefly on a development that caused Arab leaders much concern at that time. Some months earlier, in the autumn of 1919, British officers with whom Mussa Kazem and Amin were in constant touch told them that the new Political Officer appointed to General Allenby's staff, Colonel R. Meinertzhagen, could be of considerable danger to the Arab cause. He had been appointed, they were told, to ensure the

196

execution of the strict pro-Zionist policy of the Government in London and had much influence with Lloyd George and Curzon.

Soon afterwards, the Arab leaders were told that Meinertzhagen was forming a special secret intelligence service manned mainly by Arabs and Jews to keep him informed about the nationalist movements in Palestine and Syria. One of the Arabs approached by Meinertzhagen's agent, reputedly a young lady, was Amin el-Husaini. According to Amin, he consulted with his friends and they advised him to join the Meinertzhagen secret service in order to keep the Arabs informed of what was going on inside that organisation and, if need be, supply it with information which would embarrass the enemies of the Arab cause, especially the Zionists. As a result of the information thus obtained, Amin says, the Palestinian Arab leaders and their Syrian colleagues were informed of the secret messages that passed between Faisal and the Zionists. They were also aware that the troubles in Palestine, the riots in Jerusalem and Jaffa, during the first half of 1920 were provoked by Meinertzhagen's organisation so as to provide the opportunity for the British to suppress the Palestinian nationalist movement, and to purge the British Military Administration of those officers who were known to be sympathetic to the Arab cause.

I must interrupt the Arab narrative here to consider the Meinertzhagen affair – and especially the role of his special secret service to which this Arab account refers. Meinertzhagen was an extraordinary person, with remarkable abilities and outstanding courage. But he was not the best – or most consistent – judge of men and policies, and his political judgements were not always sound. Above all, one wonders whether his information was always accurate and reliable in view of his strong personal enthusiasms. But in a way this is immaterial to the situation that existed in Palestine during 1920. What is relevant is that the Arabs believed, evidently on the basis of information supplied by Amin and others, that Meinertzhagen's organisation was provoking them into conflict with the British so as to suit the Zionist cause. What is no less relevant is that Meinertzhagen was clearly not aware that Amin had been infiltrated into his organisation, but was convinced that the Military Governor of Jerusalem, Sir Ronald Storrs, and the Chief of Staff to the Chief Administrator, Colonel Waters-Taylor, were encouraging the Arab extremists and supplying them – and also Faisal – with secret and confidential information about British intentions and Zionist activity.

197

The Meinertzhagen and the Waters-Taylor complex made an un-
doubted impression on the Arab and Zionist leaders and furthered their
mutual suspicions. They were an essential element in the development
of the crisis of 1920 based as it was on suspicion and distrust between all
the parties concerned, and within all the parties. This, then, was the
essential factor in the disturbing situation that confronted Faisal as he
came back a second time from Europe – empty-handed in the eyes of the
nationalists.

Aref el-Aref has recorded the mood with which he and his colleagues
greeted the return of Faisal. For the first time Faisal seemed to them
to be dispensable. They might have more success in winning their
national aspirations without him than by following the Hashemite
leadership. Moreover, Faisal was suspected by the Palestinians of
encouraging the Zionists in Palestine so as to weaken the position of the
Palestinian nationalists opposing Faisal in Damascus. *Syria el-Jenoubia*,
edited by Aref el-Aref, gave public voice to the open rift that was
developing between Syrians and Palestinians. It might be better, the
paper said, if the Palestinian Arabs were to fight their own cause rather
than link it with that of the Syrians. For the Palestinians the threat of
Zionism was greater than that of Western domination over the Arab
countries. The Palestinians no longer had the identical interests to the
Syrians. The Palestinians were anti-British while the Syrians were anti-
French. The Palestinians were prepared to reach an agreement with the
French directed against the Zionists; the Syrians considered the French
to be their principal enemy.

It was the beginning of the parting of the ways which was to have
as one of its unforeseen consequences the formation of a separate
Palestinian nation encouraged ironically by its influential paper which
still carried the name *Southern Syria*. The Syrian papers for their part
concentrated their fire on the French, appealed to the Arab world to
fight the French invasion, but made no mention of Zionism.

As the year – 1920 – advanced from spring to summer and the British
troops in Syria were withdrawn, fighting developed in many parts of the
country between Arab guerrilla forces and the French; and with the
fighting came the rumours, and more specific reports, that British
officers were assisting the Arab guerrillas. In Damascus, the popular
mood had become pro-British but not pro-Hashemite. Faisal remained
under a cloud of suspicion. The French retaliated by telling the
Palestinians "that the Zionists were about to establish a Jewish state, a

Bolshevik Colony, in Southern Syria and that it will be a menace to Moslems everywhere". But all this was overshadowed when the Syrian National Congress voted Syrian independence with Faisal as King on 8 March 1920. The resolutions were treated by the Syrian and Palestinian nationalists as the equivalent to an accomplished fact that a Greater Syria, including Palestine, had been established. In Jerusalem, Jaffa, Nablus, Hebron and Gaza thousands of jubilant Arabs demonstrated. In Jerusalem and Jaffa they paraded outside the British Governor's home with banners and slogans, shouting "Long Live Faisal!", "Down with the British!", and "Death to the Jews!" in spontaneously graduated violence. In Jerusalem the demonstrators were led by Mussa Kazem, the Mayor, accompanied by Amin el-Husaini and by Aref el-Aref. Aref's paper, *Syria el-Jenoubia*, published a special edition with massive banner headlines proclaiming: "Arabs Arise! The end of the foreigners is near. Jews will be drowned in their own blood!"

In the face of this sudden militancy the British were helpless; troops and police disappeared from the streets. The Arabs were the masters of Jerusalem. The Government in London was most annoyed and instructed Storrs to dismiss Mussa Kazem as Mayor of Jerusalem and to appoint someone more amenable to the British. After Storrs had done this and appointed Ragheb Nashashibi as the new Mayor, Mussa Kazem met with Colonel Waters-Taylor and a number of other senior British officers who had been acting as his informal advisers. According to Mussa Kazem's account of this meeting, Waters-Taylor told him that his dismissal could be the opening of the way to Arab independence. He said that if the Arabs are not deterred by British reprisals and maintain their open revolt to British rule then they will succeed in containing the Zionist danger.

Faisal had also been encouraged at first by the response to his own militancy. For a short time he appeared to have regained his popularity – at least in Palestine. But he soon realised that he was playing with fire and that the Palestinian leaders were not at all concerned with the future well-being of the Hashemites, nor with the French presence in Syria. He therefore summoned the Syrian nationalists for an exchange of views and impressed on them that their radical alliance with the Palestinians could in the end unite the French and the British against them. "He appealed to the Syrians not to be led astray by the Palestinians and to rely on the British. But the Syrian nationalist leaders would not hear of it. They accused Faisal of wanting to inflict upon the Arabs 'the Jewish plague'."

Meanwhile Meinertzhagen had come to Damascus to persuade Faisal to attend the San Remo Conference due to take place in April 1920. This was to settle finally the questions of mandates for Syria, Palestine and Iraq. But Faisal felt his position was too uncertain for him to risk another prolonged absence in Europe. Instead, he turned once more to the Zionists. He sent a message to Jerusalem suggesting that the Zionist leadership should consider his proposal for a Syrian Federal State of which Palestine would be one of the federated states with Faisal as King. He had heard that Herbert Samuel was in Jerusalem for consultations (he had not yet been appointed as High Commissioner) and Faisal invited him to come to Damascus for further talks. After consultations with the Government in London, Samuel replied that he was in Jerusalem "on purely administrative business and could not engage in political conversations".

Faisal felt himself completely isolated but still inclined to risk the journey to San Remo for one more direct appeal to the British and French. "Before he made his definitive decision, however, the Syrian Minister of War received a secret message from Colonel Waters-Taylor who, together with a number of other British officers, made no secret of their pro-Arab sympathies, in Jerusalem. He informed the Syrian Government and also Faisal of the warning Waters-Taylor had sent. This advised the Syrian authorities that at the San Remo Conference Palestine was to be made into a Jewish state under British mandate. The British were already arming the Jews in Palestine, the Waters-Taylor message continued, so that they can secede from the Syrian state. Unless the Arabs actively oppose this move at once, Waters-Taylor, one of the most senior officers in Palestine, told the Syrian War Minister, their fate will be settled for years to come and they will have to accept Jewish domination supported by the British Government."

In a further message, Waters-Taylor told the Syrian Government that the British Government would soon send out Samuel as High Commissioner to implement the Zionist policies. The Military Administration in Palestine was however opposed to Samuel's appointment. This opposition might still be successful if the Arabs themselves were to manifest their own radical opposition to this British intention. In view of the imminence of the San Remo Conference it was necessary that the Arabs should act without delay and in a more radical way than they did after the Damascus Congress in March.

This message coming from the British Chief of Staff in Palestine made a deep impression on the Arab leaders in Damascus. Youssef el-Azma, the War Minister, convened a meeting of nationalist representatives and it was agreed to present an ultimatum to Faisal.

He was told that unless he opted for armed resistance to the French and the Zionists they would act without him in Syria and Palestine. They advised him to go to San Remo so that they could stage a military uprising without compromising his diplomatic fight against the British and the French. When Faisal asked them whether they had sufficient arms and ammunition Youssef el-Azma assured him that the British had promised them adequate supplies. Faisal still hesitated. They told him then that the Palestinians would go ahead in any case and the first thing they would do would be to expel Faisal from Damascus and sever all links with the Hashemites. Faisal continued to question their decision. He wanted to know who was the Palestine Committee of National Defence that dictated this action to the Syrian Government?

Faisal was told that the Committee was made up of a well-organised group of the Husaini family with Mussa, Amin and Jamal as the leaders who exercised great influence over the Palestinian youth, and they were supported by Mussa Kazem, the former Mayor, and others. Faisal replied that he required time for consultations and that he would give his answer to the Palestinian delegation that was coming to Damascus to congratulate Faisal on his nomination as King of Syria. When they met and stated their terms, Faisal told them that he appreciated their enthusiasm but that "he expected his Palestinian brethren to obey his orders and not to act rashly. He would in due time safeguard their national aspirations with the help of the British."

At the same time, Faisal ordered strict security measures and supervision of extremists, especially the Palestinians. He decided to stay in Damascus and not go to San Remo. He sent General Nuri[15] instead. But most important of all, he wrote an urgent and private letter to

[15] Later Prime Minister of Iraq. Assassinated in 1958.

Allenby in Cairo. He implored Allenby to use his influence in London to prevent any pro-Zionist decision at the San Remo Conference. He repeated his offer to be crowned as King of Palestine, federated to Syria, and to calm the anti-Zionist and anti-British agitation by mediating between Arab and Jew. Allenby referred Faisal's appeal to General Bols in Palestine. He suggested that Bols should invite Faisal for talks in Jerusalem. Allenby also informed the Foreign Office of Faisal's urgent appeal.

But events overtook Faisal's diplomacy. On 4 April, Easter Monday, a great and excited demonstration in Jerusalem exploded into a mass assault on the Jewish population. The Jews were obviously anticipating such an attack and resisted the Arab crowd. The British withdrew police and soldiers from the Old City and after two days of rioting there were five Jewish dead and 211 Jewish wounded and four Arabs dead and 21 wounded. "Amin and Aref el-Aref, who led the demonstration together with other members of the Arab Defence Committee, did their best to keep the Arab masses under control, and appealed to them not to attack British soldiers and not to assault Christians." However, as the "so-called Jewish Self-Defence group under a Jewish Army Officer, Vladimir Jabotinsky, was approaching the homes of the Mufti and of Amin in order to assassinate them, the Arab Committee requested Amin to put into operation the plan to launch Arab *Fedayoun* against a selected number of Zionist leaders who were to be removed from the Palestinian scene. Among those chosen for action by the *Fedayoun* were Dr Weizmann, Menahem Ussishkin, Dr David Eder, Israel Sieff and a number of other Russian and British Zionists; no American and no Palestinian Jews were included in the list of those who were to be killed." British Intelligence heard of this planned action by the *Fedayoun* and took counter-measures. Amin and Aref had to flee to Transjordan after being accused by the British of having provoked the riots.

The most striking feature of the Jerusalem riots and their aftermath was that they evoked no reaction at all in Syria. The French were delighted. The British were pleased. The Zionists were relieved. But the Syrian failure to respond to the Palestinian initiative made its most significant impact on Amin and the Palestinians. They became involved in an angry exchange with their British friends, especially Waters-Taylor who had expressed his astonishment to Mussa Kazem immediately after the riots "at the failure of the Arab Defence Committee to exploit their chances in a more radical manner since the British military had

202

given them the opportunity for a straight show-down with the Jews. Aref el-Aref, who had been acting Chief of Staff for the Committee, explained to the British that the risks were too great for once the crowd had embarked on a course of looting and destruction, the British would have been compelled to intervene against the Arabs."

Amin, however, insisted that the Jerusalem uprising was the turning-point in the struggle for Palestinian independence, it was the beginning of the Palestinian show of force. The Palestinians, without help from the Syrians or from any outside source, had expressed in deeds their resolution to resist the Zionists and the British. The Syrians had remained passive because they still expected British help against the French. They were mistaken. Amin admitted that the Arabs would have to make alliances that would assist their cause but the Arab cause now must remain in the hands of a Palestinian leadership. He warned the Arabs that they had to be as subtle as their enemies. They had to court the English and the Jews without making fundamental concessions and they had to drive a wedge between the English and the Jews without appearing to do so. The Zionists were anxious to have friendly relations with the Arabs because they realised that they could not succeed without them – and they were prepared to pay a price. The important thing was to isolate the Jews from the English. And Amin and his friends prepared to assume the mantle of Arab leadership that was perceptibly slipping from Faisal's shoulders.

Faisal was not alone in his disillusionment with the British. Their handling of the Jerusalem riots had shocked the Zionists even if it had not surprised them. Despite a sense of anticipation the actual occurrences had a traumatic effect on the Zionist leadership. Weizmann had been in a buoyant mood when he sailed from Europe, but landed in Alexandria to meet a very different situation from that which he had anticipated. He wrote to his wife soon afterwards – on 21 March 1920 – about the deluge of bad news that greeted him as he came off the boat in Alexandria: Murder in Upper Galilee, Metullah attacked. Six Jews killed "among them Trumpeldor and the two girls to whom you spoke at Tel Chai. . . . A demonstration in Jerusalem. The Administration terrified and therefore lenient towards the Arabs; they want to disband the Jewish battalion and to get rid of Meinertzhagen! . . . Samuel – so I am assured – is weak, frightened and trembling." And there is more at which Weizmann only hints, "I have decided to tell the whole truth about the Administration in Jerusalem; I am convinced that they will all have to go. Otherwise the thing will just collapse. . . . The story about Faisal is not particularly pleasant. . . ."[16]

And a week later, from Jerusalem, Weizmann was writing about the dangerous situation he had found there. "The English are behaving abominably towards us, and all the promises made to us at home have the sound of bitter irony here. And every time the English treat us badly, Arab impertinence and arrogance increases. They are really riding high and the English encourage them." He calculated that perhaps five or six British officials in the whole administration treated the Zionists decently, the rest were their secret or open enemies. "Faisal's conduct – which the British supported – is making the situation worse. I have had two conversations with Allenby and one with Bols (he is still decent!); also one with Waters-Taylor. I have told them categorically that I consider their conduct dishonest, they were ruining our cause and gravely harming that of the British, that their entire conduct has become a public lie and that I wanted no more dealings with them until they show proof that they mean to carry out Zionist policy."[17]

The bitter memories remained with him on his way to Genoa for the San Remo conference. Writing still about his latest experiences he tells his wife that he was not in a position to describe what he believed to have actually happened in Jerusalem. "Meinertzhagen and Deedes are the only two Englishmen who are adequate to the situation – the others are just jackals." He was proud of the way the Jews had behaved and had it not been for the British intervention "we could have managed the Arabs very well from the very first day". But the British disarmed the Haganah and "arrested our people (Jabotinsky among them)". He was very dubious about the outcome of the San Remo conference. "In future I shall not accept any more paper promises or proclamations. I don't trust any of these wolves. After all, in Palestine . . . the English!!"[18]

Weizmann reported also to his colleagues in Jerusalem and London but he did little more than record the final phase of the Faisal period in Arab-Jewish relations – without being fully aware that this marked the end of the first epoch of Zionist-Arab relations, and that they would have to contend with entirely different and more aggressive forces than the Hashemite princes. It is necessary to dwell on this briefly as it was

[16] Weizmann to Vera Weizmann, 21 March 1920.
[17] Weizmann to Vera Weizmann, 29 March 1920.
[18] Weizmann to Vera Weizmann, 19 April 1920.

an essential part of the Faisal phase – for a few months Zionist and Hashemite fate became closely intermingled – and neither seemed to be aware of the Palestinian factor that was to be their – temporary – undoing.

Thus, faced by the emergence of the Palestinians in the March demonstrations in Jerusalem and elsewhere, Weizmann reported to the Zionist Commission in Jerusalem on 25 March entirely in terms of the British attitude and of Faisal's position. The Palestinians were not mentioned: The present situation in Palestine had come as a surprise to him after his arrival in Cairo where he had met Meinertzhagen who had explained that the officials of the present administration were not "friendly disposed towards us". They gave the impression as if they were succeeding in forcing a revision of the Government's Zionist policy. Yet, despite this, Meinertzhagen was optimistic, Weizmann told his colleagues. He was of the opinion that the anti-Zionist demonstrations earlier that month "were organised by the French representative and that the French Government had spent a lot of money on it". Meinertzhagen also gave an account of the Zionist speeches made by General Bols and himself in Nablus and told Weizmann of an interview which Meinertzhagen had just had with Lord Milner. Milner had said that Zionism was necessary for England and that he believed in a Jewish state in Palestine. Meinertzhagen agreed with Milner and said that he believed in "a Jewish state from the Arabian Desert to the Euphrates". Weizmann reported this interview with Meinertzhagen with evident satisfaction and added that Meinertzhagen had also told him that the Zionists had no friend in Cairo except Allenby and that all the British there consider the Balfour Declaration to have been a mistake.[19]

Weizmann's mercurial temperament, his rapid switch off from hope to despair, from near euphoria to blackest depression, puzzled the Arabs. They thought it was a part of the Zionist Machiavellian diplomacy. But, curiously, the Zionists themselves – who generally followed Weizmann's temperamental excursions – seemed to be unaware of this lack of political constancy. Only a few, such as Sieff and Sacher, were very conscious of this quirk in Weizmann's usual scientific calm and balance which had become part and parcel of Zionist diplomacy.

Weizmann emerged in a hopeful frame of mind from the San Remo

[19] Minutes of Meeting of the Zionist Commission, 25 March 1920.

205

conference and – with the Palestinian disturbances almost forgotten – wrote to his wife from San Remo on 20 April 1920.

> . . . The Mandate has been approved and with it the Declaration. There will be a change in the Administration. Herbert Samuel will be our first Governor in the new Palestine . . . A new era is setting in and a great deal will depend on us now . . . Lloyd George, Balfour and even Curzon behaved very well; also the Italians. But our French friends – what a trash! . . . A dramatic chapter has been closed and now we build the new Palestine. Samuel is delighted . . . The Arabs here walk about with long faces. . . .[20]

But in the weeks that followed Weizmann became increasingly conscious of the inability or incompetence of the Zionist Commission in Palestine especially in its handling of the Arab question – an item that figured prominently at the major meeting of the Zionist Executive in London on 7 May 1920. Instead of discussing what should be Zionist policy in relation to the Arabs – particularly in view of the evident crisis which faced Faisal in Damascus – the discussion centred on the kind of personalities who understood the Arabs and had good connections with them, men like Kalvarisky and Yellin. Weizmann proposed that they should be brought into the Arab Department and offices opened for them in Jerusalem, Cairo and Damascus. No one appeared to notice the gulf that separated the rather unpolitical idealistic Kalvarisky from the new men who were at the head of the Palestinian Arab movement. It was almost incredible how little the Zionist leadership knew of this Arab national movement in political terms and even more how little it understood the Arab nationalists and their objectives.

Just when such a Zionist reorientation in Arab relations was becoming necessary because of the eclipse of the Hashemites, Weizmann found himself totally preoccupied with his own camp, and by early June 1920 he was confronted by a crisis not with the Palestinian Arabs but with the Palestinian Jews and some of their most prominent leaders. They were harassing Weizmann, demanding impossible action which Weizmann believed to be of no value whatsoever in constructive terms. "There is apparently a spirit of bitterness and vindictiveness abroad that will make it very difficult for Mr Samuel," he wrote to David Eder in Jerusalem by way of comment on the letters and reports the Zionist

[20] Weizmann to Vera Weizmann, 20 April 1920.

Executive in London was receiving from Palestine. Drastic measures would be necessary to make an end to the state of hysteria "into which a part of the Palestinian population had apparently worked itself". Weizmann was speaking of the Jews, not the Arabs. They seemed to excel "in cheap heroism and fictitious martyrdom" and Weizmann was "beginning to sympathise with the British administration more now than I ever did". And after denouncing the irresponsibilities of "the Dizengoffs and Jabotinskys" Weizmann tells Eder that he had made up his mind to finish with this state of affairs: "the pampering tactics which the Zionist Organisation has adopted towards the pioneers and the heroes will have to cease definitely once and for all".[21]

Much of this internal Zionist conflict stemmed from the shrewd tactics of the new Palestinian leadership which encouraged these differences between the Palestinian Jews and the Zionist leaders. Amin's hit-and-run tactics were designed to provoke and unnerve the Palestinian Jews and he succeeded on both counts. Moreover, the Faisal story was moving to its sad and ineffective conclusion as far as the association with the Zionists was concerned. Faisal had been Weizmann's great hope – as he had been Clayton's, one of the essential pillars of the Grand Design. But when he met with Dr Eder in Haifa on 6 August Faisal was a refugee without kingdom and without following. The drama and futility of the Faisal-Weizmann association was packed into that last interview in Haifa about which Eder reported to Weizmann.

> The general position which I adopted was this: We favoured a United Arab Nation, outside the limits of Palestine, with one representative with whom one could treat. . . . We had of course no personal feeling of loyalty to Faisal such as his followers had (two of them were in the room and acted as interpreters) but ours was based entirely on political considerations. If Faisal was the chosen representative and could make himself accepted by the Great Powers, we should cordially be in favour of his leadership of the Arab people.

Eder lacked the suppleness and tact of Weizmann and his talk with Faisal had therefore an air of blunt reality which was usually lacking at the meeting of two such polite and respectful gentlemen as Faisal and Weizmann. Perhaps, the fact that Faisal was now a king who had lost his throne rather than one about to be anointed also contributed

[21] Weizmann to Eder, 8 June 1920.

to the change in style. For Weizmann had never spoken to Faisal in the manner in which Eder now addressed him.

I had to point out to him he had tried to be too clever; he was a Zionist in Europe; he backed the anti-Zionists at Damascus; he was trying to play off the French against the English and *vice versa*. He must pursue a straightforward policy if there was to be any chance of success – the recognition of the French Mandate in Syria, the recognition of the Balfour Declaration and all its implications, which I detailed, in Palestine. He asked how we could help him and what we expected from him.

Eder told him that the Zionists had no quarrel with France, they were under a British mandate in Palestine but Weizmann and Sokolow would use their diplomatic influence in Paris and London, and Brandeis would do the same in Washington. Moreover, it had to be remembered that the Zionists were no military power. Faisal then said that he knew that "the power of the Jewish press was great, could it not be mobilised in his favour?"

Eder replied that Faisal was mistaken; there was no Jewish press influence in the way Faisal imagined it. But instead of entering on this question Eder re-stated the Zionist demands on Faisal. They would want him to use his influence with the Arabs to halt the anti-Zionist propaganda, and "to recognise fully the Zionist influence in Palestine and to abandon all cries for a United Syria". Eder concluded his report with a personal assessment of the fallen monarch:

I believe Faisal is still in favour with the British. The Arabs, including some of Faisal's entourage, attribute his defeat to the anti-Zionism of his extreme Party. I doubt, after studying Faisal during my interview whether he is strong enough to rule an Arab people. He has plenty of intelligence but I should judge that he is not a born leader; he sees too many sides of the question.[22]

It was a sad interview for Faisal and an even sadder commentary on the manner in which the Zionist leadership viewed its relations with the Arabs in a kind of vacuum quite apart from the mainstream of Arab development. With the passing of time, Weizmann had more opportunity to reflect on these shortcomings and towards the end of 1923 he

[22] Eder to Weizmann, 9 August 1920.

wrote a personal note to Samuel in Jerusalem in which he voiced some of the changed ideas he had developed on the subject of the Palestinians.

> I think the whole problem of the Arab Federation might become of great value to all parties concerned if the Zionists were allowed freer scope to negotiate with the Arabs, and particularly with the Arabs of Palestine, on that plane. Thus the Arabs would be convinced that we would favour the creation of an Arab Federation as long as an honest agreement could be arrived at by which the Arabs consent to an unhampered development of a Jewish National Home.[23]

But it was very much a case of shutting the stable door much too late. It was also the perfect example of the incompatibility that was to develop between the Arab and the Zionist leadership, so much so that not even the fiction of the Faisal-Weizmann collaboration could be maintained. For meanwhile, the changes in the Arab leadership had become fully effective. The stage was set for an Arab-Zionist relationship that could be resolved only by conflict and force and no longer by agreement. That might just have been possible had Faisal prevailed, but only just, and after many adjustments by Arabs and Zionists alike. But Faisal was no longer a factor and his place had been taken by the new Palestinian Arab dispensation under the leadership of Amin, Aref and their militant colleagues. Weizmann's diplomacy was no match for them for they were not concerned with diplomacy; above all, the Zionist leadership failed to understand the change which had taken place – and they opened the road for Amin and the new Arab policy, the Palestinian policy that was the rock on which Faisal had foundered and on which Weizmann's Zionist diplomacy was also to be wrecked. How this came about has to be seen through Arab eyes.

Amin returned to Jerusalem after he had been pardoned, together with Aref el-Aref, by the High Commissioner, Herbert Samuel. He returned to work with Mussa Kazem at the Arab Executive but his mind was preoccupied with other matters. He was the only Arab leader who seemed to have the capacity to look ahead and to seek to shape Arab policy accordingly. "In the first instance," Amin confided to Aref el-Aref, "it was necessary to shape an instrument for the Arab struggle against the Zionists and the British, a political instrument that was attuned to the changed conditions of British rule from those which had prevailed under the Turks. For with the British occupation, Palestine

[23] Weizmann to Samuel, 14 November 1923.

ceased to be a Muslim country and became a state comprising three communities, Jews, Muslims and Christians. What was necessary for their purpose," Amin argued, "was to create an institution which would be completely independent of the British and at the same time the recognised authority and spokesman of the Muslim community." For this purpose the Supreme Moslem Council was established in March 1921 and Amin was elected its President the following January. The authority of the Council was virtually unlimited as it could always refer to Moslem Law for its justification and it became an effective government within the Government in Palestine; in its way it paralleled the Zionist Organisation as the spokesman for the Arab population – and it had the additional advantage of being the most important all-Arab religious body based on Jerusalem.

When Kamel el-Husaini died in 1921, there were four candidates for the succession as Mufti of Jerusalem. The first three candidates received 18, 17 and 12 votes respectively. Amin was the fourth with nine votes and he showed his general political ability by successfully getting the High Commissioner to appoint him as Mufti and to make Aref el-Aref the District Commissioner, first for Jenin and then for the strategic areas of Nablus, Gaza and Beisan respectively. In his new position Amin seemed almost a moderate at first, and Samuel was reassured by his choice. Some of Amin's colleagues even suspected him of trying to continue the secret talks with the Zionists which Faisal had initiated. In fact, Amin pursued a cautious and responsible policy towards the British and the Jews while he consolidated his grip on the Supreme Moslem Council. But at the same time, he was directing Arab policy in negotiations with the British and successfully created the new climate which practically nullified any possibility of an agreed settlement. He was the author of the Memorandum which Mussa Kazem presented to Winston Churchill, then Colonial Secretary, at Government House in Jerusalem on 28 March 1921. In it Amin set the guidelines for Palestinian resistance to Zionism which every patriotic Arab leader followed. His purpose then was the same as in 1918: he wanted to isolate the Zionists and drive a wedge between them and the British. He set the tone for the disturbances that were to follow in May 1921. These were very different from the riots of April 1920, and they showed how much progress Amin had made along the new course which he was charting for the Arabs.

In April 1920 the Arab demonstrators had denounced the British as

210

much as the Zionists and, in a sense, drove them into each others' arms. Not so now that Amin had assumed control. The demonstrating Arab masses linked their anti-Zionist slogans with declarations of loyalty to the British Administration – to Samuel! They marched shouting "Death to the Jews" and "The Government is with us". It was an effective move by Amin and it showed that the Zionists had to face a worthy antagonist. But far more damaging to the Zionists than the demonstrations and the Arab identification with the British, was the calculated forethought of Amin's policy which was set out in the memorandum handed to Churchill. It demanded the dismantling of the entire Zionist superstructure in Palestine including the very concept of a Jewish National Home, the formation of a national Arab Government, the halting of Jewish immigration and of pro-Zionist legislation, and the reunion of Palestine with Syria and Transjordan.

Amin knew that such requests would not even be considered by the British but he also knew that the Arabs would understand what they meant. There was to be no recognition of the Zionists, no acceptance of their presence and no negotiations with the Zionists. In case there might be a misunderstanding on this point, as Churchill had misunderstood Amin's first approach, when he replied to the delegation that they should negotiate directly with the Zionists, Amin had its meaning spelled out at a further meeting with Churchill in London on 12 August 1921. Churchill had told the Palestine delegation that he wanted them to meet with Dr Weizmann. Fully briefed by Amin on this occasion, the secretary to the delegation, Shibly Jamali, replied on their behalf that "we do not recognise Dr Weizmann. We recognise the British Government." They would parley only with the British and would have no direct negotiations with the Zionists.

Despite this there was a meeting between some members of the Arab delegation and the Zionists but this only served to confirm Amin's policy. The Zionists demanded Arab recognition of their rights in Palestine, the Arabs demanded British abrogation of any special rights granted to the Jews. They were prepared to accept the Jews as citizens of Arab states but in no other way. There was total deadlock. The Zionists were unable to reach accommodation with or acceptance by the Arabs, and the British would not proceed on Zionist lines without Arab agreement. Within a matter of months Amin had established the Arab right of veto which effectively blocked Weizmann's diplomacy, and when on 14 May 1921, Samuel announced the suspension of Jewish

211

immigration, it looked as if Amin's formula had been wholly successful. He had made the one factor that the Zionists ignored or rejected – the Palestinian Arabs – into the most effective obstacle that barred the Zionist road to Arab acceptance. It did not matter that politicians and princes had private meetings with Weizmann and others; what mattered was that by mid-1921 Amin had made it impossible for any Arab politician publicly to propose a settlement with the Zionists on terms that would be acceptable to the Zionists. He had blocked any kind of negotiation and refused every form of recognition. His triumph was total – except for something which had remained outside Amin's calculation.

For 1921 was the year of decision – and recognition – for the Zionists, though both decision and recognition took many years to germinate. But once the British limited immigration at the behest of Arab pressure, they left no alternative to the Zionist leadership but to go all out to create the conditions which would enable them to be in control of this immigration. Amin in fact set in motion the two most potent forces that were to play the dominant role over the next half-century or more in Palestine: first, he established the Arab refusal to accept the Zionists in any form, or negotiate with them directly in any way, or conclude a treaty with them. And, secondly, he compelled the Zionist leadership to abandon the Weizmannist policy of seeking accommodation and prepare the conditions for complete statehood and control over Palestine. It was Amin who set the Arab guidelines in 1921 which survived 50 years later that there must be no peace in Zion with the Zionists. It took the Zionists a long time to understand the full implications of Amin's success; it took the Palestinian Arabs even longer.

# INTERLUDE
## 1923-1967

# Chronology of Events

**1923**

25 May    Proclamation of Transjordan independence under Emir Abdullah.

29 May    Palestine Constitution suspended by British Order in Council because of Arab refusal to co-operate.

24 July    Lausanne Peace Treaty signed by Greece, Turkey and the Allies.

29 Sept.    British Palestine Mandate comes into force.

**1924**

3 Oct.    King Husain of the Hejaz abdicates; succeeded by his son Ali.

**1925**

20 July    Druze uprising in Syria (until June 1927).

12 Oct.    Syrian uprising against French Mandate.

**1926**

8 Jan.    Emir ibn Saud becomes King of Hejaz after defeating Hashemites; name changed to Kingdom of Saudi Arabia.

23 May    France proclaims Republic of Lebanon.

**1927**

20 May    Britain recognises Saudi Arabia's independence.

14 Dec.    Britain recognises Iraq's independence (subject to a special treaty relationship).

**1928**

20 Feb.    Britain recognises independence of Transjordan, subject to a special treaty relationship.

9 June    France convenes Syrian Constituent Assembly with Nationalist majority.

1929

Aug.   Arab attack on Jews in Palestine following dispute at the Temple Wall in Jerusalem; many Jewish dead in Hebron and Safed.

1930

20 Oct.   British "Passfield White Paper" proposes halt in Jewish immigration into Palestine and restricts sale of Arab land to Jews.

1932

3 Oct.   British Mandate over Iraq terminated.

1933

July–Aug.   Massacre of Assyrian Christians in Iraq.
8 Sept.   Death of King Faisal of Iraq; succeeded by his son Ghazi.

1934

May–June   Six-week war between Saudi Arabia and Yemen.
3 Nov.   Syrian Parliament indefinitely prorogued.

1935

14 Jan.   Iraq–Mediterranean oil pipeline from Kirkuk to Haifa and Sidon opened.

1936

25 April   Arab Higher Committee formed in Palestine.
28 April   Farouk succeeds Fuad I as King of Egypt.
March   Arab general strike in Palestine.
Aug.   Arab rebellion in Palestine (until Aug. 1939).
26 Aug.   Anglo-Egyptian treaty ends military occupation of Egypt except in the Suez Canal Zone.
29 Oct.   General Sidqi Bakr seizes power in Iraq.

1937

7 July   British Royal Commission publishes partition plan for Palestine.
11 Aug.   General Sidqi Bakr, Iraqi dictator, assassinated.
1 Oct.   British declare Arab Higher Committee in Palestine an illegal body.
16 Oct.   Mufti of Jerusalem escapes to Syria.

1939

Jan.–March   Round-table conference on Palestine called in London.

216

17 May  British White Paper providing for an independent
Palestine, with Arab majority and severe limits on Jewish
immigration and land-purchase; Jewish Agency statement:
"Jews will never accept the closing against them of the
gates of Palestine, nor let their national home be
converted into a ghetto."

3 Sept.  Palestine Jews declare wholehearted support for Britain's
war against Nazi Germany; 119,000 register to serve
Britain in any capacity.

## 1941

3 April  Pro-Axis Government under Rashid Ali set up in Iraq.

May–June  British expeditionary force reoccupies Habbaniyah and
Baghdad.

22 May  Rashid Ali and pro-Axis leaders seek asylum in Teheran
and Berlin.

June  Free French and Australian troops occupy Syria and
Lebanon; Britain and France guarantee Syrian
independence.

## 1942

Dec.  Under pressure from British and Arabs, Free French
agree to relinquish mandatory powers over Syrian and
Lebanese Governments.

## 1945

22 March  Arab League founded in Cairo offer consultations between
Eden and Nuri.

May–June  Crisis in Syria and Lebanon; ultimatum from British to
French results in French undertaking to withdraw forces.

Aug.  President Truman proposes Britain admit 110,000 Jews to
Palestine.

Sept.  British limit Jewish immigration into Palestine to 1,500
a month.

Nov.  Anglo-American Enquiry Commission for Palestine
appointed.

## 1946

March  New Anglo-Transjordan treaty negotiated in London;
British recognise Emir Abdullah as King of Transjordan.

April  Last British and French troops leave Damascus.
Report of Anglo-American Enquiry Commission for
Palestine published and rejected by Arab and Zionist
spokesmen.

|        |                                                                                                                 |
| ------ | --------------------------------------------------------------------------------------------------------------- |
| June   | Amin el-Husaini escapes from detention in France; given sanctuary in Cairo. Terrorism increasing in Palestine; British occupy Jewish Agency HQ, and detain most Zionist leaders in Palestine. |
|        | Anti-British riots in Baghdad.                                                                                  |
| 22 July | British Military HQ in King David Hotel, Jerusalem, blown up by the Irgun.                                     |
| Aug.   | British start deporting illegal Jewish immigrants to Cyprus.                                                    |
| Sept.  | Palestine round-table conference opens in London.                                                              |

1947

| Feb. | Britain refers Palestine issue to UN after Arab and Zionist leaders had rejected British proposals. |
| --- | --- |
| May | UN Assembly appoints Special Committee on Palestine (UNSCOP). |
| July | Three Jews hanged for participation in Acre prison break; Irgun executes two British sergeants as reprisal. |
| Sept. | UNSCOP recommends partition. British announce decision to terminate Mandate and withdraw troops from Palestine. |
| Oct. | USA and USSR support partition of Palestine by 1 August 1948. |
| 29 Nov. | UN General Assembly endorses partition. |
| Dec. | Arab League says it will oppose creation of Jewish state. |

1948

| Feb. | Anti-British riots in Baghdad against new Anglo-Iraqi treaty lead to fall of pro-British Government. |
| --- | --- |
| March | Provisional Jewish Government formed in Tel-Aviv. |
| April | UN proposes temporary UN trusteeship for Palestine. |
| 14 May | British High Commissioner leaves Palestine; State of Israel proclaimed. |
| 14–15 May | Arab armies cross Palestine frontier. |
|  | UN General Assembly appoint Count Bernadotte mediator for Palestine. |
| 15–17 May | USA and USSR recognise Israel. Siege of Jerusalem starts. |
| 28 May | Jews in old city of Jerusalem surrender. |
| 11 June | Four weeks' truce proclaimed in Palestine. |
| 28 June | Bernadotte's first Peace Plan: Jerusalem to be Arab. |
| 30 June | Last British soldier leaves Palestine. |
| 7 July | Israel accepts, Arab League refuses, UN request for extension of truce; Egyptian attack resumed in southern Palestine. |
| 18 July | Second truce proclaimed. |
| 17 Sept. | Bernadotte assassinated in Jerusalem. |

| 20 Sept. | Bernadotte's final Palestine proposals published and rejected by Arab League and by Israel. |
| 16–22 Oct. | Fighting breaks out in Negev; Egyptian reverses. Security Council orders cease-fire. Israelis take Beersheba. |
| 29–31 Oct. | Israeli successes in central Galilee and southern Lebanon. |
| Dec. | UN General Assembly calls for internationalisation of Jerusalem. Renewed fighting in Negev; Israelis advance into Egypt. |

## 1949

| Jan. | Israeli and Egyptian forces withdraw behind their frontiers; British troops occupy Aqaba. |
| 24 Feb. | Armistice between Israel and Egypt. |
| March | Armistice between Israel and Lebanon. Israelis reach Gulf of Aqaba. |
| 20 July | Armistice between Israel and Syria. |

## 1950

| Jan. | Wafd win Egyptian elections; Nahas Pasha becomes Premier. |
| April | Britain gives *de jure* recognition to Israel and to the Hashemite Kingdom of Jordan. |
| May | Britain, France and USA issue Tripartite Declaration that Middle East security and stability is their common interest. |

## 1951

| 2 May | Persian Premier Mussadiq nationalises Persian oil industry. |
| 20 July | King Abdullah assassinated; Talal succeeds to throne. |
| 4 Oct. | Last British leave oil refinery at Abadan, Persia. |
| 8 Oct. | Egypt abrogates Anglo-Egyptian treaty of 1936. |

## 1952

| 26 Jan. | Riots in Cairo; 76 people reported killed; martial law. |
| 23 July | General Neguib's military coup in Cairo. |
| 26 July | Farouk abdicates in favour of 7-month-old son; leaves Egypt. |
| 11 Aug. | Talal of Jordan abdicates; 17-year-old Husain proclaimed King. |
| 7 Sept. | Neguib assumes premiership of Egypt. |

## 1953

| 18 Jan. | Moscow accuses "Zionist agents" of murdering Zhdanov and attempting to murder other Soviet leaders. |
| 18 June | Republic proclaimed in Egypt, with Neguib as President and Prime Minister. |

219

|         |                                                                                    |
| ------- | ---------------------------------------------------------------------------------- |
| 7 Sept. | Ben-Gurion resigns Israeli premiership; succeeded by Moshe Sharett.                |

**1954**

| 19 Oct. | Anglo-Egyptian evacuation agreement signed. |
| 3 Nov.  | Nasser becomes Head of State in Egypt.      |

**1955**

| 24 Feb. | Baghdad Pact formally signed by Turkey and Iraq.         |
| 28 Feb. | Israeli army attacks Gaza; 38 Egyptians reported killed. |
| 2 Nov.  | Ben-Gurion becomes Israel's Premier.                     |
| 3 Nov.  | Iran joins Baghdad Pact.                                 |

**1956**

| 29 Feb.     | Husain of Jordan dismisses General Glubb, Commander of Arab Legion. |
| 13 June     | Last British troops leave Suez Canal base. |
| 24 June     | Nasser elected President of Egypt. |
| 19–20 July  | USA and Britain withdraw offer to help Egypt finance the Aswan Dam. |
| 26 July     | Nasser nationalises the Suez Canal. |
| 26–31 July  | Britain, France and USA announce financial retaliation against Egypt. |
| 16 Aug.     | London conference on Suez Canal boycotted by Egypt. |
| 10 Sept.    | Egypt rejects 18-nation proposals for Suez Canal. |
| 19 Sept.    | Second London conference on Suez. |
| 23 Sept.    | Britain and France refer Suez dispute to UN Security Council. |
| 12 Oct.     | Britain informs Israel she will assist Jordan against further Israeli attacks. |
| 25 Oct.     | Egypt, Syria and Jordan establish unified military command. |
| 29 Oct.     | Israeli troops invade Sinai Peninsula. |
| 30 Oct.     | Anglo-French ultimatum to Egypt and Israel to withdraw troops 10 miles from Canal; accepted by Israel, rejected by Egypt. |
| 31 Oct.     | Anglo-French aircraft bomb Egyptian airfields. |
| 2 Nov.      | Israelis occupy Gaza and most of Sinai; 3,000 Egyptian prisoners. |
| 4 Nov.      | UN Assembly adopts Canadian-sponsored resolution to send UN force to Egypt; Israel votes against, Britain and France abstain. Soviet forces attack Budapest. |
| 5 Nov.      | British paratroops land at Port Said. |
| 6 Nov.      | USSR threat to use rockets unless Britain, France and Israel withdraw. |

7 Nov. Premier Ben-Gurion announces Israel's readiness to withdraw as UN troops move in. Anglo-French cease-fire.

14 Nov. First UN troops arrive.

22 Dec. British and French withdraw.

### 1957

22 Jan. Israel withdraws from Sinai.

8 March Israel withdraws from Gaza.

25 March Suez Canal opened to shipping.

### 1958

1 Feb. Egypt and Syria proclaim union as United Arab Republic.

14 July Revolution in Iraq, led by General Kassem; King Faisal II, the former Regent and Nuri es-Said murdered.

15 July US Marines land in Lebanon at request of President Chamoun.

17 July British paratroops land in Jordan at King Husain's request.

23 Oct. Soviet loan to Egypt to finance Aswan Dam.

2 Nov. British troops leave Jordan.

### 1961

29 Sept. Syria secedes from union with Egypt.

### 1962

27 Sept. Army coup in Yemen; Abdullah al-Sallal proclaimed Premier.

29 Sept. Egypt announces her backing of Yemeni revolution.

5 Nov. Saudi Arabia severs relations with UAR.

### 1963

14 March Unity talks open in Cairo between Egypt, Syria and Iraq with a view to setting up a federation (abandoned Aug. 1963).

16–24 June Ben-Gurion resigns Israeli premiership; succeeded by Levi Eshkol.

### 1964

9 May Soviet Premier Khrushchev in Egypt for opening of Aswan Dam.

8 Nov. Cease-fire in Yemen war.

### 1965

6 March President Bourguiba of Tunisia proposes Arab recognition of Israel on terms of the 1947 UN resolution.

1966

31 March  British troops leave Libya.

11 Oct.  Syrian Premier, Dr Zuwayen, declares Government
support for al-Fatah.

Oct.-Nov.  Increasing terrorist attacks against Israel by Palestinian
guerrillas from Syria and Jordan.

13 Nov.  Large Israeli reprisal action against the village of Samu
near Hebron, followed by anti-Husain demonstrations
by Palestinian Arabs in Nablus and Jenin.

25 Nov.  Security Council condemnation of Israeli attack on Samu.

1967

Jan.  Unemployment in Israel 117,000 – 12 per cent of working
population.

7 April  Fighting on Syrian-Israeli border; 6 Syrian MIGs reported
shot down.

12 May  Premier Eshkol threatens reprisals against Syrians if
they continue to support al-Fatah attacks on Israel.

18 May  At Egypt's request, Secretary-General U Thant orders
withdrawal of UNEF.

23 May  Egypt closes Straits of Tiran to Israeli shipping; large
Egyptian reinforcements move into Sinai Peninsula.

2 June  General Moshe Dayan joins Israeli Cabinet as Minister
of Defence.

5 June  Israel attacks Egyptian air force bases and advance
positions in Sinai and the Gaza Strip. Jordan guns shell
Jerusalem. Iraqi troops advance to West Bank of Jordan.

9–10 June  Cease-fire.

13 June  USSR, Czechoslovakia, Bulgaria, Hungary, Poland and
Yugoslavia sever diplomatic relations with Israel.

19 June  Eban at UN Assembly: "Our watchword is 'Forward to
peace'."

29 Aug.–1 Sept.  Arab summit in Khartoum decides "no peace, no
negotiation and no recognition" policy with regard to
Israel. Arab oil states resume supplies to West, and pay
Egypt and Jordan annual subsidy of $135 million.

5 Nov.  President Sallal of the Yemen overthrown.

22 Nov.  Security Council unanimously adopts British-sponsored
Resolution 242 on an Arab-Israeli settlement; appoints
Gunnar Jarring as UN special representative.

# The Need for Oil

"I do not care under what system we keep the oil," Balfour had told the Dominion Prime Ministers in mid-August 1918, "but I am clear that it is all-important that this oil should be available." Hankey's memorandum had alarmed the War Cabinet to the implications of Middle East oil – and the alarm continued to ring for the next 50 years, and has not stopped to this day. Whatever initial reasons the British and the French had for their interest in the Levant, whatever caused the Americans to disinterest themselves after the Peace Conference, became altogether immaterial with the emergence of the oil factor which Hankey had discerned in the critical days of 1918. And because of Hankey's percipience, the British were to enjoy a decisive advantage when it came to the oil share-out; but not her two partners in the Middle East adventure, the Arab nationalists and the Zionists: they had missed the boat altogether. Completely inward looking as these two were during the formative years after 1917, entirely preoccupied with their own special interests, they failed to see the significance, for their own cause, of the oil factor. On the contrary, both Arabs and Zionists saw the British, French and American concern for Middle East oil as a rival attraction with which they had to compete. They did not see it as the trump card which they could have held and played had they understood the larger game of which unknowingly they were a part.

The Arabs and Zionists failed to do this; worse, they succeeded in impressing on the British that neither Zionism nor Arab nationalism had anything much to contribute to the reshaping of the Grand Design for the Middle East. Admittedly, as imperial designs go, the revised version lacked the grandeur and the imaginative possibilities of the Clayton-Weizmann-Faisal concept, but it had its compensations. It promised to be very profitable; it was firmly rooted in the City of

223

London, and it offered a presence in the Middle East unencumbered by the political complications which Arabs and Zionists had managed to arouse. It also had that strongest of all moral – and political – justifications to back it up: it was an essential element in Great Britain's national security. You had no need to be pro-Zionist or pro-Arab to be pro-oil. It was in every way an attractive and welcome alternative. And that was the crux: after 1922, neither Zionists nor Arab nationalists had much attraction for the British or the French – or for the Americans – in terms of practical Middle East politics. Neither would be of help in consolidating the imperial position in the control and exploitation of the oilfields because the thought had never occurred to them. By 1922, Zionists and Arabs were more concerned with being a nuisance to the British than with the originally conceived partnership. Because of this, oil became, as it were, a Third Force in competition with Arab and Zionists. And as the nationalist causes flagged and wilted by 1922, after the first flush of enthusiasm, the cause of oil gathered momentum and strength and, 50 years later, threatened to transform the world situation.

There is no need to tell once more the history of the rise in importance of Middle East oil, but, though the basic facts have become generally known, there are one or two rather fundamental and curious exceptions to the general rule. What we need, therefore, is a corrective emphasis on some of the main elements in the role of Middle East oil and of its progenitors.

It started respectably enough with the British Admiralty's concern for the fuel supply to the Royal Navy, which was being converted from coal to oil-firing. Its broader implications for national defence were subsequently traced by Hankey and Geddes, as we have seen. But within months of the Armistice in November 1918, other and more material factors became apparent – sufficiently apparent for the British authorities to refuse permission to the American Sinclair Oil Company to send exploration teams into Mesopotamia. The San Remo Agreements in April 1920 not only settled the Anglo-French differences about Syria and Palestine, but also established an effectively closed shop, restricted to the British and French, for Arabian oil exploitation. It took the Americans six years from the commencement of talks with the British and French in 1922, before they reached the so-called Red Line Agreement in 1928, which allowed for limited American participation in the Anglo-French oil developments as the element of potentially rich profits became an added incentive for the international oil companies.

It took the Americans no time at all, during the second world war, when the French and British were in dire difficulties and needed American aid, to cancel the Red Line Agreement when it would have assured British and French participation in the rich new oil discoveries in Saudi Arabia. Even so, before this happened, back in 1933, the British-controlled Iraq Petroleum Company could have shared with the Americans in the development of the Saudi Arabian oilfields, but they considered King Ibn Saud's cash demand outrageously high. It is an acid comment on the fallibility of experts and the acumen of the oil tycoons, when one recalls that the Shell geologists advised the Iraq Petroleum Company that there was not much prospect of oil in the Saudi Arabian Hasa oilfield, and the Company decided that they would not offer more than £10,000 for the oil concessions; they could have had it for £20,000. The Americans wanted to make sure. They put down £50,000 and got it. The profits derived from this deal have mounted beyond the billion dollar mark, but clearly, in the 1930s, the later largesse of the oil business was not yet apparent among the older companies, the British and the Dutch. They were making very large profits for very little expenditure. But all this changed with the coming of the second world war.

By 1943 American oil policy was taking shape, freed from the shackles of the Red Line Agreement. The Americans had stalled a British request for talks, made earlier in the year, in which the British wanted to convince the Americans of "the greater importance of the Middle East to the British Commonwealth" than it was to the United States. Under the circumstances, Eden thought that the Americans could be persuaded "to allow us a certain local political initiative".[1] But the Americans were not so inclined. Roosevelt's special representative, Halford B. Hoskins, advised the President that this was now the first real opportunity the United States had of developing its own post-war economic interests in the Middle East. Even if it acted as a junior partner to the British, Washington had now to recognise the substantial American oil position involved. "In line with this thought he also recommended that the United States oppose Zionist claims and in fact the attainment of control over oil now assumed top priority in American

[1] L. Woodward, *British Foreign Policy in the Second World War*, p. 395.

Middle East policy."[2] "There should be full realisation of the fact that the oil of Saudi Arabia constitutes one of the world's greatest prizes," Secretary of State Hull told the Secretary of the Interior, Harold Ickes, who was also President of the Petroleum Reserves Corporation; Hull called for the proper protection of American interests against British long-term intentions "to build up their post-war position in the Middle East at the expense of American interests there". He counselled, therefore, that the British should be assisted to expand their oil interests only insofar as this was absolutely necessary for the immediate war requirements.[3]

The sense of urgency in Washington induced by the realisation of this Saudi Arabian oil bonanza was not confined to those immediately concerned with it. Shortly after Hull had sent his message to Ickes, the Navy Secretary, James Forrestal, telephoned the President with this recorded message. He told Roosevelt that the oil people whom he happened to know were anxious to have Government backing in Saudi Arabia but no Government participation. ". . . the main thing is that stack of oil is something that this country damn well ought to have and we've lost, in the last ninety days, a good deal of our position with this Sheik – Eben Sihoudo, whatever his name is, and we are losing more every day." He then informed the President that, under the guise of naturalists operating against locusts, the British had sent some 500 men into Saudi Arabia "to see what the hell we are doing and what we've got".[4]

The British were not unaware of this sudden feverish interest in Washington with Middle East oil affairs – and especially with "this Sheik", King Ibn Saud. Churchill felt constrained to cable Roosevelt in blunt simplicity that there was apprehension in Whitehall "that the United States has a desire to deprive us of our oil assets in the Middle East on which, among other things, the whole supply for our Navy depends". Roosevelt replied crisply that he was disturbed by the rumour "that the British wish to horn in on Saudi Arabian oil reserves". Churchill recognised the danger signal to the alliance and decided to bring down the temperature in a characteristic personal message to

[2] See Gabriel Kolko's *Politics of War*, pp. 297–302, for an instructive summary of the American position at this time.

[3] Hull to Ickes, 13 November 1943, Foreign Relations of the United States, 1943, Vol., IV, pp. 942–3.

[4] Telephone conversation of 22 December 1943, see Kolko, pp. 298 and 649.

Roosevelt. He thanked the President for the assurances "about no sheep's eyes at our oilfields in Iran and Iraq. Let me reciprocate," Churchill responded "by giving you fullest assurance that we have no thought of trying to horn in upon your interests or property in Saudi Arabia." Britain sought no territorial or other advantages from the war but "she will not be deprived of anything which rightly belongs to her . . . at least not so long as your humble servant is entrusted with the conduct of her affairs".[5]

These were, in their way, the romantic, rumbustious and buccaneering days of Middle East Oil, and the men who were concerned with it, in government and in the oil business, were fitted for the role. Some were concerned with national security, others with national economic advantage, some with personal gain and the making of big money – by the standards of those days. But the political undertones were also present, though not yet dominant.

But with the ending of the war, there came a change of gear, a total change of outlook and the prospect of a petroleum Shangri La for the oil companies. The contrast between the new men, the new tone and the new perspectives of 1946 and the traditionalist oil philosophy of 1944 was stark. And the transition for the old guard unaccustomed to the new post-war world was hard, and many of them did not make it, did not want to make it, could not make it. A case in point was Sir William Fraser, the dour tough boss of the Anglo-Persian Oil Company. No one outside his boardroom knew the secrets of his company's operations in Iran or how much actual profit the company had made from its oil extraction in the country. The balance sheets and accounts generally were designed to disguise information rather than reveal it. What was known was that the Persian Government had received annual royalty payments ranging from £2 million to £4 million on oil that sold for around £70 to £100 million. The most searching enquiries and independent investigation by Persian experts and American competitors did not reveal the real cost of this oil product or the extent of the profit made by Anglo-Iranian. However, a Committee of the 80th US Senate produced a sample costing on the basis of oil produced in Saudi Arabia. Conditions there were similar to those in Iran, except that the royalty paid by the Americans was substantially higher than that paid, at this time, by the British. Allowing for this difference, the gross profit

[5] Churchill to Roosevelt, 4 March 1944, Foreign Relations, 1944, Vol. III, pp. 96–103. See also Kolko, p. 301.

made by the Anglo-Iranian Oil Company on its purely Persian operation in ten years from 1934 to 1943 was estimated to be $800 million and the royalties paid to the Persian Government over this period were around $100 million.

Curiously – or perhaps perceptively – the Persians at that time were not asking for larger royalty payments. When I discussed this with the Head of the Iranian National Bank in Teheran at the end of the war in 1945, Abol-Hasan Ebtehaj, an able economist who knew a lot about the oil business, said that all the Persians wanted was a minimum of participation, a recognition of the Iranian part of the "Anglo-Iranian" – just two Iranian nationals on the Board of the Anglo-Iranian. It did not seem much to ask, I thought, but Sir William Fraser understood the implications. When I put it to him that he could buy Iranian peace with just such two appointments, he reacted with angry indignation: "What, have them look into our books!" And that was it. The Ebtehaj proposal was the thin end of the wedge – and some wedge it would have been. For, with the end of the war, came the golden days of oil.

The reconstruction of Europe and the new demands in the United States outpaced all anticipation of demand for oil. Europe was thirsting for it and the people who could supply it in abundance were the international companies controlling the oilfields of Iran, Iraq, Saudi Arabia and the Persian Gulf. Under these conditions, the oil companies wanted no Iranian or Arabian cuckoos in their directorial nests; they would rather pay more, much more, by way of royalties. They could afford this. But they could not afford to open their books to the Iranians, the Iraqis and the Saudi Arabians – nor, for that matter, to the British and American consumer and taxpayer. For, by now, the British-controlled companies were powerfully entrenched in Iran and Iraq, and the Americans in Saudi Arabia. They controlled most of the foreign exchange of Iran and Iraq, and virtually all of Saudi Arabia. The powerful Public Relations and Press Departments of the oil companies in Teheran and Baghdad helped not only to guide the foreign journalist along the path to a proper understanding and appreciation of good work done by the oil companies in and for these countries, but they also assisted the local press and journalists over their financial difficulties and with their orientation problems. The expenditure on such "assistance" was generous and fairly undiscriminating by the standards prevailing at the time. Politicians and Ministers were also able to avail themselves of this timely assistance provided by the oil companies, and they were not slow in showing their appreciation for it in their newspapers or in the Majlis. In the immediate post-war years, despite some extremist rumblings, the position of the oil companies appeared to be virtually impregnable in Iran, Iraq, and in Saudi Arabia. And so it was that, despite the severe shocks suffered by them – when these had passed – the oil companies were still there, sometimes with new names, but always with rising profits and undiminished influence. They had to pay more but they were not doing badly – for meanwhile, they had acquired another contributor to their income: the British and American taxpayer.

After the end of the second world war, in 1946, the total royalty payments to Middle East countries amounted to barely £10 million while the largely undisclosed profits of the oil companies was in excess of £100 million. We were impressed, at the time, by the enormity of these figures and the discrepancy between the benefits derived by the host countries and the operating companies. Since then there have been at least three major oil crises in which future supplies – especially to Europe – were said to be in danger. There have been revolutions and wars and serious political upheavals, in every Middle East country concerned. At the end of it all, in 1972, after 25 years of such turmoil, payments made to the Middle East host countries in one year, by way of royalties and taxes, added up to $10 billion – from £10 million in 1946 to £4,000 million in 1972. And the seven major oil companies were still not doing too badly. The purely Middle Eastern proportion of their net income for 1971 has been calculated at some $2½ billion or £1,000 million, out of a total recorded income of $5¼ billion.[6]

Before we turn to consider the political implications of this oil bonanza for the 1970s, the full weight of the profits derived from the Middle East oil connection merits further consideration. The contours of these operations are particularly interesting and they apply, with some difference in the overall sums involved to all the major oil producers except Libya, which was a latecomer. Saudi Arabia offers a typical example which is duplicated by Iran and Kuwait and, on a somewhat lower level, also by Iraq.

Thus in the first decade from 1948 to 1957:

[6] The seven companies are Standard Oil of New Jersey, Texaco, Gulf Oil, Mobil, Royal Dutch/Shell, British Petroleum; see *Petroleum Press Service*, May 1972, p. 166, for details.

229

the Saudi Arabian Government received $1,785 million by way of oil income.

During the same period the Arabian-American Oil Company, Aramco, recorded a net profit of $3,029 million from its oil operations originating in Saudi Arabia.

During the second decade from 1958 to 1967:

the Saudi Arabian Government received $5,155 million, while Aramco's recorded profits rose to $4,700 million.

During the *five* years from 1968 to 1972:

the Saudi Arabian Government received $7,834 million, and Aramco's net profits, still rising, were estimated at $5,400 million.

The general trend was the same for Iran and Kuwait, and lately also for Libya and the Gulf States. Yet within these figures there were three major oil crises. That of 1946 when Europe, the Soviet Union and the United States anticipated acute shortages of supply to meet their rapidly expanding economies; that of 1956 when the Suez Canal was closed and President Nasser threatened to bring Europe to its knees by blocking its supplies of Arab oil; and the crisis of the aftermath of the 1967 war when the Suez Canal was closed and remained shut. Each one of these major crises was absorbed by greater expansion, larger payments to the host Governments, and more substantial profits for the companies. The host Governments did not suffer; they waxed rich. The international oil companies did not suffer, though they had to make use of some of their accumulated fat. They paid out much more and they retained a much smaller proportion of their total income. But in absolute figures this continued to increase. And here, they had a problem. Like most other technical and financial problems, the oil industry managed to overcome it. It proved to be another bonanza.

It is one that has been kept very quiet by the international companies, by the British Treasury and by the United States Treasury Department. The man who discovered this chink in the oil companies' balance sheets was the Iraqi dictator, General Abdul Karim Kassem, who may have had many faults and shortcomings, but he knew his oil business. When a British team came to meet with him to discuss a new agreement with the Iraq Petroleum Company, Kassem challenged the chairman of the oil company to deny that in fact the royalty payments which they made were no burden on the company's finance since the British Government permitted them to deduct payments made to the Iraqi Government from the Company's British tax payments. In other words, oil royalties and other oil payments were tax deductible and were paid therefore, not by the company, but by the British taxpayer.[7]

Nothing more would have been heard of this extraordinary tax innovation which was not made public nor presented to Parliament at any time, had it remained a bargaining counter in the private negotiations between the chairman of the Iraq Petroleum Company and General Kassem. But Kassem had the conversation recorded without the knowledge of the British negotiators and then had the conversation edited, translated and broadcast over Baghdad Radio.

I came across the broadcast in my daily check of the BBC Monitoring Reports. Before using this intriguing news item, I asked the Shell press department for confirmation and elucidation: on my reckoning the Treasury dispensation had saved the oil company and cost the taxpayer some hundreds of millions of pounds by 1960. After some hasty and embarrassed explaining by the Iraq Petroleum Company's executives with their legal and financial advisers participating, the following facts emerged: at some time in the late forties, when Sir Stafford Cripps was in charge, a minute was agreed by the Treasury permitting the Iraq Petroleum Company to deduct royalty payments made to the Iraqi Government from tax which the Company had to pay in the United Kingdom. A similar arrangement existed with all major oil companies, I was told, in the United States and in France. On this basis, the Iraq Petroleum Company alone had been able to deduct, in the 20 years between 1952 to 1972, some $7 billion from its tax bill in the United Kingdom which meant that it paid virtually no tax at all on its share of the profits which were at least as large as those accruing to the Iraqi Government. The same applied to most other oil companies registered in the United Kingdom, France or the United States. Since detailed information has been withheld about the actual amount involved, one must assume that it was a worthwhile discretion on the part of those who benefited.

This, then, was the contrivance that featherbedded the oil companies against the shock of higher royalty payments which the unsuspecting taxpayer has been meeting. Altogether, the oil companies have sought

[7] See BBC Monitoring Report, Part IV, for 30 September 1960, also *Oil and Public Opinion in the Middle East*, by D. Hirst, pp. 87–92.

to lower their profile the more their income soared. They managed to ride the crisis of 1956 which was a European crisis, and the closing of the Suez Canal in 1967 hardly caused a ripple except that it sent up costs and profits; but there was no shortage of oil either for Europe or for the United States.

But by the end of 1972, in the wake of President Nixon's re-election, a new kind of crisis was anticipated by the oil specialists. This time it was not Europe, always dependent on the Middle East, that faced an energy crisis; it was the United States herself that was confronted by the noisy and much publicised spectre of an oil shortage. It was not the first time, and we may gain some insight and perspective by recalling earlier occasions which, in retrospect, appeared to be not entirely unconnected with the longer-range interests of the supercompanies of the oil industry.

The tone was set by the Petroleum Adviser of the US Department of State, Charles Raynor, himself a man of considerable standing in the American oil industry. In a statement made on 30 October 1946, shortly after a high-level conference between the British and Americans on matters concerning oil supplies, and circulated by the US Government's Information Service, Raynor drew attention to the grave prospects confronting the United States with regard to its oil supplies. By 1965, he said, American oil consumption will run at the rate of 325 million tons a year while oil production in the United States would be "at the most" 200 million tons. By 1965, he added the supply situation will have become acute; even by 1955 shortages will become noticeable.

About the same time, Stalin was discussing the oil crisis of the Soviet Union with the newly arrived American Ambassador in Moscow, General Bedell Smith. Stalin was bitter about the way the United States and the British had blocked Russian attempts to obtain more oil concessions, especially in Iran. He talked of the Soviet Union's need for a greater share in the world's oil resources. "You don't understand our situation as regards oil and Iran," he said to Bedell Smith. They were so dependent on the vulnerable Baku oil fields that he had to do something about it: "We are not going to risk our oil supply."[8]

On 6 February 1948 the State Department published a further survey which claimed that the oil supply situation was so serious that consumption by the European countries receiving Marshall Aid might have to be severely cut back and that substantial imports from the

[8] *Moscow Mission*, by Walter Bedell Smith, 1946–1949.

Middle East might become immediately necessary for the United States. The *Financial Times* reported from Washington that "Unless sufficient quantities are got out of the Middle East, the whole oil situation as it affects the European Recovery Programme may have to be reviewed."[9]

More reports along similar lines were issued by various agencies. The Department of the Interior made public an alarming forecast of an acute oil crisis in 1955 when it published the report prepared by the National Petroleum Council in the summer of 1951. It was in every way a fashionable theme and it was encouraged by independent forecasts and analyses by such specialists as the Chase Manhattan Bank and other similar institutions. The international oil industry – especially the American sector – responded with alacrity to the challenge; so much so that cynics were inclined to conclude that the industry might well have induced it since it was to benefit so hugely from this turn of events.

Thus when the alarm was sounded in 1946 the latest oil production figures available for the United States and the Middle East were those for 1945 – 227 million tons produced in the United States and 27 million tons in the Middle East. By 1951, the first dateline for crisis, the United States had increased production to 300 million tons and the Middle East to 100 million, and by 1955 Middle East production was up to 165 million; by 1965 – Raynor's year of crisis – Middle East production had reached 475 million. United States oil output was 390 million tons, just about double the Raynor forecast; consumption was 550 million tons as against the forecast of 325 million tons; and imports of 130 million tons represented no problem. There was no crisis. By the end of 1967, unaffected by the June fighting, Middle East oil production had climbed to 580 million tons and then almost doubled in the following five years. In 1972, Middle East oil output, including that of Libya, topped the 1,000 million ton mark and was still rising fast. During the same period the American controlled oil companies changed places with the British-Dutch controlled companies. At the commencement of the period, the Americans were the junior partners: they accounted for a mere 12 per cent share of the oil produced in the Middle East in 1945. By 1951 this had advanced into a majority holding of 58 per cent, and by 1972 – despite pressures from the host countries – American controlled oil companies held a dominating position in the Middle East and North Africa.

[9] *Financial Times*, 7 February 1948, Report from Washington.

Admittedly, their projections – and the resulting alarms – had been mistaken in 1946, in 1948, in 1951 and again in 1956 and 1967. The managerial and technical departments of the oil industry successfully overcame the most difficult problems with remarkable aplomb, but their political and analytical staff showed little faith in their own industry when they prepared their gloomy forecasts – and they are still doing it. However, on closer inspection, the recurring near panics about American and European oil supplies were not without their positive features in the balance sheets of the oil companies. They were without a doubt an important factor in bringing about the remarkable tax concession which the companies received from Sir Stafford Cripps and from the American Treasury Department; they provided increased capital and other facilities for the development of Middle East oil – especially in the bonanza years immediately after the war; and they helped to restrict the share of imported oil in the steadily rising oil consumption in the United States.

The looming threat of an oil crisis had also its political and foreign policy aspects. President Truman had recorded the concern of the State Department and the Joint Chiefs of Staff in 1946 – at the time when the Raynor reports were being prepared – lest American policy in the Middle East failed to take account "that control of oil in the Middle East was a very serious consideration and . . . that no action should be taken which would commit US armed forces, or turn the peoples of the Middle East away from the Western Powers, since we had a vital security interest there. The report put military leaders on record. They were primarily concerned about Middle East oil and in long-range terms about the danger that the Arabs, antagonised by Western action in Palestine, would make common cause with Russia."[10]

There was, of course, genuine justification for the concern by the Joint Chiefs of Staff, as there was for the oil industry's worry about the future status of the United States with the Arab host countries. In fact, their preoccupation was shared by the British Imperial General Staff and by the Government in Whitehall. Nor were the fears expressed by the Joint Chiefs to President Truman at the same time about the possible intrusion of the Soviet Union into the Middle East altogether without foundation. These opinions were based on a realistic assessment of the situation and not primarily the product of anti-Zionist machinations as they were thought to be by many Jews and their sympathisers.

[10] *Truman Memoirs*, Vol. II, p. 159.

But the process did not end there. We have no means of telling whether this co-ordination of events – the oil warning by Raynor, the Joint Chiefs of Staff warning to the President not to go too far in his Zionist enthusiasm because of the Arab-Oil factor involved, the drive for greatly increased oil production, and American economic presence in the Middle East were just coincidental or accidental! It could have been – once, or even twice; but not four times or more. Oil companies are not prone to coincidences and accidents without there being some understanding guiding spirit to direct events in this convenient way.

So we come to the political essentials of the energy crisis that once more settled on the United States and the Western world – once again through the good services of the National Petroleum Council – in December 1972, on the eve of President Nixon's policy declarations for his second term. In London, the *Observer* prominently headlined the report ENERGY CRISIS FRIGHTENS AMERICA. That was on 17 December 1972. In Israel, the *Jerusalem Post* reprinted a report from the *Wall Street Journal* with its own indicative headline FEAR OF ARAB BLACKMAIL SAID WORRYING U.S., on 1 February 1973. And in the United States, on 22 January 1973, *Newsweek* devoted its cover story to AMERICA'S ENERGY CRISIS. In its essentials the arguments and the conclusions were no different from what they had been in 1946, 1956 and in 1967. *Newsweek* summed up the political implications in 1973 in almost identical terms to those used by the Joint Chiefs of Staff in 1946. "Internationally, the crisis could force a whole new order or priority in American diplomacy. The US could ultimately find itself alienating its Israeli allies as it tries to improve relations with the Arab nations that control most of the world's oil reserves."

It was an understandable position in 1946 and it remained so in 1973. The United States, Great Britain and Western Europe had to put their own interest first – and their oil interest was a very substantial item in their security and in their economic well-being.

Where the major oil companies appear to have been mistaken, consistently so, was in their assumption that there was a relatively easy way of assuring their good relations with the Arab host countries by not giving aid or comfort to and by not trading with Israel. When, for example, Shell scrambled to get out of Israel in the 1950s, and sold off its valuable properties and rights at a knock-down price to the Israelis rather than be identified with the country, it did not really change the Arab nationalist attitude towards the international oil corporations, it did not lessen their hostility or reduce their demands. If anything, it acted as an incentive to press all the harder on the oil companies. What the oil companies did not seem to understand in the days of Truman and still did not seem to comprehend in the days of Nixon was that the question of Israel was largely an irrelevancy in the Arab attitude to the British and American oil companies. The issue between them was the same as that which had produced the Iranian oil crisis in 1951 – the unfair division of spoils in the earlier years of the industry and the understanding by the Arab host countries that they were in a position to demand their due – plus a little extra.

One Shell executive, who represented his company at OPEC[11] meetings, explained to me in 1970 that Shell and every other major oil company had in fact written off the Middle East as a source of profit some years ago. What they were doing was "to lean on the present situation" – these were his words – and everything they got out of it was treated "as an additional windfall" – some windfall! The more perceptive oil executives did understand by 1972 that no matter how much support the Arab Governments would receive from the United States and Great Britain against Israel, even if Israel were wiped off the Middle East map as a consequence, it would make no difference to the Arab pressure on the international oil industry; on the contrary, Arab nationalists would probably be greatly encouraged to press all the harder.

But that was no longer the nature of the Middle East balance of power in 1972. Even before the American energy crisis became a public issue at the end of the year, a major strategic transformation had taken place in the Middle East with profound consequences for all the parties concerned in the energy crisis. We need to recall at this stage that at the end of 1922 the British Government came to the evident conclusion that neither the Zionists in Palestine nor the Arab nationalists could ensure the security and stability of the area and of its strategically and economically invaluable oil supplies. Subsequent British policy was accordingly shaped without undue consideration for the Zionists or the Arab nationalists but entirely with a view to ensuring security and stability and the uninterrupted flow of oil and safe passage through the region. That was in 1922 and that was the dominant theme in the intervening 50 years – including those of the second world war and those which led the British to oppose the establishment of the State of Israel. And when the British made way for the Americans after their Suez,

[11] Organisation of Petroleum Exporting Countries.

Iraqi and Jordanian débacles in the later 1950s, American policy remained oriented, with some change of emphasis, along the same basic lines concerning the dominant importance of ensuring the safety and free flow of Middle East oil – especially to Europe which depended on the Middle East and North Africa for some two-thirds of its oil requirements.

The Americans increased the strategic dimensions of the Middle East's role in world politics, and introduced the enlarged US Sixth Fleet into the Mediterranean as the symbol of the American presence and interest. But in terms of these world considerations, the Zionists in the shape of Israel, and the Arab nationalists represented by Egypt's President Nasser, played only marginal and local parts. Neither was an essential plus or minus in the new security system which the Americans had established and manned in place of that which the British had abandoned. This remained the essence of the Arab and Israeli relationship with the Americans in the 1960s. Basically, the position was not any different on 1 June 1967 to what it had been on 1 June 1922; neither the Arab nationalists nor the Zionists were indispensable to American security and the defence of the massive United States oil interests in the Middle East. And then began the transformation. It was not immediately evident after the Six Day War; for that was rated as a great Israeli victory, but still only in local terms, against Nasser, against the Arabs.

It was not until 1969 when President Nasser launched the "War of Attrition" across the Canal and the Israelis began to respond and escalate the challenge until it embraced the Russians in Egypt that the real change in the Middle Eastern balance of power took place. With massive American aid in arms and sophisticated equipment, and as a result of her own industrial expansion and development, Israel established as a fact in 1970 what had appeared to be only a flash in the local pan in June 1967. Israel had become the major military factor in the Middle East; she was the only power capable and able to take decisive action since the two superpowers had accepted their mutual status of parity. This meant that the United States and the Soviet Union could not act in the region without incurring counter-action by the other superpower. Israel was not inhibited in this way and could strike at will with only the tacit approval of the United States Government to support her.

This was the decisive development in the interregnum since 1922.

237

There was now one country that had become indispensable to the United States. What Weizmann had failed to achieve in 1922, Dayan had achieved in 1972 – and, as we shall see, it was Dayan who did it, not Mrs Meir or anyone else. He had established a third force – a real military force – in the Middle East which by its nature had to become a central element in the security of the Middle East's oil supplies to the United States and, no less so, to Europe. Indeed, as Japan's dependence on Middle East oil was so complete – almost 90 per cent of her requirements came from the area – and her direct interest increased, a new community of interest between Japan and Israel had to develop. Israel became the only possible sanction that the Americans, the Europeans and the Japanese could call upon in their confrontation with the Arab and international oil barons of 1973 on whose goodwill their oil supplies for the rest of the decade would depend.

The rulers of Iran, Saudi Arabia, Kuwait, Libya and Iraq, and the Sultans and Sheikhs of the Gulf were no longer the exploited poor of the developing world. They now held Europe and Japan and to some degree also the United States to ransom. They had the oil, the others had need of it. But the equation was no longer that simple. The oil companies had the money and the oil barons wanted it and – what is more – needed it. They had developed a style of life which they could no longer abandon except at great risk to their own power and to the well-being of their countries. In the decade from 1963 to 1972, the four principal oil producers received $37 billion in revenue from the oil companies. The Shah of Iran received $9½ billion, Libya $9 billion, the Sultan of Kuwait $8 billion and the Saudi Arabian rulers just over $11 billion. Their estimated income for the following three years from 1973 to 1975 is put at $34 billion. In the case of Saudi Arabia, Libya and Kuwait, this oil income constitutes three-quarters or more of the total revenue of the country and in the case of Iran, it makes up something like two-thirds of the Shah's income. Without this income, despite their reserves abroad, the economies of the oil states would soon seize up, their influence would diminish and the fading attraction of their rulers would quickly be replaced.

The dependence of the Western world and Japan on Middle East oil is in fact equalled only by the dependence of the Middle East rulers on the oil incomes from the Western oil companies and – no mean factor this – the military presence of Israel in the Middle East. It is this combination of circumstances which was not present in any previous

238

energy crisis, real or imagined. It is this combination that conditioned the discussion on how the oil requirements of Europe, the United States and Japan were to be met.

For one thing, the Israelis and Arabs had to recognise what they failed to appreciate at the time of their first opportunity in 1918–1923, that they were part of a larger whole, and that they could not separate their own national requirements from those of the world community. At that time – and in the present – there was much said about the concern for the Holy Places of the three religions centred on Jerusalem, but the real concern even then was not the sanctity of the shrines but the safety of the oil. What the excitement about the energy crisis in the winter of 1972–1973 had achieved was to focus once more the Great Power and superpower interest on the Middle East and to make all concerned understand that this was no marginal interest – that this was one area from which the United States could not withdraw or from which Europe (including the Soviet Union) and Japan could not disinterest themselves.

With the proclamation of the American energy crisis in the winter of 1972 came in effect the proclamation of the recolonisation of the Middle East by the superpowers. And the question loomed large as it had done 50 years earlier in 1922, would the Zionists or the Arab nationalists prove themselves to be indispensable? In 1922 the British found that both were expendable in terms of world strategy and British oil interest; in 1972 the Americans found that both were indispensable and that they had to find a new equation to provide for this condition. But had the Israelis understood this? Had the Arab leaders – Sadat, Qaddafy and the remaining Kings and Sultans?

For answer we have to turn to the transformation which took place at the time when oil supplies became the predominant factor. How Israel and Egypt coped at that juncture is the subject of the concluding part of this enquiry.

# PART II

## 1967-1973
## THE LAST CHANCE?

# ONE

# The Palestinians

Israel faced her most serious crisis not in the summer of 1967 but in the bleak winter of 1966. It was then that Israel's entire social, economic and ideological structure was at risk; when more Jews emigrated – many of them veteran settlers not disillusioned newcomers – than new immigrants came into the country; when the Government seemed to be no longer in full control of the deteriorating situation on the home front; and when it ceased to be frank about the realities of Israel's problems with its own people and with its Jewish supporters in the Diaspora. Only the armed forces were unaffected by this all-pervading malaise.

In May 1967 Israel was confronted by an altogether different and much more limited crisis which stemmed rather from the indecisions and lack of leadership by the Government and from the crisis of self-confidence which this induced in the general public, than from the military nature of the Arab threat.

This Government was the product of Israel's peculiar party system which has been dominated for 30 years by the Labour movement. After many vicissitudes, Mrs Meir and some of her colleagues – especially Sapir and Peres – had brought the three main Labour groupings into one united Israel Labour Party. All the same, the separate party identities – and organisations – survived as part of the uneasy alliance. They consisted of the most powerful establishment party, Mapai, led by Mrs Meir, Ahdut Ha'Avoda led by Israel Galili and Yigal Allon, and the breakaway Ben-Gurionist Rafi Party led by Dayan and Peres.

In electoral terms the Labour Party did not have an absolute majority and required the support of the National Religious Party and of Mapan, a more Leftist Labour Party which had maintained its own organisation though associating with the Labour Party.

The opposition was made up by the union of the Herut and Liberal Parties in the Gahal Party led by Beigin, and by the Communists and some very small parties with only one or two members in Parliament.

The Arab threat was real enough for the Israeli public; it was heightened by the seeming inability of its own Government to take effective counter-action and compounded by evidence of diplomatic hesitation on the part of the Great Powers to respond to Israel's desperate appeals. This was how it seemed to the great majority of Israelis and – what is much more surprising – to the majority of the Eshkol Government.

It was not so for those who knew of Israel's actual military capacity and of the real state of the Arab threat. One would have thought that among those who were able to make this correct assessment were Israel's Prime Minister and Minister of Defence, Levi Eshkol, the Foreign Minister, Abba Eban and the Labour Party's *éminence grise*, Mrs Meir. They showed no evidence that they did understand the real situation during those critical days of May 1967. Because of the actual military balance of power in June 1967, the military situation did not present a threat to the existence of Israel: Israel's defence forces were fully prepared for it. However, there was a psychological crisis of the Israeli public and a real crisis of Government and leadership at the top; it was in many ways a hangover from the previous winter: the June 1967 crisis, therefore, can be understood only in the context of the much greater threat of December 1966, and in that perspective the Six Day War turned out to be more in the nature of a salvation than a crisis.

The nature of the winter emergency is best reflected in contemporary comments by those who were most aware of it. Thus, on 13 November 1966 – the morning after the Israeli defence forces had carried out a particularly punishing retaliatory raid against the village of Samu near Hebron – one of Premier Eshkol's most senior civil servants, a man of outstanding ability who had worked with Ben-Gurion, Eshkol and Mrs Meir and knew them well, talked to me about the situation which worried him greatly. He was not a politician or a party man, but he understood the nature of Israel's politics better than most – and came to occupy in 1973 one of the half-dozen most important Government posts in the country.

His first words made me decide to take down verbatim what he proposed to say. He began by assuring me that he was fully conscious of the gravity of what he proposed to say and of its possible implications, and then he continued – and these were his own words:

I must admit that I still felt an element of doubt when I began my enquiries, perhaps one per cent or possibly even a five per cent doubt; my job breeds a certain humility towards the so-called accuracy of facts. But none of these doubts now remain. Apart from dealing with professional affairs, I have spent the best part of my time in re-checking my views with the most independent and unimpeachable sources; I have deliberately avoided the declared opponents of Eshkol and of Mapai.

The present difficulties [he continued] are only incidentally due to economic problems; what these have done is to intensify and to concentrate the basic problem which we have to overcome. At the root of everything is the lack of confidence in the Government, especially in Eshkol and in the Labour Party, Mapai. Moreover, after the most recent events, there is also some uncertainty about the soundness of judgement in the leadership of the armed forces. That the other political parties have also their own varieties of leadership problems and do not enjoy any more public confidence is really immaterial in this context. For, unlike Mapai, they are not the central element in the fabric of the state.

The present crisis of confidence [he repeated] stems largely from Eshkol's failure to govern – his indecision, his lack of self-confidence which has been greatly increased by the insistent questioning of the soundness of his political judgement and intentions. This has concentrated primarily on the economic policy of the Government and also on important areas of foreign policy – especially Eshkol's ambivalent attitude to the Soviet Union which has greatly disturbed some of his closest colleagues. As a result, there has been an almost open discussion, even among those in Mapai who are considered to be most loyal to Eshkol, about possible alternative Prime Ministers.

This process of internal disintegration has affected Mapai itself. The "Gush", the powerful Tel Aviv Party Organisation, has come out against Eshkol and Golda Meir, because they say, Eshkol has sacrificed the interests of Mapai in order to win the support of the Ahdut Avoda Party of Galili and Allon. The so-called Young Mapai – the *Zeirim* – led by such Mapai loyalists as Liova Eliav and Ofer

245

has also rebelled against the Eshkol-Meir policies and against what they call the Tammany Hall methods of the Eshkol-Meir leadership. In fact, as a result of these processes, the internal divisions in the Party and the remoteness of the leaders from the rank-and-file, there is virtually no grass-roots local organisation of Mapai left in the country. All that exists now is the party-machine geared to get the votes at election time at any cost and by every means. When you think back of what Mapai used to be the change is incredible and incredibly tragic.

He went on to picture the other side:

A few men have stood aside and remained uninvolved. The Mayor of Haifa, Abba Hushi, is one of these, and he might have been a possible alternative to Eshkol. But he is not prepared to expose himself until he is sure that it is safe to do so and those who had looked to him for leadership are turning elsewhere – but without much hope of success. Another factor in the national demoralisation is the knowledge now widespread in the country of the kind of Byzantine relationship which Pinhas Sapir, the Minister of Finance, has imposed on some of his close colleagues and on those who are dependent on the Finance Ministry's general goodwill and support.

But unquestionably the most disturbing aspect of the present situation is the one I have already referred to – the almost total breakdown in communication between Government and the people, between the Mapai leadership and its members, and, in fact, between the Establishments – all of them: Government, Jewish Agency, Histadrut, the political parties and even Wizo – and the general Israeli public, especially, though not exclusively, with the under-forties. The result of this is the extraordinary state of national apathy and fatalism in the country. The general mood of the public is that there is nothing that can be done about it, nothing they can do. For the first time since the establishment of the state I have heard acquaintances (in their thirties and forties) who are considered to be pillars of the nation tell me that they were scared about the future. I have heard this phrase repeated in Tel Aviv and Jerusalem – "I am scared".

The fact is [he concluded] that we are passing through a transition of our society and the mechanisms and checks which have operated hitherto are working no longer. We need something that will effectively replace the framework of pioneering, patronage and the party

246

system – and Government – which Mapai used to provide and which was so effective and decisive in the past. My own feeling is that the country needs a new ideological impetus which puts the national interest before all else linked with a national consensus around a nationally accepted and competent personality at the head of a national Government.[1]

This senior official had no doubts about the one man that could fill this position. By far the best suited, he said, was Yigael Yadin, the former Chief of Staff and the present Professor of Archaeology at the Hebrew University. He would have the support of Mapai and of Ahdut Avoda, of leading Rafi personalities such as Shimon Peres and of the new Gahal Party, which had emerged from the merger of the Liberals and Beigin's Herut. As the head of a national Government, he would overnight transform the spirit of the people.

He was right. I sounded the leading personalities he had mentioned – and others – and with only very few exceptions the idea of a Government led by Yadin and reflecting a national consensus was everywhere received with hope and doubt: hope that it might be possible and doubt that the forces in authority were too strongly entrenched to permit such a development within the Israeli party system. It might be possible, though, if the pressure for change was reinforced by representative Jewish figures in the Diaspora.

Israel Sieff had also been in Israel at this time and had also observed the critical situation. He had meanwhile received a life peerage for his contribution to British public life – he had become head of the Marks & Spencer organisation, President of the Zionist Federation of Great Britain, and a powerful figure in the World Jewish Congress. For all that, he was accepted by all as a person who sought neither personal profit nor advancement in Israel and who gave without expecting to receive. He had established himself as an elder statesman whose counsel was sought and whose advice was occasionally taken and who was held in respect second to none. And now he decided to offer his counsel not only in private, but also in public.

He was greatly concerned by what he had found in Israel, but not depressed. He found that in industry, manufacturers and workers had the feeling that they were operating a going concern which was bene-fiting from efficient planning and greater productivity. It was the con-

[1] Memo by J.K., 13 November 1966.

247

trast between this spirit and that of the Government that worried Sieff. The Government gave the impression of being unable to cope. He had himself taken up the case of families in Beersheba who had not enough to eat despite all the official statistics to the contrary; and there was evident hunger among the immigrant population of Beisan. He regretted that the Minister of Labour, Yigal Allon, had again postponed the starting date from which the unemployed – over 100,000 – would receive unemployment benefit.

These and many other examples suggested to Sieff that what was wrong was not the capacity of the country to manage, nor its ability to make another leap forward, but the machinery of Government and, in some cases, the men in the Government. It seemed to him quite wrong that men like himself should have to come to Israel and tell the authorities what they should do, or where there was urgent need for them to intervene with positive action. The Government should be sufficiently and accurately informed on these matters without the help of outsiders; but they evidently were not . . . Israel could not afford anything to be second-rate, be it men or methods, be it the machinery of the Government.[2]

It so happened that Yadin had come to London for the opening of the Massada exhibition. Before leaving Israel he had been sounded on the general idea of a change of Government in which he might play a central role as the need for drastic action on the home front became increasingly apparent. It was not just the grimness of the economic situation, Israel had been through worse periods, but the combination of the economic depression with the psychological depression that was different. The steam of Zionism and Israeli pioneering appeared to be running out and the gap between the haves and have-nots was widening perceptibly. It was, in fact, no sudden turn for the worse; it was merely that for a variety of largely irrelevant reasons – and because of some publicity which the Government had wanted to sweep under the carpet there was a sudden awareness of problems that had been there all along.

In a sense, the December crisis was the accumulated product of the post-Ben-Gurion regime of Eshkol, Sapir and Golda Meir. It was the pay-off of the new team that had replaced Ben-Gurion's in 1963. The problems were still the same, only the style and the sense of purpose had been lost in the intervening three years.

[2] See Sieff to J.K., 12 January 1967; Sieff Interview in *Jewish Observer*, 20 January 1967; *Bank of Israel Annual Report* 1966, pp. 213–18.

248

By the winter of 1966 this showed itself more sharply than at any previous time in the history of the state. The hard-core poverty which affected close on 300,000 Israelis who were living in conditions euphemistically described as under-privileged, was growing larger not smaller. The Chairman of the Jewish Agency had estimated that, when Eshkol took over from Ben-Gurion in 1963, there were some 150,000 children living in homes with over five children to a room, and he had asked what chance had they of equal opportunity or of an adequate education.[3] In the winter of 1966 their number had swollen and their opportunities had diminished still further. The new development towns in the north and the south were often blind alleys built with much ado and money by the Jewish National Fund and other Jewish Agency organisations. Social need was often sacrificed for the sake of fund-raising propaganda and the blackness of the conditions of the poor was emphasised abroad where it helped to get money and generally dismissed at home where it cost money and required long-range and careful planning.

At the other end of the social pyramid, a comparatively small but influential group of manufacturers, merchants, entrepreneurs, bankers, lawyers, doctors and farmers grew inordinately rich, frequently with the help of the Ministry of Trade and Industry or the Minister of Finance who dispensed a vastly complicated but profitable system of subsidies and financial inducements which no businessman worth his salt could resist. And as business became more profitable and more aggressive, so did the trade unions, the Histadrut – and since both were powerful and both had much to gain from this handout policy by the Government, they had their way in most things. In the middle sat the weak Government of Levi Eshkol, presided over by a weak Prime Minister.

Ben-Gurion has described the shock he experienced early on when Eshkol was his Finance Minister, when Ben-Gurion came to understand that Eshkol was not sure of himself, that he would take no decisions without consulting any number of people and at the end would still avoid reaching a decision because he could not make up his mind between the usually contradictory advice offered him by his friends. Ben-Gurion explained how he had tried to impress on Eshkol what leadership meant: "A leader was not made by the people who followed him, but a leader was made from within himself; that is the test." Eshkol failed a second time when Ben-Gurion appointed him to

[3] Louis Pincus to J.K., 17 November 1963.

head the Committee of Seven on the Lavon Affair. "It was his opportunity, I told him," Ben-Gurion said, "if you find the officer guilty, you will have made your reputation; and so you will if you find him not guilty of misconduct. Instead of deciding, Eshkol waffled." Eshkol's Premiership was his third opportunity, and he failed this as well. In Ben-Gurion's opinion, there was no single major mistake which Eshkol had made; it was simply again the moral failure of not being sure of himself and not knowing what he really wanted to do.[4]

Teddy Kollek, who had been Ben-Gurion's Director-General for many years, and then had been with Eshkol for a short time, saw the problem of Ben-Gurion's successor in a broader light. It was not just that Eshkol was constantly consulting instead of deciding, but he was concerned with matters on a lower scale. The biggest change in the wake of Ben-Gurion's replacement by Eshkol, as Kollek saw it, was that somehow the magnetic touch which affected everything that Ben-Gurion handled had disappeared:

. . . There is no one now who thinks ahead in terms of Israel's Grand Strategy. Ben-Gurion had a concept, five years, ten years and even twenty years ahead. He saw Israel's relationships with the United States, with France, with Germany and Africa, and with China as a possible alternative to Russia, in concrete terms. These may not always have been immediately realistic, but they gave a perspective and sense of purpose to Israel's outlook which is totally lacking now. The country is living ideologically as well as financially on a hand-to-mouth basis and on day-to-day decisions. This was particularly reflected in the general blurring of principles which had become a feature of the Eshkol approach.[5]

What Kollek had observed in 1964, from his vantage point inside the Eshkol establishment, became more generally apparent by 1966. Kollek had noted at that time that there was no evident alternative to Eshkol's leadership. Dayan was the only man who had the ability to look ahead, as did Ben-Gurion, and he had a brilliant mind, but he was politically isolated and contained by the establishment and the party machine. Moreover, Eshkol and Mrs Meir and the party hierarchy were taking care to neutralise any possible opposition centres of power that might

[4] Ben-Gurion to J.K., 25 March 1966.
[5] Kollek to J.K., 26 May 1964.

250

be associated with Dayan and his friends. Shimon Peres, Ben-Gurion's Deputy Defence Minister, was now working quite well with Eshkol who, like Ben-Gurion, had also taken charge of the Defence Ministry. But it was a one-sided affair. Eshkol had re-organised the army establishment, and among senior officers – especially those in command positions – there was virtually no one left who considered himself to be Mapai or close to Peres and Dayan. Most of them had come from the Palmach establishment and were associates of Allon and Galili. These changes had considerably undermined Peres' position at the Ministry.[6]

In the run-up to the winter crisis of 1966, there was one further area of Government operation that was of particular significance in the setting of the 1967 salvation. In June 1965 Eshkol went to Washington for talks with President Johnson about Israel's military preparedness. The talks had, of course, been carefully prepared in advance by Israel's defence staff, but as Eshkol put it on his return, "we got what we wanted – and more".

The British Government had asked President Johnson to use his influence to persuade the Israelis to buy the new British "Chieftain" tank, but the Israelis preferred the modified "Centurion", which had served them so well, rather than the more costly, untried and heavier "Chieftain" – especially as the Israelis wanted quicker deliveries than would be possible with the "Chieftain"; had they chosen otherwise, it would have been doubtful whether Israel's armoured forces would have been as well equipped as they were in June two years later. Johnson did not stop at that. He arranged, while Eshkol was in Washington, a complicated financial arrangement whereby the German Government paid the British for the "Centurion" tanks to be delivered to Israel as part of a long-term loan to Israel.

But the most important decision taken during Eshkol's visit to Washington was to arrange for a periodical joint US-Israeli survey of the military situation in the Middle East which would go beyond the usual exchange of intelligence information. It would be, in fact, a form of very detailed contingency planning for the most likely eventualities (though the Americans were anxious that this term should not be used). In all but name this came very close to joint military planning. The Americans had come to the discussions with the Israelis with plans and complete details of units and capabilities which they had available in the Middle East, and with precise indications what they could do in a given

[6] Kollek, ibid.

situation. The Americans were, however, less enthusiastic about Eshkol's assessment of Khrushchev as a moderate who would follow "a milder line". Anyhow, Khrushchev did not stay long enough for either Eshkol or the Americans to discover who was right. Eshkol and Peres – who had done much of the preparatory work – were greatly struck by the manner in which the Americans had put themselves out to meet the Israeli requirements, and not only just to make the Israelis happy. Peres was particularly aware of the potential importance of the American connection.[7]

This new relationship with the United States was no passing gesture. It developed rapidly, so rapidly that it began to have a momentum all of its own, almost independent of the policy-makers. The Israelis thought that most of it was due to their initiative; the Americans – especially the Pentagon and the Central Intelligence Agency – had a longer perspective and were looking beyond the purely Israeli features of the new relationship. They had become convinced that the Soviet interest in the Middle East and North Africa was real, that the Russians had valid interests which they proposed to protect. In a sense, so the Americans argued at the time, the United States and the Soviet Union had parallel interests in the Middle East and the Mediterranean to prevent a situation which could bring about a head-on clash of the superpowers. Eshkol, during his 1965 visit to Washington, had encouraged this type of thinking and had seen himself as the honest broker between the superpowers in the Middle East. The Americans thought this to be rather naive but did not discourage this line of Israeli thinking.

On the contrary, they saw the new Israeli Foreign Minister, Abba Eban, who had taken over the Ministry from Mrs Meir, as a rather effective pacemaker for this probing of Russian intentions on which the Americans had embarked. Eshkol's unusually friendly relations with the influential Soviet Ambassador in Israel, Chuvakhin, might provide a channel of useful information and an indication of Soviet intentions. Eban, himself, had taken over the Ministry Mrs Meir had left with the firm intention of making a clean sweep of her policies and personalities if that could be done without kicking up too much dust. Eban felt that so many changes were necessary that it would require a better alibi than the programme of a newly installed minister and relatively junior party member. He thought it might be possible, however, to appoint "some-

[7] Kollek to J.K., 15 June 1965; *Jewish Observer*, 19 June 1965.

thing like a Royal Commission to report on the need and nature of change required by the Foreign Ministry".[8]

He also proposed important changes in the policy routines of the Ministry. The Israeli public had to be kept better informed than it had been under his predecessor to overcome the recurring problem that "whenever any kind of new foreign policy initiative had to be undertaken, the Government was handicapped by their fear of public opinion at home. As a result we usually act on the basis of what the public would like or not instead of doing what is necessary in a given situation."

Typical of this, Eban reflected, "was the annual hysteria over the refugee discussion at the United Nations. The amount of time and money wasted over the years on half a sentence that was forgotten no sooner than it had been voted, was impossible to estimate."

He felt that Mrs Meir's characteristic persistence in this field had often annoyed and irritated Israel's best friends, and he wanted to change all that. In the same way, he was convinced that the "whole arms' balance campaign" conducted by his predecessor in the United States had been a mistake; it was rather phoney and, since the American administration knew that, even if no one else did, it could do no good.

In fact, the arms delivered to Jordan, about which Mrs Meir had protested, had been provided by the Americans in agreement with the Israeli Government – and Israel was getting her monthly share of tanks at the same time, only on a much larger scale. The Americans had become part of Israel's arms-supply system, and the important thing now was not to bother the President in the way this had been done in the past, with minor and constant requests, but to reserve discussions on that level for problems of major policy, such as, "how to fill the Middle East vacuum as the British leave, and as the continuing Western influence in the region becomes less evident. Israel wanted to talk to the Americans now on how to bring in the Russians on a basis of mutual agreement, though they realised that there was not much hope of this happening in the near future." However, Eban was certain that the Russians would welcome such a move and, if nothing else, it would be good public relations.[9]

But events and the American initiative had gone way beyond Eban's

[8] Eban to J.K., 30 January 1966.
[9] Eban to J.K., 30 January 1966.

253

initial intentions. Just how far the Americans had gone – and what this might ultimately mean to Israel's foreign policy and independence – could be seen best through the eyes of a shrewd and perceptive diplomat and politician, the then Minister at Israel's Embassy in Washington, who had been transferred to this key position after an unusually successful tenure in London, Ephraim Evron.

Evron had been greatly impressed by Eban's visit to Washington. It had been a tremendous success and Evron had been proud of his Foreign Minister. He had excelled himself in his presentation of the four major issues which confronted Israel, which he had put in lucid and sympathetic form in 14 minutes. Evron was less happy about the substance of the new foreign policy: "Its style was magnificent but there was relatively little new to back it up." Evidently, having surveyed the political landscape, Eban had concluded that his planned reforms might kick up more than just dust – and that Israel's most powerful politician would continue to exercise her all-pervading influence inside or outside the Government, now that Mrs Meir had become General Secretary of the Labour Party.

However, none of this affected the central fact of Israel's relations with the United States. These were ubiquitous and yet were largely outside the mainstream of the customary foreign relations. Evron had been surprised by this when he arrived from London and "it was a shock I felt almost every day since I arrived in Washington; things were so very different to what one had been led to expect, or what one had suspected relations were like with Washington." It was incredible on how many different points Israeli and American relations touched each other, where Israel relied on the United States. Evron thought that the sheer extent to which Israeli Government departments, business concerns, institutions and every conceivable type of organisation looked to the United States to help them get out of trouble, harboured possible and serious dangers. Evron found that the consequence was "an Israeli dependence on the United States which was almost frightening".[10]

Thus a curious duality developed in Israel's relations with the United States. By the spring of 1967, Israel was a liability for the Americans in diplomatic, political and economic terms – a problem, a drain and an embarrassment; but in military terms, Israel had become a desirable associate. The Americans, that is those who had to advise the President, were of the opinion in April 1967 that the military factor might soon

[10] Ephraim Evron to J.K., 6 May 1966.

254

outweigh all others and that the United States was well advised to hold on to and further reinforce this link despite the continued uncertain state of Israel's home front. President Johnson had appointed an inter-departmental committee under a senior diplomat, Julius Holmes, to assess American commitments in the Middle East and what these involved. The Central Intelligence Agency, and other secret agencies, had established close links with the Head of Israel's exceptionally able Military Intelligence, Brigadier Aharon Yariv, and with the Head of the Secret Service, Meir Amit. Richard Helms, the Director of the Central Intelligence Agency in Washington, was a frequent visitor to Israel and an unusual degree of collaboration on this level had developed by the spring of 1967. On one of these visits a senior American official wrote to me privately what was, in effect, the assessment of the general situation by the American and Israeli intelligence establishments. The letter was posted from Tel Aviv on 17 May 1967 and it shows how suddenly the war crisis developed and how it escalated out of control of its principal participants.

After noting first the state of Israel's home front, the American official commented that strange as it may seem, it looked as if the period of economic regression and austerity was at an end. Not because the *Mitun*, as the Israelis called the economic slow-down, had achieved its purpose, but because the Government had panicked at the political consequences of maintaining the squeeze, largely because the whole operation had got out of hand. The Government had revised its policy and was again budgeting for a I£400 million deficit and was pouring money into the economy at a reckless rate intent on reducing the un-employment figures and on curing the depression.

The economists, such as Dan Patenkin, were warning the Govern-ment against launching another inflationary boom that would be a spectulators' paradise and would not put the economy on a sound basis. However, the Government was basking in sudden and undeserved popularity after the air force had shot down six Syrian MIG planes, and after Sapir's economic deal with the Rumanians which had been built up out of all proportion to its real value. The remainder of this letter I propose to quote verbatim – remember the date when it was written, 17 May 1967: four days before Nasser closed the Gulf of Aqaba to Israeli shipping. Note also that this was a confidential account of the way the American and Israeli intelligence in Israel assessed the military situation on that day:

255

From London the present tension on the borders probably looks much worse than it does here. Although it does seem pretty serious, we do not think here that it will develop into a hot war, but anything can happen now that the UN is pulling out. This latest development has taken everybody by surprise. The move of the Egyptian troops into Sinai was interpreted by the Israelis as an Egyptian attempt to save their reputation in the Arab world. They really had no choice; they had to do something after Eshkol's warning to the Arabs otherwise they would have publicly displayed their total impotence. The Egyptian troop movements have therefore been accepted by the Israeli authorities as one more gambit in the complex game of inter-Arab politics – dangerous, but not alarming.

This view has been somewhat qualified in the light of the UN withdrawal during the last 24 hours. The reasoning of their intelligence people for changing their position is roughly as follows – and broadly we go along with it: The Egyptians do not want to go to war at present, but without the restraining presence of the UN troops, the local situation could easily get out of hand. Escalation into war need not be the result of a deliberate policy in Cairo, but could result from the Syrians and Palestinians misreading this new Egyptian belligerence. They may resume their raiding and acts of sabotage on the assumption that Israel will not react because of the Egyptian presence in Sinai. But there is no immediate sign of this. The Syrians are keeping very quiet, evidently anxious not to spark off something.

Here in Israel there is total calm; there is no war hysteria, no run on the shops, no panic, not even much excitement. Most people – and that includes those who matter – are carrying on, business as usual. This is no act. They really believe that even if there is more trouble with the Syrians and the Israelis mount another reprisal raid, the Egyptians will not intervene.[11]

And then everything changed in a matter of days. Nasser closed the Gulf of Aqaba on 21 May. But he showed no overt signs of going to war until 26 May, when he was assured by his air force pilots at Bir Gafgafah that they were the masters, that they could take on the Israeli air force and defeat it in a matter of hours and that the Israeli cities would be at their mercy. From that moment Nasser seemed intent on provoking the Israelis into an attack.

[11] Letter to J.K., 17 May 1967.

It was precisely for this situation that the Israel defence force had made its contingency plans and had prepared itself to the smallest detail. Rabin, Hod and Yariv were ready to go on 27 May, while the Egyptians in Sinai were still deploying and in a state of chaos and Husain had not yet been drawn into the war front.

Israel was ready, but not the Israeli Government. It became evident that Eshkol and Eban had wholly misunderstood the special relationship with the United States. All these matters about which Evron had spoken were seen as American goodwill for Israel which had to be repaid by a form of political and diplomatic conformism. In short, they accepted that Israel was a client state of the United States and therefore had to do nothing that would displease the President or embarrass American interests. And the Americans were for peace and international action. The President had said so and the State Department had enlarged on it. At all costs the Israelis must avoid taking the initiative.

At the same time, Israeli public opinion was becoming worried and agitated by the noisy propaganda broadcasts from Cairo and Damascus, and even more by the Government's seeming inactivity and lack of leadership. And the armed forces were getting restless. For the first time since the establishment of the state, senior officers distrusted the political leadership and distrusted even more its political, let alone military, judgement. After Eban had returned from Washington and Paris in the midst of these agitated discussions, Brigadier Yariv informed the Prime Minister that the information which the Foreign Minister had given to the Cabinet was not confirmed by independent reports of the position taken by the Americans and by General de Gaulle. In fact, the Foreign Minister's assessment was catastrophically mistaken, even though he might himself believe that his reports to the Cabinet had correctly interpreted the American position – and that of General de Gaulle.

What Eban had seemed to misread, and this may well have been Eshkol's fault for not co-ordinating the civilian and the military foreign policy, was that there were two American policies operating on two distinct levels. Officially, the Americans were correct in every way. They went along with the United Nations, with the British and the French, and endeavoured to find an international solution. But they were convinced that the United Nations would remain ineffective, and that all the British might succeed in doing was to get the Americans involved in a conflict in the Middle East. The more they saw of the attitudes of the parties concerned – the Egyptians and Syrians, George Brown, Foreign Secretary in the British Labour Government, and the French, the less the Americans liked the prospect.

In secret talks which they had with Yariv and Amit, Israel's Military and Secret Intelligence Chiefs, the Pentagon and the CIA were satisfied that Israel could well take care of the situation so long as the Great Powers did not intervene. The Israelis were, therefore, informed on two distinct levels of the American position. Johnson and Rusk played their version of the Middle East charade with Eban, but did not realise that Eban was taking it all seriously and was unaware of the other half of the American proposal. Helms told his Israeli colleagues that Israel would have to conjure up all her inner strength to withstand pressures from the outside. Even the Americans might find it necessary to join in these pressures for they had to protect themselves at all cost against the suspicion of collusion – and they could do so only by ensuring that there was no collusion. But – and this was conveyed to Yariv rather than spelled out in as many words – if Israel wanted to have tangible results this time, she would have to be as solid as a rock and not weaken before, during, or after the actual military encounter. No less important in the eyes of Israel's defence establishment was an undertaking by the Americans that once hostilities had commenced they would immediately inform the Russians that the United States would not intervene. The Americans were sure that the Russians would get the message and would act accordingly – which they did. They stayed out of the conflict while it lasted.

In effect, what happened during the last days of May was that the United States had reached an understanding with Israel's defence forces which cleared the way for the 5 June initiative, but the whole operation nearly came unstuck because of Eshkol's indecision and of Eban's entirely mistaken assessment of the American position. The "client complex" died hard and it nearly wrecked the plans of Israel's General Staff on the eve of the outbreak of the war. While this is now a somewhat hypothetical question, and no one is particularly anxious to discuss it, there was no doubt at the time that a number of leading army commanders and staff officers would not have stood by idly if the composition of the Eshkol Government had not been changed and if no action had been taken in the face of the gathering Arab storm.

There were, in fact, two quite distinct sides to the country's leadership on the eve of the war. The political leaders had been unable to develop a common language and a common sense of trust between the political establishment of the parties and the military establishment which had to act on its own because of the ineffectiveness and inactivity of the civilian leadership.

These inner contradictions which had beset the Israeli leadership would have continued unchanged into the post-war period had not the exigencies of the war forced the Mapai establishment – Eshkol, Meir, Sapir and Eban – to accept changes in the composition of the Government which under normal conditions they would not have considered and which they opposed even in the critical days on the eve of the war. What produced the change, what brought Dayan into the Defence Ministry was not popular opinion; Israel's leading politicians take note of that only when it suits their book. In the case of Dayan, it was the fear of an army coup, however formulated, that forced the Government's hand. And behind that was the completely different outlook of the contesting forces. Eshkol, Eban, Sapir – and also Mrs Meir, despite her reputation – were essentially Weizmannists who had grown up to shape policies to meet immediate needs, to act from positions of weakness and to seek to obtain that which seemed possible. Like Weizmann – and unlike Ben-Gurion – they had no long-range sense of direction, they had no clear ideas what they wanted and they were not even sure what they meant by peace and by secure frontiers. The Israel defence forces had an altogether different outlook. In their way, they were the real Ben-Gurion legacy; they were confident of their strength and ability; they had clear-cut objectives and they knew how to get them. But they still lacked the perspective ahead that Ben-Gurion might have given them. For with victory came opportunity. But there was no one to pick it up.

Dayan, perhaps the only Israeli leader at that time who had the influence and the ability to act and, in his own way, managed to look beyond the immediate daily requirements, could have filled the gap left by Ben-Gurion's withdrawal. But he was immediately muzzled, constrained and restricted by the Cabinet establishment and by the selective operation of the rule of the collective responsibility of the Cabinet. Dayan and his military advisers, especially Shlomo Gazit, recognised the potentiality of a settlement with the Palestinians on the West Bank immediately after the war when the Palestinians still felt that they had been liberated rather than conquered by the Israelis.

The Palestinian leaders "telephoned" their desire for an immediate settlement. About 40 of the West Bank notables and radicals put their names to a call for a provisional Palestinian Assembly. But there was no reply. Dayan was told by the Cabinet that this was not his affair as military commander, but that it belonged to the Foreign Minister and the Prime Minister who would deal with it. They did. A month later, on 17 July 1967, the Prime Minister's most senior adviser wrote to me about the fate of the Palestinian initiative which I had personally witnessed:

Our good friend Levi [Eshkol] is not interested in a quick solution. It is so much easier to muddle through than to reach a decision. The special committee concerned with policy matters affecting the West Bank continue to meet, but there is no longer much point to it. The Arabs have been quick to sense the change of mood of the Israeli authorities and they have adjusted their own attitudes accordingly. No one speaks any longer about the establishment of an independent Palestinian state as an immediate target as was so common two or three weeks ago. No one in fact talks about an independent State at all. For the word has been passed round that, by agreement with the Israelis, King Husain is coming back and will rule again over the West Bank. This means for the West Bank Arabs that they must not be seen to co-operate too much with the Jews and they must avoid making statements which would be considered as traitorous by the returning Hashemite authorities. This change of mood is particularly evident among the hard-core Palestinian nationalists in Nablus. A few weeks ago they spoke quite openly of having been liberated from the oppressive Jordanian occupation regime; now they claim piously that all they want is to return into the fold of their beloved King.

What is more [the letter continued] the Prime Minister's advisers on Arab affairs accept these opportunist claims at their face value. Moise Sasson and Chaim Herzog, the Military Governor of Jerusalem, have actually welcomed this change of mood as an encouraging step towards a peace, and, understandably, the West Bank Arabs take this as a confirmation of an Israeli deal with Husain. Thus the Husain dance is on, and every one from Eshkol and Eban downwards (with the exception of Dayan and his circle) are preening themselves as the would-be bearers of peace from Amman. They don't seem to see that the more Husain's name is bandied about the less the Arabs want to co-operate.

260

A month ago [he concluded] Palestinian newspaper-owners and editors were begging for permission to re-start their papers on the West Bank; now that they have the permits, they don't want them. They tell us "Let's wait and see first if Husain comes to terms with you" – and this applies right across the board. Dayan gave instructions the other day that there was to be no economic discrimination against the West Bank Arabs, that in their day-to-day affairs and living, they were to be treated the same as Israelis. Two days later the Government reversed Dayan's orders and we now have the crazy situation of Israeli customs posts between Ramallah and Jerusalem. The Arabs think we have gone mad and at times I feel the same. But then one needs to understand that while the war against the Arabs may be over that against Dayan has only just begun.[12]

Twelve days later this conviction that Husain would be back in the saddle on the West Bank any day was so general that "the merchants on the West Bank dare not go to bed with Israeli pounds still in their possession. Every evening they hawk their Israeli currency earned that day to black marketeers who are making fortunes buying this Israeli money for Jordanian Dinars or Dollars at outrageous rates of exchange. There are also other causes for trouble – not least the way the Israeli Ministries of the Interior, Transport and Religion have dealt with East Jerusalem. I was with Teddy Kollek the other day and he was livid at the manner in which officials from the ministries were operating. They had undone all the good work he and the municipality had already achieved in Jerusalem."[13]

Moreover, the majority of the Government had only limited time for the problems of the West Bank for it also had to conduct its intensive campaign against the proposed merger of Rafi, with Dayan and Peres at its head, with Mapai and Ahdut Avoda. This was to be the principal theme for weeks to come. It was opposed by Eshkol, Mrs Meir, Galili, Allon and especially Eban, who had returned from his mission to the United Nations as a kind of conquering hero. He was at this time "wreathed in glory, one of the most popular men in the country", and Mapai made the most of it. All the same, a strong minority still favoured Dayan and Rafi, even inside the Labour Party. At the Central Committee meeting of the party early in August, Eshkol and Mrs Meir

[12] Letter to J.K., 17 July 1967.
[13] Letter to J.K., 29 July 1967.

261

were in a minority when they proposed that the merger talks should be frozen for six months.[14]

But by the beginning of September, while the Arab leaders were meeting at Khartoum to decide on their further policy towards a possible settlement, the Israel Government had moved into the first of the fixed positions which were to dominate all further talks about peace and withdrawal in the coming years. Even before the Prime Minister had been enabled to read the verbatim text of the discussions at the secret summit conference of Arab leaders at Khartoum which Israel's Secret Service had obtained for him,[15] the Israel Government's position was "that we need not be in a hurry about anything. We are staying put until the Arabs make the first concrete move (and the later that is, the better it is for us). The intransigent Syrians and Algerians are doing the work of 'Zionist agents', if only they realised it!"[16]

The full details of the discussions at the Khartoum summit conference of Arab leaders held in September 1967, showed the Israelis that there was not the remotest inclination by Nasser or by any other Arab leader – including Husain – to consider seriously any kind of peace settlement with Israel. It was not just that they stipulated terms which would be unacceptable to the Israelis; they simply would not consider any step that would lead to the recognition of Israel as part of the Middle East scene. Nasser's speech especially struck the Israelis as particularly negative. In the light of the actual record of these discussions, and of Husain's own contribution, Husain's later explanations to his British biographer Peter Snow are not very convincing.[17] Husain said that he had explained the so-called "Three Noes" on which the Khartoum Conference decided to the then British Prime Minister, Harold Wilson.[18]

He had told him that the term "peace" meant something different in Arabic than in English. It did not convince the Prime Minister and it did not convince the Israelis. All the same, at least some Israelis, especially Eban, believed that whatever Husain might say – and there was little that he had not said over the years – he was still the natural heir to the Faisal-Weizmann Agreement. And as Eban prepared himself for the critical UN Assembly in the autumn of 1967 that was to produce

[14] Ibid.
[15] See Eshkol's statement.
[16] Letter to J.K., 2 September 1967.
[17] *Hussein*, by Peter Snow, pp. 198–9.
[18] Ibid.

a settlement for the Middle East, he summoned his Ambassadors and outlined to them his general strategy for the Assembly. This is how it was reported to me at the time by one of the participating Ambassadors:

Eban believes that the UN Assembly could be stalemated; then Husain would make a peace move to which Israel should respond by giving him back the West Bank – and more. Eban was of the opinion that Husain was now the strongest ruler in the Arab world and should be backed to the hilt by Israel. In short, Israel and Husain should partition the Arab world East of Suez. They should conclude an alliance in which Israel would guarantee the Hashemite Kingdom, and this might possibly again include Iraq. Israeli troops would be stationed on the Jordan river and, if need be, also at H5 [the oil pumping station on the pipeline from Kirkuk to the Mediterranean situated on the Jordan-Iraqi border]. Syria would then be isolated and Nasser, who is waiting for Husain to make the first move towards a settlement, will then join him in reaching an agreement with Israel. This is the basis of Eban's policy of keeping all options open.

In the event, there was no more substance in Eban's Husain solution than there had been in Weizmann's Faisal Agreement. Like Faisal – and more so – Husain kept meeting Israeli representatives, always furtively and under conditions of ill-kept secrecy. He met them in rising seniority as the prospects of a settlement receded and Husain's need for an effective occasional ally became greater than his need for a friend. In the years between the Khartoum Conference in 1967 and his re-emergence as a spokesman for an Arab initiative in the winter of 1972/3, Husain met more senior Israeli officials, Ministers and soldiers than probably any other statesman – including the Americans. He met with Yaacov Herzog who paved the way at the outset, then he met with Eban in London and Allon in Aqaba, with Dayan and ultimately also with Mrs Meir. At the end of this sustained acquaintanceship the Israelis had a good idea of Husain's thinking, and Husain was able to understand what the Israelis wanted. The mutual revelations helped to establish a pragmatic relationship, but did not further the cause of peace.

Eshkol, Mrs Meir and Eban had discovered at the end of five years of furtive diplomacy what any well-informed Israeli junior officer serving on the West Bank could have told them in the summer of 1967.

Husain, like his grandfather, King Abdullah, was not able to make a public settlement with Israel, not even one limited to a Pact of Non-Aggression unless either Egypt or Syria approved or moved first.

There was one real chance of a settlement on the morrow of victory; it was lost when the Israel Government turned to Husain instead of inviting the Palestinians to come home and take over their rightful heritage as of right and not on sufferance, to enable the Palestinians to do what they had been unable to do under Ottoman rule, under British rule and under Jordanian rule – to establish their own National Home in Palestine alongside the Jews. When Eshkol delayed action at Eban's behest so as to allow Eban to win over international opinion at the United Nations Assembly, he sacrificed at least the hope, if not certainty, of a real peace.

Eban went on to score his greatest diplomatic triumph at that Assembly and returned home as the hero and darling of his people. Yet rarely has a political triumph been bought at so high a price. For despite all his shortcomings and weaknesses, Eshkol was essentially a man of peace and he would have welcomed a Palestinian settlement, strongly backed as it might have been by Dayan and other members of his Government. But that chance was lost at the UN Assembly and it died with Levi Eshkol on 26 February 1969. Yet when we look back 50 years to 1918, we can see that this curious Israeli refusal to consider the Palestinian solution was in the true tradition of Weizmann's own approach in the early years after the Balfour Declaration.[19] It was as if the assertion of a Jewish nation required the rejection of the existence of a Palestinian nation. It was in its own way the Israeli contribution to the Khartoum Resolution of the "Three Noes" – no formal peace with the Palestinians, no recognition, no negotiation. It survived from Amin to Arafat. This was the reality, not Husain's "peacemaking", not even Dayan's valiant attempt to reach an accommodation with Nasser which nearly succeeded when Nasser died.

Eshkol had in fact ceased to be de facto Premier some time before his death. An inner Cabinet consisting of his "friends" met at least once a week at Eshkol's home and decided all major policy issues. Those who played the key roles in the secret Cabinet were Pinhas Sapir, the Finance Minister; Golda Meir, the Party's General Secretary, Shapiro, the Minister of Justice, Galili and Allon representing the Ahdut Avoda wing. Rafi and Dayan were not invited. They met as usual on Friday

[19] See Part I, Chapter Two.

264

evening, 14 February 1969 – 12 days before Eshkol died. Eshkol said that in view of the published criticism of his premiership, he had decided to resign. He was told by Sapir, and especially by Mrs Meir in her measured tones, that it was not for him to decide when to resign. This would be decided for him by his colleagues who were at that meeting.

In fact, they had gone to quite extraordinary lengths to maintain Eshkol in office – evidently because the preparations for the succession had not been completed.

The situation within the Party leadership remains tense and strained for Eshkol is very ill and has been so for some time. His "friends" are doing everything to keep it quiet and the public does not suspect that in fact Israel has no Prime Minister at this critical time. A little while ago, Eshkol collapsed at home and when the doctor came, he ordered his immediate removal to hospital. The ambulance arrived at the same time as some members of his "inner circle". His "friends" firmly vetoed the doctor's order and insisted that Eshkol should remain at home and that nothing be said about the gravity of his illness. The public was told that the Prime Minister was indisposed.[20]

Unknown to the other members of the secret Cabinet, Sapir proceeded to prepare for the succession and to make sure that the Premiership should pass to Mrs Meir and not to the front-runner, Yigal Allon.

Sapir confounded his opponents and confused his allies without any apparent effort. At his bidding, the party voted almost unanimously for the ageing and ailing Golda Meir, and this despite the fact that during the last year she seemed to have spent more time in hospital than out. She had also suffered a steep decline in public popularity since she had opposed the formation of a national coalition in the last days of May 1967 and had strongly opposed the appointment of Dayan as Minister of Defence. A few days after Eshkol's death she polled only just one per cent in the popularity stakes for the succession. The party machine directed by Sapir devoured all opposition, popular and political, in order to place Mrs Meir at the head of the coalition which she had so strenuously opposed.[21]

Four years later, the vigorous, healthy and dominant Mrs Meir, Prime Minister, 74 years old, visited Eshkol's grave on the anniversary

[20] Letter to J.K., 18 February 1969.
[21] Letter to J.K., 8 March 1969.

of his death, a warning to those who form rash judgements, and an example of the remarkable recuperative potency of high office and power. We had seen it in men such as Churchill and Adenauer, de Gaulle and Franco – but they had not been ailing when they started, but Golda Meir was unique, not only because of her sex.

She had served a long apprenticeship and had developed ways of handling the powerful into a fine art, so much so that there was no politician in Israel, friend or foe, who did not quake when Mrs Meir approached with something she wanted done or, more often, about something or someone she did not like. She had no scruples about using her special feminine aids if they helped to get what she wanted. Ben-Gurion would do anything rather than have his Foreign Minister dissolve in tears, or retire to the Sanatorium in Motza while she recovered from a hurt, real or imagined, which she felt had been done to her. Before she became Prime Minister, in the fifties and sixties while she was at the Foreign Ministry, she was protected against criticism of her policies and of her Ministry. Ben-Gurion, Peres and others would go to any length to dissuade a politician or a journalist from questioning Mrs Meir's policies in public. It was different in private, it is still different in private. Golda Meir assumed the Premiership only weeks after Richard Nixon had become the President of the United States. It was a time of uncertainty in Israel about future United States policy and it set the tone for the first phase of Mrs Meir's American trauma, one of the strangest political relationships in modern diplomacy.

# TWO

# The Meir Era

By the time Mrs Meir assumed the mantle of Prime Minister in name as well as in fact, in March 1969, she was no longer a free agent in shaping Israel's policies. For she had inherited from her predecessor the consequences of the victory of June 1967 and it was these that largely dictated and shaped her subsequent actions – not least her attitude to the United States. The most satisfactory feature of this aftermath was the actual military situation in the occupied territories and on Israel's borders. There were difficulties, but these were adequately dealt with by the Minister of Defence, Moshe Dayan, and by the Israel Defence Forces. They presented no problem that could not be managed.

It was, however, the Israeli failure to compel or induce the Arab leaders to come to the peace table, which left its indelible mark on Israel's and Mrs Meir's outlook and policy. It was this which gave rise to a mood of disillusioned impatience with the peace that would not come. And this mood encouraged Israel to welcome the other unexpected aftermath of the 1967 victory – the social and economic impact of the awakened world Jewry on life in Israel and on the policies of the Government. The Israeli establishment had already under Eshkol opened the economic sluice-gates to the emotional and financial flood that poured in from the Jewish Diaspora in support of the victorious Israel, and Government and country were overwhelmed by the flood. By the time Mrs Meir assumed the Premiership this delayed-action explosion of Jewish Diaspora nationalism was well on its way to colonising the post-1967 Israel; in many ways, this was a more far-reaching "annexation" of the entire social and economic life and *mores* of Israel than was Dayan's military occupation of the Arab territories conquered by the Israeli forces during the Six Day War. The economic salvation

267

that followed June 1967 had produced consequences that were no less significant for the future of Israel than were the consequences of the military salvation.

We have to consider these two factors somewhat more closely, because they became an integral part of Mrs Meir's policy – and especially of the policy of assertive compliance which she practised in her relations with Washington. They also conditioned her attitude in the struggle for the control of the Labour movement, and thus of the country, which the Labour establishment led by Mrs Meir waged with the greatest vigour against Dayan and his friends.

The Government of Israel was in an immeasurably stronger position to obtain its objectives after the June War in 1967, than Weizmann and his friends had been when it came to the implementation of the Balfour Declaration. But the 1967 problem was very similar in its essentials to that of 1917. Would the pressure of outside factors and the interests of the Great Powers lead to the whittling away of most of the "tangible gains" that had been won as had happened in 1917 and again in 1957 after the Suez war? The difference in 1967 was that Israel had the tacit support of the Americans. As we have seen, President Johnson counselled Premier Eshkol, not through the normal diplomatic channels, but through the Secret Service link that had been firmly established, that if Israel wanted to secure her tangible gains on this occasion, she would have to remain firm as a rock in the face of every kind of pressure – even American pressure. It was this advice, which now more than anything, conditioned the mind of Mrs Meir and fixed her policies in the rigid frame proposed by the President's formula and by what she herself conceived to be also Israel's fundamental interest.

But – and here one must enter a major proviso – at the time when Lyndon Johnson sent this message to Eshkol it was assumed in Washington, and no less so in Israel, that what was understood by the term "tangible gains" was a properly secured and negotiated peace agreement between Israel and the Arab states with whom she had been at war. At that time – in the late summer of 1967 – there was no question of Israel maintaining the occupation of the captured Arab territories apart from Jerusalem and the Golan Heights and some adjustments around Latrun, Kalkylyia and a few other similar relatively minor border corrections.

In fact when General Ze'evi who is most inappropriately known as "Gandhi", one of Israel's most dynamic field commanders, advanced his considered opinion soon after the end of the war, that a premature peace could mean disaster for Israel, he was roundly and sincerely condemned by every one of his colleagues, some of whom thought him to be excessively extreme. General Shlomo Gazit, Dayan's deputy in the occupied territories, reflected the general view at the time, and also that of Dayan when he argued that the occupied territories gave Israel, for the first time, an effective bargaining counter in their negotiations with the Arabs; they now had something to offer the Arabs in return for peace with security. Gazit added that the crux of the matter was that Israel must not give up this trump card until she was assured of getting both – peace and security. This remained the attitude of most representative Israelis in the Government and in the armed forces and in the glow of the aftermath of victory there were few who doubted that if only the Israelis remained firm and patient, the Arabs would yet come to seek a peace with honour, and get it.

The Israelis waited, but the Arabs did not come. Doubts were followed by disillusionment and bitterness. The right-wing Gahal Party combining the so-called Liberals and Beigin's Herut, the bloc of religious parties, and the "patriots" within the Labour Party, saw themselves cheated out of the just consequences of victory and accused those who would consider withdrawing from the occupied territories as betraying the interests of the country. None of the Ministers of the Labour alignment actually held this view, but there was not one among them at that time prepared to risk electoral unpopularity by openly declaring themselves against the tide of chauvinist sentiment which had come in as the hopes of a peace settlement with the Arabs went out. The popular attitude which was reflected by the leadership was that "if the Arabs don't want peace then to hell with them; we'll hold on to what we have". The Government had not initiated this policy, but it embraced it; it followed the public mood, it did not guide it. In a way, when the Arab summit at Khartoum passed its resolution of "no peace, no recognition and no negotiation" with Israel, it set the seal to the Israeli mood. Henceforth, the Israelis were content to accept the Arab formula. It suited them.

Yet there was a peculiar double-take in the Israeli position. The establishment – from Mrs Meir downwards – sincerely wanted a peaceful settlement and was prepared to make considerable sacrifices in order to get one. At the same time, the same establishment – from Mrs Meir downwards – was utterly convinced that every step proposed towards a settlement, whether by friend or foe, was nothing but a gambit designed to bring about an Israeli withdrawal from the occupied territories. Therefore every proposal linked to an Israeli withdrawal, whether made by the Egyptians or the Americans, or by "naive" Israelis, and, in the most significant instance, by Dayan himself, was viewed by Mrs Meir and her Cabinet friends with deep suspicion as something that had to be scotched before it would develop into a threat to Israel's security or to the unity of Mrs Meir's Cabinet coalition. When therefore the Israeli Government – and especially Mrs Meir and her Foreign Minister, Abba Eban – spoke of Israel's desire for peace, they were giving voice to a hope and not proposing a policy. Mrs Meir and her colleagues rejected the charge that there was an element of hypocrisy in this attitude since it posited that their priority was not peace, but the preservation of the status quo. They argued – with considerable weight on their side, as we shall see – that under prevailing conditions in the Arab world, and in view of the outlook of its leaders, any change during these five years would have been detrimental to Israel's interests. We shall consider this further in the context of Israel's American relations, but first we need to consider an altogether different reason for Mrs Meir's resistance to change.

For the aftermath of the war in 1967, the sheer size of the military victory and the enthusiasm which it aroused in the Jewish Diaspora, the negative attitude of the Arab leaders towards a peace settlement, the success of Dayan's occupation policy, and the economic boom which displaced the depression of the pre-war days, created a new social base for the post-war version of a Greater Israel – Mrs Meir's Israel. The enthusiasm of Diaspora Jews expressed in massive financial support and the backing of Israel's wealthy and loyal sympathisers not only made their mark on Israel's economy, but also transformed the political and social base of Israeli society. After the war, Diaspora Jewry had become a potent factor which could not be ignored as it has been before June 1967. World Jewish financial support became a more significant factor in Israeli policy-making than did the new immigrants or the members of Israel's parliament. World Jewry – especially the money-providing sector – became an essential element of the new Israeli society and politics, a constant and mounting challenge to the more egalitarian and socialist Israel of the pre-war days.

It was of course not a simple or sudden transition. The elements of change had been present before the war. Israeli society had become

ISRAEL: BOUNDARIES

4 JUNE 1967 — — —
11 JUNE 1967 ·········

LEBANON

SYRIA

Tyne

Safad
Akko
Haifa
Tiberias
Nazareth
Afula
Hadera
Jenin
Nablus
Damiya Bridge
Tel Aviv
Jericho
Allenby Bridge
Amman
Ashgelon
Jerusalem
Gaza
DEAD SEA

MEDITERRANEAN SEA

Port Said
El Arish
Rafah
Beersheba
El Quantara
Ismailiya
Gebel Libni
Bir Gifgafa
Bir Hasana

ISRAEL

JORDAN

Suez Canal

Suez
Nakhl

Elat
Aqaba

SINIA

GULF OF SUEZ

GULF OF AQABA

SAUDI

ARABIA

EGYPT

Mt. Sinai

0 10 20 30    60
MILES

Ras Nuzrani
Sharm el Sheikh

RED SEA

271

increasingly divided between the rich minority and the poor minority with a large grey mass in between. But before the war the rich were not politically influential – and certainly not the Diaspora rich. In the post-war years, Mrs Meir's policy became a reflection of the new deal with world Jewry; this assumed almost greater importance in the eyes of the official establishment than did the need for a Middle East settlement. For one thing, it was immediately attainable.

It was the first time since the establishment of the Jewish State in 1948, that the majority of Jews in the world – including many living under Soviet rule – had openly and publicly expressed their sympathy, support and identification with Israel. There were no inhibitions about dual loyalty or being recognised as a Jew. Israel's victory appeared to have removed these psychological blocks which had prevailed for 2,000 years. It found expression in many ways of offering direct support for Israel – and the most impressive was the financial contribution of world Jewry. While the official figures do not tell the whole story, they do provide a fairly accurate indication of the extent to which the war of 1967 was Israel's economic, as well as military, salvation, as the following comparisons will show:

In the five years from 1962 to 1966, Anglo-Jewry donated through the Joint Palestine Appeal, a total of £11 million or $30 million.

In the five years from 1967 to 1971, Anglo-Jewry donated three times as much – £32 million or just under $90 million.

In the last year before the war, in 1966, Anglo-Jewry donated £2½ million or $7 million; in the year of the war, 1967, this rose to £17 million, $45 million dollars from a Jewish community of 400,000.

In the United States, the comparison of the United Israel Appeal reflects a similar trend. In five pre-war years, 1962–1966, the Appeal raised $300 million; in the five post-war years, 1967–1971, the total raised was a billion dollars, $1,000 million. In the last pre-war year, 1966, the amount donated to the Israel Appeal in the United States was $70 million; in post-war 1967 this rose to $240 million.

The total amount of funds transferred by way of donation on the part of world Jewry in Israel in the five pre-war years was $400 million, in the five post-war years, 1967–1971, it rose to $1,200 million. The full amount donated, before deductions were made for local overheads and other payments, was considerably larger – probably around $1,600 million in the five post-war years. We also have here the same contrast between the last pre-war year, 1966, when transfers to Israel amounted to $120 million and the war year, 1967, when Jewish contributions transferred to Israel reached a record total of $430 million.

The dynamic response of world Jewry to the challenge of the Six Day War seeped through every sector of Israel's economy and revitalised it. The donation boom was accompanied by an investment forward leap of similar dimensions, allowing for the necessary time-lag for this type of financing. The change is best illustrated by three sets of figures showing Net Domestic Investment in Israel. First for the two lean years – 1966 and 1967 – it amounted to I£3,200 million. For the following two years, 1968/9, it rose to I£5,000 million and climbed even more steeply for the next two years, 1970/71, when it reached the remarkable total of I£7,700 million.

Foreign financial and industrial concerns – mainly American, Canadian, German and French, and a few British firms – followed in the wake, assisted and encouraged by some of the leading banking houses of the United States and Europe. Many of these were not Jewish firms and acted on strictly business reasons in launching their Israeli business operations – but the great majority were sponsored by prominent American Jews and such international financial interests as the Warburgs and the Rothschilds. The First Pennsylvania Corporation invested $16½ million in setting up the first international banking house in Israel; others who invested substantially to establish themselves in Israel were the Ford Motor Company, General Telephone and Electronics, Motorola, Monsanto, Allied Chemicals, Samuel Osborne of Sheffield, Bethlehem Steel, Eagle Star Insurance, Barclays Bank (Discount), Miami Corporation, Sam Rothberg's Israel Investment Corporation, Coca-Cola, Shidlowski's Aero Engines, the German Trade Union-controlled "Bank fuer Gemeinwirtschaft", the Canadian Bronfman interests, ITT, RCA, IBM and California Computers, and many others. By 1970 they were investing about $150 million a year in bringing these new industries and concerns to Israel.

British Jews, apart from the Wolfson complex, invested relatively little in Israel industry or commerce. Lord Sieff's argument in the early days of fund-raising for Israel was that he did not want to make a profit out of his support for Israel and most of the principal contributors from Great Britain followed the example set by Lord Sieff. They made substantial donations to the Joint Palestine Appeal and gave large sums to specialised interests such as the Weizmann Institute of Science, the

Hebrew University, the Technion in Haifa, the Israel Museum in Jerusalem. Insofar as British Jews invested money in Israel it was mainly in the purchase of property and villas and, to some extent, in hotels. But Anglo-Jewry had had its fingers burnt in the earlier investment spree in Israel and was holding back in the general rush to invest. However, the Wolfson interests were substantial and included the highly profitable Paz Petroleum Company which they acquired for a throw-away price from Shell International in the fifties when Shell was anxious to disembarrass itself of its Israeli business, which it claimed was not very profitable. It was also something of an embarrassment for a company with so many important links in the Arab world.

The combination of this massive domestic investment and the interests of large foreign concerns linked to the large inflow of capital – donations, the sale of bonds, foreign loans and aid – created a new Israeli elite, a new establishment that to a considerable extent displaced the old, or embraced part of it into its amply financed New Deal. This resulted in a new parallel power-structure to that which had dominated Israel for the previous 30 years, even in the days before the State was established. Thus, alongside the old establishment – the political parties, the Jewish Agency, the Histadrut, the Kibbutz organisations and the armed forces – there grew up the new elite, which was no longer dependent on the restrictive patronage of the old establishment but was strong enough and had the financial resources to exercise its own form of patronage and influence.

The "Captains of Industry" who owned the most prosperous concerns and could be counted as Israel's "Hundred Families" that disposed over a very large share of the wealth of the country in private hands, maintained, however, a remarkable self-restraint when it came to public affairs. Either from choice, or because of the risks involved, they largely opted out from the exercise of political influence, except where it directly affected their own interests. They had discovered early on that in the peculiar closed shop climate of Israeli politics it was easier to achieve worthwhile objectives which would serve their interests by selective patronage and other non-political but quite legitimate methods of winning friends and influencing decisions without stepping into the political minefields.

Most of these wealthy "Captains" had at one time served the State or its civilian and military institutions before and after 1948. They had contributed greatly to the economic upswing. Most of them had become

274

very rich and by the nature of things contrasted strongly by their wealth and style of life with the great majority of Israelis. But they were not, as in so many developing countries, a parasitic or anti-social element. The problems of the social imbalance which had been created lay rather with official policy than in individual conduct. But the end product was the same – a hard core of great wealth tuned in to the wealth coming into the country from the Diaspora and other outside sources. They were the bridge to the wealth of American and British Jewry – and others. They mattered more to the Israelis than the Zionist General Council or the World Jewish Congress. They were not to be found connected with either of these organisations and, by and large, were also keeping aloof from the political parties in Israel – whatever private aid they might offer one or the other when the electoral need arose.

The roll-call of this unusual elite of wealth in Israel belongs to this record. Among the foremost are Friedman, Pecker, Glickman and Guzman (Central Trade & Investment Company); Recanati, Tolkowsky – a former air force commander – and Shlomo Lahat (discount bank); Gesundheit (Electro); Klier (Argaman); Moshevitz and Frumchenko (Elite); Moller (Ata); Mayer Bros. (Wolfson, Clore and Mayer); Martin Gehl (Dubeck); Rokach, Isaacson and Pollani (citrus groves); Bejerano (Assis); Sacharoff (timber and insurance); Taiber (insurance); Ben Zion (Anglo-Israel Bank); Ellern (banking); Gorodeski (Amcor); Berenstein & Elman (Ampa); Susayeff (industrialist); Y. and S. Federman (hotels); Illin, Buxenbaum, Goldberg and Lubinski (motor-cars and spare parts); Meridor and Brenner (shipping); Kamerman (timber).

Alongside these was another group of "Captains" who had no part in the ownership or wealth of the concerns which they directed, but who carried considerable political influence. Most of them had been, until fairly recently, part of the Governmental or military establishments and had come from one or the other major political parties – but most of them had been associated with the Labour movement. These were men who had succeeded in other fields and then turned their abilities to public corporations, banks, industrial concerns and suchlike positions from which they exercised considerable influence on the political and economic policies of the country.

Among them was Meir Amit, a former Chief of the Secret Intelligence, Makleff, a former Chief of Staff, Limon, a former Commander of the Navy, politicians, lawyers, doctors and academics. But probably the largest number of these new industrial executives were drawn from the armed forces. Of the 75 senior officers who retired between 1952 and 1970, 22 took charge of executive positions in private and public industry. The impact of these men was reflected on the life of Israel and of its standards.

The Central Bureau of Statistics released figures to show that at the end of 1972, nine out of ten Israeli families owned a refrigerator, four out of five had a gas stove, half the population owned washing machines and two out of three a television set. The ownership of these "durables" had doubled in three years, statistically speaking. In fact, it had increased even more among the Western Jews and those born in Israel and rather less among those of Oriental origin. However one looked at it, affluence was spreading, living conditions were improving for many, if not all, and the modernisation of the economy was going ahead at a great pace under the impetus of the flow of funds and the continued Arab threat. The combination was irresistible.

Inevitably these developments introduced a subtle – and sometimes not so subtle – social and political change. The new Zionist elite was in the upper economic brackets or in an equivalent managerial rank. Pioneering had moved from the land to industry, defence and finance. In the past, the Zionist elite had often been a largely bureaucratic body without real connections with the masses; but in the years after the June War, the new Zionist elite was almost totally cut off from the mass of the Israelis by a difference in outlook and wealth, by altogether different social aspirations and interests, and by an altogether different assessment of Israel's role in the life of the Jew. In place of the balanced society of classical Zionism came the concept of the efficient state derived from models which owed more of their concepts to the modern supermarket and merchant bankers than to the ideologies of Herzl and Weizmann. This change was recognised by the World Zionist Organisation when it re-organised the Assembly of the Jewish Agency in 1971 in such a way as to place the wealthy donors and the fund raisers in a commanding position in the counsels of the World Zionist movement with considerable influence in Israel itself.

All this had a profound political implication, for this expanding Israeli economy had need for an expanding base, an expanding reservoir of labour and for the necessary connections abroad. It was not only Dayan or Allon or even Mrs Meir who decided on the policy which Israel wanted to pursue in relation to the occupied territories and a peace

276

settlement. It was not only Mrs Meir's inclination, or resistance to the Palestinians and to Dayan, that shaped her policies; it was also conditioned by the economic imperative of her "Greater Israel" on which the post-war economic boom had been constructed.

But it was not only the continued possession of the occupied territories and the more secure frontiers which Israel's hungry economy demanded for its fare. This economic Greater Israel had need also of the American connection. This had to be preserved at almost any cost except a premature peace with unrequited concessions. In order to secure this American aid and support, Israel had to consider its own Grand Design that would attract the Americans and ensure their backing for Israel. But Israel's Grand Design soon ran into trouble. For the Americans began to have ideas about their own American-patterned plan which was rather different from that espoused by Mrs Meir. As a result, within days of Nixon's election as President, the two Designs crashed headlong into each other and the curious relationship of Mrs Meir and William P. Rogers, Nixon's Secretary of State, was on its extraordinary way even before Mrs Meir succeeded to the Premiership.

Meanwhile the Egyptians – first Nasser, then Sadat – were giving shape to a Design of their own which was also aimed at the United States, on "neutralising America" in the Arab-Israel conflict. These three Grand Designs, with Russia's added as a fourth on the sidelines, were to dominate the post-war years – especially since all the Designs – unlike that of the British during the Great War – were little more than crude outline shapes that needed to be filled and completed. This placed a premium on indecision and uncertainty – the two principal elements of the post-war failure to achieve a settlement. We must look now at these unfinished political symphonies in greater detail.

Tuesday 8 October 1968 was a kind of watershed for the future of the Middle East. On the record, U Thant's special United Nations' envoy, Ambassador Gunnar Jarring, had noted wearily that since the beginning of the year he had made 128 air journeys to meet with the Foreign Ministers of Egypt, Jordan and Israel and had not seen either his family or his embassy in Moscow for ten months. But rather more significant were his off-the-record thoughts which were communicated to the Secretary-General of the United Nations, and to the representatives of the four principal Powers concerned, those of the United States, the Soviet Union, Great Britain and France.

277

In his own individual and very restrained style, Dr Jarring was saying that he had arrived at certain conclusions and that the time had come for the Great Powers to take note of them and act accordingly. 8 October, in a sense, was the last date on which an alternative approach might still have been possible, if Israel's Foreign Minister Eban had on that day substituted a specific Israel peace initiative for the more general rhetoric of his nine-point plan which he presented to the UN Assembly that day.

For Dr Jarring understood only too well what all the praise for his mission had meant and why both the Eastern and the Western bloc Powers, and both the Arab world and Israel, were pleading with him to continue his seemingly fruitless mission. Throughout his travels and talks Jarring had said little, put nothing to paper, and listened a great deal. He had also, in his private thoughts, made up his mind even before 8 October. That day only confirmed him in his conclusions.

He believed that a Middle Eastern settlement was possible without recourse to a further major military conflict – but only on certain conditions. He had been convinced by the Egyptians, and rather less so by the Jordanians, that direct negotiations, as understood by Israel were not practicable. He believed that the formula used by Dr Ralph Bunche in 1949, which led to the armistice talks on the island of Rhodes, offered a far more fruitful field of progress. It was on Dr Jarring's suggestion that U Thant included this proposal in the introduction to his Annual Report to the UN Assembly. However, Jarring was as surprised as U Thant by the strong Israeli denunciation and opposition to this suggestion; it appeared to be so hasty that there were doubts whether the Israeli leaders had read the full text of U Thant's proposal before making their negative comments.

But even such a settlement would be difficult, in Dr Jarring's view, unless it could be grounded within the framework of a Four Power agreement, a settlement underwritten by the United States, the Soviet Union, Great Britain and France. The real meaning of 8 October had to be sought therefore not so much in the aftermath to the proposals made by Eban on behalf of the Government of Israel, as in the conclusions drawn by Jarring that a Four Power agreement must precede a Middle Eastern settlement.

But what were the chances?

For the time being – despite some laboured optimism at the New York UN Assembly during the first weeks of October – not really very great. After having achieved a fairly clear position which had been applied with some consistency ever since June 1967, United States policy was suddenly again in a state of uncertainty and change. This could not be explained simply by the imminence of another Presidential election, the likelihood of a radical change in the Washington administration or the significance of the Jewish vote for the Democratic and Republican candidates.

The new hesitations in Washington stemmed far more from the complex combined impact of the war in Vietnam and the aftermath of the Soviet occupation of Czechoslovakia. For the first time since the end of the second world war, leading American policy-makers (and especially some who were then connected with a prospective Nixon administration) were reconsidering the role played by the United States in Europe and the Middle East.

The question was framed, and answered by Henry Kissinger shortly before his appointment as National Security Adviser to President Nixon in this manner: the United States will not be prepared to risk anything from 40 million to 120 million dead in a nuclear war over the security of Berlin or Belgrade, or for that matter for any part of Europe or the Middle East. It was an extreme, though an authoritative, formulation which placed a distinct limitation on the nature of a United States guarantee in a Four Power agreement shared with the Soviet Union. In a sense, it was the first momentous warning of the changing balance of power in the world.

It was the recognition of this altered role of the United States, or at least the assumption that such a change was taking place, which led to the major Soviet and Arab diplomatic effort in the Middle East being concentrated on the United States. At first, the Soviet leaders – and also President Nasser – concluded (and said so publicly) that the only way a political settlement of the Middle East conflict would still be possible would be by a preliminary withdrawal of all Israeli forces from the territories occupied in June 1967; and since Israel would not do this on her own accord, the only country that could force her to do so without going to war was the United States.

But another line of thought began to assert itself in Cairo. Its sponsors drew rather more far-reaching conclusions from what they understood to be the changed balance of power. There was a sudden increase of tension on the Suez Canal border. On 10 September 1968, this erupted into a major artillery exchange along a 70-mile front, during which the Egyptian guns were estimated to have fired some 10,000 shells into the Israeli positions on the East Bank of the Canal. The Israelis shelled Egyptian positions and the towns of Suez and Port Tewfiq. For the next ten days it seemed as if those bombardments were the pre-liminaries to another outbreak of limited fighting for the possession of the Canal. Almost 100,000 Egyptian troops, comprising the 7th and 8th Egyptian Army Groups, were alerted in the Canal zone. The Israelis called up reserves and alerted the entire Sinai area.

There was some difference of opinion between the politicians and the military about the extent of Egyptian preparedness to go to war. The Foreign Ministry in Jerusalem sought to minimise the risk of war and attributed the tension on the borders to a calculated Arab-Soviet plan to prepare the ground for the UN Assembly to intervene to stop this alleged threat to war. In general, Israeli political and press opinion was that there was no risk, only political and tactical hullabaloo encouraged by the foreign press. It was a view not shared by Dayan or the Israel defence force commanders. On the face of it, they argued, Egypt was not ready for a major war, but she had substantial forces and there were unpredictable and unknown connections with the Soviet navy and the very large number of Soviet specialists serving in Egypt; all of which made Dayan wary of unpredictable developments.

The opening of the UN Assembly switched the emphasis again to talks and negotiations, but the thoughts in Cairo moved rather along different lines. Possibly, the best explanation came from Hassanein Haikal, the Editor of *al Ahram*. He described Cairo's thinking on the changed balance of power in his weekly article published on the eve of the UN Assembly, on 3 October 1968. He called it "The Primacy of Military Strength". These were his main points:

United States' political influence in the Middle East has dwindled altogether. It no longer plays an effective part in determining the course of events in the area. This applies equally to those countries which maintained good relations with the United States and to those whose relations with the United States were marked chiefly by tension. . . . The growing Soviet presence in the Mediterranean is outflanking NATO at a time when, as a result of the Czechoslovak issue, the West has become more acutely aware of the weakness in the NATO alliance. . . . No matter what we may hear in the days or weeks to come, no matter what we may answer, we must fully realise that a political solution is neither near nor easy. I would almost add that a political settlement is impossible. . . .

It is true there are advocates of a political settlement. Yet such a settlement is dependent on the state of the Arab military force. I can almost say that if there were a real opportunity for a political solution, it would arise only with an Arab military force that would do its work and carry out its role of implementing the provisions and articles of such a solution. But a solution is not the first priority now. The rebuilding of the Arab military force, and specifically the Egyptian force, is the incomparable priority. Through military force, we shall be able to act in accordance with the dictates of our Nation's rights, security and interests.

There was rather more significance than usual in this Egyptian declaration for it came after some three weeks of intensive though informal talks between Egyptian and American representatives which had been conducted both in Cairo and in Washington; moreover, Soviet diplomats had also participated in the shaping of these new assessments which were accepted by President Nasser and his colleagues in September 1968. In fact, the Egyptians had emerged from these discussions greatly reassured. For the first time in years it seemed as if the United States would not intervene directly to support the Israeli position on the question of direct negotiations and the timing of an Israeli withdrawal from the occupied territories. The test of American good faith and changed attitude, conveyed, it was said in Cairo, by the retiring State Department Under-Secretary Lucius Battle, was the President's refusal to sanction the sale of supersonic "Phantom" aircraft to Israel. So convinced were the Egyptian leaders by these American assurances that Haikal wrote a long article reflecting the Egyptian view that the American decision had basically changed the balance of power in the Middle East in Israel's disfavour; Egypt's military leaders – and seemingly their Soviet advisers – had come to believe that a limited military operation against the Suez Canal, for example, might be effective, and would expose the hollowness of the American position in the Middle East.

By the time the National Assembly of the Arab Socialist Union assembled in Cairo on 14 September, it was evident that this had become a major preoccupation of Government and people in Egypt. President Nasser's own speech and frequent interventions encouraged this mood.

They had entered a new phase, he told the Assembly. They had to liberate their territory "and our armed forces represent the principal means for doing this". This was now their sacred duty. He also told delegates of his own meetings with the two American Presidential candidates who had come to see him in Cairo, Humphrey and Nixon. He recalled their talks and quoted the expressions of understanding for the Arab position of which both Humphrey and Nixon had assured him. President Nasser thought that their expressed support for Israel was something that was temporarily conditioned by the electoral campaign rather than a basic American interest. Just like Haikal, Nasser was becoming convinced that the combined Soviet and Arab persuasion had led the administration in Washington to reconsider its aid to Israel ; and the "Phantom" deal was the test. Indeed, it began to look as if these "Phantoms" were assuming rather more political than military significance.

This was still the situation when Israel's Foreign Minister presented his proposals for a settlement to the UN Assembly on 8 October. It was clearly a carefully thought-out scheme but it still lacked the essential information about Israeli intentions without which the Arab Governments would not even consider any form of negotiations. It said nothing about the time factor, nor about which frontiers Israel wanted secured and permanent, nor what it proposed to do for the refugees. It was its omissions rather than its contents that would decide the fate of this Israeli initiative; but more striking than anything was the omission about the future of Palestine. It was not surprising when Egyptian Foreign Minister, Riad, followed Eban on 10 October and rejected the Israeli "Peace Plan" on the grounds of its lack of precision and, with some justice, because it really did not add anything new to previous Israeli declarations.

But between the two speeches of Eban and Riad something had happened which changed the whole balance of assumptions and produced a profound reaction in Cairo. The United States announced that it would begin negotiations for the sale of supersonic "Phantom" fighter-bombers to Israel. The statement could have only one meaning for Cairo – and Moscow. As in May 1967, the United States had again decided "to unleash" the Israelis, to place the onus of defence on the Israelis themselves, and to provide them with the necessary assistance to effectively ensure Israel's position of a deterrent force, and, should the deterrent not work, to enable her to take care of the military situation. It looked like the abandonment by the United States of any prospect of a Four Power guarantee for the Middle East.

Instead, the message was clear for those who wanted to read it: in future, the United States would have to rely as much on Israel for support in the Middle East as Israel would have to rely on the United States. Israel's "client status" had undergone a fundamental change. It was altogether surprising that the Egyptians did not appreciate the implications of this transformation on their policy of attempting to "neutralise the United States in the Middle East". For the United States could henceforth not afford to lose the Israeli factor in the area. What was much more surprising, however, was the time it took Mrs Meir and her political colleagues before they understood what had happened to their American relationship. Dayan's defence establishment – and the Russians – had realised much sooner what it meant and had acted accordingly.

Mrs Meir might be excused for this failure to appreciate fully what had happened, for her early months as Prime Minister were preoccupied with her colleagues' fear that the pre-eminence of the old guard of Labour politicians who controlled the party, and also Mrs Meir's Premiership itself, could be challenged by Dayan and his Rafi break-away Labour Party. They were also aware of the known inclination of Dayan and his collegaues to withdraw from their association with the Labour Party's so-called "Alignment" in order to form their own independent party for which there was much support and enthusiasm in the ranks of Labour supporters and especially among the young. These internal difficulties competed for Mrs Meir's attention with the increasing pressures and casualties of the "War of Attrition' on the Suez Canal which had first been signalled by Nasser on 26 October 1968, and then resumed in earnest in March 1969, as Mrs Meir assumed the Premiership.

Her first testing time came in July that year when she made her appearance at the Convention of the Rafi Party in Tel Aviv before two thousand young – mostly under-thirties – delegates. For once she failed to sense the mood of her audience and talked to them about world socialism and the need for unity in the face of the enemy. She praised Pinhas Sapir who had most strongly opposed Dayan and told an interruptor that she would leave if there were any more remarks from the audience. One of the most respected members of Rafi, Ben-Porat, thereafter reminded her that she had told them to think about issues and not individuals; yet she, Golda Meir, had opposed the appointment of Dayan in June 1967, though he was unquestionably the best Defence Minister that could be chosen: "Was that thinking in terms of issues and not individuals?" he asked. At that, Mrs Meir rose in evident anger and left the hall. Her abrupt departure made a terrible impression on the young delegates who had looked forward to a real dialogue with the new Prime Minister. The pressure on Dayan to leave the alignment and form a new party greatly increased from the young rank-and-file and from many of his Rafi and Labour colleagues. But Dayan stayed; far bigger events were in the making on the Suez Canal.

On the night of 20 July 1969 Dayan responded to the challenge of Nasser's war of attrition and unleashed the struggle for the mastery of the air over the Canal zone and over Egypt itself which was to involve not only the whole of the Egyptian air force, but also Soviet combat personnel and aircraft. The crunch came just two weeks after Mrs Meir's dramatic walk-out from the Rafi Convention and overnight the Israel defence forces moved from the defensive which they had maintained since the first of the Egyptian attacks almost a year previously, towards a new kind of initiative, one that had significant political overtones.

That night Israeli forces occupied the rock fortress of Green Island and destroyed its installations before withdrawing, but the major move came 11 hours later when the Israel air force attacked Egyptian defence positions and missile sites in strength and engaged the Egyptian air force. Until then, the Israel air force had not been used as an independent strike weapon since the June War. The details of the operations were of less consequence in the long run than their aftermath. The Israelis noted that there had been no Soviet reaction although some of the attacks were directed at sites which had Soviet experts attached to them and others were aimed at targets near Port Said, a sensitive area with Soviet ships stationed there. Equally significant was the reaction from Washington; it was "far from disapproving".

But one difficulty the Israelis could not overcome. They could not convince the Egyptians – from Nasser downwards – that they had again suffered a decisive setback, and that they were courting another disaster. The make-believe and false reporting on what had happened started with the Egyptian officers in the field and went right through the chain of command until it reached Nasser himself. The Egyptians had in fact convinced themselves that they had won a great victory. They were sure that they had driven the Israelis from Green Island and they had shot down 19 Israeli planes. Nasser believed it and so did the General Staff; why should the press and public disbelieve it?

Yet the Egyptians were not alone in misreading the implications of these events. The Israeli politicians – as distinct from the defence establishment – did not seem to understand the new American role in Israeli affairs and Mrs Meir continued to set the tone of suspicion of United States' intention which was taken up by most of her non-military colleagues and the press. It was as if the confusion about American policy that reigned in the days before the June War in the Israeli Cabinet was being re-enacted. However, after two days in Washington in September 1969, and after meeting with President Nixon, Mrs Meir returned "with a much lighter heart than when I came". But a great many matters had not been resolved and Israel's needs were still presented in Washington on almost a charitable basis.

The role of Israel in the American Grand Design, first envisaged by President Lyndon Johnson in 1967 and then further developed by Richard Nixon, appeared to be still hidden from the Israeli politicians, and not least from Israel's Prime Minister. However, Israel's defence leaders – Dayan, Barlev, Hod, Yariv and others – read and understood the signals from Washington and proceeded accordingly. They had to clear up, for one thing, an internal division of opinion which agitated the Middle East specialists in the Pentagon and State Department following the overthrow of the Libyan monarchy on 1 September 1969 – just three weeks before Mrs Meir came to Washington. The view expressed in both the Pentagon and the State Department that the downfall of the Western-orientated regime in Libya was due to the excessive American support for Israel, and that if American policy continued unchanged it would lead to the downfall of every Western-orientated regime in the Arab world. There was, however, also the contrary opinion voiced by some of the more important officials in both departments that the overthrow of King Idris and his pro-Western regime in Libya was further evidence of how little trust the United States could afford to place on these pro-Western Arab regimes and that the United States would be better advised to assist Israel militarily and economically in becoming a firm and independent bastion in the Middle East.

But old suspicions died hard. Mrs Meir's satisfaction with the impression she had made on the Nixon administration did not survive the proposals for a new approach to a Middle East settlement which the us Secretary of State, William P. Rogers, made in a widely advertised speech on 9 December 1969. It was the sort of diplomatic exercise that had something for everybody, and everything was qualified to allow for every kind of interpretation. But quite apart from its content, the Rogers initiative affronted Mrs Meir since it devalued the supposed success she had had in Washington in September. Neither Nixon nor Rogers had said anything about the proposed move. Eban also was incensed. He had been in Washington only a few days before the Rogers speech and he had not been advised or warned of its imminence. Eban reacted with unaccustomed gloom and for once fully approved and shared Mrs Meir's negative reactions. But there was more to it than just the personal affront which Mrs Meir and Eban saw in the Rogers proposal.

The Cabinet feared that the Americans might go further in offering concessions to the Soviet-Arab axis in order to achieve a detente in the Middle East. They thought that the more noise they made the more it would discourage Nixon from making further concessions. Privately, a number of the most vocal Ministers admitted that the Rogers proposals were not really as negative as the Israel Government had made them out to be, but they were particularly sensitive about outsiders making suggestions since the Government itself had neither a plan, a map or a consensus of opinion among its members on what Israel wanted as the price of peace and what they were prepared to concede.

President Nixon and many Americans were frankly puzzled by this ill-tempered Israeli response to the Rogers initiative. It did not fit the image of the strong self-reliant Israel of June 1967. When the usual diplomatic exchanges provided no satisfactory elucidation, he sent the Assistant-Secretary of State, Joseph S. Sisco, to consult with the Egyptian and Israeli leaders on the spot in Cairo and Jerusalem and see for himself what caused this Israeli agitation. Nasser's response to Sisco's arrival in mid-April 1970 was characteristic of his temper which had changed so much in recent years. He had lost the old cool calculating habit that had served him so well in earlier years. Instead, he reacted to the Americans in much the same way as he had acted in May 1967. He would show the Americans that Egypt was not to be trifled with, and he proceeded to do so after a series of fruitless talks with Nixon's special envoy. He had received no assurances from Sisco that the United States would halt the supply of "Phantom" planes to Israel before Sisco flew off to Jerusalem on 14 April 1970 for talks with Mrs Meir and Dayan.

For Nasser the critical and significant day was 18 April 1970, a day of unseasonal sandstorms and heavy clouds over the Suez Canal; it was the Sabbath, Israel's traditional day of rest. Shortly before dusk an evidently carefully prepared Egyptian air attack was launched against Israeli targets on the canal. It was the largest and best-staged Egyptian air assault since the June War; it exploited the bad weather conditions which favoured the attack and it demonstrated – as it was designed to do – that President Nasser had not been bluffing when he had taken a hard tough line with Sisco earlier in the week. The attack signified a new phase in the re-activation of the Suez Canal Front and was seen in particular as underlining President Nasser's argumentation in his talks with Sisco, that a return to the cease-fire arrangement of 9 June 1967 would simply play into Israel's hands. He was not prepared to do that.

Sisco was both surprised and impressed by the vehemence of Nasser's presentation. It was, moreover, an argument that, as Sisco knew from his recent meetings with the Soviet Ambassador in Washington, had the pointed support of the Soviet Government. In fact, President Nasser's presentation of Egyptian policy to Sisco conformed to an extraordinary degree with the explanation which he had given to the secret session of the Egyptian National Assembly on 25 March. Sisco left Cairo convinced that the hard-liners prevailed in Cairo and that President Nasser and the Soviet leaders were fully supporting them. He did manage to resume the American-Egyptian dialogue, but that was the extent of his success. When he left Cairo, the Egyptian-Soviet position appeared to him far more uncompromising than it had been when Rogers made his proposals for a negotiated settlement on 9 December 1969, which in the event had led to a cease-fire seven months later.

Sisco's talks with Mrs Meir hardly advanced the process of settlement. He was more fortunate in the course of a private exchange of views with Dayan. These received further backing from an unexpected quarter. For some time, the Israel air force had been making deep penetration raids into Egypt, over Cairo and other targets outside the Canal zone. Dayan had opposed this policy as causing a maximum of political irritation to Nasser and producing a minimum of military effect. Dayan also feared that it would provoke the Russians to intervene

287

more directly than they had done hitherto. Dayan's objections were overruled by Mrs Meir and the Cabinet, as usual, followed her lead. "We are not really either hawks or doves," a Cabinet member explained self-deprecatingly; "we are sheep. Golda is the shepherd and we are her flock." Normally, Mrs Meir brooked no nonsense or opposition once she had made up her mind – and the Cabinet and the higher echelons of the administration knew it. It was not wise to challenge her decisions or question her policy. She had a way of effectively neutralising those who tried to cross her.

But this time Dayan had an unintended ally who could not be dealt with in this way. On 29 April 1970 the Israel Government issued a communiqué which indicated that Soviet pilots had been flying operational missions against Israeli planes near Cairo and Alexandria. It was a risk Dayan did not seek and would not take – and which the Americans insisted that Israel should not take. Even before the official announcement, and the day after Dayan had met with Sisco, Dayan addressed a group of Israel army cadets and told them that henceforth the main problem they had to be concerned about was the Soviet involvement in the Middle East. It was his opinion that Israel had to avoid becoming engaged in a direct conflict with the Soviet Union. More privately, Sisco had conveyed the opinion that it was the American interest that there should be no overt clash between the Soviet Union and Israel which might involve the United States. Dayan understood.

From these Dayan-Sisco talks in April, there came the American initiative for an Egyptian-Israeli cease-fire which was addressed to the two Governments in identical letters from Secretary of State Rogers on 19 June 1970. In these letters Rogers proposed that the two sides make a beginning of negotiating through the United Nations representative, Gunnar Jarring, and that in order to facilitate the preliminaries to such indirect negotiations, there should be a limited cease-fire for 90 days. The impact of the Rogers letter on the Cabinet was extraordinarily revealing. Better than any hindsight is a letter from one of the participants of the Ministerial discussions which reflects the mood of those days. "This is an important moment in our history. The American initiative has released and brought into the open the doubts which so many of us have felt about the Government's policy. The Cabinet discussions of the last week are without a doubt among the most crucial at which I have been present."

The writer of the letter then proceeds to describe the divisions in the

288

Cabinet and the general argumentation over the letter from the Secretary of State. "There were three distinct reactions among Ministers. The first which was led, surprisingly, by our ambassador in Washington, Itzhak Rabin, and by the Foreign Minister, Abba Eban – surprisingly, because the two have been very much at loggerheads – urged the Government to go along with the Americans, except that is for the limited cease-fire. On this issue there is general acceptance that such a restricted cease-fire will not be acceptable to Israel." However, neither Rabin nor Eban really thought that anything would come from the Rogers plan. But for tactical reasons, they believed it was imperative that Israel should show greater flexibility in discussions of a future peace. Therefore, Israel should not be the first country to reject the American initiative, but should give every encouragement to the Americans. This view was supported also by the Finance Minister, Pinhas Sapir, by the Mapam Ministers and by Moshe Kol, the Independent Liberal.

Dayan's response to the Rogers initiative was very different. He saw it as a means for further clarifying – and strengthening – Israel's special relationship with the United States, a continuation of the private talks he had with Sisco in April; he also saw it as a lever that might force the Cabinet in Jerusalem to take a stand as to its peace aims. To bring this about he proposed that the discussion with the Americans should be conducted in private and not through the press fed by "leaks" from interested ministers and that Israel's proposed "map" of her new frontiers should be shown to the Americans on a confidential basis which should be strictly observed in Washington and Jerusalem. At the same time, the Americans should be told that as formulated the Rogers cease-fire proposal was not acceptable. Mrs Meir herself inclined to Dayan's interpretation. The Gahal Party view, urged on the Cabinet by Beigin, that the American proposals should be publicly rejected, was not acceptable to any of the other parties represented in the Government.

But what deserves attention was that at this crucial moment, no one in the Cabinet really believed that a cease-fire was possible or that the Americans were genuinely concerned in bringing one about in a way that would not be damaging to Israel's security and future negotiating position. It was Dayan who broke openly during these discussions with the "hawks" represented by Beigin and opened the way for the Cabinet to extricate itself from an impossible position into which it had manoeuvred itself. Dayan formulated a number of security issues on which he suggested the Government should obtain President Nixon's "clarification". Dayan had a fairly good idea of the answers that would be forthcoming in view of the close private links which he had established with the Service Chiefs in the United States. Dayan formulated the questions, Eban drafted them, Mrs Meir sent them and President Nixon replied. The contents of Nixon's message to Mrs Meir were immediately leaked by Cabinet sources to the Israeli press so as to explain to a puzzled public why the Government might after all accept the noxious Rogers proposals for a cease-fire despite the critical and negative attitude with which Mrs Meir had initially received them.

According to these leaks, President Nixon had given assurances on the following points:

The US would not press for any withdrawal of Israeli troops from occupied territories until a contractual peace settlement had been signed.

The US would not demand a large scale return of Palestinian refugees to Israel as part of the solution of the refugee problem.

The US would continue to seek a balance of arms between the contending sides, or, in other words, would continue to supply Israel with the arms she needed so long as the Soviet Union did the same for Egypt.

These assurances were elaborated upon in talks between Ambassador Rabin and senior American officials. The Americans were most forthcoming on such subjects as no withdrawal before peace, no swamping of the Jewish state by returning refugees, and effective supervision of the limited cease-fire. With such assurances in her pocket, Mrs Meir could hardly have taken any other decision when the choice finally came between coalition with Gahal or alliance with the Americans. Yet the process of decision-making was not an easy one. Up to the spring of 1970 there had been no retreat from the official Israeli formula of nothing less than direct negotiations between the contending parties, with no pre-conditions or promises of withdrawal.

Three factors contributed to the change in the Israel Government's attitude; outside pressures, direct Soviet involvement, and international discontent. The first signs of a change came after Assistant Secretary of State Sisco's visit to Israel on 14 April 1970. Sisco conveyed American disapproval of Israel's intransigence in the strongest possible terms.

The Israeli press, radio and television highlighted these criticisms. The Government found itself compelled for the first time to defend its policy and to explain it more fully.

Added to these pressures, both from outside and inside, came the completely new military situation on the Egyptian Front caused by the direct Soviet involvement. For the first time, the Government felt it was getting out of its depth. Ezer Weizmann, the Gahal Minister of Transport at the time, summed up this feeling in his usual succinct manner: "If I have to face the Red Star of Russia instead of Egypt's two stars then I prefer not to play." The creeping advance of the Soviet ground-to-air missile sites towards the Canal and the arrival of the "electronic summer" which General Dayan had so accurately predicted, made the Israeli Government realise that Israel was more dependent than ever on her continuing alliance with the US. She needed the US politically to neutralise the Soviet presence, and she needed her military assistance in the form of sensitive and complicated electronic equipment to counteract the Soviet missiles on the Canal and to maintain Israel's mastery of the Middle East air.

The Israelis were preoccupied in all their discussions about the cease-fire with only the local balance of power on the Canal. They failed to take note of the change that was taking place in the superpower balance in the Mediterranean and failed to see its implications for Israel. It not only changed the nature of the Israel-Arab confrontation but it also changed the entire character of Israel's relationship with the United States. And what Mrs Meir and her political colleagues failed most to comprehend was that these changes were working in Israel's favour and gave her a powerful bargaining position when she made her requests for arms and financial aid in Washington. The Israeli Government – with the lone exception of Dayan – totally misread the changed situation, and they made a major error as a result in estimating how Israel could best approach the Nixon administration in order to get it to undo the parts of the Rogers proposals which Israel considered damaging to her interests.

As in May 1967, the Government – though not the Dayan circle – underestimated Israel's own strong standing in the calculations of the Americans. The President and his National Security Adviser, Henry Kissinger, had already reached the conclusion which was not to be made public for another year that by 1973 – if not before – the most that the United States could hope for in the Mediterranean and Middle

291

East was a position of parity with the Soviet Union in the strategic weapon field.[1]

In fact, by the time the Rogers proposals for the cease-fire were under discussion in the high summer of 1970, the United States had as much need of a strong and self-reliant Israel in the Middle East as an essential element of the new concept of parity with the Soviet Union, and not as an anti-Soviet factor as some Israelis, as for example Mrs Meir and Brigadier Haim Herzog, preferred to present the case. President Nixon therefore decided to state publicly what he had said privately to Mrs Meir. He intended not only to reassure the still unaccountably unsure Government of Israel, but also to indicate to the Soviet Union that United States interest in Israel was of a more fundamental character than the Jewish vote and Jewish public opinion in the United States.

Dayan understood the enormous implications and advantages for Israel – and also the political drawbacks of this relationship. But not Mrs Meir. She was still beset by distrust of the Arabs – with some justification, and by suspicion of the Americans – especially of the State Department and its Secretary of State. But above all, she seemed unable to grasp the broader implications of the new strategic situation, the role of Israel in the new American Grand Design. Where Dayan understood the changed dimension of the association with the Americans, Mrs Meir remained preoccupied with personal relations, likes and dislikes. It was to lead her into a series of misunderstandings, mis-interpretations and mishandling of the Americans which might have had much more disastrous consequences for Israel but for the timely and repeated interventions by Dayan and the defence establishment. It had been his initial soundings of Sisco in April that laid the basis for the cease-fire which came into force on 7 August 1970. It was again Dayan's intervention by threatening punitive action that resolved the crisis caused by the missiles which the Egyptians had moved into the cease-fire zone in the days immediately after its commencement; and it was Dayan again who, by persuading his colleagues to agree to a partial withdrawal, under certain conditions, from the Suez Canal, enabled the diplomatic log-jam to be broken in his private talks with Secretary of State Rogers, and subsequently with his Assistant-Secretary Joseph Sisco during their visits to Cairo and Jerusalem in May 1971.

[1] See statement by the US Secretary of Defence at a news conference at the Pentagon on 13 October 1971.

It was, in fact, the initiatives largely inspired by Dayan and ably executed by Sisco, before the cease-fire in August 1970, which laid the foundation for the transformation brought about in the Middle East by the three cease-fire months. These were cruel months for established reputations. The civil war in Jordan wrought havoc with the standing of King Husain (despite his successes) and with that of the Palestinian guerrilla leaders: Arafat, Habash, Hawatmeh and their spokesmen emerged tarnished and battered. They had lost both their charisma and their credibility.

Then came the death of President Nasser with its explosion of grief, both sincere and political, which passed almost as swiftly as it had risen and left in its wake the sour taste of political machinations to ensure the kind of succession which would not offend either the Soviet Union or the army officers in Egypt who had been made increasingly restless by the gradual hardening of the arteries of the Nasser regime. The Nasser legacy, the great hopes of Egypt's Arab revolution, passed into the faltering hands of two pedestrian politicians, Anwar Sadat and Mahmoud Fawzi, whose only claim to credit was that they would ensure "continuity" – but continuity of what?

One only had to look at the record. The cost of the war of attrition along the canal: 600,000 Egyptian evacuees, or de facto refugees, from the Canal zone (according to official figures, many more according to a more reliable unofficial estimate); 10,000 Egyptian casualties (mostly soldiers) during the three months before the cease-fire, victims of the war of attrition declared on Israel; the greater Soviet commitment and direct influence on Egyptian policy-making and life generally; and, not least, the blow to Egypt's international credibility as a result of the curious interpretations of the so-called standstill agreement embodied in the cease-fire which undermined the even slight prospects of the projected renewal of peace talks under the auspices of the United Nations' special representative, Dr Jarring.

Continuity of such a policy offered not much encouragement to the Egyptians or to the prospects of peace. In fact, "continuity" was the last thing that the Egyptian interest demanded – and this, perhaps, was the saddest comment of all about the final phase of the Nasser era. But not even Nasser's limited though sincere interpretation of his acceptance of the Rogers plan was continued by his successors. The brave and constructive step which President Nasser took when he defied Palestinian and other Arab opinion, was in fact, buried with him.

President Sadat spoke of 700,000 Egyptians under arms confronting the Israelis; on 1 October the Arab heads of state, meeting for President Nasser's funeral in Cairo, resolved that they would "liberate the whole of Palestine"; the "Voice of the Palestine Revolution", broadcasting from Baghdad pronounced as its aim the establishment of a Palestinian state "from the Jordan to the sea". Four weeks after Nasser's death the Arab world – especially Egypt, Jordan, Iraq, Syria and Libya – had been shaken up internally far more than they had been four weeks after the disaster of the Six Day War. But the greatest impact of Abdul Nasser's passing from the political scene was on the Palestinians. Those who – like President Nasser – had come to the conclusion that the only remaining hope for a Palestinian national revival was in an independent state co-existing with Israel, had argued that they could take a political initiative in this direction only under Nasser's protection. They looked to him to save them from the threats of Fatah and the Popular Front. They also looked to Nasser to speak for the Palestinians in Arab and international councils. There had been a great upsurge of hope when President Nasser accepted the Rogers proposals for a cease-fire and for subsequent negotiations. There was now no Nasser to rally them and protect them. During their most critical days they therefore did not rally, did not speak, did not act.

The Israelis for their part were also affected by the events that led up to the acceptance of the Rogers plan, the cease-fire, and by the implications of the Jordanian civil war and President Nasser's death. But even more than all that, Israeli thinking was becoming increasingly preoccupied with the lengthening shadow of Soviet influence over Israel's neighbours and, especially, by the effects of the global strategies of the Soviet Union in relation to the United States.

This was reflected by a series of informal diplomatic sorties – all officially denied in Jerusalem – with which the name of Israel's Defence Minister, Moshe Dayan, had been associated. The first was said to have sounded the Soviet leaders about realistic terms for a settlement, but this effort was said to have been unproductive. The second was far more significant. This was addressed to the Americans in the State Department and the Pentagon and was intended to reach the Russians and Egyptians.

The proposals which Dayan aired in this connection could be very roughly summarised under the following "assumptions" of Dayan's thinking:

294

1   A renewal of fighting on the Canal would be patently against Egypt's interests; it could well be catastrophic in its consequences. Israel's interests are also served by not resuming the fighting. On this score Egypt and Israel have a major common interest.

2   This being so, it should be possible to work out a formula which would make the renewal of fighting unnecessary for both parties.

3   The Israelis recognise that in this context their demand for the negotiation of a formal peace treaty has become unrealistic since the Egyptian Government could not possibly agree to it. For Israel to continue to insist on it is therefore to perpetuate the state of tension on the Canal.

4   What is required is in the first instance a form of "Arrangement" which would establish a de facto peaceful co-existence which both sides want and need.

5   Such an arrangement could begin with the establishment of a demilitarised belt along both sides of the Suez Canal which would enable the Egyptians to reopen the Canal and to rebuild the shattered front-line cities in the Canal zone.

6   In sum, what is suggested from this quarter is that Israel would be willing to withdraw from the Canal in return for an arrangement which would fall short of her demand for "a total peace or nothing".

These suggestions caused a good deal of commotion below the surface of Israeli politics, for in the context of the existing Israeli policies they were revolutionary proposals, but they had behind them a formidable backing which went far beyond the usual count of Dayan's supporters. The Americans made no secret that they found them greatly encouraging. Even more interesting had been the Soviet reaction fully developed in the so-called new Soviet peace plan and the *Pravda* article of 15 October 1970. Despite its polemical tone, the hard core of the Soviet proposals came closer to what might be called "the Dayan concept" than any other international statement yet made. All the six assumptions listed were covered in the Soviet proposals.

But as far as the Cabinet in Jerusalem was concerned there was no such thing as a Dayan Plan or a proposal for a partial withdrawal from the Suez Canal linked to a settlement with Egypt which might lead to a state of co-existence if not formal peace. No official recognition of Dayan's proposal came from either the Government or the Foreign

Ministry. Even the Israel press had ignored it until some time in November 1970, and then only to report that it had been rejected by the Cabinet with Yigal Allon, Israel Galili and Justice Minister Shapiro leading the critics. But Dayan had succeeded in at least unnerving his fellow ministers and making them understand that there was a limit to their policy of "sit tight, say nothing, and do not budge one inch" which had dominated Israeli thinking about a peace settlement once the initial post-war euphoria had been dissipated in 1967. Dayan warned his colleagues that peace was not inevitable and that the Arab Governments might not be strong enough to prevent another war which, from the Israeli interest, would be costly, senseless and solve nothing.

Instead of grappling with this question our Cabinet meetings are largely devoted to the question whether we should return to the Jarring talks and whether it was wise to break them off after the Egyptians had broken the cease-fire agreement by moving their missiles up into the front line on the Canal. Dayan had demanded that we return to the Jarring talks in order to break the stalemate and prolong the cease-fire. He was very outspoken and he upset Golda Meir with his frank talking. She accused him of being tactically unwise and naturally her loyal following in the Cabinet followed suit. Nor was it any surprise to me to see the Cabinet discussion and attacks on Dayan reappear in the columns of the "Court journalists" to whom the anti-Dayan clique resorts as a way of carrying their Cabinet war to the general public. They accused Dayan of lacking Cabinet discipline and seeking to steal the limelight for his coming visit to the United States. The real problem of course is not so much the issue of the Jarring talks but of defining what we really want. Eban is in Washington and reports that the Americans are very forthcoming and are not exercising any pressure on Israel to take a quick decision – it is the usual Eban line from Washington. For once, Eban's optimism is shared by Mrs Meir who has come back from Washington satisfied that she will get all she asked for. As so often before, she had assured us that there will be no weakening in the Israeli negotiating position, and as so often before she has made precisely those concessions to the Americans which she would have condemned in the strongest terms if either Dayan or Eban had proposed them. I can well understand why Nixon is so fond of her; he gets his way by presenting the outcome as if Mrs Meir has got her way. Dayan is an altogether different case and he operates on a much higher level of policy. Despite the Cabinet's refusal to go along with him, he has forced us – for the first time in three years – to give serious thought to our ultimate objectives. So far, I regret to say, it has produced no worthwhile results.[2]

There was no agreement in the Cabinet and among its principal advisers. Rabin from Washington insisted that it was important to return to the Jarring negotiations without pre-conditions; Eban insisted that certain pre-conditions must be first fulfilled; Galili insisted that they had not even agreed in principle to resume talks with Jarring. Mrs Meir told the Cabinet that there was no Dayan plan; the Minister of Defence had no connection with any of the proposals which had been reported in his name, the Government spokesman told the press. Barely a week later, the same spokesman told the same Israeli public that Dayan would be putting his proposals before the Nixon administration in Washington on his coming visit. But what were the Dayan proposals, as understood by the Cabinet? Dayan himself was very much in the dark on the eve of his departure for Washington. He knew what he would propose but he knew also that it would be impossible to give a coherent account of Governmental thinking on this subject.

Ambassador Rabin in Washington had bluntly informed the Prime Minister Mrs Meir – he was hardly on communicating terms with the Foreign Minister at that time – that the Government had been guilty of a series of blunders in breaking off the negotiations with Jarring and making impossible conditions for Israel's return. Dayan had not been involved in these disputations. Before leaving on his American journey he publicly restated his opinion that the Government must take every opportunity to prevent another outbreak of war. "We have demanded total peace and this the Arabs are not prepared to grant us. The Arabs have demanded total withdrawal and this we are not ready to grant them. So let us have an arrangement which would give us something less than total peace and them something less than total withdrawal." And with that Dayan went to Washington, and the Israel Government presently returned to the Jarring talks.

But the Israelis were strangely defensive. There was something else that observers had noted – especially those in Washington more acutely attuned to the Israeli vibrations. While Israel's military and general

[2] Letter to J.K., 13 November 1970.

intelligence was clearly second to none in this field, Israel's political intelligence – which required no secret operations – appeared to be often appallingly misguided, lop-sided, nervous and defensive. This was also the key to Israel's position at the resumed talks with Dr Jarring. There was no follow-up to the Dayan initiative; on the contrary, at the London embassy, Israel's Ambassador Comay replied to a member of his staff who wanted to know the position with regard to the Dayan plan that "since he had received no formal communication from the Foreign Ministry mentioning the existence of such a plan, it did not exist as far as he was concerned and he wanted no further discussion about it". In New York, Ambassador Tekoah received his instructions for the resumed negotiations. He was told that the Government's policy was for the time being to wait-and-see and it was Tekoah's job to stay at the wicket and bat as long as possible by using every recognised form of stone-walling. This cricket parlance sounded even more effectively destructive in the original and classical Hebrew of the Foreign Minister.

Thus the final stages of the foreign policy of the Meir-Eban era were ushered in with yet another version of the charade of making peace – only this time the United Nations and the Americans were playing their parts in place of the British 50 years earlier. The Arab and Israeli performers were on stage as before.

The eighth of January 1971 was the day the UN special envoy, Ambassador Gunnar Jarring arrived in Jerusalem for talks with Mrs Meir and Eban. They progressed better than had been expected, and when Jarring left for New York the Israelis concluded that he was no mean figure in the peace-making process and that he was not unfriendly towards Israeli aspirations for a genuine peace settlement in the Middle East. But – as so often in recent Israeli diplomacy – the Israeli ministers involved were better talkers than listeners. They therefore failed to comprehend fully what Dr Jarring had been trying to tell them – how he would take the initiative to get the talks going if there was no real advance by either the Egyptians or the Israelis.

The Israelis still believed at the end of January 1971 that the Nixon administration was generally pleased with the Israeli attitude, but Government spokesmen continued to be strangely defensive in their public pronouncements. For example, on 29 January the *Jerusalem Post* reported that Mrs Meir had told a student meeting the previous day that Israel's return to the Jarring talks had been justified "because otherwise

298

our arms supplies would have dried up". However, Government spokesmen, and especially Eban, were increasingly enthusiastic about the Jarring mission; it was treated at the beginning of February 1971 as one of the most important components in the search for a political settlement.

Meanwhile, the Egyptian reaction to the impending Jarring intervention was very different. For one thing, President Sadat would have an early occasion on which to declare Egypt's position on the renewal of the cease-fire – and since the eyes of the world were focused on this statement of Egyptian intent, it was a ready-made opportunity for an Egyptian initiative.

Before President Sadat made his planned peace initiative, a member of his inner circle at the Presidency was sent on a very private mission to Washington to sound out the authorities there. Major Khaled Fawzi (no relation of the then Prime Minister) arrived in Washington on 3 January, had a series of very confidential meetings with representative senior officials and returned to Cairo on 2 February. Meanwhile in Cairo there was daily consultation with the Soviet Ambassador Vinogradov. In London the observant Foreign Office noted this unusual expansion of American-Egyptian collusion with, it seemed, Soviet approval. But at the same time it was also noted that in the Four Power meetings in New York, the United States representative continued to oppose any move by either the Soviet Union or France that could be inimical to Israel.

Thus the stage was set for 4 February and the emergence of President Sadat as the peacemaker. He renewed the cease-fire, but attention was focused on his proposal to open the Canal if the Israelis withdrew to a line beyond el Arish. The most important part of his speech was his agreement in a last-minute addition to the text to a partial withdrawal by the Israelis from the Suez Canal as the first stage of a time-table. This gave the Israel Government an opportunity to seek an alternative form of settlement to the introduction of the Four Powers which the Israelis have always disliked and opposed. On 9 March, five days after President Sadat's speech, Mrs Meir told the Knesset that Israel was ready for such talks with Egypt about the opening of the canal.

But before anything more could happen Dr Jarring launched his own initiative, which he had signalled to the Israelis a month earlier. On 8 February 1971, while the Israeli Foreign Ministry specialists were still debating what to do in response to President Sadat's speech, there arrived the Jarring letter. A message in identical terms was delivered to the Egyptian Government.

The Israel Government was taken wholly unaware by Dr Jarring's questions and reacted with shocked and angry petulance. The UN special envoy was accused of having exceeded his mandate, was told that he had no authority to act as mediator and was advised that the Israel Government would not answer his letter. However, the Egyptian Government sent a speedy reply and the Israel Government then decided to send a reply but to address it directly to the Egyptian Government and deal with the Egyptian answers to Dr Jarring instead of with his questions to Israel. In the event, the Egyptian Government refused to accept the communication addressed to it and Dr Jarring had to tear off the address part of the Israeli reply before it could be delivered in Cairo. All this was still hidden from the public view, since no details of the Jarring exchanges had been published at that time: all that was known was the Israel Government's annoyance – and something more. Mrs Meir and her close associates in the Cabinet were becoming convinced that the Jarring initiative as well as that of President Sadat had been prepared in collusion with the US State Department as instruments to impose the Rogers Plan on Israel. And this conviction increased as the days passed and was to lead the Israel Government into making yet another major diplomatic miscalculation.

Meanwhile, however, President Sadat again seized the diplomatic initiative in an interview with the Editor of the US magazine *Newsweek* on 15 February 1971. Egypt, he said among other things, was prepared to negotiate a peace agreement with Israel provided the Israelis withdrew from the Canal and the Sinai Peninsula to a line behind el Arish as a first step. The Egyptian Government gave a similar and more qualified undertaking to negotiate a peace in its reply to Dr Jarring sent also on 15 February. This was the first time any Arab leader had declared himself in these terms in public and in private although here again there remained a number of unclarified provisos and qualifications. But – so it seemed to the innocent outsider – the door was opened sufficiently for a switch from political warfare to serious probing questions and discussions between Egypt and Israel with Dr Jarring acting as go-between.

But that was not how the matter was seen in Jerusalem. The Prime Minister and the Foreign Ministry had already overruled the urgent advice tendered by Israel's embassy in Washington – and especially by the Ambassador himself, General Itzhak Rabin. He had courted the displeasure of his Prime Minister and Foreign Minister – and experienced it in full measure – by insisting that both the American position and that of Dr Jarring should not be strained too much by what looked in Washington like stubborn incomprehension by the usually so sophisticated government in Jerusalem. But neither Rabin nor the embassy made any impact in Jerusalem; Mrs Meir's mind and those of most (though not all) of her colleagues were made up; they faced a Jarring-Rogers-Sadat collusion that might at any moment expand to embrace the Russians, the French and the British. Israel would then be isolated and find it difficult to object to what would in effect become an imposed settlement on Egyptian terms. This reading of the situation became the centre-piece of Israeli Government thinking about the middle of February 1971, and it became also the basis of the response to the Jarring initiative which the Cabinet had asked Mrs Meir and Mr Eban to draft. However, on the urging of Israel's Washington embassy, the draft was shown to the State Department for comment before being despatched to Dr Jarring. The Americans suggested that the last sentence in paragraph four of the Israeli reply, which stated that "Israel will not withdraw to the pre-June 5, 1967 lines", should be taken out of the Israeli reply.

The Americans argued that almost every official statement or speech by Israeli leaders contained this sentence and it was also implicit in the remainder of the Israeli argument. But stated boldly in this context and at this time it might so rock the frail craft that President Sadat had launched as very likely to upset it altogether. This American intervention convinced the Cabinet in Jerusalem that the Americans were in league with Jarring and Sadat and that to take out this sentence would expose Israel to the full rigours of the Rogers plan. Come what may – even displeasure in Washington – the offending sentence would stay at the end of paragraph four. The Americans, that is the President and Kissinger with Rogers and Sisco, were not so much displeased as surprised and a little worried by the course that events were taking and by the uncharacteristic provincialism of Israeli thinking. Had they not known that Mrs Meir and her friends really believed and were seriously worried by the prospect, as they saw it, of the great powers ganging-up with Egypt, the Americans might have concluded that the Israelis were engaged in some particularly Machiavellian ploy; for those who had no sympathy for Israel it really looked like that.

For Mrs Meir and her advisers now decided to pre-empt this looming crisis with the United States, to seek a showdown while conditions still favoured the Israelis, and so compel the United States to withdraw from the positions particularly which, the Israelis maintained again and again, the United States had adopted. Mrs Meir had said and continued to say throughout March that the Rogers plan envisaged virtually total Israeli withdrawal from the occupied territories and a Four Power guarantee as a substitute for secure frontiers. American assurances and explanations that this was not US policy, that in fact the American position was quite different and far more approximated the Israeli than the Egyptian position, made no impact on the Israeli attitude; if anything, it became increasingly tough about the nature of the new frontiers and on the question of guarantees. Now the Americans were getting puzzled and seriously worried. For the first time, serious doubts were expressed about Israeli credibility when Israelis spoke about seeking a peaceful settlement. The Israelis seemed to be scaling up their demands as the Egyptians were inclined to scale theirs down.

This was all the more surprising since the Israelis had been told by the United States that Egypt would not demand total withdrawal and that President Sadat was prepared to enter into direct negotiations on the question of opening the Suez Canal. Thus, during the first week of March 1971, a completely artificial "crisis" developed between Israel and the United States based entirely on mistaken assumptions and inspired newspaper articles in Israel and the United States. Ambassador Rabin in Washington said bluntly that the reports in the Israeli papers about a crisis in relations between the two countries were lies fed to the press by interested politicians or officials. But the harm had been done; worse still, the Israel Government now began to believe its own propaganda. Just at the moment when the earlier "assumptions" about collusion between the Americans and Egypt were shown to be in error, the propaganda was elevated to policy and despite an appeal by Eban on 10 March for a return to "quiet diplomacy without scoring goals in public", his diplomacy was accompanied by an officially inspired campaign of press warfare. It took just two weeks before the campaign collapsed on 25 March.

The intervening time-table is instructive. On the same day as Eban had made his appeal for quiet diplomacy, the diplomatic correspondents of the Israeli papers reported that the purpose of Eban's forthcoming visit to London, New York and Washington was to make clear to

302

Jarring – and his supporters – that Israel would not retreat from its stated withdrawal formula. Eban had been instructed by the Prime Minister to take a tough line in Washington and New York. On the same day, Israel's Washington embassy issued one of its periodic "pink-papers" which set out the hard Israeli line "without verbal cosmetics"; they had taken their instructions from Jerusalem very literally.

Meanwhile, of course, President Sadat had made another speech on 7 March, this time not formally renewing the cease-fire and also evidently concerned at the prospect of achieving an Israeli withdrawal of some kind before his own home pressures began to build up to danger point. But for the time being the Israelis appeared to be more concerned with the Washington than with the Suez Front. By 12 March it was evident that the lead to the Israeli papers was coming from the Prime Minister's office rather than from the Foreign Ministry. It was made clear that the document issued by the Washington embassy reflected the new determination of the Government; so had Mrs Meir's tough statement at a meeting of the Knesset alignment faction. Once again, the *Jerusalem Post*'s diplomatic correspondent conveyed current Government thinking. Washington was convinced, he wrote (meaning that this was how the Israel Government saw it), that the Arabs would not agree to any settlement short of almost total withdrawal and that the US now expected Israel to "deliver the goods" in exchange for international guarantees and some kind of American involvement. He also reported that the Government felt that it was succeeding with its tough line; Washington was already on the defensive.

The same evening, however, Ambassador Rabin told Israeli television viewers some home truths, but they seem to have passed almost unnoticed amid the welter of preconceived opinions. In an answer of significant content, Rabin said that "the United States had made its position clear to Egypt as to what she considered an acceptable political solution in the same way she had made it clear to Israel. Egypt has more or less accepted the principles of the United States' position with some reservations. These principles are that there can be no withdrawal without peace and no peace without withdrawal." And then Rabin made an important addition. "When the United States says that there should be only minor border adjustments," he said, "in line with the statements made by President Johnson and President Nixon, this did not apply to the Egyptian-Israeli frontier. On this point, the United States has

303

remained loyal to its earlier position to this day." On the following day, 13 March, *The Times* published its interview with Mrs Meir in which she spelled out some of the territorial adjustments which Israel would require.

There was much speculation about Mrs Meir's reasons for breaking her own silence. Her close friend, Pinhas Sapir, the Minister of Finance, did not beat about the bush. He said the interview was a good omen in that it took away from Mr Dayan the political initiative "in territorial formulations". The Americans were also encouraged, and when Ambassador Rabin met with Sisco at the State Department shortly afterwards the us official wondered why the terms of *The Times* interview were not conveyed to Dr Jarring as a formal paper. And then came the final phase of this unhappy chapter.

On 16 March 1971 Mrs Meir spoke in the Knesset in answer to a vote of no confidence and proceeded to somewhat devalue the positive elements in her interview which had produced the debate. Later that same day, us Secretary William P. Rogers held an important press conference at the State Department. In this he went to great pains to reassure the Israelis by spelling out those matters that had seemed to worry the Israelis most: the nature of international guarantees as supportive to a settlement, not in place of it; borders agreed by Israel and a peace negotiated by Egypt and Israel, not anyone else. It clearly constituted one of the most important policy statements made by the Secretary of State. It received short shrift in Israel from Mrs Meir and the press generally. In Jerusalem a Government spokesman had evidently taken the trouble to read the transcript before commenting. Rogers had allayed the Government's "worst fears" by his insistence that guarantees could be only "supportive" and not a substitute for secure frontiers, he said. But in the Histadrut Hall, Mrs Meir was addressing the Central Committee of the Labour Party during a foreign policy discussion. Her speech, an authoritative government spokesman informed the press, "should be regarded as the Israel Government's reply to Mr Rogers' press conference the previous day", details of which, the spokesman added, "were received in Jerusalem with considerable dismay and concern". Mrs Meir for her part ignored the explanations given by Mr Rogers at his press conference and said that she strongly objected "to a substitute arrangement of guarantees and international police forces" in place of secure borders. Israel most "definitely and categorically" would not budge from Sharm el-Sheikh,

Gaza and "from important adjustments" at Tulkarem on the West Bank. Mrs Meir warned that Israel would become the object of "strong pressure" and added that Israel "could not trust what Mr Rogers offers us even if he does it with the best of intentions".

Elsewhere, however, Dayan, speaking to the more critical audience of students and teachers at the Weizmann Institute of Science at Rehovot, warned them that Israel was facing the moment of truth, which was revealing new realities to them. "There must be careful assessment of the situation because this is the first time that Arab leaders have openly talked about peace and lasting borders with Israel." But this was not the prevailing mood in Jerusalem. On 19 March, a Friday, Eban met with Rogers and later in the day briefed 40 influential senators on the essence of the Israeli position and why Israel was opposed to Rogers' peace proposals. This was how the Foreign Ministry in Jerusalem and the Israeli press reflected the events of that Friday. After the Eban talks it was emphasised that "only direct talks can rescue the Jarring mission". Eban had "given Mr Rogers no encouragement to believe his recommendations, that Israel should formally answer Dr Jarring's last message, would be complied with – even if this refusal would be represented on some sides as a lack of desire for peace" on Israel's part.

But most significant was Israeli satisfaction that the tough posture of non-co-operation was bearing dividends in Washington. Reports reaching Jerusalem, wrote the *Jerusalem Post* on 23 March, "suggest a growing public backlash against Mr Rogers' somewhat clumsy campaign to mobilise opinion-moulders – mainly press, radio and the Congress – in support for international guarantees as a substitute for defensible borders". The report goes on to speak of the widespread criticism of Mr Rogers for his "blithe dismissal" of Israel's right to defensible frontiers and his "implied attempt" to impose a dictated solution. The guarantee idea had now come under fire from leading senators – evidently after they had heard Eban on that Friday.

The backlash came – but not the way it had been anticipated in Jerusalem. On Tuesday 23 March, Secretary Rogers asked for a private meeting in closed session with the senators that were in the capital. Out of 80, 67 attended. Among them were most of those who had been to the Eban briefing – including many of Israel's staunchest supporters. When Rogers had finished and they emerged they were unanimous in their praise for the Secretary of State; they also said that they had been under a misapprehension about the administration's policy and they approved of the Rogers approach to the problem.

There remained the lesson to be learnt by all concerned. It was clear that in diplomacy, when there is so imprecise a basic document as the Balfour Declaration or the Security Council's Resolution 242 as the principal guideline, imprecision is inevitable and can be disastrous. Yet imprecision was the essence of the Security Council Resolution of 22 November 1967, as we have seen from the record.[3]

The Resolution voted unanimously on 22 November 1967, concocted by the British Foreign Secretary, George Brown, with the help of his Arab Affairs Adviser, Sir Harold Beeley, and Lord Caradon, the British representative at the United Nations, became a largely meaningless formula to be used by each party according to its needs, a substitute rather than a prescription for peace, an alibi for helpless politicians, an obstacle to any realistic settlement. Everybody subscribed to it and no one believed in it, since neither Arabs nor Israelis, Russians or Americans could agree on what the Resolution meant. Not even its authors were prepared to commit themselves to a definition. The United Nations and the Security Council Resolution clearly were not going to pave the way to peace.

But what were the alternatives? Mrs Meir and her associates in the Cabinet offered none, but there were distinct signs in the reaction of the Israeli public that it was becoming restless at the *immobilisme* of its Government. Mrs Meir had turned down the UN special representative, Dr Jarring; he had offended her with his letter of 8 February and there was to be no further communication with him until he withdrew that letter. He did not.

Almost at the same time Mrs Meir, assisted by the Israeli press and radio, had unleashed her crisis of confidence in Mr Rogers; and the Israeli public was told once more that American friendship was "eroding". It was virtually a repetition of the procedure of a year previously. Dayan attempted to set the record straight. On 16 March he told the Israelis that "Israel was stronger than it has ever been" and that she was receiving military supplies from the United States on a level never before achieved. It made no impression on the masochistic rampage on which Mrs Meir and the Foreign Ministry had embarked. This reached its climacteric in another personal encounter between Mrs Meir and Mr Rogers when the US Secretary of State came to

[3] See above, Chapter One, pp. 85–6.

Jerusalem on 6 May 1971. Their talk was completely deadlocked. Once again, it was Dayan and Sisco who met next day in a private session who eased the way to a renewal of the understanding. It was – as on earlier and subsequent occasions – a wholly artificial and largely self-induced crisis which stemmed from the over-developed sense of suspicion with which Mrs Meir viewed the Secretary of State. An indication of this could be seen in Dayan's insistence that Mrs Meir's personal political adviser and a tape-recorder should be present during his private conversation with Sisco, so as to reassure Mrs Meir that the two would not be plotting against her and Israel's interests.

The Dayan-Sisco initiative did not get far because of the crisis which developed in Cairo when President Sadat had his leading Ministers arrested and accused of plotting against him. For once, the Russians and the Israelis agreed that President Sadat had enough problems to contend with and should be given time before being confronted by the supreme difficulty of having to make peace, not war.

However, when Rogers again spoke in his customary vein at the UN Assembly on 14 October 1971, the whole gamut of the "erosion scenario" was again displayed by the Israelis, but this time the follow-up was different. Mrs Meir came to Washington in the midst of the American preoccupation with the India-Pakistan war. There was no great interest at the UN Assembly for the Middle East debate which proceeded before hundreds of empty chairs. But Mrs Meir's meeting with President Nixon was probably the most important in her long career, and even more important for American-Israeli relations. For Nixon and Kissinger had decided that the time had come to make the Israelis understand and accept the American position. That they decided to do this was largely the outcome of many private and secret consultations on the more confidential level of the defence establishments.

White House sources did not, of course, subscribe to the inspired reports which appeared in the Israeli papers, and were circulated by Mrs Meir's entourage, that the outcome of her visit had been singularly successful in changing American attitudes to an Arab-Israeli settlement. On the contrary, there was evident satisfaction in the White House that the President had at last got through the American message to Mrs Meir, and that, as a result, she had abandoned her own and her Government's critical attitude towards the Secretary of State and to United States' policy as propounded by Mr Rogers. It was accepted after the subsequent meeting between Mrs Meir and Mr Rogers, which Mrs

307

Meir described as "wonderful" that Mrs Meir now fully understood and approved of the American position. But it was not the end of this American odyssey.

Senior White House and State Department officials – President Nixon among them – watched with fascinated admiration (and with some concern) the way in which Mrs Meir managed to carry through a major change in Israel's foreign policy without any apparent awareness in Israel of what had been taking place. Since the change involved Mrs Meir in a substantial revision of her own previous position on the matters agreed between her and President Nixon during their talks in Washington on 2 December, it was accepted that this aspect should be rather slurred over in the Israeli accounts of the Meir talks. It was understood in Washington that domestic politics and *amour propre* required that the full extent of the Israeli retreat in the Washington talks should not be unduly emphasised.

But by the middle of January the White House and State Department became somewhat concerned by a new factor in this difficult equation for the Israeli Government. It looked in Washington that what they had believed would become a public relations exercise to reassure the Israeli public and the American Jews had turned into something quite different. For all the news coming from Jerusalem, based on the most authoritative sources which could be only those emanating from the Prime Minister herself, indicated that the Israeli Government did not see this as the coating that sugared the pill of the Washington agreement but as the essence of the agreement itself. The Israelis, it seemed to the Washington observers, had begun to believe their own propaganda. Inspired statements from the Minister generally thought to be closest to Mrs Meir, Israel Galili, and from the Prime Minister's office generally, left no doubt about the way Mrs Meir saw the outcome of her Washington visit, or, at least, how she wanted her Government colleagues to understand it.

This was that Mrs Meir had made it clear to President Nixon that until the United States lifted her embargo on the further supply of "Phantom" and other aircraft to Israel, the Israeli Government would not make any further steps towards a partial or total settlement. It was also emphasised – particularly by Galili – that Mrs Meir gave no undertaking of any kind that once the supply of "Phantoms" was agreed in principle, Israel would be prepared to make at least some of the concessions which the Americans had wanted her to make.

This was not how President Nixon had reported his "understanding" with Mrs Meir to his colleagues following the Washington talks in December 1971. He was in no doubt that Mrs Meir had agreed to consider the practical military measures that could lead to the re-opening of the Suez Canal, and to consider the so-called Rogers proposals in the context in which these were explained to her both by the President and the Secretary of State. As part of this package deal the United States would agree to the resumption of the supply of "Phantoms".

All this was fairly openly discussed in the Israeli press after Mrs Meir's return from Washington in December 1971 but rather as an achievement by Mrs Meir than as a major revision of her policy. This was not unusual for politicians and the Americans fully understood that the Israel Government thought it best that its public opinion should not be unduly shocked by the outcome of the Washington talks. But even this limited admission of what had been conceded by Israel in return for the resumed "Phantom" deliveries disappeared from all public discussion in Israel as soon as the "Phantom" deal was made public. It is this that disconcerted White House and State Department observers. Because of it, more than usual interest centred on General Dayan's visit to the United States early in February for the Americans had noted that Dayan's had been the only authoritative voice repeating the message to the Israelis that what they need is peace – not more war; and that they must make up their mind what price they can afford to pay for a peace settlement.

Before he arrived back in Israel in mid-February, Dayan gave a warning to the Israeli public in an interview with the Israeli radio which went largely unnoticed in the welter of self-congratulation and adulation for Mrs Meir's reported success in her "tough and unbending" negotiations with the Americans. What Dayan said was the key to much that was happening, it was his way of tactfully telling the Israeli public not to take everything it was told from high up at its face value. Dayan chose his words with great care:

*I do not want the Israeli public to believe that everything takes care of itself because Israel now sits on the Canal, gets the weapons she wants, and because the Americans are said to like us. Israel cannot afford to go on sitting with folded arms; it still remains urgently necessary for us to progress towards a political settlement.*

In the politest and least offensive way possible Dayan said that, for one thing, the policy pursued by the Meir Government had not really settled anything and that the emphasis remained on a settlement, not on a static position of "holding what we have". But even more significant was the fact that on close reading Dayan's comment was almost identical with that made by President Nixon in his State of the Union address to Congress shortly before Dayan's arrival in Washington. Dayan was in fact trying to tell the Israeli public through the smoke-screen of the officially inspired half-truths about relations with America, that the real test for Israel was still to come when the Cabinet would have to make up its collective mind about the terms of a political settlement. It was all very well to talk about negotiations without pre-condition but the Cabinet must know what conditions will be acceptable to the negotiators and what directives to give them.

The Government in Jerusalem had persistently shirked this question and Dayan's warning was addressed as much to them as to the public. What he conveyed to them was that Mrs Meir's "Phantoms" were bought at a price and that the Israelis had better realise that this price would have to be paid when the time came for making peace – probably later rather than sooner.

This was not the only case in which Mrs Meir's Government had tried to be "too clever by half" and had landed itself in serious trouble as a result. The sudden conflict with the African mediation team headed by the Senegalese President Senghor was another example. During the UN Assembly in New York in December 1971, puzzled observers found that Eban and the African representative gave totally different versions of the terms of settlement proposed by the four African heads of state who had visited Israel and Egypt. In fact, Eban told the UN Assembly that Israel was happy to go along with the African version as against that of Dr Jarring, which was unacceptable to Mrs Meir's Government, but then came President Senghor of Senegal, who had been a good friend to Israel, and charged that the Israelis had either bamboozled him or had gone back on their word; they had told him and his three African colleagues that Israel wanted no annexation of Arab territory. But Israel's position at the UN Assembly was in direct conflict with that undertaking, Senghor claimed. Mrs Meir thereupon despatched post haste one of her ablest diplomats, Walter Eytan, former Director-General of the Foreign Ministry and former Ambassador in Paris, to Dakar with a personal explanation for President Senghor.

What had happened was that in its explanation to the four African presidents, the Israel Government had declared that "Israel has no desire to annex territory, and that for her it is only a question of 'secure and recognised borders'." The Africans understood this to mean that, after a peace settlement, Israel would not demand any Arab territory beyond the 1967 frontiers, though it was understood that Jerusalem and the Golan Heights would require separate definition. What Mrs Meir's envoy was to explain to President Senghor was that, as the Israelis understood it, annexation was a unilateral act carried out without agreement; what Israel wanted was to negotiate terms by which some territories would be ceded to her with the agreement of the Arab countries concerned. To the African leaders – and others – it sounded like double-talk which, in a way, it was. Moreover it was a not untypical example of the trouble into which the Israeli Government was getting because it believed that playing with words was a desirable substitute for a possibly unpopular policy. It was preferable, and necessary, so Dayan thought, for the Israeli public to be told the whole truth. It would pay the Government not only at home but also abroad.

All the same Mrs Meir rode the storm triumphantly, despite Dayan's oblique warnings, for it was the considered opinion of the majority of the Cabinet – and especially of Mrs Meir – that on the international front Israel had never had it so good in political, military or diplomatic terms. Moreover, a majority of the Israel public shared this view and credited Mrs Meir with this success of her tough policy. It had brought American aid on a scale never before thought possible; it had strengthened Israel's armed forces to a point where they were the masters of the Middle East and it had given Israel the secure boundaries for which she had yearned.

Why then, asked Mrs Meir and her assenting adult colleagues, should Israel risk this strong position by making concessions to Egypt or anyone else; particularly so, it was added with much satisfaction – one could almost say, self-satisfaction – in view of the American swing to this firmly held Israeli position. The question was echoed and affirmed by the Israeli press and public opinion. "Why change", became the slogan for 1972, and for the run-up to the election in 1973. Israel had everything she could want – except peace. And Mrs Meir and her colleagues, backed by public opinion, did not believe that peace was obtainable at the price which Israel might be willing to pay. This last proviso was crucial. It was the considered opinion of the majority of the Government with Dayan standing rather imprecisely aside. It was based on a careful assessment of all the sources available to the Government, including the usually well-informed Israeli intelligence services, and the assessments of friendly outside sources in the United States and elsewhere.

As a result the Israel Government was convinced that despite all public statements to the contrary, the Egyptian Government was not prepared to consider any settlement with Israel – total or partial – which did not include an Israeli withdrawal from all occupied Egyptian territory. Since Mrs Meir was determined not to agree to such a settlement on any terms, she was certain that there was therefore no chance even for an interim settlement. And without any kind of settlement, naturally, the Israeli position, as it was, was the best possible obtainable. The Government therefore believed that the best thing they could do in this climate was to go on making sympathetic noises for a peace settlement, to be generally accommodating without making any commitments, and to rely on the Arab leaders to reject any American initiative, and to go on quarrelling among themselves.

Crucial, however, in this Israeli calculation was the assumption of continuing American support, diplomatic, military and financial. The majority of the Cabinet believed that they could rely on this for some years to come in view of the new agreements concluded with the Nixon administration; the Government felt sure that President Nixon would be re-elected for a second term and that therefore there would be continuity in American support for Mrs Meir's firm policies at least until 1976. And so it seemed as the months passed and Israel's relationship with the United States became more special and more firmly rooted in mutual aid and understanding. The Moscow summit conference in May 1972 passed without justifying some fearful Israeli anticipations about a Soviet-American "deal" on the Middle East at Israeli's expense. Then came November and Nixon's re-election as President. But there was now a new climate and the making of a new policy and, as before, Dayan was again the swallow that signalled the change of season. He had been briefly in Washington after Nixon's return to office and his private reports on his return indicated the need for considerable revision of the earlier "assumptions".

President Nixon's unexpected re-appointment of the Secretary of State, William P. Rogers, was among other things, the first flashing of a warning light to the Israelis. It did not come altogether as a surprise in Jerusalem for Dayan's report to the Prime Minister had been rather different to his vetted public statements. For Dayan had come back

312

convinced that the Americans meant to tackle the Middle East situation once Vietnam really was out of the way. What was more important, he was sure that the Americans would not abandon the Israelis as they might the regime in Saigon.

But – and it was a very big "but" – there was an important proviso in the new American position. The impression which the Americans – especially Kissinger – left on Dayan was that there need be no difficulties between Israel and Washington about the new "Grand Design" so long as the Israelis understood that there would have to be negotiations and some give-and-take.

What the Americans wanted the Israelis to understand – and both Dayan and Allon were made aware of this – was that the two super-powers wanted a Middle East without wars and crises of wars; and that they meant to get it. It would therefore be far better for Israel to tailor her policies so as to be a part in the shaping of this process rather than attempt to stand against it; and when Mrs Meir came to Washington at the end of February 1973, she accepted and approved of the Nixon Doctrine for the Middle East. Dayan had reacted differently. He did not like the idea of a superpower condominium for the Middle East. He understood its inevitability and its preferability to more war, but he was not reconciled to it all the same. There were other possibilities of avoiding another war and Israel's best hope of pre-empting such a superpower settlement on the lines desired by President Nixon without at the same time upsetting the relationship with the United States was by seeking to establish the kind of situation that would make superpower intervention unnecessary.

There were two major complications that would have to be over-come if a realistic settlement was to be obtained without superpower dictation in whatever guise it might be presented. One was the growing concentration of superpower interest in the Middle East oil role which existed quite independently of the Arab conflict with Israel; the other, was the conviction of Dayan's intelligence advisers – which was shared by the Americans – that there was not one Arab regime that either could or would make any kind of peace settlement with Israel, partial or total, on terms that could be acceptable to Israel. There was in the spring of 1973 no basis for any kind of formal settlement either with Egypt about the Canal or concerning the Palestine future. It was this situation – not an early prospect of peace – that had to be woven into the new concept of strategic parity and political détente of the United States and the Soviet Union. What the aftermath of the June War had shown – and it took the best part of five years or more to demonstate it – was that the superpower requirements of parity, détente and stability in the Middle East could be attained only so long as Israel and Egypt did not feel that their security was threatened.

And in 1973 it was understood by the Americans and the Russians, by the Israelis and by the Egyptians that for the time being – possibly for the next decade – this could be best achieved by a policy of maintaining the status quo (with some minor adjustments) rather than by seeking a fully fledged peace settlement; by a policy of neither peace nor war. The charade of seeking an understanding and peace would be continued to be played by all concerned as it had been 50 years before. That there would be no peace was certain, that there would be no war was likely, but less so.

It was in its way a reassuring conclusion for President Nixon and for Mrs Meir – and even for the Egyptians. Was this then the fulfilment of the Zionist dream, or of the Arab national aspirations? Was this the stamp of success or the mark of failure? Was Weizmann right when he foresaw the inevitability of Arab failure, when he reported to the Zionist General Council on 26 July 1926? He told them of the approach made by the French High Commissioner in Syria, M. de Jouvenel, to the Zionist organisation in which he had discussed the Jewish colonisation of that part of Syria adjoining Palestine, the Hauran or Golan Heights. The Zionists had also opened negotiations with the Emir Abdullah of Transjordan to consider the possibilities of Jewish colonisation along the Eastern Bank of the Jordan river. Weizmann explained that he had discussed the Syrian project with the leader of the French Socialist Party, Leon Blum, and had his approval; he had also urged the French to aim at "a Boer peace with the Syrians, not a Carthaginian peace. All the same," Weizmann told the Zionist General Council, "the Arabs would always say we were Circassians, but we need not trouble about that except that at the first opportunity we must act as best accords with our interests. He had emphasised to Leon Blum that our colonisation of any part of Syria would be done only in peaceful co-operation with the Arabs . . . We could offer the Arabs what they had not got, that is to say, organisation, means, etc. The Arabs could offer us what we had not got; they must accept the Balfour Declaration." Weizmann then added these pregnant words: "He was convinced that the Jewish state, whatever form it would take, would extend from the

314

Euphrates to the Mediterranean Sea, and it was our duty to achieve this. M. de Jouvenel's proposal for the colonisation of the Hauran fell in with this idea, and it would do much good if it were pursued tactfully and carefully."[4]

Where then did Israel draw the line? So long as there was no clear intent the Arabs would remain distrustful, fearful and on guard. Was the aftermath of the military triumph in 1967 then to be another charade in which the Israelis, the Americans, the Russians and the Arabs again participated rather than declare frankly that they had failed to produce a settlement because they had failed to produce the terms, the conditions and the frontiers without which there could be only more double-talk, more formulae, more unrest?

But was such a statement of intent possible in 1973, five years and more after Israel's June victory? The answer had to come in the final analysis not from Jerusalem nor from Washington or Moscow but from Cairo, from Damascus, from Tripoli – and from the Palestinians. It was the measure of the failure of Israel's diplomacy under Eshkol and Mrs Meir, though the country had prospered, and though militarily it reigned supreme, that on the one outstanding question which mattered in 1973 as it had done in 1923, the initiative remained, now as then, with the Arabs – the Palestine Arabs. Dayan had been a lone voice, supported only by a majority of Israel's public opinion but with no weight in the councils of establishment parties. He had recognised this and vainly sought to rectify it. And so Mrs Meir led her country into the General Election without it knowing where it was going, without the Arab countries knowing what Israel really wanted, with a marriage of great convenience with President Nixon's America and with a great question mark hanging over the future – the aftermath of the Meir Era: for the unstated issue of 1973 was the same as that of 1923 about which Weizmann spoke at the Zionist General Council in July 1926 – not peace, but recognition. "They must accept the Balfour Declaration," as he had put it. But they did not do so in 1917 or in 1947 or in 1967. Could Israel compel or induce recognition in 1977 or before? Or could Israel afford to do without this Arab recognition and impose a new form of co-existence on the Middle East, one that was independent of Arab recognition or acceptance and which replaced the era of imperialist

[4] Minutes of the Actions Committee held in London, 22 July to 2 August 1926; Morning Session Monday, 26 July 1926.

and superpower domination by a *Pax Israeli* since no other peace was possible?

But the initiative was not Israel's. Mrs Meir had forfeited that by her considered policy to refuse to chart Israel's future course – and so as the Meir era moved into the elections of 1973 and towards its close, the prospect of a negotiated peace with the Arab world seemed as remote as it appeared to Weizmann in the disillusioned days 50 years previously. The alternatives that were left for the time being was either an Israeli peace or a superpower peace – and as we shall see in the concluding account of this period – it was in 1973 as in 1923 the broader canvas of world events that dictated the outcome, not the local conflict of Arabs and Jews.

# THREE

# The Superpowers

By 1973 the nuclear balance of terror had forced the two superpowers to become vegetarians. They could fight wars only by proxy; in Indo-China, in the Indian sub-continent, in the Mediterranean, and in the Middle East. And even that had become unrewarding as détente and strategic "parity" and the emergence of the Peoples' Republic of China into the Great Power arena established new priorities. Future policies could no longer be guided by traditional methods. The experience of the superpowers in conjunction with their allies in the Middle East in the hot summer of 1967 was the real watershed – the beginning of the new diplomacy, the start of a long-range re-orientation of all the parties concerned in the Middle East, and a revision of the concepts which had prevailed since the Balfour Declaration of 1917 and the Versailles Settlement of 1919. The Arab-Israeli war of June 1967 was the catalyst. It was short; but the dissolution of the old order which it ushered in was slow, very slow.

Despite the endless stream of revelations of "inside" reports and memoirs, the most extraordinary aspect of the Six Day War was that six years after the event there remained so many unexplained mysteries about it – and all the evidence pointed to the decision by the authorities concerned to ensure that the "mysteries" should remain locked away in the archives for many more years.

Yet at the same time there were searching investigations being conducted by the Russians, the Americans, the Egyptians and the Israelis in order to clearly identify those unresolved questions about the Six Day War on which future policy would depend. Typical of this process was the conduct of the enquiry in the Soviet Union. The man chosen to investigate what had gone wrong was the man who had been at the centre of events in Tel Aviv, Soviet Ambassador Chuvakhin, the man who was personally held to be responsible for the outbreak of the war

317

by many leading Israelis, Egyptians and Americans. Chuvakhin had been instrumental – so it was said at the time – in advising Moscow and Cairo in May 1967 that Israel was preparing to launch a major attack on Syria – a report for which there had been no valid justification.

Chuvakhin disappeared from the public view after his return to Moscow in the summer of 1967 and it was assumed that he was in disgrace and paying the penalty for his costly mistaken intelligence. But evidently, this was not the way the Soviet rulers saw his role in Israel; there was subsequent suspicion that Chuvakhin had acted on instructions from the Defence Ministry in Moscow when he sent the reports about an imminent Israeli assault on Syria. For reasons of their own, the Kremlin's leaders were clearly anxious to get a complete picture of what had happened during that May and June and who had been really responsible for Chuvakhin's reporting, for when he returned to Moscow in 1967 they installed him in a special department at the Moscow Institute of Oriental Studies on retirement pay which was higher than the salary of a Cabinet Minister and with exceptional privileges and access to all official sources. He was charged with preparing a detailed report on the origins and course of the Six Day War. The Chuvakhin Report is unlikely to be published but was sure to have some very attentive readers among the members of the Politburo who commissioned it. For whatever the war did for Israel – and it was much; whatever it did to Nasser and Egypt – and that was also much, its most significant long-term consequence was what it did to – and for – the Soviet Union. It was a traumatic experience for the Kremlin: all information and every calculation had been wrong: about Egypt, about Israel, about United States' policy. In Egypt there was a partial reckoning with those held responsible – but not with the real principals. In Moscow, the reckoning had yet to come. And all the evidence indicated that the Politburo was preparing for the day, however long it might have to wait. In preparation for this domestic settlement Brezhnev had continued to lavish aid on Egypt on an unprecedented scale – Soviet military and other aid was estimated to have reached a total close to $8 billion on the fifth anniversary of the 5 June disaster.

Brezhnev also assumed personal control of the Soviet Union's relations with Egypt and other Middle Eastern states. This was first fully reflected by the diplomatic happenings during the 33 days between 25 January and 26 February 1972 that radically transformed the strategic-diplomatic pattern of the Middle East. In Washington and in Jerusalem it had been assumed – mistakenly it would seem – that the Soviet leaders would hold their hand until after the Moscow meeting with President Nixon in May 1972 before reacting to American initiative reflected in the agreement with Mrs Meir in December 1971 and Nixon's subsequent talks in Peking. Instead of remaining passively on the sidelines, however, the Soviet leaders unfolded in these 33 days one of the most concentrated efforts at high-pressure diplomacy in the history of Soviet foreign policy. The execution of this Soviet counter-thrust to the American initiative showed few signs of the improvisation with which it must have been conducted. It looked outwardly like a well-prepared series of ripostes but, judging by all the available evidence, it was in fact a hasty and extremely well-improvised operation. All indications point to the presence at the helm of a firm hand and a flexible mind – always a formidable combination in diplomacy; in fact, there was considerable evidence that Leonid Brezhnev, the Secretary-General of the Soviet Communist Party, was the principal architect of this February diplomacy.

In preparation for the Moscow summit, the Soviet leaders were concerned to establish bargaining positions of political and diplomatic strength, and to this end they sought, among other things, to neutralise or, if possible, paralyse the effective United States presence in the Mediterranean and the Middle East. As they saw it, they had to contain and restrain what they considered to be the two principal instruments of United States' policy, the US Sixth Fleet and the Israel defence forces. This aim was pursued during February and March by a calculated policy of establishing new positions of Soviet strength in the Middle East and the Mediterranean.

It seemed to take the Soviet leaders some time to recover from the unpleasant surprise they got from the Meir-Nixon talks in Washington on 2 December 1971. These had resulted in a much wider-ranging agreement than they had anticipated on future American arms deliveries and Israeli acquiescence in the American diplomatic initiative. At first, the Indo-Pakistani conflict had overshadowed the immediate implications of the Nixon-Meir understanding. This understanding had left both Americans and Israelis in positions of exceptional strength in the context of the Arab-Israeli conflict, but it was largely over-looked for a time under the impact of the setback suffered by President Nixon and United States' policy on the Indian sub-continent.

It was not until the end of January 1972 that the Soviet leaders made their first counter-move, and they did so in a somewhat oblique manner. They summoned a conference of Warsaw Pact leaders to Prague on 25 January. On the agenda for the two-day meeting was a major declaration covering all aspects of Soviet diplomacy – one of those model declarations to which every communist country can subscribe with a clear conscience. It declared that "frontiers now existing between European states, including the frontiers that took shape as a result of the second world war, are inviolable". This was followed by a renunciation of the use of force, and an assertion of the ideal of peaceful co-existence among all states. Many observers thought it was rather pointless to bring together the political leaders of the Soviet Union and East European member states of the Warsaw Pact to talk over mere generalities this way. There clearly had to be more to it; and there was. Within a week of the Prague meeting, the Soviet diplomatic offensive in the Middle East was under way.

On 2 February, "President Sadat paid a friendly visit to the Soviet Union", as the official communiqué described it when he departed two days later. This was an unusual and curious way of describing the arrival of President Sadat; in contrast with the cases of the other Arab leaders who were to follow him that month, the communiqué said nothing about his having been invited by the Soviet Government. The rest of the communiqué was similarly singular in its wording. It was almost effusive in its reference to the talks between Sadat and the Soviet leaders. They had been conducted "in an atmosphere of trust, complete mutual understanding and friendship". Yet there was a marked absence of the kind of unilateral Soviet commitment that there had been in virtually all previous Soviet-Egyptian declarations. On the contrary, this time there was a recurring emphasis that everything would be done jointly by Egypt and the Soviet Union. "The sides," as it was phrased, "again considered measures to secure the lawful rights and interests of the Arab peoples and to render assistance to the Arab Republic of Egypt, in particular in the field of strengthening its defence capacity." The "sides" were also going "to struggle for a just settlement on the basis of UN Security Council Resolution 242 and above all for the withdrawal of Israeli troops from all Arab lands occupied in 1967". This was to be done through the good offices of Ambassador Gunnar Jarring and not through those of the United States.

There were also aspects of policy which the Soviet leaders were keen to stress in a way that had not been possible in the actual text of the communiqué of 4 February 1972. This was made clear in a widely circulated comment on the Sadat talks by the political commentator of the official Novosti news agency, Vladimir Katin, which was broadcast on the Moscow home service and in many other Soviet radio transmissions. Katin was particularly concerned to counter reports of growing tension in Soviet-Egyptian relations and said that the statement in the official communiqué that there was "trust, mutual understanding and friendship" was a "precise picture of the actual relations which existed between them". He then formulated the central theme of the discussions with President Sadat. In Katin's words, the Soviet leaders were convinced that the greatest attention had to be paid to the Middle East. "A dangerous situation fraught with the risk of explosion still exists." In the Soviet view, Israel was still putting obstacles in the way of a just settlement. But even so, the Soviet leaders, in Katin's words, were trying to see "if there is a way out of this situation; is a relaxation of the inflammable atmosphere in the Middle East possible?"

Then came two further important elucidations of Soviet policy. Katin stressed that all consultations between the interested Arab countries and Israel should be carried out by their "legal plenipotentiaries and Ambassador Jarring, but in no case by the United States". The second elucidation was more significant. In direct contrast to almost every speech made during the previous six months by President Sadat and by Soviet spokesmen in the Security Council, Katin asserted that the "Soviet Union and the Arab Republic of Egypt cling to the firm conviction that a normalisation of the Middle East is possible on the basis of the Security Council resolution." And in discussing the terms of the resolution Katin repeatedly stressed that both the Arab countries and Israel must take measures to fulfil *"all its clauses"*.

However, in a speech by Soviet Premier Kosygin on 11 February, the posture of the Soviet Union in the Middle East came out strikingly at variance with the "peaceful co-existence" theme adopted by the Warsaw Pact leaders. An Iraqi delegation, headed by Sadam Hussein Tikriti, had suddenly arrived in Moscow the day before, six days after the departure of President Sadat. At the luncheon given in its honour the day after its arrival, Kosygin began his speech by saying that the Central Committee of the Communist Party of the Soviet Union and the Soviet Government (in that order) attached great importance to the visit of the party and Government delegation (in that order) from Iraq. "The

321

Middle East," he said, "is one of the parts of the world where the forces of progress are waging a ceaseless struggle against the forces of reaction and imperialism. The imperialists are doing everything in their power to hold on to their positions in that area and to undermine the progressive regimes in the Arab states. . . . Some people in Israel and the United States presume that in the present situation the Arab peoples will in the final analysis reconcile themselves to the occupation of their territories. Such hopes are devoid of any foundation. . . ."

Sadam Hussein was treated by the Soviet leaders with rather more attention than President Sadat had received the previous week. This was all the more noticeable since he did not hold any formal Government position in Baghdad. He was in fact the Deputy General Secretary of the Regional Baath Party and Vice-Chairman of the Iraqi Revolutionary Command Council (officially designated in that order). Sadam Hussein was also the man in Baghdad who controlled more levers of real power than any member of the Government or any senior officer in the armed forces; he was a Communist and a much-feared personality.

The joint communiqué issued as the Iraqi party prepared to leave for home on 17 February reflected the keen interest the Soviet leaders had shown in this new connection. The Soviet Union undertook to assist in the establishment of a national oil industry in Iraq and to support the Iraqi Government in its resistance to growing Iranian influence in the Persian Gulf. Tactfully, the communiqué made no mention of support of the UN Security Council resolution or for the need of a political settlement of the Arab-Israeli conflict, both of which were rejected by the Iraqi Government. Instead, the Soviet and Iraqi Governments declared that "a lasting peace cannot be established in the Middle East without the liberation of all Arab territories occupied as a result of Israel's imperialist aggression and without ensuring the legitimate rights of the Arab people of Palestine".

And then came a strange footnote, which was to be repeated in the Soviet-Libyan communiqué ten days later. It said that "Iraq expressed high appreciation for the decisions of the Warsaw Treaty member-countries as a very important contribution to the strengthening of peace in Europe." It was an indication of the shape of things to come, of the Russian desire to have the Middle East countries participate in the shaping of European security.

While the Iraqi talks were in their final stages, the Soviet Defence Minister, Marshal Andrei Grechko, left Moscow on 14 February 1972 for four days of talks with the leaders of the Somali Democratic Republic, situated opposite Aden and alongside the entry into the Red Sea from the Indian Ocean. Grechko left the Somali Republic on 18 February. His talks, it was officially stated that day, had resulted in "complete mutual understanding on the question of Soviet-Somali military co-operation and its further development". Grechko then went to Cairo on what was described as an "official friendly visit". He spent only three days in Egypt and then issued a statement jointly with his Egyptian hosts in which they "expressed satisfaction with the development of co-operation between the armed forces of the Soviet Union and the Egyptian Arab Republic". They had also exchanged views on further strengthening and expanding Egypt's armed forces so as to improve Egypt's defensive capacity. Then he flew back to Moscow.

As Marshal Grechko made his way back to Moscow on 21 February yet another Soviet mission was flying out, this time to Damascus. It was headed by the First Deputy Prime Minister, Kyril Mazurov, and among its 14 members were the Deputy Defence Minister and General Sokolov. On the first full day in Damascus the Mazurov mission signed an agreement with the Syrian Government for Soviet economic and technical assistance. But the real purpose of the mission was unfolded only during the following four days of intensive discussions. These not only concentrated on the customary diplomatic and defence matters but also showed that the new Soviet interest in the area had a strong political content, for they manifested a new approach to stabilising the regimes in the countries friendly and important to the Soviet Union. The official communiqué at the end of the talks turned out to be an important document. As with the Iraqis, no mention was made in it of the Security Council Resolution for an Arab-Israeli settlement, and Soviet aid is defined – and limited – to "the just struggle of the Arab peoples for an Israeli withdrawal". The communiqué then touched on all the areas of conflict with the United States, as did the Iraqi communiqué, and expressed enthusiasm and support for the decision of the Warsaw Pact countries to convene a European Security Conference. But then comes the crunch. The communiqué noted – and this is unusual in this type of Soviet declaration – that the two sides had also "signed important documents on further development of economic co-operation, on the links between the Communist Party of the Soviet Union and the Baath Party, and on assistance in the strengthening of the defence potential of the Syrian Arab Republic".

323

The unaccustomed speed with which Soviet diplomacy had been working became apparent in Damascus ten days after the signature of these "important documents". On 7 March the Baathist leaders in Damascus announced that a "Syrian National Progressive Front" had been formed comprising all major political groupings in addition to the ruling Baath Party. The Communist Party, the Arab Socialist Union and the Arab Socialist Movement were named as constituents of the new Front. That same evening, the Syrian Vice-President broadcast the full text of the Charter of the Front which set out its authority and policy. Both clearly stemmed from the discussion with the Mazurov mission.

The National Front in fact superseded the authority of the Government in vital sectors of the administration. Under Article One it was charged with "the liberation of the Arab territory occupied after June 5th, 1967". This was to take priority over all other objectives. Article Two declared that the Front will in the future be the relevant authority to "decide on peace or war"; and Article Three gave it executive authority over the whole field of economic planning. The future policy of the Front was spelled out in great detail in Article Six. This restated the Palestinian Arab people's inalienable national rights to its territory. This clause also repeated the Khartoum formula that "there will be no peace nor negotiation with the Zionist state and no relinquishment of any part of the occupied Arab territories". It undertook, moreover, to give complete support to the Palestinian Resistance, to protect it against attacks and "to give it freedom of movement". It declared that "World Zionism and its protégé Israel is the foremost and direct enemy of our Arab nation. The main conflict is between our nation on the one hand, and Zionism, Israel and world imperialism headed by the United States, on the other". And then came the other side of the coin. The friendly socialist states headed by the Soviet Union were the principal backers of the Syrian Arab Republic the Charter said. It was they "who provide every kind of military, economic and political support". But even while the Syrian deal was being made in Damascus, a new Soviet step into the Mediterranean was being taken amidst somewhat confusing and contradictory circumstances.

At 12.30 p.m. GMT (the time is significant) on 23 February 1972, Moscow announced that Libya's second-in-command, Major Abd as-Salam Jallud, had arrived at the head of an official Libyan mission which included the Minister for Oil Affairs and an unnamed deputy chief-of-staff. At Moscow airport, Major Jallud said that the purpose of his visit, the first contact of its kind with the Soviet Union, was "to strengthen the bonds between the Libyan revolution and the Soviet Union". He added that he was looking forward "to political, economic and military results" to his talks. The same evening, at 9.00 p.m. GMT, the Libyan Foreign Ministry which was under the personal control of Colonel Qaddafy, the Chairman of the Revolutionary Command Council, issued a statement which must rank as one of the curiosities of Arab diplomacy. It was evidently very carefully prepared and was given maximum publicity by the Libyan Government radio and press. It said: "It is almost confirmed that fraternal Iraq is about to conclude a treaty with the Soviet Union. The Libyan Arab Republic expresses its extreme concern at this trend which takes Iraq back to the days of the Baghdad Pact and Western imperialist treaties . . . We still hope that Iraq will resist this trend and preserve what is left of her dignity." The message was clear; the Arab States should steer clear of all commitments, whether to the Communist bloc or the Western powers.

Next day, Major Jallud had an opportunity to explain his chief's strange conduct when he met for a long talk – it was said to have lasted over three hours – with Soviet Premier Kosygin. The Russians put out a carefully worded statement after this encounter which emphasised that Jallud had been "received" by Kosygin and that they had had "a friendly talk during which they discussed the development of Soviet-Libyan relations and several urgent world problems such as the situation in the Middle East". Two days later, the Libyan delegation signed an oil agreement on routine technical assistance lines with Soviet Deputy Minister Novikov. Jallud was then supposed to depart for Bucharest for more oil talks with the Rumanians. But the departure was delayed. Nothing more happened for three days and then a curt announcement said that Jallud had met with Soviet President Podgorny on 29 February. What it did not say was that they had talked for five hours and 15 minutes – an exceptional high-level marathon even under Soviet conditions. Their subject matter had been the relations between Libya and the Soviet Union "in various fields" and international questions, "the foremost of which is the occupation of Palestine and related issues". Meanwhile, at home in Tripoli, Colonel Qaddafy was continuing his guerrilla war against Jallud's evident progress in Moscow. The Libyan press and radio reported – while Jallud was talking with Podgorny – that Colonel Qaddafy had refused to receive the Iraqi

325

Ambassador to Egypt, who had come specially from Cairo with instructions "to explain Iraq's views on the Soviet-Iraqi treaty".

However, this did not seem to affect the striking progress of the Jallud mission in Moscow. On 2 March Jallud met the Soviet leader who invariably takes precedence in all official announcements over the President and Prime Minister – the Soviet Communist Party Secretary, Leonid Brezhnev. They talked for four hours and 45 minutes. Thus Jallud had spent 13 hours with the three Soviet leaders who matter. They were clearly not concerned with the minor problem of how the Libyans were managing the formerly British Petroleum oil field which they had nationalised; something much bigger was at stake.

Some inkling of this fact was provided by Jallud in an interview he gave to Tass which was not reported by the Libyans at home. Moscow, however, broadcast his views not only in its home services but also in its powerful Arabic transmissions. Jallud said that "the Soviet Union has an important role to play in enabling the revolutionary Arab forces to defeat the Zionist settler-type colonialism which is backed by the United States . . ." He added with a bluntness for which he is renowned, but which one does not usually hear on the Soviet radio, that he was convinced "the Soviet Union could do a lot more to increase the defence capability of the Arab world . . . and to enable the Palestinian people to regain their homeland and recover their lands."

Evidently encouraged by Jallud's outspokenness, *Pravda* took a hand in the unmistakable tug-of-war between Jallud in Moscow and Qaddafy in Tripoli. "Certain people," wrote *Pravda* on 5 March, "do not like to see the mutually advantageous relations which are developing between our two countries. There are people in Libya who wish to make difficulties between Libya and the Soviet Union and to drive a wedge of distrust between them." Short of naming Colonel Qaddafy as the source of the opposition, *Pravda* made clear the political gulf that existed between the two leading members of the Libyan Government. The differences extended even to the text of the communiqué that was agreed upon at the end of the Jallud visit on 7 March. An Arabic version of the supposedly agreed text was broadcast by the Libyan State Radio on 7 March; the Soviet text was not issued until a day later and it showed a number of variations.

The Arabic version, but not the Russian, emphasised that lengthy talks took place with Brezhnev, Podgorny and Kosygin, and that they were conducted in an atmosphere of mutual understanding and frank-

326

ness when they reviewed Soviet-Libyan relations. The Soviet version was much more curt and omitted the passage in the Arabic text which stated that "the two sides demanded the closing of all military bases in the region to make it an area of security, tranquillity, peace and stability for all people". For the rest, the text followed the Iraqi and Syrian declarations: it denounced the United States and expressed support for the Warsaw Pact plans concerning European security and for the African liberation struggle. It was evident that Major Jallud had returned home with the blessing and substantial backing of the Soviet leaders.

Thus the pattern of the Soviet diplomatic and strategic countermoves was taking shape in the early spring of 1972. It was designed to form a political-strategic ring around Israel and provide the Soviet Union with political and military positions of strength. For the Soviet leaders had clearly been concerned that though they might occupy positions of diplomatic strength, the Arab world was singularly affected by internal stresses which could undermine the Soviet diplomatic and strategic structure. The political deflation of President Sadat in Egypt had been considerable. The Palestinian debacle was highlighted by the defeat by Husain of the Palestinian guerrilla organisations, with only the prospect of a switch to sheer terrorism as a possible Palestinian alternative; this would greatly embarrass the Russians and other Arab leaders and add to the overall instability in the area.

The judicial ruling by the Cairo court trying the alleged killers of the former Jordanian Prime Minister, Wasfi-Tal – which allowed a defence submission that the killing of Tal was legitimate tyrannicide – had added and not lessened concern in this direction. The Soviet leaders had also expressed to visiting statesmen their concern over the role played by the Peoples' Republic of China in stirring up discontent among the 35 million Muslims who live in the Soviet Union principally along the border with China. Broadcasts from China have for some time denounced the Soviet policy of giving permission to Soviet Jews to travel to Israel. Altogether, the Soviet diplomatic offensive which had been launched was a much more thorough affair than previous moves of this kind. For the first time, the Soviet Union was also seeking to ensure for itself a degree of direct rule in the Arab countries.

The combination of a Soviet military presence in Egypt, reinforced by substantial security representation in the Egyptian state apparatus, by the political formation of National Progressive Fronts with com-

327

munists or para-communist representation, and by the conclusion of friendship treaties which could embrace Egypt, Iraq, Syria, the South Yemen, the Somali Democratic Republic and possibly Libya was no longer a Moscow pipedream. Its purpose was to change the balance of political and military power in the Middle East and the Mediterranean despite the new arrangements between the United States and Israel and despite the presence of the US Sixth Fleet and NATO in the Mediterranean. It was the most ambitious and dramatic initiative which the Soviet Union had undertaken in the Middle East – or so it seemed, to the Soviet leaders and to Western observers. But Brezhnev, like Bismarck before him (and whom he resembles in many ways) had more than just the Arab iron in the fire. He had put one in for Nixon as well.

Hindsight has its uses – and pitfalls. The temptation to re-write the history of Soviet-Egyptian relations in the light of the Soviet "expulsion" from Egypt in July 1972 is understandably great. We now realise that there was a good deal of double-talk in all those official speeches, declarations and communiqués from Cairo and Moscow with which we were regaled until that 18 July 1972. But can we be all that certain that there was not as much double-talk in the confessions, revelations and explanations that we heard – mainly from Cairo and Beirut – in the revisionist accounts claiming to tell what really had taken place between Sadat and the Russians? Some reserve in accepting the revised version of what had taken place during the year of decision in Soviet-Egyptian relations appeared to be warranted if only because the main source of the new truth was President Sadat himself. In fact, on closer inspection, it would appear that he was the only source. No one else intimately concerned in the negotiations and rupture had said anything about the details of the process. Such other accounts as have been made public, as those in *al Ahram*, all go back to President Sadat himself. The other two principals involved have maintained a significant silence: the Russians and the leaders of the Egyptian armed forces have revealed nothing about their part in the affair. The Sadat version monopolised the stage. And that in itself was of no mean importance. Clearly, the Soviet leaders and the spokesmen for the Egyptian armed forces (who were the only effective political power in Egypt) wanted it that way. But why?

It looked as if these other parties actually encouraged President Sadat to popularise his position, to keep on explaining and, at the same time, contradicting himself and devaluing everything that he had said

328

before July 1972 about the nature of Egypt's alliance with the Soviet Union: how essential and invaluable Soviet help had been in saving Egypt from an Israeli invasion and preparing her for the ultimate confrontation, not only with Israel, but with Zionism – a battle which Sadat had estimated at various times during these months (before July 1972) might well take 50 years or more. One thing must have been evident to the more thoughtful: both accounts could not be true; one of them was false. But which one? – or both? President Sadat himself has given a number of his own versions to the Egyptian people, in press interviews, in private conversations with friendly Ambassadors and in a rather significant off-the-record talk to Egyptian Editors a few days after the public announcement of the "expulsion" of the Soviet personnel in Egypt on 18 July. In many ways this appeared to be the least inhibited and least contrived of Sadat's explanations and, from the accounts of some of those present, Arnaud de Borchgrave, the Senior Editor of *Newsweek*, reconstructed what Sadat had said. His version has been confirmed by others present although Sadat said rather more than was printed in *Newsweek* of 7 August. The following is a fairly free but accurate rendering of Sadat's main line of explanation to the Editors:

You cannot imagine what my life has been like since I became President. There has hardly been a quiet day without some quarrel with the Russians. They never trusted me. They said I was pro-American and selling Egypt out to the Americans. When I went to Moscow in March 1971 and made my first request for MIG 23s they told me after much argument that the MIGs would come very soon and that they would begin training Egyptian pilots immediately. The MIGs never came. Instead the Russians tried to overthrow me with the Aly Sabry coup in May 1971. When Soviet President Podgorny came to Cairo later that same month – May 1971– he pulled out a treaty and said I should sign it. This was the first indication I had about the treaty. I said we had no need for it but he insisted and said he could not return to Moscow without it. He gave me his solemn word that if I signed we would get the first MIG 23s within four days of his return to Moscow.

I decided to sign the treaty because I thought that this would also reassure the Russians that I was not America's man and that they could trust me. Nothing happened. The Russians knew that I had decided that 1971 was to be the year of decision for the liberation of our occupied land but it was becoming clear to me that they were not going to provide us with the equipment we needed for this purpose. The cornerstone of their policy was that there should be neither peace nor war in the Middle East. I was again in Moscow in October 1971. Podgorny – the man who had given me his solemn word – was nowhere to be found. I was left alone with Kosygin to be joined by Brezhnev on my last day there.

We concluded another agreement. I was promised it would be fulfilled before the end of the year. Again nothing happened – except the Soviet airlift to India. This showed me that when the Russians wanted to support a country they were not deterred by the fact that the United States supported the other side. I decided therefore that the time had come for a total clarification of our relationship with the Soviet Union. I told the Soviet Ambassador that I wished to visit Moscow before the end of the year. This was on 11 December 1971. They replied on 27 December and suggested a meeting in February. I told Vinogradov that my patience was nearly exhausted but for the sake of our friendship I would wait until February. After that visit I went again to Moscow in April just before the Russian summit meeting with Nixon. I wanted to make sure that the Russians did not agree to restrict arms deliveries before Israel had evacuated our country.

I received more empty and unfulfilled promises and, after waiting a month, I sent a seven-point questionnaire to Brezhnev in order to clarify our relations. I told him that Egypt's policy would depend on his answers. By 15 June 1972 I had not received any reply, so I wrote another letter to Brezhnev. After another three weeks, the Soviet Ambassador informed me that he had received Moscow's reply. He came to see me and gave me Brezhnev's letter, which was written in Arabic. I asked my assistant to read it to me. The first page of the letter reminded me of the warm and friendly spirit that had governed Soviet-Egyptian relations. The second page attacked Haikal as the man responsible for our worsening relations. The third page continued the attack on Haikal. And then, nothing. This made me very angry and I decided to act there and then in the presence of the Soviet Ambassador. I dictated my orders:

1  All Soviet advisers in the Egyptian armed forces were to leave within ten days, starting on 17 July.

2 All Soviet military installations were to be placed under Egyptian control.

3 All Soviet military equipment was to be sold to Egypt or taken out of the country.

4 All further negotiations between Egypt and the Soviet Union would be conducted in Cairo and nowhere else.

Vinogradov left at once for Moscow. Asad of Syria was coming to see me direct from his talks in Moscow. Asad asked me how I could have done such a thing as ordering the Russians out when he had just signed an agreement with the Soviet Union for arms worth $700 million. I told him not to worry about us and do what he thought was best for Syria. Finally I was informed that the Russians wanted a high-level Egyptian delegation to go to Moscow to explain to them all the reasons for my action. I decided to send Prime Minister Sidky and I told him to make one more effort to get the MIG 23s. It was useless. You know the rest of the story.

This was Sadat's confidential account to a small group of picked Cairo Editors, and at least one of them left the meeting wondering whether they really knew what Sadat had called "the rest of the story". For one thing there were some striking contradictions between this private off-the-record version and Sadat's earlier account, his first public statement on 18 July. In his talk to the Editors, Sadat had insisted that it had been Brezhnev's evident refusal to answer Sadat's seven-point questionnaire sent to Moscow on 1 June 1972 which had led Sadat to tell the Russians to quit. But in his report to the Arab Socialist Union on 18 July, Sadat said that after he had received the Soviet explanation about Nixon's talks with the Soviet leaders, in May, he had reached the conclusion that the time had come for making a pause in Egypt's friendship with the Soviet Union. He then added a curious proviso, especially if this is set against the background talk to the Editors. He added that all that he had said "in no way affected the essence of Soviet-Egyptian friendship" which he visualised as expanding into a new and more understanding phase. And he concluded with a twin assurance which seemed to be addressed more to the Soviet leaders than to the Egyptian public. He emphasised that the battle against Israel was Egypt's battle and would be fought only by "our soldiers"; nor did he seek to bring about a confrontation between the Soviet Union and the United States. These were the main lines of his

331

policy. And it was for this policy that he wanted the Soviet Union to supply him with offensive weapons – the MIG 23s and certain types of surface-to-surface missiles.

Sadat also confided to the Arab Socialist Union assembly that he had assured the Soviet leaders of this Egyptian position at each of their four meetings in Moscow in 1971 and 1972 and that this was Egypt's policy – and this still remained his policy. Sadat repeated this same declaration of intent in his major speech to the Arab Socialist Union on 24 July 1972, and on many other occasions. It was in fact the central theme of Sadat's explanation for his action in "expelling" the Russians.

One curious feature of this repeated accusation by Sadat was that at no stage did the Soviet leaders make any attempt to reply to it directly or to put the record straight indirectly through their massive publicity potential – the Soviet press and radio. One could express a similar curiosity about the American silence when President Sadat levelled charges against Rogers and Sisco and accused them of lying in his keynote speech on the anniversary of Nasser's death which he gave to the Arab Socialist Union Assembly on 28 September 1972. The Russians certainly could have answered Sadat most effectively and charged him with – to say the least – tampering with the record. For Sadat had left out some very relevant aspects of his policy in relation to the Soviet Union and the United States; indeed, the Russians might well have thought that he had omitted the single most important element of his policy.

There is considerable evidence that from the time when he took over the Presidency in October 1970, President Sadat had been convinced that the only way Egypt could regain her lost territories was by bringing about a direct confrontation of the Soviet Union and the United States. It was without a doubt the idea that concerned him most even though at first it was never fully spelled out – certainly not to the Russians and Americans. But Sadat's intimate circle – which included many of Nasser's former colleagues – knew of this thinking and were greatly disturbed by it. And since these circles included a number of prominent men such as the former Prime Minister and Sadat's Vice-President, Aly Sabry, who had a close relationship with the Soviet leaders, it was a fair assumption that Moscow was not altogether ignorant of the general line of Sadat's thinking.

However, if they had any doubts, these were resolved in October

332

1971 following the visit to Moscow of the spokesman for the Egyptian Information Minister and the Foreign Office, Tahsin Beshir. Beshir, to use his own words, had been "co-ordinating information policy with the Soviet authorities" for the preceding two weeks. In London, he gave a confidential background briefing of current Egyptian thinking to the Foreign Editor of the London *Times*, Louis Heren, and this was given prominent front-page treatment on 7 October 1971 by *The Times*, but without attribution to Beshir. During his few days in London, Beshir also briefed the Foreign Office and some private groups along similar lines. In the light of subsequent events what Beshir had said assumed exceptional importance – particularly in view of President Sadat's explanations after 18 July 1972. According to Beshir, who had gone to Moscow also to prepare the ground for President Sadat's forthcoming visit (it took place later that same month), President Sadat would make clear to the Russians that unless the Soviet Union met Egypt's requirements for an early settlement with Israel (presumably the offensive weapons which Sadat had demanded) Egypt would bring about a confrontation of the superpowers in such a way that they would be compelled to intervene in order to produce a Middle East settlement acceptable to Egypt.

Beshir may have been indiscreet in his talk with *The Times*. One may also surmise that it was a calculated indiscretion designed to bring some pressure to bear on the Russians, to warn them that Sadat meant business. For much more had since become known from authoritative Egyptian sources. Far from saying at that time, during the October 1971 summit in Moscow, that he wanted no direct Soviet military aid and that he did not seek to involve the Russians and Americans with each other, President Sadat had convinced himself and his immediate colleagues that the Soviet leaders had no alternative but to come to the aid of Egypt even if this involved confrontation with the Americans. Nor was this one of Sadat's passing fancies. He had developed the concept before the October summit and assumed a posture at the Moscow talks which left the Russians puzzled and not a little disturbed. Sadat seemed so sure of himself and of his reading of the situation: the Russians would have to go along with him whether they liked it or not. The Soviet leaders realised – perhaps for the first time – that Sadat really meant what he said about this being "the year of decision" and that the Russians would have to go along with him.

We know now from President Sadat's account of that meeting that the Soviet leaders evidently became alarmed by the way Sadat was pushing them into a headlong conflict with the Americans. Brezhnev faced by this unpleasant reality had two options: he could break with Sadat there and then and send him packing, but the Soviet Union was neither politically nor militarily prepared for this. Or the Russians could play for time. This they did. They appeared to go along with Sadat. They agreed to most of his requests but stipulated that the new deliveries which Sadat wanted would not be possible before the end of the year. They also agreed on a formula which the Russians read very differently from what Sadat understood it to be. It was in fact a formula that laid the basis for the denouement of 18 July. The Soviet formula accepted that President Sadat might have to go to war against Israel but excluded the Soviet Union from direct participation. President Sadat agreed because he was convinced that under the prevailing circumstances the Soviet Union was so involved in every phase and on every level of Egyptian war-making that it would be unrealistic for Brezhnev to attempt to stand aside. As soon as Sadat returned home he gave orders for an attack on the Israeli positions across the Canal to be launched at the end of November, but this was subsequently to be delayed until 9 December 1971. Sadat has himself given the details of these plans at a meeting of the Arab Socialist Union and described them in rather more general terms on 13 January 1972. He added that he had been compelled to call off the attack because of the outbreak of the Indo-Pakistan war and the involvement in it of the Soviet Union.

Sadat made no mention of this planned attack across the canal, or its implications, when he described Soviet-Egyptian relations after the July breach. Yet it must have been the decisive element which caused the Soviet leaders to withhold offensive weapons from Egypt – even at the risk of a break with Egypt. Sadat's projected December offensive confirmed the Soviet leaders in their decision to disengage from the Egyptian-Israeli confrontation. It must be admitted that President Sadat's version of his plans for the November-December showdown was received with undisguised scepticism the world over, not least in Egypt and the Arab world. But there were two exceptions to the almost universal derision with which Sadat's claims were received. One was General Aharon Yariv, then Chief of Israel's Military Intelligence, and the other was Dayan. Both were convinced at the time that President Sadat was deploying his troops for a limited attack across the Canal. Both had prepared for it and both had concluded that the attack had been abandoned or postponed because Soviet supplies intended for Egypt had to be shipped to India.

What bothered the Israelis then was the precise Soviet role in the scheduled attack. The Israelis were convinced that the Soviet leaders must have known of Sadat's intentions. Therefore it was vital for Israel to know whether the Kremlin was actually a party to the plan, or whether the Russians disapproved of it, and whether Sadat was in a position to go ahead without Soviet approval, or even directly against the expressed Soviet wish. The central question for the Israelis – as for Sadat – was to know just how deep was the Russian involvement in Egypt and how far they were able and willing to control the situation. Could they prevent Sadat from going to war? Or were they willing and prepared to take part in a limited or not so limited war against Israel and risk involvement with the United States?

What we did not know then, but what we do know now, was that the Soviet leaders were similarly preoccupied with the same questions. They also made a number of decisions which were to lead ultimately to the withdrawal of the Soviet personnel from Egypt. They decided not to supply Egypt with offensive weapons; they decided to withdraw at once all Soviet military personnel from the front line positions on the Canal and to hand over the forward missile sites to the Egyptians; and they decided to seek an accommodation with the United States in the Middle East and the Mediterranean at the price of abandoning the Soviet positions in Egypt and the military confrontation with Israel. Once these decisions were taken there was no longer any valid political or strategic justification for a Soviet presence in Egypt. It was costly, risky and unpopular at home. It also no longer offered any particular advantage in relations with other Arab countries nor had it facilitated relations with Black Africa. On the contrary. The only remaining benefits were Egypt's port facilities for the Soviet Fleet in the Mediterranean and these were to be retained for the time being.

The Soviet leaders delayed a final decision until they were quite clear and satisfied with the outcome of the Indo-Pakistani fighting, especially with the central fact that it had not damaged Soviet-American relations. The answer to Sadat's further request for an urgent Moscow summit was therefore delayed. It was not handed to Sadat until 27 December 1971, and it proposed that the meeting should take place on 2 February, immediately after the Soviet leaders had returned from a scheduled Warsaw Pact Conference at the end of January. That meeting, which took place in Prague on 25 January 1972, was given unusual importance by the Soviet leaders although there was no evident reason for it. In fact, it marked the first major revision of Soviet Middle East policy. The emphasis placed in the resolution passed at this meeting of all important leaders of the Warsaw Pact countries on the renunciation of the use of force and the peaceful co-existence of all states assumed unusual significance in the context of the talks with Sadat a week later.

When one remembers the great importance which the Russians place on words and formalities, the writing on the wall ought to have been clear after Sadat's visit to Moscow in February. For he was received with studied casualness. The official statements showed that he had not been invited but had come at his own request. He left again for home after two days of talks during which the Russians stressed the inconceivability of a confrontation policy which might involve the United States at a time when they were preparing for President Nixon's visit to Moscow. On the basis of reliable and substantive accounts of the talks in Moscow it was evident that Brezhnev and Sadat did discuss the withdrawal of Soviet personnel from Egypt. The initiative came from the Russians but they linked it with a further suggestion that nothing overt should be done until after the Nixon visit to Moscow. The Egyptians maintain, however, that it was Sadat who had told Brezhnev that unless the Russians produced the required arms he would demand the withdrawal of all Soviet personnel in Egypt. There is truth probably in both the Soviet and Egyptian versions: both Brezhnev and Sadat were calling each other's bluff at the February meeting – and both really wanted to wait for the Nixon meeting before taking action.

It was Sadat's calculation at that time – as we now know – that he would be able to use the continued "stategic presence" of the Russians in Egypt as a bargaining lever with the Americans. The Soviet leaders were closely aware of this and went along with Sadat only as long as it suited them – until after the Nixon meeting. But Sadat sadly underestimated Brezhnev if he thought the Soviet-leader would be prepared to play the role for which Sadat cast him: to act as the catalyst for an American-Egypt rapprochement. If there were any doubts left in the minds of the Soviet leaders about their future course in Egypt, these were removed by President Sadat's fourth and final visit before the break, on the eve of the Nixon visit, on 27 April 1972. Sadat again stayed three days – and this time, the Russians have let it be known, they were really alarmed by their continued close link with Sadat.

Sadat had set the tone for the meeting by a speech which he made the day before leaving for Moscow, 26 April – the eve of the Prophet's birthday – in Alexandria. It was one of Sadat's most uncompromising declarations. By this time next year – April 1973 – he said that he would have liberated all Arab territory, including Jerusalem, which "belongs to the Islamic nation". Moreover, Egypt would proceed "to destroy the Israeli arrogance" and Israel would cease to be a factor in the Arab world. Sadat clearly believed this himself and argued along similar lines with the astonished Soviet leaders. Sadat really frightened the Kremlin by his unshaken determination to proceed along his set course, and he again gave voice to his thoughts on his return from Moscow, at a May First demonstration in Cairo. He repeated what he had said a few days earlier – only in even more forcible terms. "My goal will be not merely the liberation of occupied Arab territory but also the destruction of the intolerable Israeli arrogance." He was prepared to sacrifice a million men in the next war and "Israel should be prepared to do the same". But to the utter amazement of the Soviet leaders Sadat added that he had the full support of the Soviet Union for his policy. Egypt's enemies, he told this May Day gathering, had tried to sabotage his visit to Moscow by predicting his failure to get Soviet arms and Soviet support. He therefore advised them to study the communiqué issued in Moscow after his talks and to read it "two, three and four times".

The Russians – always inclined to suspicion – evidently saw this latest Egyptian move as a deliberate attempt to involve them in a renewal of the conflict which they knew would be disastrous for Egypt and for anyone associated with her. Moreover, they were aware that Sadat was speaking against a background situation that was full of pitfalls for the Russians. During April, Sadat had received a memorandum signed by four former members of Nasser's original Revolutionary Command Council, Abdul Latif Boghdady, Kamal Eddin Hussein, Zakaria Mohieddin, and Hassan Ibrahim, by a much respected former Mayor of Cairo, and by other former ministers and leaders of the Medical Association, the radio and television operatives. There were two documents. One called on Sadat to form a national Government composed of men known for their absolute loyalty to Egypt in order to confront the existing "grave and unprecedented situation". The second document demanded that a Government thus formed should put an end to the activity of Leftists in Egypt and that it should abrogate the treaty with the Soviet Union, expel the Soviet personnel in Egypt and reactivate the Jarring mission.

At the same time labour and student unrest continued in Egypt despite the official silence and the press censorship of these events. The disturbances were not critical but they were symptomatic of a growing malaise which could not have reassured the Russians about future prospects for their involvement in Egypt. But possibly the most telling factor in Soviet calculations at that time was the information which became generally known to Western Governments some time in April and May and which must have been even more fully evident to the Soviet intelligence and military circles concerned with the Arab-Israeli confrontation. What was known then was made public some weeks later by the then commanding officer of the Israel air force, General Mordechai Hod.

The substance of this information – which General Hod discussed in an interview on 15 July 1972 – was that the gap between the Israeli air force and the Egyptians had widened still more and by his confident assertion that, in effect, the Israelis had "cracked" the Soviet-Egyptian missile defence system along the Canal. Western military observers had been aware of this development for some time, and it must be assumed that the Russians could hardly have been in ignorance of this central fact. Indeed, it explains the withdrawal of all Soviet personnel from these defence sites many months before the Soviet "expulsion" from Egypt. This then was the scenario with which the Soviet leaders entered into their relatively brief discussion over the Middle East with President Nixon in May 1972. Brezhnev apprised President Nixon of the Soviet intention to disengage from the Egyptian-Israeli conflict and warned the United States of the risks which the Americans might incur by dealing with President Sadat's unpredictable temperament. What the Soviet leaders had clearly not anticipated was the timing and the manner in which President Sadat would pre-empt the planned Soviet disengagement.

However, neither Moscow nor Washington reacted to Sadat's "expulsion" of the Russians; both virtually ignored its supposedly far-reaching implications. Neither Brezhnev nor Nixon made the mistake which most other observers and Governments made – including the Israelis – of assuming that the Soviet withdrawal had brought about a fundamental change in the Middle East alignment and had increased

338

the prospect of a negotiated settlement between Israel and Egypt. This is not to say that there was no change in the situation. There was. But as a result of the Nixon-Brezhnev talks, not because of the Soviet withdrawal. The Russians, we have seen, had already before the Moscow summit won United States' acceptance of a state of strategic parity in the Mediterranean. The logic of this "adjustment" required further agreements, however tacit.

The strategic, political and economic interests of both the Western alliance and the Soviet bloc necessitated measures to prevent another outbreak of war by some form of Soviet-American understanding based on an agreed political and strategic parity on land as well as at sea. Soviet policy, however, was moving faster and looking further ahead than did the American or European Governments. Rightly or wrongly, the Russians were less concerned with what would happen in Egypt, or by the continued massive presence of the Americans in the area, than by the possible emergence of a new and powerful Middle Eastern alliance based on the two stronger military powers in the area – Israel and Iran, and with a possible accession of Turkey to this powerful local combination.

In Soviet eyes, the Shah was a central figure to be reassured and courted, as was evident from the royal reception accorded to the Iranian royal couple during their ten-day visit to the Soviet Union which began on 10 October 1972. For the consequences of Arab opposition to any formal settlement with Israel on terms which might be acceptable to the Israelis was a further incentive to encourage the formation of such a new alliance which in time could also attract and protect those Arab Governments which were willing and prepared to seek a formal peace settlement.

What appeared to have been left open during the Middle East discussion – which was not very exhaustive – at Nixon's Moscow summit in May 1972 was whether the Soviet Union and the United States should encourage this trend in the Middle East or whether they would oppose it as a possible divisive element. But the Russians have evidently treated their withdrawal from Egypt as a modern example of the Leninist precept of one step back and two steps forward. The new axis of Soviet interest extending through Syria, Iraq to Southern Yemen and into Africa was reinforced by the extensive courting of Iran, Afghanistan and India. For the Russians meant to maintain their Middle East presence from positions of strength unaffected by the withdrawal from

339

Egypt. They were not alone. The Americans also understood that the Middle East was not South East Asia, not Vietnam nor Pakistan, and that it would require some form of American presence that would help safeguard the oil resources of the area for the benefit of the world consumer against the threats from outside and even more from the "owners" of the oil – the host countries and the international companies. Both superpowers – the United States and the Soviet Union – had a stake in that; similarly, both superpowers were concerned by 1973 that the rest of the world should not become infected by the conflicts of the Middle East, by the Arab conflict with Israel and Iran, or by the internal conflicts of Arab regimes.

They understood, as Clayton had come to understand half a century before, that the Palestine question would not be resolved by their generation, that Arab leaders would come and go – a Nasser, a Kassem, a Sadat, a Qaddafy; that Israel could and would develop within the limiting conditions of peaceful co-existence with her neighbours and the Palestinians – but without peace. But no matter what happened it would have to take place within the framework of superpower and world interests and this would be the criterion of success or failure of every country in the region, be it Egypt, Israel or Iran. For the resources of the Middle East – her vast oil reserves – had become too precious for the superpowers and the rest of the world to be left to the tender mercies of the host countries, their friends and their enemies – or placed at risk by the Arab-Israeli conflict. The Balfour Declaration had come home.

Because they failed to take account of the demands of the British Grand Designs in 1918, the Jewish and Arab nationalists failed in 1923; and because they failed again to adjust to the superpower world design geared to Middle East oil and strategic parity, they failed again in 1973 and so opened the gates for the return of the superpower condominium in place of the imperialism of 50 years before. For as the twentieth century entered on its last quarter, the only historical hangovers left from the first quarter and the Versailles Settlement of 1919 were the Jewish and Arab nationalisms in the Middle East. They had failed to find a peaceful settlement because from the first they failed to keep faith with each other, and continued to say one thing and to mean another.

They were thus destined to live with this failure to co-exist and do so under the protective umbrella of the two superpowers for many years to come. They forfeited the opportunities and challenges of real independence until a new generation with different concepts of national aspirations, co-existence and peace will learn to speak with frankness and honesty to each other. I can see no hope of that for the present – only a slow awakening, and a few men who over the years are prepared to pioneer the New Deal between Arab and Jew in Israel, between Palestinians *and* Israel, not Palestinians *or* Israel.

# Appendix I

## THE BALFOUR DECLARATION

Foreign Office
2 November 1917

Dear Lord Rothschild,

I have much pleasure in conveying to you, on behalf of His Majesty's Government, the following declaration of sympathy with Jewish Zionist aspirations which has been submitted to, and approved by, the Cabinet.

"His Majesty's Government view with favour the establishment in Palestine of a national home for the Jewish people, and will use their best endeavours to facilitate the achievement of this object, it being clearly understood that nothing shall be done which may prejudice the civil and religious rights of existing non-Jewish communities in Palestine, or the rights and political status enjoyed by Jews in any other country."

I should be grateful if you would bring this declaration to the knowledge of the Zionist Federation.

Yours sincerely,

Arthur James Balfour.

# Appendix II

The Security Council,

Expressing its continuing concern with the grave situation in the Middle East,

Emphasising the inadmissibility of the acquisition of territory by war and the need to work for a just and lasting peace in which every State in the area can live in security,

Emphasising further that all member States in the acceptance of the Charter of the United Nations have undertaken a commitment to act in accordance with Article 2 of the Charter,

1. *Affirms* that the fulfilment of Charter principles requires the establishment of a just and lasting peace in the Middle East which should include the application of both the following principles:

   I. Withdrawal of Israeli armed forces from territories occupied in the recent conflict;

  II. Termination of all claims or states of belligerency and respect for and acknowledgement of the sovereignty, territorial integrity and political independence of every State in the area and their right to live in peace within secure and recognised boundaries free from threats or acts of force;

2. *Affirms* further the necessity

A. For guaranteeing freedom of navigation through international waterways in the area;

B. For achieving a just settlement of the refugee problem;

C. For guaranteeing the territorial inviolability and political independence of every State in the area, through measures including the establishment of demilitarised zones:

3. *Requests* the Secretary-General to designate a special representative to proceed to the Middle East to establish and maintain contacts with the States concerned in order to promote agreement and assist efforts to achieve a peaceful and accepted settlement in accordance with the provisions and principles in this resolution:

4. *Requests* the Secretary-General to report to the Security Council on the progress of the efforts of the special representative as soon as possible.

# A Note on Sources and Books

The sources and bibliography of contemporary history – especially if the author has been a writer on contemporary affairs for some 35 years – tend to be somewhat different from those of the academic historian. Many years of harsh experience observing actual events as they happen, and dealing with the principals concerned in person, creates a strong sense of doubt and questioning about the so-called documentation which is the mainstay of the professional historian. I say this without decrying the invaluable work of the "professionals" without whose groundwork we would be lost. But they see only the public and proven face of history whereas those who often "were there" are also aware of other aspects. In this book I have sought to marry these two concepts but have relied primarily on the direct and first-hand sources that were made available to me and which I had accumulated myself over the years of reporting, researching and discussing the matters dealt with here. It would be idle and pretentious to parade a list of these sources but in view of the special character of Chapter Three I would like to express my appreciation to colleagues of the former Mufti on the Arab Higher Committee who helped me to understand his important role in these events – especially Aref el-Aref, Awny Abdul Hadi, his cousin Jamal al-Husaini, Thabet Khalidi, Ahmad Shukairy, and to the founder of the Muslim Brotherhood, Hassan al-Banna. For the rest, I learnt much at first hand from Dr Weizmann and Mrs Vera Weizmann, from Sir Leon Simon and Mr David Ben-Gurion, and particularly in many years of discussion and consultation with the late Lord Sieff. But the reader will find the references – where it is possible to identify them precisely – in the text; for the more recent period the cloak of anonymity must still be used where officials or politicians remain in positions which make it impossible or undesirable to name them. But I have used this course only where I considered this to be absolutely necessary. Both kinds, politicians and officials, often talk freely to journalists because they know that they are not going to be accountable when they really ought to be. I have therefore used my own discretion in these matters and used the public right to know as the ultimate standard without, however, causing unnecessary hurt or embarrassment. But sometimes either or both these consequences cannot be avoided if one wishes to deal with events as they really happened and not as politicians and officials would like the public to believe.

345

My bibliography is therefore confined to books that have on the whole helped me and which I would recommend. The student who wishes for a more extensive bibliography will find them in Walter Laqueur's *History of Zionism*, in Howard Sacher's *Emergence of the Middle East* and Elizabeth Monroe's *Britain's Moment in the Middle East*. Of immense value are the two volumes of Documents in J. C. Hurewitz's *Diplomacy in the Near and Middle East* to which Professor Hurewitz is soon adding another two volumes to bring them up-to-date, and the two volumes of Khalil's *Arab States and Arab League*. So is Menahem Mansoor's great seven-volume chronology of the political and diplomatic history of the Arab world from 1900 to 1967 which has been published by the University of Wisconsin and computerised on a Micro Card edition. There is nothing quite like it to help the student of Middle Eastern affairs.

In addition to the personal files to which I have referred, anyone writing about this period must lean heavily – but not too heavily – on the files in the Public Record Office in London, the Wingate Papers and the Clayton Papers at Durham University, Sir Mark Sykes' papers in the possession of his family at Sledmere and at St Antony's College, Oxford, and on the German files in Potsdam and Bonn. F. R. Manuel, *The Realities of American-Palestine Relations*, provides a valuable addition of American sources to those listed by Howard Sacher.

But by far the most valuable collection of material is now to be found in the Weizmann Archives in which has been assembled a wide range of documentation, in the Israeli State Archives and in those of the Zionist World Organisation in Jerusalem. St Antony's College, Oxford, is seeking, with considerable success, to fill the gap caused by the absence of parallel Arab archives, and Albert Hourani and Elizabeth Monroe deserve every student's gratitude for this imaginative step. For the second part of this book there are as yet few really valuable first-hand documents available other than those published and described by Laqueur and by David Kimche and Dan Bawly in *The Sandstorm*.

The following list, then, contains some of the books which I have used and found either instructive, stimulating or infuriating.

# Bibliography

AARONSOHN, ALEXANDER, *With the Turks in Palestine*, London, 1917.
KING ABDULLAH, *Memoirs*, London and New York, 1950.
*My Memoirs Completed*, Washington DC, 1954.
ABU-LUGHOD, IBRAHIM, *The Transformation of Palestine*, Evanston, 1971.
ADELMAN, M. A., "Is the Oil Shortage Real?" in *Foreign Policy*, New York, Winter 1972/3.
Adelphi Papers published by the International Institute for Strategic Studies:
   No. 41 – M. HOWARD AND R. HUNTER, "Israel and the Arab World; the Crisis of 1967", London, 1967.
   No. 51 – C. GASTEYGER, "Conflict and Tension in the Mediterranean", London, 1968.
   No. 59 – R. HUNTER, "Soviet Dilemma in the Middle East", London, 1969.
   No. 73 – R. BUSS, "Wary Partners; the Soviet Union and Arab Socialism", London, 1969.
AHMAD, F., *The Young Turks*, Oxford, 1969.
AHMAD, J., *Intellectual Origins of Egyptian Nationalism*, London, 1960.
AKINS, J. E., "The Oil Crisis – This Time the Wolf is Here", in *Foreign Affairs*, New York, April 1973.
AMERY, L. S., *My Political Life*, 3 Vols (especially Vol. 2), London, 1953.
ANDERSON, M. S., *The Eastern Question*, London and New York, 1966.
*The Great Powers and the Near East, 1774–1923*, Documents, London, 1970.
ANTONIUS, G., *The Arab Awakening*, London and Philadelphia, 1938.
ARON, R., *De Gaulle, Israel and the Jews*, London, 1969.
ASHBEE, C. R., *A Palestine Notebook, 1918–1923*, London, 1923.

Bank of Israel Annual Reports (especially for 1966, 1967 and 1971), Jerusalem.
LORD BERTIE, *The Diary of Lord Bertie of Thame*, 2 Vols (especially Vol. 2), London, 1924.
BODENHEIMER, MAX, *So wurde Israel*, Frankfurt-am-Main, 1958.
BOLLING, L. R. (editor), "Search for Peace in the Middle East, a Quaker Study", London and New York, 1971.
"Truth and Peace in the Middle East, a critical analysis of the Quaker Report", by A. M. Soloway and others, New York, 1971.

"Towards Middle-East Dialogue, responses to the Quaker Report", by A. Solomonov and others, New York, 1972.

BURNS, E. L. M., *Between Arab and Israeli*, London and New York, 1962.

CAMPBELL, JOHN C., *Defence of the Middle East; Problems of American Policy*, New York, 1961.

CASSAR, G. H., *The French and the Dardanelles*, London, 1971.

CATTAN, H., *Palestine, the Arabs and Israel*, London, 1969.

Chatham House, "Great Britain and Palestine, 1919–1939", London, 1939.

"Great Britain and Palestine, 1919–1945", London, 1946.

"British Interests in the Mediterranean and Middle East", Report of a Study Group, London, 1958.

CLAYTON, GILBERT F., *An Arabian Diary*, edited and introduced by Robert D. Collins, Los Angeles, 1969.

COHEN, AHARON, *Israel and the Arab World*, London, 1970.

DAGAN, A., *Moscow and Jerusalem*, London and New York, 1970.

DE NOVO, JOHN A., *American Interests and Policies in the Middle East, 1900–1939*, Minneapolis, 1963.

DICKINSON, G. LOWES, *Documents and Statements relating to Peace Proposals and War Aims, December 1916–November 1918*, London, 1919.

DODD, C. H. *and* SALES, M. E. (editors), *Israel and the Arab World*, Documents etc., London, 1970.

ELWELL-SUTTON, L. P., *Persian Oil*, London, 1955.

EVANS, LAURENCE, *United States Policy and the Partition of Turkey, 1914–1924*, Baltimore, 1965.

FISCHER, FRITZ, *Griff nach der Weltmacht*, 3rd edition, Düsseldorf, 1964 (English edition 1970).

"Revolutionierung und Separatfrieden im Osten", in *Historische Zeitschrift*, Vol. 188, Part 2, October 1959.

"Weltpolitik, Weltmachtstreben und deutsche Kriegsziele", in *Historische Zeitschrift*, Vol. 199, Part 2, October 1964.

FISCHER, LOUIS, *The Soviets in World Affairs*, 2 Vols, London, 1936.

GABBAY, R. E., *A Political Study of the Arab-Jewish Conflict*, Geneva, 1959.

GENDZIER, I. L., *Frantz Fanon*, New York, 1972.

(editor), *A Middle East Reader*, New York, 1969.

GILBERT, MARTIN, *Winston S. Churchill*, Vol. 3, 1914–1916, London, 1971.

GOLDMANN, NAHUM, *Der Geist des Militarismus*, Berlin, 1915.

*Memories*, London, 1970.

GRABILL, J. L., *Protestant Diplomacy in the Near East, 1810–1927*, Minneapolis, 1971.

GRAFTEY-SMITH, L., *Bright Levant*, London, 1970

GROBBA, FRITZ, *Manner und Mächte im Orient*, Göttingen, 1967.

GUINN, PAUL, *British Strategy and Politics, 1914–1918*, Oxford, 1965.


HAIM, SYLVIA G., *Arab Nationalism, An Anthology*, Berkeley, 1962.
HALPERN, MANFRED, *The Politics of Social Change in the Middle East and North Africa*, Princeton, 1963.
HANKEY, SIR MAURICE, *Supreme Command*, 2 Vols, London, 1951.
HARKABY, Y., *Arab Attitudes to Israel*, Jerusalem and London, 1972.
HARTSHORN, J. E., *Oil Companies and Government*, London, 1967.
HATTIS, S. LEE, *The Bi-National Idea in Palestine during Mandatory Times*, Tel Aviv, 1970.
HEADLAM-MORLEY, SIR JAMES, *Studies in Diplomatic History*, London, 1930.
HEIKAL, M., *Nasser, the Cairo Documents*, London, 1972.
HENTIG, OTTO VON, *Mein Leben*, Göttingen, 1962.
HIRSZKOWICZ, L., *The Third Reich and the Arab East*, London, 1966.
HIGGINS, R. H., *U.N. Peacekeeping, 1946–1967*, Vol. 1, "The Middle East", London, 1969.
HIRST, D., *Oil and Public Opinion in the Middle East*, London, 1966.
History of *The Times*, 4 Vols, especially Vol. IV, Part 1, London, 1935–1952.
HMSO, *Documents of British Foreign Policy*
    First Series: Vol. IV    1919, "Adriatic and Middle East", London, 1952.
                 Vol. VIII 1920, "International Conferences", London, 1958.
                 Vol. XIII Jan. 1920 – March 1921 "Near and Middle East", London, 1963.
HOPKINS, H., *Egypt, The Crucible*, London, 1969.
HOSKINS, H. L., *British Routes to India*, London, 1928 and 1966.
HOTTINGER, A., *The Arabs*, London, 1963.
*10 mal Nah-Ost*, Munich, 1970.
HOURANI, A., *A Vision of History*, Beirut, 1961.
*Arabic Thought in the Liberal Age, 1798–1939*, London, 1962.
HOUSEPIAN, M., *Smyrna 1922*, London, 1972.
HOWARD, H. N., *The King-Crane Commission*, Beirut, 1963.
HUREWITZ, J. C., *Diplomacy in the Near and Middle East*, 2 Vols, Documents, Princeton, 1956.
*The Struggle for Palestine*, New York, 1950.
*Middle East Politics, the Military Dimension*, London and New York, 1969.
(editor) *Soviet-American Rivalry in the Middle East*, New York, 1969.


INGRAMS, D., *Palestine Papers*, Documents 1917–1922, London, 1972.
"International Petroleum Cartel", Report to the US Senate, 22 August 1952, Washington DC, 1952.
ISSAWI, C., *Egypt in Revolution, an Economic Analysis*, Oxford and New York, 1963.


JAMES, A., *The Politics of Peacekeeping*, London, 1969.

KARPAT, KEMAL H. (editor), *Political and Social Thought in the Contemporary Middle East*, London and New York, 1968.

KEDOURIE, E., *England and the Middle East, 1914–1921*, London, 1956.
  *The Chatham House Version and other Middle Eastern Studies*, London, 1970.

KERNEK, STERLING, "British Government's Reactions to Wilson's 'Peace Note' ", in *Historical Journal* XIII, 4 (1970), London.

KERR, MALCOLM, *The Arab Cold War 1958–1970*, 3rd revised edition, Oxford, 1970.

KHADDURI, MAJDIA D. (editor), *The Arab-Israeli Impasse*, Washington DC, 1968.

KHADDURI, MAJID, *Independent Iraq – 1932–1958*, 2nd edition, London, 1959.
  *Republican Iraq*, London, 1969.

KHALIDI, WALID (editor), *From Haven to Conquest*, Beirut, 1971.

KHALIL, M., *The Arab States and the Arab League*, Documents, 2 Vols, Beirut, 1962.

KIMCHE, JON, *Seven Fallen Pillars*, London, 1950.
  *The Unromantics*, London, 1968.
  *The Second Arab Awakening*, London, 1968.

KIMCHE, JON *and* KIMCHE, DAVID, *Both Sides of the Hill*, London, 1960.

KIMCHE, DAVID *and* BAWLY, DAN, *The Sandstorm*, London, 1968.

KIRKBRIDE, SIR ALEC, *A Crackle of Thorns*, London, 1956.

KLIEMAN, A. S., *Foundations of British Policy in the Arab World, the Cairo Conference of 1921*, Baltimore and London, 1970.
  *The Soviet Union and the Middle East*, London, 1970.

KONZELMANN, G., *Vom Frieden redet Keiner*, Stuttgart, 1971.


LALL, ARTHUR, *The UN and the Middle East Crisis, 1967*, New York, 1968.

LANGER, W. L., *Diplomacy of Imperialism, 1890–1902*, 2nd edition, New York, 1950.

LAQUEUR, W. Z., *The Struggle for the Middle East, 1958–1968*, London, 1970.
  *The Road to War, 1967*, London, 1968.
  *Israel-Arab Reader*, London and New York, 1970.
  *A History of Zionism*, London, 1972.
  (editor) *The Soviet Union and the Middle East*, London, 1959.

LEWIS, BERNARD, *The Arabs in History*, London, 1950.
  *The Emergence of Modern Turkey*, London, 1961.
  *The Middle East and the West*, London, 1964.

LICHTHEIM, R., *Die Geschichte Deutschen Zionismus*, Jerusalem, 1954.

LIPSKY, L., *A Gallery of Zionist Profiles*, New York, 1956.

LUBELL, H., *Middle East Oil Crises and Western Europe's Energy Supplies*, Baltimore, 1963.


MANSOOR, M., *Arab World: chronology of political and diplomatic history, 1900–1967*, 7 Vols, Wisconsin, 1972.

MANUEL, F. R., *The Realities of American-Palestine Relations*, Washington DC, 1949.

MARLOWE, JOHN, *The Seat of Pilate*, London, 1959.

*Perfidious Albion – Origins of the Anglo-French Rivalry in the Levant*, London, 1971.

MAY, E. R., *World War and American Isolation 1914–1917*, Cambridge, Mass., 1959.

MAYER, ARNO J., *Wilson versus Lenin, Political Origins of the New Diplomacy, 1917–1918*, New York, 1959 and 1964.

*Politics and Diplomacy of Peacemaking, 1918–1919*, London, 1968.

MEIER, H. (*and* others), *Israel, Edition Zeitgesehen*, Hannover, 1970.

MEINERTZHAGEN, COLONEL R., *Middle East Diary, 1917–1956*, London, 1959.

*Army Diary, 1899–1926*, London, 1960.

"Middle East Record 1967", Shiloah Middle East Institute, Jerusalem, 1971.

MILLER, W., *Ottoman Empire and its Successors*, London, 1913 and 1966.

MONROE, ELIZABETH, *Britain's Moment in the Middle East, 1914–1956*, London, 1963.

MORAN, T. H., "The Politics of Oil: (1) Coups and Costs", in *Foreign Policy*, New York, Autumn 1972.

MUNAJJID, SALAH AL-, *Wohin treibt die Arabische Welt?*, Munich, 1968.


NASSER, GAMAL ABDUL, *The Philosophy of the Revolution*, Cairo, 1953, Washington DC, 1955.

NEVAKIVI, JUKKA, *Britain, France and the Arab Middle East, 1914–1918*, London, 1968.

NICOLSON, H., *Peacemaking 1919*, London, 1933.


PARKES, J., *A History of Palestine, 135 AD to Modern Times*, London, 1949.

PERES, S., *David's Sling*, London, 1970.

*Petroleum Press Service*, Monthly, London, 1970.

PRESLAND, JOHN, *Deedes Bey*, London, 1942.

PRICE, M. PHILIPS, *War and Revolution in Asiatic Russia*, London, 1918.


*The Quran*, Arabic Text and English Translation by Muhammad Zafrullah Khan, London and Dublin, 1971.


RA'ANAN, U., *The Soviet Union, Arms and the Third World*, Cambridge, Mass., 1969.

RATHMAN, LOTHAR, *Stossrichtung Nahost, 1914–1918*, East Berlin, 1963.

Report of the Palestine Commission, Cmnd 5479, London, July 1937.

RODINSON, M., *Mohammed*, London, 1971.

ROSKILL, S., *Hankey, Man of Secrets*, Vol. I 1877–1918, Vol. II 1919–1931, London, 1970–72.

ROTHWELL, W. H., *British War Aims and Peace Diplomacy, 1914–1918*, Oxford, 1971.

351

"Mesopotamia in British War Aims, 1914–1918", in *Historical Journal* XIII, 2 (1970), London.

RUPPIN, A., *Memoirs, Diaries and Letters*, edited by A. Bein. Afterword by M. Dagan, Jerusalem, 1971.

SACHAR, H. M., *The Emergence of the Middle East, 1914–1924*, New York, 1969.

SACHER, HARRY, *Zionist Portraits*, London, 1959.

St Antony's Papers, Middle Eastern Affairs:

Number IV    London, 1958.
Number XI    London, 1961.
Number XVI   London, 1963.
Number XVII  London, 1965.

SAFRAN, NADAV, *From War to War, the Arab-Israel Confrontation*, New York, 1969.

SAM'O, E. (editor), *June 1967 – the Arab-Israeli War*, Wilmette, Illinois, 1971.

SCOTT, C. P., *Scott Journal*, Political Diaries 1911–1928, edited by T. Wilson, London, 1970.

SEALE, P., *The Struggle for Syria*, London, 1965.

SHABAN, M. A., *The Abassid Revolution*, Cambridge, 1970.
  *Islamic History, AD 600–750, a new interpretation*, Cambridge, 1971.

SHARABI, H., *Arab Intellectuals and the West, 1875–1914*, Baltimore and London, 1970.
  *Palestine and Israel*, New York, 1969.

SIDEBOTHAM, H., *England and Palestine*, London, 1917, new ed. 1936.

SIEFF, ISRAEL M., *Memoirs*, London, 1970.
  Foreword to *The Unromantics* by J. Kimche.

SNOW, P., *Hussein*, London, 1972.

SOKOLOW, N., *A History of Zionism, 1600–1918*, 2 Vols, Preface by A. J. Balfour, London, 1919.

STEIN, LEONARD, *The Balfour Declaration*, London, 1961.

STEWART, DESMOND, *Temple of Janus*, New York, 1971.

SPECTOR, I., *The Soviet Union and the Middle East*, Seattle, 1959.

STEVENSON, F., *Lloyd George, A Diary*, London, 1971.

STOCKING, G. W., *Middle East Oil*, London, 1971.

STORRS, SIR RONALD, *Orientations*, London, 1937.

SYKES, CHRISTOPHER, *Two Studies in Virtue*, London, 1953.
  *Crossroads to Israel*, London, 1965.

SYKES, MARK, *The Caliph's Last Heritage*, London, 1915.

TAYLOR, A. J. P., *The Struggle for Mastery in Europe, 1848–1918*, Oxford, 1954.

TEMPERLEY, H. M. V., *England and the Near East*, London, 1936 and 1964.

TILLMANN, HEINZ, *Deutschlands Araberpolitik im 2 Weltkrieg*, East Berlin, 1965.

TEVETH, S. L., *Moshe Dayan*, London, 1972.

TOYNBEE, A. J., *Acquaintances*, London, 1967.

TRUMPENER, ULRICH, *Germany and the Ottoman Empire*, Princeton, NJ, 1968.
TÜETSCH, H. E., *Facets of Arab Nationalism*, Detroit, 1965.
TUGENHAT, C., *Oil – the Biggest Business*, London, 1968.

URQUHART, B., *Hammarskjold*, London, 1973.

VATIKIOTIS, P. J., *The Egyptian Army in Politics*, Bloomington, Indiana, 1961.
  *Politics and Military in Jordan, 1921–1957*, New York, 1967.
  *Conflict in the Middle East*, London, 1971.

WAGNER, H., *Der Arabische-Israelische Konflict im Völkerrecht*, Berlin, 1971.
WAVELL, VISCOUNT, *Allenby*, London, 1946.
WEISGAL, M. M., . . . *so far*, London, 1971.
WEIZMANN, C., *Trial and Error*, London, 1949.
WEIZMANN C. (*and* others), *Zionism and the Jewish Future*, edited by H. Sacher,
  London, 1917.

ZAYID, M. J., *Egypt's Struggle for Independence*, Beirut, 1960.
ZANDER, W., *Israel and the Holy Places of Christendom*, London, 1971.
ZECHLIN, EGMONT, *Die deutsche Politik und die Juden im 1 Weltkrieg*, Göttingen, 1969.
ZEINE, Z. N., *The Emergence of Arab Nationalism*, Beirut, 1958 and 1966.
  *The Struggle for Arab Independence*, Beirut, 1960.

# Index

There is continual debate on the correct transliteration of many Arabic names. Accordingly, when such names appear in direct quotations, they have been left as they appeared in the original letters or memoranda.

355